MW00534924

# CHARLES R. SWINDOLL

# SWINDOLL'S
# LIVING
# INSIGHTS

## NEW TESTAMENT COMMENTARY

# GALATIANS, EPHESIANS

*Tyndale House Publishers, Inc.*
*Carol Stream, Illinois*

Swindoll's Living Insights New Testament Commentary, Volume 8

Visit Tyndale online at www.tyndale.com.

*Insights on Galatians, Ephesians* copyright © 2015 by Charles R. Swindoll, Inc.

Designed by Nicole Grimes

Published in association with Yates & Yates, LLP (www.yates2.com).

---

**Library of Congress Cataloging-in-Publication Data**

Swindoll, Charles R.
  Galatians, Ephesians / Charles R. Swindoll.
    pages cm. — (Swindoll's living insights New Testament commentary ; Volume 8)
  Includes bibliographical references.
  ISBN 978-1-4143-9376-6 (hc)
  1. Bible. Galatians—Commentaries. 2. Bible. Ephesians—Commentaries. I. Title.
  BS2685.53.S95 2015
  227'.407—dc23                                                          2015033837

---

Previously published by Zondervan under ISBN 978-1-4143-9740-5

Printed in the United States of America
21   20   19   18   17   16   15
7    6    5    4    3    2    1

# CONTENTS

# AUTHOR'S PREFACE

For more than sixty years I have loved the Bible. It was that love for the Scriptures, mixed with a clear call into the gospel ministry during my tour of duty in the Marine Corps, that resulted in my going to Dallas Theological Seminary to prepare for a lifetime of ministry. During those four great years I had the privilege of studying under outstanding men of God, who also loved God's Word. They not only held the inerrant Word of God in high esteem, they taught it carefully, preached it passionately, and modeled it consistently. A week never passes without my giving thanks to God for the grand heritage that has been mine to claim! I am forever indebted to those fine theologians and mentors, who cultivated in me a strong commitment to the understanding, exposition, and application of God's truth.

For more than fifty years I have been engaged in doing just that—*and how I love it!* I confess without hesitation that I am addicted to the examination and the proclamation of the Scriptures. Because of this, books have played a major role in my life for as long as I have been in ministry—especially those volumes that explain the truths and enhance my understanding of what God has written. Through these many years I have collected a large personal library, which has proven invaluable as I have sought to remain a faithful student of the Bible. To the end of my days, my major goal in life is to communicate the Word with accuracy, insight, clarity, and practicality. Without informative and reliable books to turn to, I would have "run dry" decades ago.

Among my favorite and most well-worn volumes are those that have enabled me to get a better grasp of the biblical text. Like most expositors, I am forever searching for literary tools that I can use to hone my gifts and sharpen my skills. For me, that means finding resources that make the complicated simple and easy to understand, that offer insightful comments and word pictures that enable me to see the relevance of sacred truth in light of my twenty-first-century world, and that drive those truths home to my heart in ways I do not easily forget. When I come across such books, they wind up in my hands as I devour them and then place them in my library for further reference . . . and, believe me, I often return to them. What a relief it is to have these resources to turn to when I lack fresh insight, or when I need just the right story or illustration, or when I get stuck in the tangled text and cannot find my way out. For the serious expositor, a library is essential. As a mentor of mine once said, "Where else can you have ten thousand professors at your fingertips?"

In recent years I have discovered there are not nearly enough resources like those I just described. It was such a discovery that prompted me to consider becoming a part of the answer instead of lamenting the problem. But the solution would result in a huge undertaking. A writing project that covers all of the books and letters of the New Testament seemed overwhelming and intimidating. A rush of relief came when I realized that during the past fifty-plus years I've taught and preached through most of the New Testament. In my files were folders filled with notes from those messages that were just lying there, waiting to be brought out of hiding, given a fresh and relevant touch in light of today's needs, and applied to fit into the lives of men and women who long for a fresh word from the Lord. *That did it!* I began to work on plans to turn all of those notes into this commentary on the New Testament.

I must express my gratitude to both Mark Gaither and Mike Svigel for their tireless and devoted efforts, serving as my hands-on, day-to-day editors. They have done superb work as we have walked our way through the verses and chapters of all twenty-seven New Testament books. It has been a pleasure to see how they have taken my original material and helped me shape it into a style that remains true to the text of the Scriptures, at the same time interestingly and creatively developed, and all the while allowing my voice to come through in a natural and easy-to-read manner.

I need to add sincere words of appreciation to the congregations I have served in various parts of these United States for more than five decades. It has been my good fortune to be the recipient of their love, support, encouragement, patience, and frequent words of affirmation as I have fulfilled my calling to stand and deliver God's message year after year. The sheep from all those flocks have endeared themselves to this shepherd in more ways than I can put into words . . . and none more than those I currently serve with delight at Stonebriar Community Church in Frisco, Texas.

Finally, I must thank my wife, Cynthia, for her understanding of my addiction to studying, to preaching, and to writing. Never has she discouraged me from staying at it. Never has she failed to urge me in the pursuit of doing my very best. On the contrary, her affectionate support personally, and her own commitment to excellence in leading Insight for Living for more than three and a half decades, have combined to keep me faithful to my calling "in season and out of season." Without her devotion to me and apart from our mutual partnership throughout our lifetime of ministry together, Swindoll's Living Insights would never have been undertaken.

I am grateful that it has now found its way into your hands and, ultimately, onto the shelves of your library. My continued hope and prayer is that you will find these volumes helpful in your own study and personal application of the Bible. May they help you come to realize, as I have over these many years, that God's Word is as timeless as it is true.

The grass withers, the flower fades,
But the word of our God stands forever. (Isa. 40:8)

*Chuck Swindoll*
Frisco, Texas

# THE STRONG'S
# NUMBERING SYSTEM

Swindoll's Living Insights New Testament Commentary uses the Strong's word-study numbering system to give both newer and more advanced Bible students alike quicker, more convenient access to helpful original-language tools (e.g., concordances, lexicons, and theological dictionaries). The Strong's numbering system, made popular by the *Strong's Exhaustive Concordance of the Bible*, is used with the majority of biblical Greek and Hebrew reference works. Those who are unfamiliar with the ancient Hebrew, Aramaic, and Greek alphabets can quickly find information on a given word by looking up the appropriate index number. Advanced students will find the system helpful because it allows them to quickly find the lexical form of obscure conjugations and inflections.

When a Greek word is mentioned in the text, the Strong's number is included in square brackets after the Greek word. So in the example of the Greek word *agapē* [26], "love," the number is used with Greek tools keyed to the Strong's system.

On occasion, a Hebrew word is mentioned in the text. The Strong's Hebrew numbers are completely separate from the Greek numbers, so Hebrew numbers are prefixed with a letter "H." So, for example, the Hebrew word *kapporet* [H3727], "mercy seat," comes from *kopher* [H3722], "to ransom," "to secure favor through a gift."

# INSIGHTS ON GALATIANS

*The gospel frees us from trying to earn or retain God's favor through rule keeping, but it also keeps us from running headlong to the other extreme—willfully sinning in the name of freedom. As people saved by grace, we have been sealed by the Spirit, who works in us to help us to love and obey Christ and to serve one another. We have been freed—not to do whatever we want, but to do what God wants.*

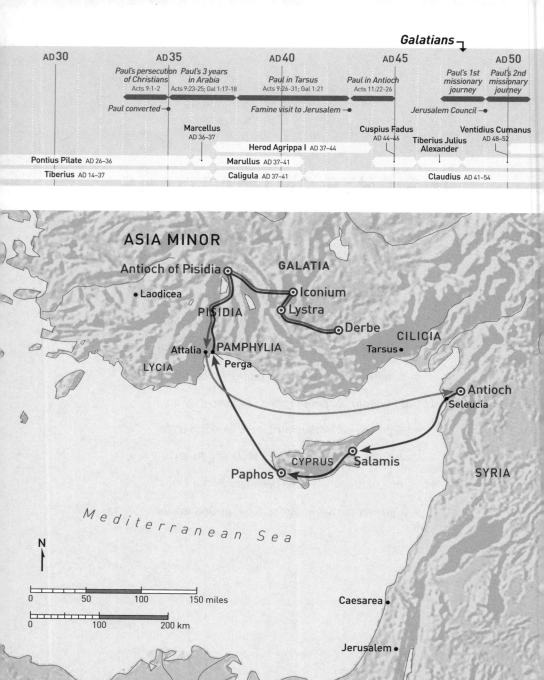

**Galatians**

AD 30    AD 35    AD 40    AD 45    AD 50

Paul's persecution of Christians
Acts 9:1-2

Paul's 3 years in Arabia
Acts 9:23-25; Gal 1:17-18

Paul in Tarsus
Acts 9:26-31; Gal 1:21

Paul in Antioch
Acts 11:22-26

Paul's 1st missionary journey

Paul's 2nd missionary journey

Paul converted

Famine visit to Jerusalem

Jerusalem Council

Marcellus
AD 36-37

Cuspius Fadus
AD 44-46

Ventidius Cumanus
AD 48-52

Tiberius Julius Alexander

Herod Agrippa I  AD 37-44

Pontius Pilate  AD 26-36

Marullus  AD 37-41

Tiberius  AD 14-37

Caligula  AD 37-41

Claudius  AD 41-54

**ASIA MINOR**

Antioch of Pisidia

**GALATIA**

Laodicea

Iconium

Lystra

**PISIDIA**

Derbe

**CILICIA**

Attalia  **PAMPHYLIA**

Tarsus

**LYCIA**

Perga

Antioch

Seleucia

**CYPRUS**  Salamis

**SYRIA**

Paphos

*Mediterranean Sea*

N

0      50      100      150 miles

0         100        200 km

Caesarea

Jerusalem

**Paul's first missionary journey** began in Antioch in about AD 47 when the Holy Spirit revealed that he and his co-worker Barnabas were to bring the gospel to the Gentiles (Acts 13:1-3). After traveling across the island of Cyprus (13:4-12), they reached the southern coast of Asia Minor in the region of Pamphylia, then continued deeper into the mainland, visiting various cities in the southern half of the province of Galatia (13:13–14:18). On their journey home, they retraced their path, strengthening the new churches before returning to Antioch to report the results of their mission (14:19-28).

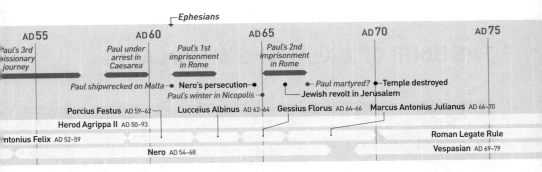

┌─Ephesians

AD 55    AD 60    AD 65    AD 70    AD 75

Paul's 3rd missionary journey

Paul under arrest in Caesarea

Paul's 1st imprisonment in Rome

Paul's 2nd imprisonment in Rome

Paul shipwrecked on Malta — Nero's persecution—

Paul's winter in Nicopolis —

—Paul martyred? —Temple destroyed

Jewish revolt in Jerusalem

Porcius Festus AD 59–62

Lucceius Albinus AD 62–64   Gessius Florus AD 64–66   Marcus Antonius Julianus AD 66–70

Herod Agrippa II AD 50–93

ntonius Felix AD 52–59

Roman Legate Rule

Nero AD 54–68

Vespasian AD 69–79

# GALATIANS

## INTRODUCTION

Though we have no record of the circumstances leading to the writing of Paul's epistle to the Galatians, the abrupt tone and explosive content of the letter give us the impression that if we had visited Paul at the time, we would not have seen a calm, collected, and composed apostle. A frustrated, agitated, and determined one is more likely. If we allow ourselves a little "sanctified imagination," we might relive the scene this way:

Paul paces the room, clearly agitated. He frowns, pauses, shakes his head, then pivots and strides across the room again. He glances out the window from the house on Mount Silpius, his gaze rising across the colonnaded street that dissects the city of Antioch from north to south. His weakened eyes prevent him from peering much farther than the palace jutting prominently from the island in the Orontes River, but he knows that beyond the hills descending to the sea, across the shore of Asia Minor, on the other side of the Taurus Mountains, the sprawling region of southern Galatia calls for his attention. "I would give anything to be there right now," he whispers under his breath.

Paul notices Barnabas at the table in the corner, who is looking on in concern as the limp in Paul's leg becomes more pronounced with each step. Paul grunts in discomfort, but the permanent injuries he suffered for the sake of the gospel at the hands of the rioters in the province of Galatia several weeks earlier feel like minor bruises compared to the deep emotional blow he just received from the messengers. "Foolish Galatians!" Paul mutters. He shakes his head again, thinking through his last visit to the cities of that region.

From Paul's perspective, things had gone well on that first journey through the provinces of Cyprus, Pamphylia, and Galatia—what their house church here in Antioch now called the "first mission." Gentiles,

# THE BOOK OF GALATIANS AT A GLANCE

| SECTION | CONFIRMING THE TRUTH OF THE GOSPEL | DEFENDING THE SUPERIORITY OF THE GOSPEL | LIVING THE FREEDOM OF THE GOSPEL |
|---|---|---|---|
| PASSAGE | 1:1–2:21 | 3:1–4:31 | 5:1–6:18 |
| THEMES | Grace is the way to life and the way of life. | | |
| | Personal Narrative | Doctrinal Argument | Practical Application |
| | The authority of Paul's apostleship vs. the falsehood of the Judaizers | The sufficiency of faith in Christ vs. the uselessness of works of the Law | The power of the Spirit in the Christian life vs. the weakness of the sinful flesh |
| | Confusion | Works vs. Faith | Don't be enslaved. |
| | Clarification | Legalism vs. Justification | Serve through love. |
| | Correction | Bondage vs. Freedom | Walk in the Spirit. |
| KEY TERMS | Law . . . Gospel . . . Spirit | | |
| | Evangelize | Faith | Freedom |
| | Anathema | Promise | Desire of the flesh |
| | | Heir | Crucify |

## KEY TERMS IN GALATIANS

*euangelion* (εὐαγγέλιον) [2098] "good news," "gospel"
The English term "gospel" comes from the Middle English compound "good-spell," where "spell" means "tale." The gospel is therefore the "good story." The Greek term *euangelion* would have been used to describe a favorable report of a messenger from the battlefield or an official proclamation that an heir to the king had been born. The good news that Paul proclaimed concerned Jesus Christ's death for sin and resurrection as well as salvation by grace alone through faith alone in Christ alone. Christ had conquered sin and death, and through Him God offers new life.

*nomos* (νόμος) [3551] "a law," "the Mosaic Law"
Paul uses *nomos* over thirty times in the book of Galatians to refer to the Mosaic Law, the code of conduct Moses received directly from God. It is clear in Galatians that Paul has a high view of the Law as an authentic revelation from God, but he argues that its function as a rule of life has come to an end with the coming of Christ (see 3:19; 5:18). The Law still reveals human sinfulness, however, driving guilty sinners to the grace and mercy of God for forgiveness.

*pneuma* (πνεῦμα) [4151] "spirit," "Holy Spirit"
Although *pneuma* is commonly used in secular Greek literature to speak of a person's immaterial soul, Paul most often uses the term in reference to the Holy Spirit, the third person of the Trinity. Paul uses phrases such as "walk by the Spirit" (5:16) or "led by the Spirit" (5:18) to mark the difference between one who lives according to God's power and one who lives according to one's own strength. The Spirit also works miracles (3:5), grants believers adoption as sons of God (4:6), gives new hope (5:5), and imparts new desires in contrast to those of the flesh (5:16-17).

starving for hope, had received the good news of Jesus Christ's death and resurrection with great enthusiasm. The Holy Spirit had wrought miracles through Paul and Barnabas that astounded even them. On Cyprus the Spirit had prompted Paul to cast a meddlesome sorcerer into a state of blindness, opening the spiritual eyes of a Roman proconsul. In Iconium, the Lord confirmed their message concerning the grace of God with signs and wonders done through their hands. At Lystra the Spirit healed a man crippled from birth, drawing awestruck crowds from the city who insisted that Paul and Barnabas must be gods who had descended from heaven. But the fact that the Spirit had confirmed the apostles' message of grace with such amazing power only made Paul all the more frustrated to receive the tragic news: *The new believers in the province of Galatia have abandoned the good news of the gift of salvation and have started depending on obedience to the Law!*

"Remember, Barnabas?" Paul asks, pounding his fist into his open hand. "Remember what we told them in Pisidia? We told them that *through Christ* the forgiveness of sins was being proclaimed to them. *Through Him alone* believing sinners are freed from everything—*every-thing*—from which the Law of Moses was powerless to free them!"

"We were very clear, Paul," Barnabas assures him, watching his companion wring his hands, "but the circumcision party has invaded their ranks and poisoned their minds against us."

"You're right," Paul responds. "Those dogs were nipping at our heels the whole time. As soon as we sailed for Antioch, they returned to gnaw our young brothers and sisters to the bone!"

Paul again commences pacing as a growing tension fills the room. Finally he stops and stares out the window. The sun is beginning to set—that much he can tell even with his weakening eyesight. In fact, the brilliant sphere seems to hover over the distant region of Galatia itself, confirming Paul's resolve to somehow pierce the darkness that is invading the world of those young believers. He turns to his companion and nods his head, the expression on his face transformed from dismay to determination. "Fetch me parchment and a pen, Brother Barnabas. Then ask Simeon or Lucius to find a messenger who can set off with a letter for the Galatians in the morning. I'll pay the expenses myself."

"What are we going to do?" Barnabas asks, rising from his seat.

Paul smiles for the first time since receiving the news of the Galatian crisis. "Since they have attacked our brothers and sisters in Galatia, we're going to bite back!"

● ● ●

It stunned Paul to learn that the Galatians had abandoned the simple and pure gospel of grace and freedom in Christ for a complex and strenuous religion of works and human bondage. Why would a slave, once freed, go back to living in bondage? Why would a debtor forgiven of his debts free and clear continue making backbreaking payments to his creditor? Why would a criminal pardoned by a gracious judge walk himself to prison to do time behind bars? These implausible scenarios make as much sense to us as the Galatian crisis of faith made to Paul and Barnabas after their first missionary journey through southeastern Asia Minor.

In fact, Paul put it bluntly to the Galatians: "I am amazed that you are so quickly deserting Him who called you by the grace of

Christ, for a different gospel" (1:6). Paul was shocked, astounded, dumbfounded—virtually at a loss for words! The "different gospel" they had received in exchange for the grace of Christ was no gospel at all, but a mixture of faith plus works—reasonable within the typical pull-yourself-up-by-your-bootstraps mentality of today and fashionable among the influential legalists then. This "different gospel" was so far from the truth of Christ that it could no longer be called "good news," only "damnable doctrine." So Paul set out to extinguish this smoldering heresy before it burst into full flame and reduced his fledgling churches to ashes.

Before working our way through Paul's letter of liberation, let's explore its background in order to get a better understanding of the world in which it was written and the situation it addressed. We will then be in a good position to appreciate an overview of the entire book.

## THEM'S FIGHTIN' WORDS!

Back in the 1980s Hollywood created what became a veritable film genre in which a bulked-up, heavily armed one-man fighting machine broke into prison camps and rescued hostages, POWs, or kidnap victims. Names like Sylvester Stallone, Chuck Norris, and Bruce Willis immediately come to mind. The plots and characters usually had as much depth as a North Texas winter snowfall, but when it came to shoot-'em-up action, those movies had no rivals. An obvious lesson jumped out of any one of those flicks: If you want to set the captives free, you need to go in with guns blazing.

This is the approach Paul took with the letter to the Galatians. Commentators have called it the "Magna Carta of Christian Liberty" or the "Christian's Declaration of Independence." Fair enough, but frankly, it reads more like a declaration of war! Clearly, Galatians is the most personal, in-your-face, no-holds-barred writing from Paul's passionate pen. Let me give you just a few snippets to demonstrate how militant the letter is:

> As we have said before, so I say again now, if any man is preaching to you a gospel contrary to what you received, he is to be accursed! (1:9)

> You foolish Galatians, who has bewitched you, before whose eyes Jesus Christ was publicly portrayed as crucified? (3:1)

> Are you so foolish? Having begun by the Spirit, are you now being perfected by the flesh? (3:3)

My children, with whom I am again in labor until Christ is formed in you—but I could wish to be present with you now and to change my tone, for I am perplexed about you. (4:19-20)

I wish that those who are troubling you would even mutilate themselves. (5:12)

These words come from a man unleashed, a man who places vital truth above courtesy and plain facts above civility. He assails the severe, faith-threatening spiritual problems of the Galatians with a three-pronged attack.

First, *he asserts a strong affirmation of freedom based on grace.* First and foremost, Galatians reminds us that Christ has already freed us from sin, death, and the Law. How have we been freed? By grace alone through faith alone in Christ alone. Why have we been freed? In order to live an unshackled life based not on an exhaustive list of dos and don'ts but on a grace-motivated, Spirit-empowered life of love for God and others. Over and over again Paul reminds his readers that grace has freed them (and us!) from the Law and its penalties.

Second, *he launches a bold assault on works-based legalism.* If Paul were alive today, he would be disappointed that so many Christians struggle under the bondage of legalism rather than thrive in the freedom of grace. What is legalism? Charles Ryrie defines it as "a fleshly attitude which conforms to a code for the purpose of exalting self."[1] In the case of the Galatians, they were succumbing to the observance of the Law "to make a good showing in the flesh" and to avoid being "persecuted for the cross of Christ" (6:12). Legalism always involves man-made rules and regulations, enforced through guilt and shame. For legalists, God seems like a severe judge ready to pounce at every infraction, a stern teacher eager to point out every mistake, or a strict father whose standards we can never live up to.

Third, *he issues a courageous encouragement for those surrounded by legalists.* Legalists have been with the church throughout history, and they have pitched their tents among us today. At the same time, those who believe, live, and proclaim God's grace and fruitful life in the Spirit continually work at tearing down the base camps of their adversaries. Paul presents himself as a warrior for the cause of grace against the insurgency of legalism, encouraging us to step into the fray and take a stand against those who would seek to enslave us to their own standards of law.

# THE GLORY OF GALATIANS

The book of Galatians sparkles like a multifaceted gem. It has at least four sides that each brilliantly reflect a vital aspect of the truth and reveal the shortcomings of opposing views.

First, *it warns against abandoning the true gospel for a cheap imitation.* After a brief greeting, Paul instantly dives into a veritable invective, calling down curses upon those who would tamper with the truth of the gospel (1:6-8). These aren't the words of a raving lunatic or a dogmatic heresy hunter. They reflect the passion of a patriot of grace who knows that adding to or taking from the one true gospel destroys the Christian faith itself.

Second, *it upholds the significance of grace.* Except for the book of Romans, Paul's letter to the Galatians presents the clearest and most succinct articulation of the doctrine of justification in Scripture. Salvation comes by grace through faith apart from works. This simple truth stands as the bedrock of our faith. Remove this foundation of grace, and the whole building will crumble.

Third, *it presents the true function of the Mosaic Law.* Obeying the Law of Moses can't save us. In fact, it has never saved anyone. Never has, never will. Nobody (except Jesus) can ever keep the Law perfectly, although legalists like to pretend they can. Paul acknowledges, however, that the Law serves a good and necessary purpose: It reveals our sin and need for grace, and it reminds us of God's nonnegotiable standards of righteousness.

Fourth, *it provides a needed balance so liberty is not abused.* The gospel frees us from trying to earn or retain God's favor through rule keeping, but it also keeps us from running headlong to the other extreme—willfully sinning in the name of freedom. As people saved by grace, we have been sealed by the Spirit, who works in us to help us to

> **QUICK FACTS ON GALATIANS**
> - *Who wrote it?* Paul the apostle (1:1), perhaps through a secretary (6:11).
> - *Where was it written?* From Antioch, Paul and Barnabas's "home church" in Syria (Acts 14:26-28).
> - *To whom was it written?* To newly established churches in the southern part of the Roman province of Galatia, including Pisidian Antioch, Iconium, Lystra, and Derbe (Gal. 1:2).
> - *When was it written?* About AD 48, shortly after Paul's first missionary journey (Acts 13:1–14:28) and just before the Jerusalem Council (Acts 15:1-35).
> - *Why was it written?* Judaizers were trying to convince new Gentile converts that they had to be circumcised and keep the Law of Moses to be saved. Paul soundly rejects this message as a false gospel (Gal. 6:11-18).
> - *What is its basic theme?* Grace—not law—is both the way to life and the way of life.

love and obey Christ and to serve one another. We have been freed—not to do whatever we want, but to do what God wants.

## OVERVIEW OF THE LETTER

The basic message of Galatians can be summed up in three sentences: Paul had heard that the Galatian Christians were in danger of falling away from the true gospel of grace by turning to a legalistic approach to salvation and the Christian life. His passion for the truth compelled him to call them back to the freedom of salvation by grace alone through faith alone. In doing so, he argued that not only is the sinner *saved* by grace, but the saved sinner also *lives* by grace.

This simple but profound message can be expressed in a single line:

Grace is the way *to* life and the way *of* life.

Paul supports this basic truth in each of the three sections of his letter. Let's walk through them.

*Confirming the Truth of the Gospel (1:1–2:21).* After a brief greeting, Paul hits the ground running, declaring that any message from any source that does not agree with the gospel he had preached to the Galatians is a *false* gospel (1:1-10). Paul expected that some would ask, "What's so special about Paul? Why is his message any better than somebody else's?" To answer them, Paul tells the story of his own radical conversion from Judaism to faith in Christ and his call as an apostle (1:11-24). Although Peter and the apostles to the Jews had affirmed their agreement with the gospel of salvation by grace through faith (2:1-10), Paul recounts a run-in he had with Peter himself over the respected leader's failure to live in conformity with the truth of the gospel (2:11-16). In this encounter with Peter, Paul made it clear that the believer is no longer bound by the Law and has been freed to live a new life of faith through Christ (2:17-21).

*Defending the Superiority of the Gospel (3:1–4:31).* Having established that his gospel is God's gospel, Paul turns again to the Galatians' defection and draws a sharp distinction between law and grace. How can people saved by grace expect to grow by slipping into legalism? Having begun by faith, how could the Galatians now depend on their own works? Even Abraham, the father of the Jews, "believed God, and it was reckoned to him as righteousness" (3:6). The Law, rather than saving us, explains God's standards and exposes sin (3:19). That is, it served as a "tutor" to bring us to faith in Christ (3:24). Christ's grace, not the Law, made the Galatians part of the family of faith, where neither race, nor gender, nor social status provides an advantage. We are all fellow heirs of the grace of God in Christ Jesus (3:28). Understandably, then, the Galatians' backsliding dumbfounded Paul, who found it incredible that they would "turn back again to the weak and worthless elemental things" (4:9). Paul crowns his doctrinal section with an Old Testament illustration, contrasting children of slavery with children of freedom (4:21-31).

*Living the Freedom of the Gospel (5:1–6:18).* Having defended both his apostolic authority and the doctrine of justification by faith, Paul finally turns his attention to a defense of the life of Christian freedom. This answers the Judaizers' objection that living by grace promotes immorality. Having been set free in Christ, the Galatians are to "keep standing firm and . . . not be subject again to a yoke of slavery" (5:1). The Judaizers' teaching—which says that circumcision and other rituals save us—is not of God (5:8). Like leaven (5:9), this heresy permeates the church and nullifies the doctrine of grace. In some of his strongest language, Paul even wishes the pro-circumcision crowd would fall victim to their own practices and mutilate themselves (5:12). No, the Galatians were not set free to fall back under the Law. Neither, however, were they liberated to live immoral lives. They were set free to love and serve one another (5:13-14) and to display true Christlike character (5:22-23). In this way, they would truly fulfill the deeper intention behind the written laws. Unlike the false teachers who wanted to boast in circumcision instead of the Cross (6:12-13), Paul desires to boast only "in the cross of our Lord Jesus Christ" (6:14).

In short, Christ has set us free! We are free from the shackles of legalism. We are free to love and live for Him. We are free to love and serve others. Are you ready to immerse yourself in the study of this liberating letter? I certainly am!

# CONFIRMING THE TRUTH OF THE GOSPEL (GALATIANS 1:1–2:21)

Since the dawn of the church, the good news of God's grace has been threatened. When I think back over my fifty years of ministry, I recall the countless times I've had to personally take a stand for grace. Therefore, I'm not at all surprised that the first letter penned by Paul dealt with the same thing—confronting legalism and championing grace. That's why the words of one of my most respected Greek professors, written years ago, still reflect the condition of the church today:

> One of the most serious problems facing the orthodox Christian church today is the problem of legalism. One of the most serious problems facing the church in Paul's day was the problem of legalism. In every day it is the same. Legalism wrenches the joy of the Lord from the Christian believer, and with the joy of the Lord goes his power for vital worship and vibrant service. Nothing is left but cramped, somber, dull and listless profession. The truth is betrayed, and the glorious name of the Lord becomes a synonym for a gloomy kill-joy. The Christian under law is a miserable parody of the real thing.[1]

Paul's letter to the Galatians sets us free. Its bold statement of liberating grace points us away from a false gospel of self-empowered works and toward the true gospel of faith and Spirit-empowered love. Its basic theme, to which we will return again and again, is that grace is the way to life and the way of life.

In this first major section of the letter (1:1–2:21), Paul confirms the truth of the gospel of grace. This includes Paul's defense of his own apostleship, guaranteeing that the gospel he preached to the Galatians was, in fact, the truth received from God and taught by his fellow apostles. In this section, which includes some of the most autobiographical elements of all his writings, Paul tells his own story of conversion in great detail. He also recounts a run-in he had with Peter over that great apostle's failure to live in line with grace. How easy it is to

## KEY TERMS IN GALATIANS 1:1–2:21

***anathema* (ἀνάθεμα)** [331] "curse," "condemnation," "damnation"

Paul uses *anathema,* perhaps the strongest Greek word for absolute condemnation, to describe those who preach a false gospel (1:8-9). In Romans 9:3 Paul uses the term rhetorically, wishing himself "accursed" for the sake of his Jewish brethren, thus demonstrating the depth of the love he has for them. In 1 Corinthians 16:22 he uses the term to describe the utterly condemned state of those who have no love for Christ. Throughout church history the term continued to be applied to those who taught heresy concerning Jesus Christ's person or work.

***euangelizō* (εὐαγγελίζω)** [2097] "to announce good news," "to preach the gospel"

Paul uses this verb seven times in the book of Galatians, six of which are in chapter 1 alone. In Galatians 1:8, 9, and 11, Paul uses the term in reference to "preaching the gospel," contrasting those who preach the *authentic* good news of Jesus Christ with those who preach a gospel *contrary* to the one preached by Paul. From this verb we derive our word "evangelism," the ministry of sharing the gospel.

believe and preach one thing while caving in to the pressure to live in a way that pleases others! Through his personal testimony of receiving and preaching grace, Paul confirms that we believers have been freed from the Law and rescued from its condemnation. That means we're empowered to live beyond its legalistic dos and don'ts.

# Another Gospel Is Not *the* Gospel
## GALATIANS 1:1-10

**NASB**

¹Paul, an apostle (not *sent* from men nor through the agency of man, but through Jesus Christ and God the Father, who raised Him from the dead), ²and all the brethren who are with me,

**NLT**

¹This letter is from Paul, an apostle. I was not appointed by any group of people or any human authority, but by Jesus Christ himself and by God the Father, who raised Jesus from the dead.

²All the brothers and sisters* here join me in sending this letter to the churches of Galatia.

**NASB**

To the churches of Galatia:

³Grace to you and peace from ªGod our Father and the Lord Jesus Christ, ⁴who gave Himself for our sins so that He might rescue us from this present evil ªage, according to the will of our God and Father, ⁵to whom *be* the glory forevermore. Amen.

⁶I am amazed that you are so quickly deserting Him who called you ªby the grace of Christ, for a different gospel; ⁷which is *really* not another; only there are some who are disturbing you and want to distort the gospel of Christ. ⁸But even if we, or an angel from heaven, should preach to you a gospel ªcontrary to what we have preached to you, he is to be ᵇaccursed! ⁹As we have said before, so I say again now, if any man is preaching to you a gospel ªcontrary to what you received, he is to be ᵇaccursed!

¹⁰For am I now seeking the favor of men, or of God? Or am I striving to please men? If I were still trying to please men, I would not be a bondservant of Christ.

1:3 ªTwo early mss read *God the Father, and our Lord Jesus Christ* 1:4 ªOr *world* 1:6 ªLit *in* 1:8 ªOr *other than, more than* ᵇGr *anathema* 1:9 ªOr *other than, more than* ᵇGr *anathema*

**NLT**

³May God the Father and our Lord Jesus Christ* give you grace and peace. ⁴Jesus gave his life for our sins, just as God our Father planned, in order to rescue us from this evil world in which we live. ⁵All glory to God forever and ever! Amen.

⁶I am shocked that you are turning away so soon from God, who called you to himself through the loving mercy of Christ.* You are following a different way that pretends to be the Good News ⁷but is not the Good News at all. You are being fooled by those who deliberately twist the truth concerning Christ.

⁸Let God's curse fall on anyone, including us or even an angel from heaven, who preaches a different kind of Good News than the one we preached to you. ⁹I say again what we have said before: If anyone preaches any other Good News than the one you welcomed, let that person be cursed.

¹⁰Obviously, I'm not trying to win the approval of people, but of God. If pleasing people were my goal, I would not be Christ's servant.

1:2 Greek *brothers;* also in 1:11. 1:3 Some manuscripts read *God our Father and the Lord Jesus Christ.* 1:6 Some manuscripts read *through loving mercy.*

Like a surgeon going after a malignant tumor that needs to be excised immediately, Paul preps his patients with a brief greeting in order to remind them of what's at stake: grace, peace, the gospel of Christ's redeeming death and miraculous resurrection, and the very glory of God. It means life or death for the churches in Galatia.

In this spiritual emergency, Paul wastes no time weighing treatment options, crafting a noninvasive procedure, preparing anesthetics, or soothing his patients with a pleasant and tactful bedside manner. Instead, he takes up his scalpel and starts cutting, declaring the main thrust of his case right up front: There is one and only one gospel of grace. Any addition to this gospel results in a corruption of the truth, leading to a cancerous plague on the Christian faith.

When it comes to this fundamental truth, Paul doesn't hem and haw. He deals with it boldly, firmly, and without fretting over the potential repercussions. The pure gospel Paul had preached was in danger of mutating into a monstrous beast that mixed Jesus and faith with the Law, works, and a number of other rude intrusions into the Christian life. The worst part of this Galatian plague was that they were embracing it voluntarily! Faith plus works sounded harmless, even helpful at first. After Paul preached his clear message of grace through faith plus nothing, the sin-sick Judaizers, carrying their viral heresy, came along and infected those new believers who had just been made well. So Paul wrote to the Galatians to cleanse them of their disease of legalism and restore them to spiritual health.

Let's take a look at the first ten verses of Galatians, where we'll discover that the legalists' improved "gospel" was really a deadly disease.

## — 1:1-5 —

Paul begins his letter in the typical fashion of his day by naming the sender, declaring the recipients, and providing a blessing. Already in this greeting we see two main thrusts of his overall message that he will develop later: his God-given authority as a true apostle (1:1) and the simplicity of the gospel of Jesus Christ (1:1-5).

Paul's self-identification as "Paul, an apostle," serves as more than the author's identification of his title. From the opening words of the letter, Paul clearly affirms what his opponents were disputing—that he was as much a true apostle as the original Twelve. Paul had learned that the Judaizers—those who had sown seeds of legalism after his departure—had first discredited Paul as an impostor. If they could instill distrust among the Galatians regarding the accuracy or completeness of Paul's message—or if they could drive a wedge between Paul and the other apostles—then the Galatians would readily listen to a more "Jewish" version that emphasized doing the works of the Law.

The early Christian use of the Greek word *apostolos* [652] (apostle) carries with it a distinct authority. It "refers to a person who has a right to speak for God as His representative or delegate."[2] The term, as commentator John Stott explains, "was not a general word which could be applied to every Christian like the words 'believer,' 'saint' or 'brother.' It was a special term reserved for the Twelve and for one or two others whom the risen Christ had personally appointed."[3]

To be an authentic apostle of Jesus Christ, a person had to measure up to certain criteria. First, apostles had to have been eyewitnesses

## NORTH OR SOUTH?

### GALATIANS 1–2

For the better part of the last century, scholars have disagreed about the destination of the letter to the Galatians.[4] Was it written to the churches located in northern Galatia or southern Galatia? The destination of the epistle largely determines the date of its composition and is crucial for harmonizing the chronology in the book of Acts with Paul's testimony in Galatians 2.

For the majority of church history, commentators have held that the phrase "churches of Galatia" (1:2) refers to the geographic region occupying northern Galatia. The inhabitants of northern Galatia were Gauls who referred to themselves as "Galatians." In the book of Acts, Luke refers to places using geographic and ethnic names instead of Roman province titles. His references to Pamphylia, Pisidia, and Lycaonia in Acts 13:13-14 and 14:6 demonstrate this. Therefore, when Luke mentions the "Galatian region" in Acts 16:6 and 18:23, he is referring to the geographic region inhabited by the Gauls in northern Galatia. Luke's mention of Galatia comes after the Jerusalem Council in Acts 15 and during Paul's second and third missionary journeys. This theory attempts to harmonize Paul's account in Galatians 2:1-10 with the events of Acts by claiming that Paul is referring to the Jerusalem Council. The north Galatian theory requires Paul to have written Galatians around AD 57–58 at the earliest.

The Roman province of **Galatia** sprawled from far north to far south through the center of Asia Minor, making it difficult for scholars to determine to whom Paul wrote the letter.

The south Galatian theory came onto the scene in the late nineteenth century. It holds that "Galatia" refers to the southern portion of the Roman province, which contained churches founded by Paul during his first missionary journey (Acts 14:21), not the land occupied by the Gauls. This view takes into consideration that Paul had a tendency to use Roman province names (rather than ethnic regions) when referring to places (1 Cor. 16:19; 2 Cor. 1:1; 8:1). Paul's use of "Galatia" in his letter would then most likely refer to the area of Galatia where he had established churches. Furthermore, if Galatians had been written later to the northern region, it would seem surprising that Paul didn't explicitly mention the Jerusalem Council in his diatribe against the Judaizers (Gal. 2:1-10). The south Galatian theory makes more sense historically, because it means Paul wrote the book of Galatians prior to the Jerusalem Council, around AD 48.

of the resurrected Christ. Paul wrote in 1 Corinthians 9:1, "Am I not an apostle? Have I not seen Jesus our Lord?" Second, apostles confirmed their God-given office through miraculous signs and wonders, as Paul wrote in 2 Corinthians 12:12: "The signs of a true apostle were performed among you with all perseverance, by signs and wonders and miracles." Finally, apostles had to have been hand selected for this unique office by the risen Lord (Acts 1:21-26). Paul had fulfilled all of these requirements because he had encountered the resurrected Christ on his way to Damascus (Acts 9:3-6), Jesus had empowered Paul to perform amazing signs and wonders during his ministry (Acts 14:3), and the Lord had specifically chosen Paul to take the gospel to the Gentiles (Acts 9:15).

Nevertheless, the false teachers insisted that Paul was not, in fact, an apostle. Hoping to discredit his message, they had pointed out some flaw or deficiency in his apostleship. Perhaps Paul was an easier target than others. Paul himself, noticing that his own selection as an apostle took an unusual route, marveled at his own calling: "He appeared to James, then to all the apostles; and last of all, as to one untimely born, He appeared to me also. For I am the least of the apostles, and not fit to be called an apostle, because I persecuted the church of God. But by the grace of God I am what I am" (1 Cor. 15:7-10).

In his introduction to Galatians, Paul reminds his readers of the simple truth: He is a true apostle, "not sent from men nor through the agency of man, but through Jesus Christ and God the Father" (Gal. 1:1). No mere human being had played even a minor role in his commission to this high office. Yes, it was true that the leadership in the church of

Antioch had laid hands on Paul and Barnabas and had sent them out on their first missionary journey, which included Galatia (Acts 13:1-3). In this general sense, Barnabas, too, was a "sent one" (*apostolos;* see Acts 14:14), though Barnabas was "sent" by the church of Antioch rather than directly by the Lord Jesus Christ Himself. This was a particular ministry assignment different from Paul's particular calling as an apostle. When God calls a person into the preaching ministry today, that general God-given calling will be worked out in a variety of specific settings throughout his life. Similarly, Paul was already identified as an apostle because of his direct calling from the Lord Jesus, which his fellow apostles had testified to and confirmed. Therefore Paul, not the legalists, had the authority to speak for the Lord. This apostolic title gave Paul the necessary authority and credentials he needed to perform radical spiritual surgery on the Galatian Christians and the legalists who were duping them.

Though Paul thought it important to assert his apostolic authority, his greeting to the Galatian believers centers mostly on the content of the gospel message itself. He wishes his readers "grace" and "peace" from God the Father and the Lord Jesus Christ (1:3). Typically, letters in the Greek-speaking world began with the word *chairein* [5463], "greetings" (Acts 15:23; Jas. 1:1). Paul, however, began his letters with a unique greeting that sounded similar but had more profound theological significance: *charis . . . kai eirēnē* [5485, 2532, 1515](grace . . . and peace). Salvation comes purely by grace and results in peace with God. That's the cause and effect of the gospel summed up in just two words.

Paul also includes the fundamental pillars of the gospel message in this opening greeting. He tells us that Christ "gave Himself for our sins so that He might rescue us from this present evil age" (Gal. 1:4). The gospel is God's rescue operation, planned and executed to liberate believers from sin's condemnation and slavery. Jesus Christ paid the full cost of this ransom on the cross. Then, because Jesus was both perfect man and perfect God, the Father "raised Him from the dead" (1:1). By placing our faith in Christ, we receive the unearned mercy of full payment for sin as well as the unmerited grace of victory over death through Christ's resurrection. Jesus Christ died for our sins and rose from the dead. That's the core of the simple gospel message. No wonder Paul ends this brief but powerful introduction with a doxology to God the Father, "to whom be the glory forevermore. Amen" (1:5).

Now here's the point of it all. God has provided salvation through the finished work of His Son, Jesus Christ. The moment a person accepts by simple faith that Christ died for his or her sins and rose from the dead, God declares that person righteous and rescues that person from this present evil age. That's called the doctrine of *justification,* which is defined as the sovereign act of God whereby He declares a condemned sinner righteous while he or she is still in a sinning state. At the moment of our justification, our names are, as it were, removed from the roll of the lost and we are enrolled as citizens of heaven . . . never to be removed.

Pretty simple message, isn't it? So simple, in fact, that even a little child could understand and believe it. No wonder Paul marveled that the Galatians had exchanged his simple, clear message of grace for a complicated, spurious gospel of works.

## — 1:6-9 —

Perhaps without even re-dipping his pen, Paul turned from glorifying the Father for His marvelous grace to chastising the Galatians for their amazing apostasy. The language indicates utter astonishment that anybody would do what the Galatians were doing. Paul found himself in a state of dumbfounded shock.

Look carefully at the word "deserting" in 1:6. It implies the complete transfer of allegiance from one thing to another. When the Galatians turned their backs on Paul's authentic message, they were walking away from Christ Himself. Not only had they defected from the gospel, but they had done it "so quickly" that it threw Paul for a loop. If Paul wrote Galatians sometime during his stay in Antioch after the first missionary journey (Acts 14:28), it may have taken only a matter of weeks before the Galatian Christians turned tail in the face of bullying from the Judaizers.

Please notice something practical in this example of the Galatians' quick desertion of the gospel. It doesn't take many years in ministry to discover that one of the characteristics of a new Christian is gullibility. If you're involved in escorting a person into the family of God, never forget how vulnerable that person remains for some time until he or she becomes grounded in the truth. Think of that new believer's spiritual life as a fragile seed freshly planted in the soil. It takes time for the faith to take firm root and grow a strong stock and bear fruit. As older, more mature believers, we need to help them during this critical time. Think about this: If people who had been under Paul's ministry turned away so quickly, don't think for a moment that it couldn't happen to those *we* lead to Christ.

The Galatians deserted the gospel of grace for a "different" gospel (Gal. 1:6), which, Paul asserts, was not simply "another" legitimate version of the truth but a perversion of it. Paul describes their gospel with the Greek word *heteros* [2087], which means "another of a different kind."[5] The Galatians considered the Judaizers' brand of the gospel a legitimate choice, but it was nothing of the kind. By adding works of the Law to the gospel of grace, the Judaizers had changed the very DNA of the gospel. Their teaching was as different from the true gospel as night from day, fire from water, death from life.

These Judaizers were disturbing the Galatians and distorting the gospel (1:7). Once they added something to simple faith in Christ's person and work—whether it be circumcision, holy days, ceremonial cleansing, or Sabbath observance—they destroyed the gospel. So how did Paul respond to the truth-twisting Judaizers? Did he schedule a collegial dialogue to let the Galatians weigh the merits of both sides in a free and open discussion of all the options? Did he publish an essay in a peer-reviewed journal to persuade his opponents by well-reasoned arguments? Or did he ignore the Judaizers' madness—refusing to dignify it—and let it blow over like a harmless fad? No! Instead, he quite literally damned them to hell!

You rarely hear leaders in evangelical circles today come down on heresy like Paul did in his day. Paul calls down God's eternal judgment on those false teachers (1:8-9). In our hypersensitive, politically correct culture, Paul's words sound harsh, don't they? Notice, however, that Paul includes even himself in the threatened curse: "But even if we, or an angel from heaven, should preach to you a gospel contrary to what we have preached to you, he is to be accursed" (1:8). Paul includes heavenly angels and his own circle of apostles—whether "sent out" by Christ Himself or by missionary-sending churches—in order to highlight the fact that nobody is off the hook. The purity of the message takes precedence over the prestige of the person. This phrasing makes the curse universal—if *anyone* were to preach a gospel different from what Paul and Barnabas preached, he would deserve to be damned.

Notice, too, that Paul repeats the curse (1:9). He is deliberate and controlled in his rebuke. Paul's curse is not a slip of the tongue, a brief fit of rage, or a regrettable exaggeration of an emotional preacher. Though he essentially damns false teachers, this language doesn't fall under the category of vulgar cursing, either. Paul isn't fiercely shaking his fist at his opponents and shouting, "Damn you!" Rather, he shakes his head and expresses a clear theological fact: Altering the gospel is

# Driving Highway 1:10

**GALATIANS 1:10**

A number of years ago I found myself facing a dreadful dilemma. The church elders were divided over a matter that had less to do with clear biblical principles than with tradition. There was no clear scriptural precept that dictated what we should decide . . . and the final decision rested on my shoulders. Let me tell you, I was in turmoil. Not so much because I wanted to be sure I was making the right decision, but because I had a lot of friends on both sides of the issue, and I didn't want to alienate anybody. I didn't yet believe the old adage that "you can't please everybody." Young, energetic, and overly idealistic, I thought there had to be a solution that would make everybody happy—which really translates as "make everybody happy with me."

I needed to figure this out, so I said to Cynthia one afternoon, "I'm going to take a drive. I may be gone overnight. I want to pray and think about this." I set out still thinking that somehow, some way, I would be able to conjure up an answer that would please both sides.

Now I know this is going to reveal something about the unforgivable driving habits of my younger years, but I'm just going to have to fess up to it. While I was driving down the highway, I actually had my Bible open on the steering wheel and was reading it, searching desperately for some key that would unlock this conundrum. I said, "Lord, I'm going to read all the way through the New Testament if I have to." Looking back, I'm sure that doing a personal Bible study while driving had to have been infinitely more dangerous than talking on a cell phone, but at that time safety was the last thing on my mind. Pleasing people meant far more to me than personal safety.

I don't know why, but I started with Galatians. I made it ten verses into that book when those inspired words in 1:10 suddenly stopped me in my place. I got an answer—not the solution I was seeking, but the freedom to make a decision free from fear. At that moment God opened my eyes to see that I had been living under the tarnished

(continued on next page)

Golden Rule of People Pleasing: "Do for others what they want you to do for them." In that moment the ancient words of the apostle Paul became my own as I applied them to my situation: Am I now seeking the favor of friends, or of God? Am I striving to please my friends or to please God? If I were still a people pleaser, I wouldn't be a Christ servant. That did it . . . I changed lanes and did a U-turn!

Though I didn't immediately get the answer about how I should approach the debated topic at the church, I was freed by God's Word to stop seeking a solution that would please everybody (an impossibility) and start seeking an answer that would please God. Although I thought I had already worked through this people-pleasing thing, that experience set me on a permanent course of driving "Highway 1:10." It's not always easy. People pleasing naturally tries to tug us to the right or left. But as I keep going back to Paul's principle of God pleasing, those words have continually kept me from driving my life or ministry into a ditch.

damnable doctrine. People's souls were at stake. The church's testimony in the region of Galatia was at stake. In fact, at this early stage in the preaching of the gospel, the very future of Christianity was at stake. With so much at stake, Paul couldn't afford to sweet-talk or beat around the bush.

## — 1:10 —

Paul's final comments about pleasing God rather than men indicate that the Judaizers had likely accused Paul of currying favor with the Gentiles by teaching freedom from the Law. They probably charged Paul with presenting a "Christianity lite" in order to make the gospel easier for the Gentiles in Galatia to swallow. Along came the Judaizers in Paul's absence to "fill in the gaps" of Paul's gospel.

Paul's sharp condemnation of the false teachers, however, would dispel any doubt about whether Paul had been the least bit interested in pleasing men rather than God. As one commentator notes, "Men-pleasers simply do not hurl *anathemas* against those who proclaim false gospels. Indeed, if the apostle had wanted to please men, he would have remained a zealous Pharisee and promoter of the Law rather than becoming a servant of Christ."[6]

If relationships needed to be damaged or bridges needed to be burned, Paul was willing to pay that price. Why? Because he knew that the gospel is worth fighting for.

# APPLICATION: GALATIANS 1:1-10

## A Hill worth Dying On

I see a lot of battle-weary faces in the church today. People are tired of fighting for everything—fighting for a job; fighting for an education; fighting with neighbors; fighting to save their marriage, their family, or their school. They fight for their political parties, their family values, and their personal freedoms. With all this fighting, it's no wonder many are calling for a time-out and wishing we could all just get along.

So what about fighting for the gospel? Sounds a bit contradictory, doesn't it? Doesn't Ephesians 6:15 call it the "gospel of peace"? Christians are called to speak "the truth in love" (Eph. 4:15), not to clobber people over the head with it. Doesn't this demand a gentle, tolerant, agreeable, and passive approach to proclaiming the gospel?

Galatians 1:1-10 gives us at least one example of drawing a clear line in the sand and saying, "This far and no farther!" And not only does Paul refuse to yield any ground, he retaliates against the Judaizers' aggressions, striking decisive blows against a primary target—the rejection of the central claims of the gospel. The church's two-thousand-year history is filled with examples of people taking a stand for the fundamental truths of the Christian faith, regardless of the personal cost. In the early church, Christians refused to worship any god or king as Lord except Jesus Christ—their one true God and King. Saint Athanasius was exiled repeatedly for refusing to fudge on the full deity of Christ. Saint Augustine took a stand against those who believed that grace wasn't necessary for salvation and that we could actually work our way into favor with God. And how about the Reformation? Strong-hearted leaders like Luther and Calvin recovered the doctrine of justification by faith alone, infuriating the established church powers and putting their own lives at risk. There wasn't a passive bone in their bodies.

True, we must choose wisely which hills we're willing to die on. The problem with evangelical Christianity today, however, isn't that we have a shortage of defended hills but that the one hill we should all be willing to die on—the gospel—is left open to attack. Part of the reason is that our churches no longer make grounding believers in a clear understanding of the gospel and teaching them the foundational doctrine of grace their highest priorities. We have countless programs, numerous activities, and overwhelming busyness, but not nearly enough people who can expound and defend the gospel.

How about you? Take a moment to reflect on your own knowledge of the gospel. If somebody were to ask you, "What is this 'gospel' you keep talking about?" what would you say? Are you able to keep the crucial aspects of this message central in your thinking? Try jotting down a definition of "the gospel" in about twenty-five words or less. Do it right now.

_____

_____

_____

_____

Now look up the following passages from Paul's writings, noting what they teach us about certain vital elements of the gospel:

- The person of Christ: Rom. 1:1-4; 2 Cor. 4:4; 2 Tim. 2:8
- The work of Christ: Rom. 2:15-16; 1 Cor. 15:1-5; 2 Tim. 2:8
- Our response to Christ: Rom. 1:16-17; Gal. 2:16; Eph. 2:8-9

After examining these passages, return to your description of the gospel. Do you need to change, remove, or add anything to keep it in line with Scripture? If so, do it. Then examine your definition carefully. *This is the truth upon which Christianity stands or falls.* If that's not worth taking a stand for, then nothing is. Being a Christian doesn't mean we spend our days looking for a fight—especially a physical fight. But when perversions of the gospel appear in our midst, we should be willing not only to teach the truth but also to expose falsehood. You can be sure of this: Those who despise the message of the gospel may attack us. So be it. The gospel is a hill worth dying on.

# Radical Transformation
## GALATIANS 1:11-24

**NASB**

¹¹ For I would have you know, brethren, that the gospel which was preached by me is not according to man. ¹² For I neither received it from man, nor was I taught it, but *I received it* through a revelation of Jesus Christ.

¹³ For you have heard of my former manner of life in Judaism, how I used to persecute the church of God beyond measure and tried to destroy it; ¹⁴ and I was advancing in Judaism beyond many of my contemporaries among my ᵃcountrymen, being more extremely zealous for my ancestral traditions. ¹⁵ But when God, who had set me apart *even* from my mother's womb and called me through His grace, was pleased ¹⁶ to reveal His Son in me so that I might preach Him among the Gentiles, I did not immediately consult with ᵃflesh and blood, ¹⁷ nor did I go up to Jerusalem to those who were apostles before me; but I went away to Arabia, and returned once more to Damascus.

¹⁸ Then three years later I went up to Jerusalem to ᵃbecome acquainted with Cephas, and stayed with him fifteen days. ¹⁹ But I did not see any other of the apostles except ᵃJames, the Lord's brother. ²⁰ (Now in what I am writing to you, ᵃI assure you before God that I am not lying.) ²¹ Then I went into the regions of Syria and Cilicia. ²² I was *still* unknown to ᵃsight to the churches of Judea which were in Christ; ²³ but only, they kept hearing, "He who once persecuted us is now preaching the faith which he once tried to destroy." ²⁴ And they were glorifying God ᵃbecause of me.

1:14 ᵃLit *race*   1:16 ᵃI.e. human beings   1:18 ᵃOr *visit Cephas*   1:19 ᵃOr *Jacob*   1:20 ᵃLit *behold before God*   1:22 ᵃLit *face*   1:24 ᵃLit *in me*

**NLT**

¹¹ Dear brothers and sisters, I want you to understand that the gospel message I preach is not based on mere human reasoning. ¹² I received my message from no human source, and no one taught me. Instead, I received it by direct revelation from Jesus Christ.*

¹³ You know what I was like when I followed the Jewish religion—how I violently persecuted God's church. I did my best to destroy it. ¹⁴ I was far ahead of my fellow Jews in my zeal for the traditions of my ancestors.

¹⁵ But even before I was born, God chose me and called me by his marvelous grace. Then it pleased him ¹⁶ to reveal his Son to me* so that I would proclaim the Good News about Jesus to the Gentiles.

When this happened, I did not rush out to consult with any human being.* ¹⁷ Nor did I go up to Jerusalem to consult with those who were apostles before I was. Instead, I went away into Arabia, and later I returned to the city of Damascus.

¹⁸ Then three years later I went to Jerusalem to get to know Peter,* and I stayed with him for fifteen days. ¹⁹ The only other apostle I met at that time was James, the Lord's brother. ²⁰ I declare before God that what I am writing to you is not a lie.

²¹ After that visit I went north into the provinces of Syria and Cilicia. ²² And still the churches in Christ that are in Judea didn't know me personally. ²³ All they knew was that people were saying, "The one who used to persecute us is now preaching the very faith he tried to destroy!" ²⁴ And they praised God because of me.

1:12 Or *by the revelation of Jesus Christ.* 1:16a Or *in me.* 1:16b Greek *with flesh and blood.* 1:18 Greek *Cephas.*

Shortly after Paul and Barnabas boarded their ship in southern Asia Minor to head back to Antioch, the Judaizers attacked the churches in southern Galatia. Attempting to hijack the new churches and to take the infant believers hostage with a false gospel of works righteousness, the Judaizers began by questioning whether Paul had really been called as an apostle after all. Think about their strategy. In order to create doubt in the Galatians' minds regarding the message, they had to create doubts about the messenger. If they could exaggerate the gap between Paul and Jesus, then the origins of Paul's gospel would be thrown into question; and if they could drive a wedge between Paul and the other apostles, then they could force their own "gospel" in through the broadening crevice.

I'm sure some of them pointed out that Paul was a Johnny-come-lately who had never even heard Jesus preach or teach. Furthermore, Paul and Barnabas had been sent by the church in Antioch, whereas the original disciples had come from Jerusalem. Finally, Paul's message itself sounded like a radical departure from everything God had done among the Hebrews for centuries. Why would God suddenly change His mind and introduce such a radical break with the past? Wouldn't it be more reasonable to conclude that somewhere along the line Paul got it wrong? The uniqueness of his testimony and the distinctiveness of his message would have made Paul an easy target for those who wanted to undermine his apostolic authority.

In Galatians 1:11-24, we read Paul's first steps toward a full-blown refutation of the Judaizers' unfounded charges. He begins by expounding on his introductory claim that his calling as an apostle was not "from men nor through the agency of man, but through Jesus Christ and God the Father" (1:1). By defending his own credibility, Paul upholds the credibility of his message.

## — 1:11-12 —

Paul begins with three negatives, likely direct refutations of his opponents' claims that Paul's credentials were untrustworthy: Paul's gospel *was not according to man*, it *was not received from man*, and it *had not been taught to him*.

These summary denials underscore that Paul's source for the gospel was not human, earthly, or natural. He didn't dream up his gospel. It did not arise through creative brainstorming or clever mental formulation. In fact, I would suggest that Paul's gospel of salvation by grace through faith alone apart from any effort on behalf of believers isn't the sort of message somebody would dream up. It's so counterintuitive, so different from every other human religious inclination, that it seems unlikely anybody would ever concoct such a way of salvation. One resource describes the common view of salvation held among cults this way:

> One teaching that is totally absent from all the cults is the gospel of the grace of God. No one is taught in the cults that he can be saved from eternal damnation by simply placing his faith in Jesus Christ. It is always belief in Jesus Christ and "do this" or "follow that." All cults attach something to the doctrine of salvation by grace through faith. . . . It is never taught that faith in Christ alone will save anyone.[7]

Had Paul's message been "according to man," or, as the NLT puts it, "based on mere human reasoning" (1:11), one would expect that it would fit the mold of other man-made ways of salvation. In fact, Paul's message breaks the mold! So unique is the notion that a person is saved by grace alone through faith alone in Christ alone that it's almost inconceivable that any human would have made it up.

This makes Paul's affirmation about where the gospel did come from even more compelling. He received it "through a revelation of Jesus Christ" (1:12). It had not been taught to him by a middleman; it came directly from the mouth of the Lord Jesus Christ. Clearly, Paul is referring to the events surrounding his conversion, which is described in Acts 9. While Paul was on his way to Damascus with authority to arrest Christians, Jesus Himself appeared to him from heaven, knocking him to the ground and blinding him with a bright light (Acts 9:3-9). In his own account of his conversion delivered to King Herod Agrippa II, Paul filled in details of Jesus' revelation to him. Jesus had said to Paul:

> "For this purpose I have appeared to you, to appoint you a minister and a witness not only to the things which you have seen, but also to the things in which I will appear to you; rescuing you from the Jewish people and from the Gentiles, to whom I am sending you, to open their eyes so that they may turn from darkness to light and from the dominion of Satan to God, that they may receive forgiveness of sins and an inheritance among those who have been sanctified by faith in Me." (Acts 26:16-18)

Already in Paul's initial encounter with the resurrected and glorified Jesus, the Lord articulated the basics of the gospel message of forgiveness of sins by faith in Christ (Acts 26:18). He also mentioned that He would appear to Paul in the future (Acts 26:16). When Paul tells the Galatians that he had received his gospel directly from Jesus Christ, he likely refers not only to this life-changing event but also to any subsequent revelations he received during the years leading up to his first missionary journey.

## — 1:13-14 —

The first chapter of Galatians gives us autobiographical information about Paul that we find nowhere else in the Bible. In the next several verses, Paul first recounts his condition prior to his conversion to Christ (1:13-14), then briefly mentions his miraculous conversion (1:15-16), and finally describes the years between his conversion and the beginning of his preaching ministry (1:17-24).

Prior to meeting Jesus on the road to Damascus, Paul was running from God while convinced he was acting in His service. In his misguided zeal, Paul had taken up the mantle of a fanatical Pharisee, bent on destroying what he and his colleagues viewed as a heretical sect of Judaism—the followers of Jesus. What motivated his hatred of Christianity? Ironically, his love of Judaism.

One might expect that the adherents of a religion molded by the Old Testament Scriptures and focused on living a righteous life in anticipation of the coming King would be the first allies of the coming Messiah. Yet already in the Gospels we see the religious leaders—and especially the Pharisees—turning their noses up at the blue-collar commoner from Nazareth. If God were to raise up a Messiah, they reasoned, He would surely do so among the rabbis, not the rabble! The young Saul, a student of the famous Rabbi Gamaliel (Acts 5:34; 22:3), would have shared these prejudices. In fact, the more Saul sought to advance in Judaism and champion the traditions of his forefathers (Gal. 1:14), the more motivated he would have been to persecute the enemy sect of Christians.

## — 1:15-17 —

Imagine that journey to Damascus. Saul (later named Paul) held in his hands what amounted to an arrest warrant—legal permission from the Jewish authorities in Jerusalem to take Christians into custody. With that permission, Saul had been deputized to carry out the order by any means necessary. The various accounts of his enthusiastic mission illustrate the seriousness with which he pursued the Christian rebels:

I used to persecute the church of God beyond measure and tried to destroy it. (Gal. 1:13)

"I persecuted this Way to the death, binding and putting both men and women into prisons. . . . I also received letters to the brethren, and started off for Damascus in order to bring even those who were there to Jerusalem as prisoners to be punished." (Acts 22:4-5)

"Not only did I lock up many of the saints in prisons, having received authority from the chief priests, but also when they were being put to death I cast my vote against them. And as I punished them often in all the synagogues, I tried to force them to blaspheme; and being furiously enraged at them, I kept pursuing them even to foreign cities." (Acts 26:10-11)

The picture painted by Paul's own vivid words presents us with a man bent on death and destruction, motivated by a misguided religious zeal, and willing to do anything to accomplish what he saw as a God-given task. Then comes one of the greatest words in every believer's testimony: "but." Allow me to break down the key phrases of his powerful conversion story in 1:15-16.

*But when God.* Notice that Paul's testimony of salvation begins with God.[8] At a time when Paul was perhaps the worst possible candidate for salvation, God broke in. Throughout the rest of this two-verse testimony, God continues to be the Actor in this salvation drama. Look at the three things Paul says God had done while Paul was still journeying toward Damascus as the arch nemesis of Christ.

*God . . . had set me apart.* Even while Paul strutted about promoting a religious system rendered obsolete (Heb. 8:13) and pushing believers to blaspheme, God had marked him for conversion. In fact, while Paul was still in his mother's womb, God had His sovereign hand on him. From Paul's infancy on, his influences, experiences, and education had been orchestrated by God to prepare him for his Gentile mission. This language of being set apart even before birth reminds us of God's call on the prophet Jeremiah: "Before I formed you in the womb I knew you, and before you were born I consecrated you; I have appointed you a prophet to the nations" (Jer. 1:5).

*God . . . called me through His grace.* Having set Paul apart before he could do anything right or wrong, God also saw fit to intrude into his life at just the right moment—not a day too soon or a second too late.

## PAUL'S ARABIAN NIGHTS

### GALATIANS 1:15-24

Paul's brief account of the three years following his miraculous conversion on the road to Damascus brings up some unanswered questions. Why did he travel east into the region of Arabia? What did he do there? Was he alone or with others?

Luke's narrative of Paul's conversion in Acts 9 explains *why* Paul ended up in Arabia. While spending some time with disciples in Damascus (Acts 9:19), Paul immediately began preaching the gospel in the synagogues (Acts 9:20, 22). The Jewish leaders in Damascus, incensed at Saul's radical change of allegiance, plotted to put him to death (Acts 9:23-24). But the Christians in Damascus discovered this plot and helped Paul escape from the hands of his assassins by lowering him in a basket through an opening in the city wall (Acts 9:25).

Though Luke's narrative fast-forwards to Paul's trip to Jerusalem in Acts 9:26, we know from Paul's report in Galatians 1:17 that after his flight from Damascus he departed east into the Arabian wilderness for some time. What did he do there? We don't exactly know. One commentator speculates:

> In this period of withdrawal, as he meditated on the Old Testament Scriptures, on the facts of the life and death of Jesus that he already knew and on his experience of conversion, the gospel of the grace of God was revealed to him in its fullness. It has even been suggested that those three years in Arabia were a deliberate compensation for the three years of instruction which Jesus gave the other apostles, but which Paul missed. Now he had Jesus to himself, as it were, for three years of solitude in the wilderness.[9]

Of course, we can't be sure what Paul did in Arabia or with whom he spent his time—if anyone. In fact, we can't be sure exactly how long he spent there. However, Jesus Christ Himself had already revealed to Paul that He would visit Paul again (Acts 26:16). He may have done so during Paul's time in Arabia.

---

Apart from anything Paul did, was doing, or would do, God called Paul on account of His pure grace. His calling came in the startling form of a rare appearance of the Lord Jesus from heaven (Acts 9). With it came a profound ministry that would change not only the character of Christianity but also the direction of world history.

*God . . . was pleased to reveal His Son in me.* In essence, Paul said, "God saved me so that His Son might be unveiled in me." God's design for salvation goes beyond merely saving souls, as miraculous as that is. He created us not only to live with Him in heaven but also to display and glorify Jesus on earth.

All of these astounding acts of God in Paul's life served one stated purpose: that Paul might preach Christ among the Gentiles (Gal. 1:16). Now, think about this calling in light of Paul's Jewish nationalism and religious fanaticism. In Paul's mind, the Gentiles were dogs, the filth of the earth. Yet Paul says, essentially, "I was so radically changed by God's grace that I realized that the object of God's plan for me was to reach people I had cared nothing

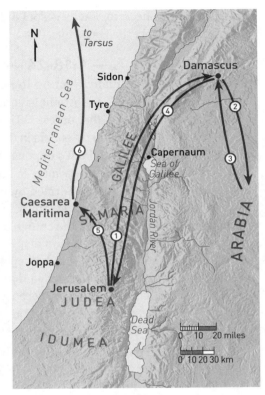

**Paul's Early Travels.** During the first three years after Paul's conversion, he spent time in Damascus and Arabia prior to visiting the original apostles in Jerusalem for the first time around AD 38.

about." Only a genuine, miraculous, heaven-sent conversion could cause a 180-degree turnaround like this.

Paul's Judaizing opponents in Galatia had claimed that Paul had conjured his gospel message of grace from his own imagination. Or that he had at least tainted the pure Jewish message from Jesus' original disciples in Jerusalem to suit his own purposes. Paul's testimony of his conversion takes a decisive swing at both lies. His testimony rules out that his gospel came from anybody other than Jesus Christ Himself. Paul then recounts his travels after his conversion to show that he did not rush to human teachers to clarify the gospel message (1:16). Rather, he first traveled east to Arabia, far from the original Jerusalem apostles. Then he returned to Damascus to begin his itinerant preaching (1:17). Nowhere in between did Paul consult with "flesh and blood" to add to, correct, or clarify the gospel he had received directly from Jesus

Christ. He had no need to. Paul's gospel didn't come from himself or from others, but from the Lord himself.

## — 1:18-24 —

After three years Paul finally went up to Jerusalem in order to meet Cephas (1:18; "Cephas" is the Aramaic equivalent of Peter's name). He also met James, the brother of Jesus. This meeting with Peter and James—the two most prominent leaders in the Jerusalem church at that time—is significant because Paul's opponents were likely contending that their own "Jewish gospel" was more in line with the original teachings of Jesus and that it was confirmed by the preaching of the Jerusalem apostles, including Peter and James. By pointing out that he had visited with those two pillars of the church after initially receiving the true gospel of grace from Christ, Paul dispels the myth that his gospel was different from that of the Jerusalem apostles. In fact, Paul points out that the churches throughout Judea that had heard of his conversion to Christ "were glorifying God" because of him (1:24). Why? Because the one who had once persecuted the church in that region was now "preaching the faith which he once tried to destroy" (1:23).

By sharing these details of his first trip to Jerusalem, Paul dealt a major blow to the Judaizers' argument. When the Galatians turned away from Paul and his gospel in favor of the Judaizers and their religion, they were not turning to a purer, earlier gospel of Jesus, Peter, and James. Instead, they were turning their backs on God and embracing a false gospel.

# APPLICATION: GALATIANS 1:11-24

## A Story to Tell to the Nations

In light of Paul's powerful testimony in Galatians 1:11-24, I want to emphasize an important lesson for today: *When God transforms a life, there's always a testimony*. The implication of this is just as important: *Testimonies are meant to be told, not hidden*. Because of these truths, every genuine believer in Jesus Christ has a story to tell.

Now, the story centers on the gospel and what Jesus Christ did for us, not on us and what we do for Him. We need to affirm that from the start. But this doesn't change the fact that God is telling a story *through us.* As we tell the story, our testimony can provide a simple yet compelling framework for delivering the gospel message.

Many of us break into a cold sweat when we hear the word "testimony." We imagine an open microphone and a crowd of strangers, or some stuffy-looking elder or deacon interrogating us for church membership. Don't panic! Sharing your testimony is actually quite simple. The following suggestions will help relieve some of the pressure.

Let me begin by suggesting four things *not* to do when you tell your story. First, *don't preach.* Just talk. When you give your testimony, don't make demands or bully the person with whom you're speaking. Let your story speak for itself. Second, *don't generalize.* Be specific. Mention places, events, and people. Share how you felt and what you were thinking. Most of all, though, be specific about how you came to the point of becoming a Christian. This will help people overcome their own obstacles on the path leading to Christ. Third, *don't be vague.* Be clear and simple. Talk straight and use plain terms. This isn't the time to impress people with any high-handed theological lingo. Put away your Christianese. Terms like "got saved" or "went forward" or "sinner's prayer" or "redeemed by grace" are meaningless to most unbelievers. Finally, *don't defend yourself.* Declare your story. You don't need to argue if somebody questions the validity of your testimony. This world is filled with cynics and skeptics, but it's also replete with eager folks whom the Lord has prepared to hear your story. Just tell your own story, explaining the difference it has made . . . then trust in the power of God to move in the hearts of those who hear. You don't need to tell all the details. Simply talk about trusting in Christ.

Now let me share three things you *should* do when sharing your testimony. First, *be brief.* If Paul could summarize his miraculous testimony in just fourteen verses, you can easily keep your story down to a few minutes. Be specific, but also be selective. Keep the focus on Christ's work in your life and leave time for questions, interaction, and listening. Second, *be logical.* Paul's example in Galatians 1 is the best model I know. Like Paul, tell what happened before you came to Christ, precisely how you came to Christ, and then how your life changed after you came to Christ. Third, *be humble.* Glorify God, not self. Focus on the transformed life after Christ, not the inglorious life of sin, stubbornness, or self-righteousness before Christ. Remember the end result of Paul's testimony: "They were glorifying God because of me" (1:24).

In light of these simple principles, take a moment right now to write out your testimony. One word of warning, though. Not everyone experiences as dramatic a change as Paul. Resist the temptation to exaggerate or overemphasize sins. So-called boring testimonies from believers who were raised in the church and came to the Lord at an early age can often demonstrate to self-righteous people that even "good" sinners need a Savior. Never be ashamed of the story God is telling through you.

On your own paper, tablet, or computer, re-create the following three-column chart to summarize each section of your testimony. Aim for an account that you can give in under three minutes.

| MY LIFE BEFORE CHRIST | HOW I CAME TO KNOW CHRIST | HOW MY LIFE HAS CHANGED |
|---|---|---|
| | | |

Now that you've thought through your testimony, share it with someone. It could be a neighbor, a colleague, a relative, a friend, someone at work, or even a stranger. Pray that God will bring you somebody with whom to share your testimony within the next few days. Then keep an eye out for this divine appointment, remembering the apostle Peter's words: "Sanctify Christ as Lord in your hearts, always being ready to make a defense to everyone who asks you to give an account for the hope that is in you, yet with gentleness and reverence" (1 Pet. 3:15).

# A Gospel worth Accepting and Affirming
## GALATIANS 2:1-10

**NASB**

¹Then after an interval of fourteen years I went up again to Jerusalem with Barnabas, taking Titus along also. ²ᵃIt was because of a revelation that I went up; and I submitted to them the gospel which I preach among the Gentiles, but *I did so* in private to those who were of reputation, for fear that I might be running,

**NLT**

¹Then fourteen years later I went back to Jerusalem again, this time with Barnabas; and Titus came along, too. ²I went there because God revealed to me that I should go. While I was there I met privately with those considered to be leaders of the church and shared with them the message I had been preaching to the Gentiles. I wanted to make sure that we were in agreement, for fear that all my efforts had been wasted and I was running

or had run, in vain. ³But not even Titus, who was with me, though he was a Greek, was compelled to be circumcised. ⁴But *it was* because of the false brethren secretly brought in, who had sneaked in to spy out our liberty which we have in Christ Jesus, in order to bring us into bondage. ⁵But we did not yield in subjection to them for even an hour, so that the truth of the gospel would remain with you. ⁶But from those who ᵃwere of high reputation (what they were makes no difference to me; God ᵇshows no partiality)—well, those who were of reputation contributed nothing to me. ⁷But on the contrary, seeing that I had been entrusted with the gospel ᵃto the uncircumcised, just as Peter *had been* ᵇto the circumcised ⁸(for He who effectually worked for Peter in *his* apostleship ᵃto the circumcised effectually worked for me also to the Gentiles), ⁹and recognizing the grace that had been given to me, ᵃJames and Cephas and John, who were reputed to be pillars, gave to me and Barnabas the right ᵇhand of fellowship, so that we *might go* to the Gentiles and they to the circumcised. ¹⁰*They* only *asked* us to remember the poor—the very thing I also was eager to do.

2:2 ᵃLit *according to revelation I went up* 2:6 ᵃLit *seemed to be something* ᵇLit *does not receive a face* 2:7 ᵃLit *of the uncircumcision* ᵇLit *of the circumcision* 2:8 ᵃLit *of the circumcision* 2:9 ᵃOr *Jacob* ᵇLit *hands*

the race for nothing. ³And they supported me and did not even demand that my companion Titus be circumcised, though he was a Gentile.*

⁴Even that question came up only because of some so-called believers there—false ones, really*—who were secretly brought in. They sneaked in to spy on us and take away the freedom we have in Christ Jesus. They wanted to enslave us and force us to follow their Jewish regulations. ⁵But we refused to give in to them for a single moment. We wanted to preserve the truth of the gospel message for you.

⁶And the leaders of the church had nothing to add to what I was preaching. (By the way, their reputation as great leaders made no difference to me, for God has no favorites.) ⁷Instead, they saw that God had given me the responsibility of preaching the gospel to the Gentiles, just as he had given Peter the responsibility of preaching to the Jews. ⁸For the same God who worked through Peter as the apostle to the Jews also worked through me as the apostle to the Gentiles.

⁹In fact, James, Peter,* and John, who were known as pillars of the church, recognized the gift God had given me, and they accepted Barnabas and me as their co-workers. They encouraged us to keep preaching to the Gentiles, while they continued their work with the Jews. ¹⁰Their only suggestion was that we keep on helping the poor, which I have always been eager to do.

2:3 Greek *a Greek.* 2:4 Greek *some false brothers.* 2:9 Greek *Cephas;* also in 2:11, 14.

In Galatians 1, Paul proved his apostolic authority by reminding the Galatians that Jesus Christ Himself was the source of both his calling and his gospel message (1:1, 11-12). In that first leg of his argument, he emphasized that his gospel had reached its maturity apart from any input by the first apostles. Paul's was an independent witness of Christ and of the good news of salvation by faith in Him. None of it was dependent on any human being. But this leaves open the possibility that perhaps—*just perhaps*—Paul's gospel was different from that of the Jerusalem apostles. Perhaps Paul received a reliable message from Jesus, but then he twisted it to his own ends. Maybe he had compromised it to suit the Gentile culture. Surely the fourteen years after his conversion had afforded enough time for pollutants to work their way into his message and spoil what had once been a pure version of Jesus' teaching.

These charges sound perfectly plausible. Most likely the Judaizers were using such reasonable-sounding arguments as wedges to create a breach of trust between Paul and the Galatian believers. Apparently that strategy was working, because Paul felt the need to prove the veracity of his version of the gospel in the second chapter of Galatians. He does this by showing not only that he was unified with the Jerusalem apostles in his message but also that they affirmed him in his ministry to the Gentiles.

## — 2:1-2 —

Paul made it clear earlier in his letter that he had received his message from God and not from people. This section explains why he went up to Jerusalem the second time fourteen years after his conversion. He did so "because of a revelation" (2:2). So, taking with him his companions, Barnabas, a Levite who had earlier introduced him to the Jerusalem church (Acts 9:27), and Titus, a Gentile convert to Christianity, Paul traveled to the "mother church" in Jerusalem. There the renowned leaders Peter, James (the brother of Jesus), and John still lived, leading the growing, international church from its original epicenter.

Since Paul's original departure from Jerusalem over ten years earlier (Acts 9:26-30), several significant events had transpired:

- Paul settled down in Tarsus, his hometown, in southeastern Asia Minor (Acts 9:30; 11:25).
- Peter received a revelation from God that the gospel of salvation was for the Gentiles also (Acts 10:1-16).
- Peter preached the gospel to the first official Gentile convert, the Roman centurion Cornelius, who converted with his whole family (Acts 10:17-48).
- Peter initially received resistance from the "circumcision party" in Jerusalem for accepting the uncircumcised Gentiles into

the church, but they changed their minds after hearing Peter's account of his revelation from God (Acts 11:1-18).

- Greek-speaking Gentiles in Antioch accepted the gospel when it was preached to them by Jewish believers who had been scattered because of the persecution after Stephen's death (Acts 11:19-21).
- The Jerusalem church sent Barnabas to Antioch to teach and lead the new Greek converts there (Acts 11:22-24).
- Overwhelmed with the ever-increasing responsibilities in Antioch, Barnabas fetched Paul from Tarsus, then spent a year ministering with him in Antioch (Acts 11:25-26).

At this point in Acts, we read of the circumstances leading up to Paul's visit to the Jerusalem church, which was precipitated by a revelation from God just as Paul mentioned in Galatians 2:2.

> Now at this time some prophets came down from Jerusalem to Antioch. One of them named Agabus stood up and began to indicate by the Spirit that there would certainly be a great famine all over the world. And this took place in the reign of Claudius. And in the proportion that any of the disciples had means, each of them determined to send a contribution for the relief of the brethren living in Judea. And this they did, sending it in charge of Barnabas and Saul to the elders. (Acts 11:27-30)

When Paul, Barnabas, and Titus arrived in Jerusalem, they not only presented the love offering to the apostles in order to assuage the effects of the famine but also "submitted to them the gospel" of salvation Paul had been preaching among the Gentiles in Tarsus and Antioch (Gal. 2:2). Paul, however, wisely chose to meet with the Jerusalem leadership privately rather than in a public forum. It is likely that, based on reports from the prophets and teachers who had come from Jerusalem to Antioch, Paul would have known that Peter's inclusion of Gentiles into the church had already caused some controversy (see Acts 10–11). The Jerusalem church had been coping with an ultratraditional party of Judaizers who were itching to push this controversy to a whole new level.[10]

Paul's worries about having been running "in vain" (Gal. 2:2) did not stem from a fear that Jesus had taught him the wrong gospel. His concerns were practical rather than theological. If leaders like Peter, James—the brother of Jesus—and John appeared to waver or waffle at all in their support for the thriving ministry among the Gentiles in their daughter church in Antioch, Paul "feared that his past and present

## BARNABAS AND TITUS

### GALATIANS 2:1

Even though we're tempted to picture a lonely Paul trudging through the wilderness with a handful of well-worn scrolls to preach the gospel to unreached peoples, we should get that "Lone Ranger" image out of our heads. From the beginning, Paul carried out his apostolic ministry with the companionship and assistance of numerous colleagues. In Galatians, Paul specifically mentions Barnabas and Titus as his companions on his relief mission to Jerusalem: "I went up again to Jerusalem with Barnabas, taking Titus along also" (2:1). Who were these two men?

Although he's never mentioned in the book of Acts, Titus appears several times in 2 Corinthians as Paul's "brother" (2:13), his "partner and fellow worker" (8:23), and a source of comfort in his distress (7:6). He was clearly a Greek, who in the midst of the Judaizing controversy refused to be bullied into circumcision (Gal. 2:3). Thus, we see Titus as a man of proven character with a heart totally devoted to the ministry (2 Cor. 8:16; 12:18). In fact, as Titus matured in the faith, Paul entrusted to him the pastoral ministry on Crete (Titus 1:5).

In contrast to the converted Gentile Titus, Barnabas was a Levite. Though his given name was Joseph, the apostles dubbed him "Barnabas," which Luke translates "son of encouragement" (Acts 4:36). In his first appearance in the biblical story we see Barnabas giving generously to the apostles' ministry (Acts 4:37). In keeping with his nickname, the "son of encouragement" came alongside Paul and vouched for him before the original apostles (Acts 9:26-27) and later persuaded Paul to aid him in the exploding ministry among Gentiles in Antioch (Acts 11:25-26). When the Spirit led the church in Antioch to send out missionaries, He chose Barnabas and Paul (Acts 13:1-3). It is true that they later had a falling out over whether to give the young disciple, John Mark, a second chance after he had abandoned their ministry team. Not surprisingly, the "son of encouragement" championed Mark's reinstatement while Paul questioned the boy's reliability (Acts 15:36-40). In all these scenes from his life of ministry, Barnabas personified grace, mercy, patience, and encouragement.

ministry might be hindered or rendered of no effect by the Judaizers."[11] That is, the potential controversy that could erupt in a public hearing could have a very disruptive outcome.

Let me illustrate Paul's concern with a modern analogy. Nobody likes to get slapped with a lawsuit. They are expensive, arduous, time consuming, stressful, and can disrupt our lives for months on end. Even people who know they can prove they are in the right will take steps to avoid lawsuits because of the troublesome and expensive nature of the legal process. Less-official mediations, arbitrations, or simple deliberations that can avoid lawsuits are always preferable to the turmoil caused by a suit and court hearing. The same was true in Paul's day. Though he was completely confident that the gospel he had been preaching was true, neither he nor Barnabas had any interest in getting embroiled in a long, drawn-out "suit" between Jerusalem and Antioch that might hinder their ministry or confuse the new believers in Antioch regarding the simple truth of the gospel.

For the sake of peace, those men "of reputation" (the Jerusalem leaders) could have temporarily pulled the plug on Paul's ministry. Or they might have attempted some kind of compromise for the sake of unity. Or perhaps they would have capitulated to the political and religious pressure from the Judaizers to protect their people from persecution. We don't know exactly what nightmare scenarios were going through Paul's head, but we do know that he wisely chose prudence and discretion over recklessness and abandon.

## — 2:3-5 —

In Galatians 2:1, Paul notes that the uncircumcised Gentile convert Titus had joined him and Barnabas on their trip to Jerusalem. Titus served as a sort of test case. Would the apostles in Jerusalem agree with Paul that salvation comes through faith alone in Christ alone? Or would the Jerusalem church leaders require Titus to undergo the normal means of conversion to Judaism—circumcision—in order to partake of the salvation originally meant for the Jewish people?

How did "those who were of reputation" respond (2:2)? Paul writes, "But not even Titus, who was with me, though he was a Greek, was compelled to be circumcised" (2:3). Let me remind you that one of the urgent challenges that incited Paul to write Galatians was that Judaizers in Galatia were compelling the Galatians to be circumcised (6:12). The same Greek phrase is used in both places. The point is that even in the center of Judaism, in the presence of the original Jewish followers of Jesus, surrounded by the most Law-loving Jews in the world, nobody compelled Gentile believers to be circumcised. What sense would it make, then, for the Judaizers to insist on enforcing the rite of circumcision for Gentile believers living in the remote regions of Galatia?

Paul then zooms in on the opponents he had been trying to avoid in Jerusalem (2:4-5). Commentator James Boice notes that Paul's descriptors of the "false brethren" constitute a "military metaphor, used to indicate the subversive and militant nature of the evil that Paul was fighting."[12]

"Secretly" . . . "sneaked" . . . "spy" . . . "bondage." Paul saw himself in the midst of a life-and-death battle, striving to protect a priceless treasure: the gospel of Jesus Christ. Judaizing spies whose loyalty remained with the old Law of Judaism were merely playing the part of followers of Christ, having infiltrated the ranks of the church in order to destroy the doctrine of grace from the inside out. And the best way to destroy grace is to enslave believers with a strenuous religious system including

- prerequisites for meriting salvation;
- rituals to receive salvation; and
- righteous works to maintain salvation.

If Paul and Barnabas had sought peace at any price, the brilliant light of the glorious gospel of grace would have been eclipsed by the waning, reflected glory of an obsolete covenant of works. And if the Judaizers had won a victory at the Christian command center in Jerusalem, the outposts of the true faith would have suffered similar attacks at the hands of an emboldened insurgency of self-righteous frauds. This is why Paul and his associates refused to yield to the demands of the false teachers "for even an hour" (2:5). The survival of the truth of the gospel itself was at stake, and Paul wasn't willing to give even an inch.

## — 2:6-9 —

At first glance, Paul's language here could sound a little standoffish and maybe even arrogant. He calls the apostles Peter and John, along with James (the brother of Jesus), "those who were of high reputation" (2:6) and men "who were reputed to be pillars" (2:9). He also makes this enigmatic parenthetical statement: "What they were makes no difference to me" (2:6). Should we read these statements as a subtle put-down of these men? Not at all! Remember, in light of the Judaizers' schemes in Galatia, the last thing Paul needed was to find himself and Barnabas on the wrong side of the original Jerusalem apostles. That would have played right into the Judaizers' hands. Besides, Paul was bringing a financial gift to that church, demonstrating love and unity with them. Controversy and schism were not on his agenda. We should instead read these statements in light of the Judaizers' attempt to put Paul in his place by overemphasizing the authority of the "super apostles" in Jerusalem (cf. 2 Cor. 11:5).

The Judaizers likely viewed James, Peter, and John as real apostles, and Paul as an impostor. James, Peter, and John had known Christ during His earthly ministry; Paul had not. They ministered primarily to

Jews; Paul brought the "unclean" people into the church and let them remain "unclean." So, the Judaizers must have expected the hammer to fall on Paul when they saw the results of his radical "anything goes" gospel: an uncircumcised Gentile believer in Christ, Titus, standing right in their midst. What a surprise those Judaizers must have had when the pillars of the church in Jerusalem not only accepted Titus as a brother in Christ but also affirmed Paul's ministry to the Gentiles!

To the consternation of Paul's enemies, Peter, James, and John accepted him as an equal. They recognized that one God was directing their different ministries, one grace was empowering their different missions, and one gospel was the driving force in everything they did. The wedge the Judaizers had tried to drive between the leaders in Jerusalem and the missionaries in Antioch became a stake driven through the heart of those false teachers trying to suck the life out of the gospel of grace. Not only did the Jerusalem leaders add nothing to Paul's gospel (Gal. 2:6), but they extended the "right hand of fellowship" to Barnabas and Paul, blessing the continuation of their work among the Gentiles (2:7-9). The win-win result must have thrilled Paul and Barnabas!

Think about why. On that epochal day, rather than being scolded in front of their opponents, put in their places, and then sent back to Antioch stripped of their ministry, Paul and Barnabas received a three-fold endorsement. First, the apostolic leaders saw Paul's distinctive contribution to the work of the ministry. They realized that Paul and Barnabas represented not a competing message but a complementary ministry (2:7). Peter had been sent to the Jews, Paul to the Gentiles.

Second, they put Paul's ministry on par with Peter's. The church leaders saw that although Peter and Paul had different ministries, their empowerment and authority came from the same source—God (2:8). Because both ministries had clear evidence of God's miraculous confirmation, it was clear that God had shown favor to each of them. The only solution was to view the situation from God's perspective: Paul and Peter represented unity and diversity in the body of Christ.

Third, they recognized the grace given to Paul and encouraged him to press on. Seeing that Paul had the gifts, skills, training, and experience to minister to the Gentiles, the apostles urged him to keep at his God-given task (2:9). Paul and Barnabas had presented a clear and compelling case that their ministry to the Gentiles was in perfect harmony with Peter's own realization several years earlier: Apart from circumcision or any other work of the Law, "the gift of the Holy Spirit had been poured out on the Gentiles also" (Acts 10:45).

## — 2:10 —

In the midst of this doctrinal discussion, however, the Jerusalem apostles did add one thing—a reminder. Understand, this wasn't something they added to the gospel message as a requirement for salvation, but something they urged Paul not to forget: "Remember the poor" (2:10). Why would the apostles interject this reminder, especially in light of the fact that the primary purpose of Paul's visit was to bring a substantial gift for the poor and suffering in Jerusalem?

It may be that the apostles recognized that an emphasis on doctrinal purity could lead to a neglect of practical ministry. I've seen this imbalance all my life—a church may have all its theological t's crossed and i's dotted, but they tremble at the thought of actually getting their hands dirty by reaching out to the poor, the needy, the helpless, and the hopeless. What a tragedy! The most generous, self-sacrificial, and philanthropic people in the world should be those who have come to terms with the theological truth of the depth of God's grace and mercy. This is why Paul responded that he wasn't about to neglect the needs of the poor. This was something he was "eager to do" (2:10).

Right doctrine and right practice. Both of these were confirmed by the Jerusalem apostles, vindicating Paul's authority as an apostle of the true gospel of Jesus Christ.

# APPLICATION: GALATIANS 2:1-10

## Wielding Zeal Well

As I ponder this great account of the face-to-face meeting between the Antioch envoys (Paul, Barnabas, and Titus) and the Jerusalem leaders (Peter, James—the brother of the Lord—and John), I'm amazed at how a meeting that took place nearly two thousand years ago resounds with relevance today. Let me point out one specific practical lesson we learn from each group.

From the Antioch contingent we learn, *in your zeal for the truth, don't forget prudence*. Think about it. Paul could have stepped into Jerusalem with guns blazing. He could have demanded an open forum in which every viewpoint would be hashed out. He could have flaunted the freedom of the gospel in ways that not only offended the erring Judaizers but also drew unneeded attention from the unbelieving Jewish establishment, which was already looking for an excuse to pounce on the Jerusalem church. In short, Paul could have stood tall and proud for the truth, belting out bold proclamations in public and thereby lighting a match in a potentially explosive situation.

But he chose prudence. I can imagine Paul and Barnabas strategizing as they walked the long, mostly uphill trek from Antioch to Jerusalem. Barnabas, with his gentle, encouraging spirit, and Paul, with his firm determination, would have talked through the perfect plan to stand for the truth in the most favorable manner. This involved a private meeting with the apostles first (2:2), which proved to be a wise move. When the sneaky Judaizers did creep into the open, Jerusalem and Antioch stood back to back against the enemies as confirmed allies in defending the gospel of grace.

This is an important lesson for us today. All too often in our understandable and even commendable zeal to stand for the truth, we forget the principle of "speaking the truth in love" (Eph. 4:15). In our eagerness to "contend earnestly for the faith which was once for all handed down to the saints" (Jude 1:3), we can forget to do so "with gentleness and reverence" (1 Pet. 3:15). We all need to get into the habit of prayerfully considering the best way to take our stand for the truth. Maybe this means waiting a day or two before we confront an erring brother or sister in Christ. Or perhaps talking it over with a wise believer who can help us think through the best approach. A levelheaded strategy always brings about a better result than a hotheaded strike. A soft answer still turns away wrath (Prov. 15:1).

Next, from the Jerusalem leaders we learn, *in your passion for right doctrine, don't neglect right living.* Galatians 2:10 reminds us that the gospel is not a list of propositions to be locked away in our heads, but a life-changing power meant to be expressed through our hearts and hands . . . from the inside out. It's easy to make this more complicated than it is. Simply put, just as we received grace from God, we should extend grace toward others. Set others free in Christ; don't hold them hostage to your own rules and regulations. Affirm the validity of a fellow Christian's mission; don't judge him or her for being different. Accept one another, just as God has accepted you.

Once we've come to terms with the theological truth of God's grace, we must begin to put this truth into practice. Accept new believers for who they are as you graciously encourage them to become all that God wants them to be. Parents, give your kids the grace to become who God wants them to be, not who you want them to be. Believers, reach out to those with real, physical needs, not shying away from people who might take a lot of our time and resources. By grace, Christ gave up everything for our sakes. The more we understand this profound truth, the more it should affect our practical living.

# Going Head-to-Head with Hypocrisy
## GALATIANS 2:11-21

**NASB**

[11] But when Cephas came to Antioch, I opposed him to his face, because he [a] stood condemned. [12] For prior to the coming of certain men from [a] James, he used to eat with the Gentiles; but when they came, he *began* to withdraw and hold himself aloof, fearing [b] the party of the circumcision. [13] The rest of the Jews joined him in hypocrisy, with the result that even Barnabas was carried away by their hypocrisy. [14] But when I saw that they were not [a] straightforward about the truth of the gospel, I said to Cephas in the presence of all, "If you, being a Jew, live like the Gentiles and not like the Jews, how *is it that* you compel the Gentiles to live like Jews? [b]

[15] "We *are* Jews by nature and not sinners from among the Gentiles; [16] nevertheless knowing that a man is not justified by the works of [a] the Law but through faith in Christ Jesus, even we have believed in Christ Jesus, so that we may be justified by faith in Christ and not by the works of [a] the Law; since by the works of [a] the Law no [b] flesh will be justified. [17] But if, while seeking to be justified in

**NLT**

[11] But when Peter came to Antioch, I had to oppose him to his face, for what he did was very wrong. [12] When he first arrived, he ate with the Gentile believers, who were not circumcised. But afterward, when some friends of James came, Peter wouldn't eat with the Gentiles anymore. He was afraid of criticism from these people who insisted on the necessity of circumcision. [13] As a result, other Jewish believers followed Peter's hypocrisy, and even Barnabas was led astray by their hypocrisy.

[14] When I saw that they were not following the truth of the gospel message, I said to Peter in front of all the others, "Since you, a Jew by birth, have discarded the Jewish laws and are living like a Gentile, why are you now trying to make these Gentiles follow the Jewish traditions?

[15] "You and I are Jews by birth, not 'sinners' like the Gentiles. [16] Yet we know that a person is made right with God by faith in Jesus Christ, not by obeying the law. And we have believed in Christ Jesus, so that we might be made right with God because of our faith in Christ, not because we have obeyed the law. For no one will ever be made right with God by obeying the law."*

[17] But suppose we seek to be made right with God through faith in Christ

Christ, we ourselves have also been found sinners, is Christ then a minister of sin? May it never be! [18]For if I rebuild what I have *once* destroyed, I prove myself to be a transgressor. [19]For through [a]the Law I died to [a]the Law, so that I might live to God. [20]I have been crucified with Christ; and it is no longer I who live, but Christ lives in me; and [a]the *life* which I now live in the flesh I live by faith in the Son of God, who loved me and gave Himself up for me. [21]I do not nullify the grace of God, for if righteousness *comes* through [a]the Law, then Christ died needlessly."

2:11 [a]Or *was to be condemned;* lit *was one who was condemned,* or, *was self-condemned* 2:12 [a]Or *Jacob* [b]Or converts *from the circumcised;* lit *those from the circumcision* 2:14 [a]Or *progressing toward;* lit *walking straightly* [b]Some close the direct quotation here, others extend it through v 21 2:16 [a]Or *law* [b]Or *mortal man* 2:19 [a]Or *law* 2:20 [a]Or *insofar as I* 2:21 [a]Or *law*

and then we are found guilty because we have abandoned the law. Would that mean Christ has led us into sin? Absolutely not! [18]Rather, I am a sinner if I rebuild the old system of law I already tore down. [19]For when I tried to keep the law, it condemned me. So I died to the law—I stopped trying to meet all its requirements—so that I might live for God. [20]My old self has been crucified with Christ.* It is no longer I who live, but Christ lives in me. So I live in this earthly body by trusting in the Son of God, who loved me and gave himself for me. [21]I do not treat the grace of God as meaningless. For if keeping the law could make us right with God, then there was no need for Christ to die.

2:16 Some translators hold that the quotation extends through verse 14; others through verse 16; and still others through verse 21. 2:20 Some English translations put this sentence in verse 19.

If there's one thing we can't seem to do without, it's *privacy*. Nobody likes strangers wandering around in their yards or snoops peeking through their windows. Nobody wants even their close friends rifling through their closets or searching through their drawers. Most of all, nobody relishes the idea of exposing the depths of their family dysfunctions or the details of household squabbles. Everything in us wants to protect our families from poking and our personal lives from probing.

This fact makes Galatians 2:11-21 all the more surprising. As Paul builds his argument against the legalistic Judaizers' twisted gospel, he crosses into the uncomfortable realm of family wrangling. Instead of keeping this particular episode of church conflict a secret, Paul exposes the details of his brief but fierce confrontation with the apostle Peter himself. He doesn't do this to simply hang out the church's dirty laundry or to meet some ideal of "total transparency." Paul knows like anybody else that not everything should be broadcast to the public. Furthermore, Paul certainly isn't trying to hang Peter out to dry. We saw in the last section that Peter and the Jerusalem apostles had given Paul and Barnabas the "right hand of fellowship" (2:9). Peter and Paul agreed on their theology and had mutually affirmed each other's ministries—to

Jews and Gentiles, respectively. They were colleagues, not competitors. Each respected the other.

So, what motivated Paul to report his conflict with Peter to the troubled churches in Galatia?

## — 2:11-14 —

The key to answering the first question comes from one small word: *but*. In the previous section, Paul described how the leaders of the Jerusalem church—including Peter—had agreed with him and Barnabas regarding the test case of Titus. Nobody required Titus, a Gentile convert to Christianity, to follow the Law—neither in order to become a Christian nor to live the Christian life. The Law contributes nothing to a person's salvation, and it adds nothing to a person's sanctification. Peter and Paul saw eye to eye on that issue.

*But* when Peter arrived in Antioch some time later, his actions openly contradicted his doctrine! Yes, Paul and Peter had agreed on the implications of the gospel while in Jerusalem, but Peter was "not straightforward about the truth of the gospel" when he faced peer pressure from Jewish Christians (2:14). In response to Peter's display of hypocrisy, Paul confronted him face-to-face. Paul included an account of this event in the letter to the Galatians in order to leave no doubt that he preached the true gospel and possessed the authority to uphold it—even if it meant rebuking the apostle Peter. This is why, when Peter played the hypocrite in Antioch, Paul "opposed him to his face," pointing out his inconsistency in front of everybody (2:11).

What specifically did Peter do to draw Paul's ire? Simply put, Peter flip-flopped in his attitudes and actions toward the Gentiles of Antioch when some Jewish hard-liners from Jerusalem showed up. Paul tells the Galatians that when Peter first arrived in that city, where the Gentile mission was exploding, Peter would enjoy uninhibited fellowship with the Gentiles around a common table. This mark of fellowship would have been forbidden under the Jewish interpretation of the Law. Eating with unclean Gentiles meant eating their nonkosher food, something a good, Law-abiding Jew would never do. But Peter's vision of the unclean animals and the subsequent unconditional conversion of the Roman centurion Cornelius (Acts 10) had convinced him that the Law had been supplanted by the gospel, that legalism should be demolished by grace. So, rather than separating himself from the Gentile believers, Peter enjoyed a meal with them.

*Until.*

Representatives from the Jerusalem church arrived in Antioch. Remember that controversy and confusion about following the Law still raged in Jerusalem, so when Jewish Christians showed up in Antioch, they brought those tensions with them. Paul describes these visitors as "certain men from James" (Gal. 2:12). Now, James had been in full agreement with Paul and Barnabas while they were in Jerusalem, but he was famous for following the Law to a tee as a testimony to unbelieving Jews in Judea. In fact, this was the common practice among Jewish believers living in Jerusalem: To Jews, they lived as Jews in order to win the Jews, a principle even Paul later advocated (1 Cor. 9:20). They obeyed the Law not to be saved or sanctified, but to adapt to the culture in which they lived in order to keep from putting a stumbling block before the Jews. But what do those same Law-abiding Jews do when they leave that Jewish cultural context? Until the Jewish Christians from Jerusalem arrived, Peter had answered that question by eating with the Gentiles in Antioch. When a number of his Jewish friends showed up, however, he reverted to his old ways.

Paul reports that Peter withdrew from the Gentiles and held himself aloof because he feared the "party of the circumcision" (Gal. 2:12). Many find it striking that Peter, who was well known for his boldness in the face of opposition, would behave hypocritically in Antioch for fear of the legalistic Judaizers. But when we retrace the steps that led from Paul's relief visit to Jerusalem (Acts 11:27-30; Gal. 2:1-10) to Peter's hypocrisy in Antioch, we begin to understand the pressures that had come to bear on that otherwise-stalwart apostle.

At the same time Paul, Barnabas, and the uncircumcised Titus came to bring famine relief to those in Jerusalem, a violent persecution broke out in Jerusalem at the hands of Herod Agrippa I, grandson of Herod the Great (Acts 12:1). In this attack, Herod executed James, one of the original twelve apostles and the brother of John (Acts 12:2). The Jewish religious leaders, likely thrilled that their attempts at destroying the church had gained governmental backing, praised Herod for his nationalism. This only encouraged him to continue further persecution. As a result, Peter himself was hunted down and thrown in prison (Acts 12:3-4). While the Jews were likely plotting to have Peter executed, as they had done several years earlier with Jesus, an angel of God conducted a covert rescue mission, miraculously releasing Peter right from under the guards' noses (Acts 12:6-18). Shortly after these occurrences, Paul and Barnabas returned to Antioch with John Mark (Acts 12:25). From there the church in Antioch sent them on the first missionary journey (Acts 13:1-3).

This brings us to the time of the clash between Paul and Peter. We are told that Paul and Barnabas remained for some time in Antioch (Acts 14:28). Peter most likely paid his visit to Antioch during this time, both to hear the report of the missionary journey and to visit with his old friends, Paul and Barnabas. But we are also told that at about the same time, or shortly thereafter, "some men came down from Judea and began teaching the brethren, 'Unless you are circumcised according to the custom of Moses, you cannot be saved'" (Acts 15:1).

It's important to point out that Peter did not himself belong to this group, which Paul calls the "the party of the circumcision" (Gal. 2:12). Rather, Peter may have been carried off into hypocritical behavior simply because he was trying to avoid another outbreak of persecution against the already brutalized church in his hometown.

In Jerusalem, following the Law was an attempt to win unbelieving Jews. Early historical testimony suggests that James, the brother of Jesus, was known among Jews in Jerusalem as "the Just" because of the unimpeachable devotion he exhibited among the Jewish people.[13] In fact, when James confessed in public that Jesus of Nazareth was the Messiah, the Pharisees announced (as if surprised), "The just man is also in error!"[14] So, for the Jewish Christians in Jerusalem, following the Law was necessary to avoid putting a stumbling block in the way of their unbelieving Jewish friends and family. It was a cultural matter related to effective evangelism, not a means of salvation or sanctification. In Antioch, however, following the Law would have meant excluding the Gentile believers. Such unloving legalism would have alienated and confused them. Worse yet, it would have unwittingly lent credence to the festering Judaizing heresy that insisted, "Unless you are circumcised . . . you cannot be saved" (Acts 15:1).

So magnetic was the pull toward hypocrisy in the face of the Judaizers' challenge that all the Jewish believers in Antioch followed Peter's lead. We can almost hear Paul's tone of disappointment—more like deep remorse—when he has to admit, "Even Barnabas was carried away by their hypocrisy" (Gal. 2:13). The Greek term for hypocrisy means "play-acting, pretending, wearing a disguise."[15] Peter and Barnabas believed one thing but did another.

What was Paul to do? Would he just sit back and watch as Peter led a brigade of Jewish Christians who acted like they were deserting the gospel? Not for a second! Instead, when he saw that Peter was acting in a way that was inconsistent with what he believed, Paul boldly confronted Peter in the presence of everybody—Jews and Gentiles (2:14).

## Grace, Legalism, Law

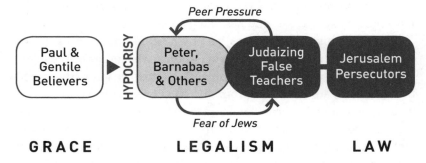

The situation in Antioch included at least three parties: (1) Paul and the Gentile believers who stayed true to the doctrine of grace; (2) Peter, Barnabas, and other Jewish believers who compromised grace for the sake of avoiding possible persecution for themselves and others; and (3) the Judaizing false teachers who could easily unleash their wrath against those who broke the Law.

## — 2:14-21 —

I can picture the scene in my mind. In a large room, dimly lit with flickering oil lamps nestled in tiny grooves in the walls, two tables have been set. On one side of the room Peter sits with his Jewish Christian friends, speaking their native Aramaic. They open their meal in traditional Hebrew prayers, perform the ceremonial Jewish hand washing, and then proceed to fellowship around the table in the name of their Jewish Messiah, Yeshua. All the while a small contingent of Pharisees, dressed to the nines in their flowing religious garb, glance disdainfully at the simple group of Gentile believers banished to a dark corner of the same room where they mumble their "vulgar" prayers in Greek in the name of Kyrios Iesous.

The message from the Jewish party is clear: If you want to sit at our table, you'll have to live like us.

Paul enters the room and quickly sizes up the situation. He looks at the Jews, then at the Gentiles . . . then back again. It doesn't take him long to realize this is a completely different picture from the one he saw the night before. Just yesterday the large, well-lit room hosted a grand table with both Jews and Gentiles singing, praying, eating, and laughing together . . . in Greek! Peter had inspired the believers with some of his most famous stories—especially the recent account of his miraculous prison break. They had experienced true spiritual fellowship—a genuine love feast, culminating in participation in the Lord's Supper in thanksgiving and remembrance of their common Lord, Jesus Christ.

Paul now sees not one church united by the Spirit, but two separate sects—the Gentiles and the Jews. It is almost as though a spell has been cast over the entire room. Even Barnabas—Barnabas, of all people!—has switched allegiances and has taken a seat beside Peter.

Gathering his composure as best as he can, Paul slowly strides across the room to the small group of Gentiles, who are surprised to see him approach. From the Jewish table, the "circumcision party" members glare at Paul for his impropriety. They had managed to build a wall of separation between them and the Gentiles, hoping to persuade them by their exclusion to embrace the Jewish Christian way of life. Yet instead of taking a seat with the Gentiles, Paul raps on the table several times, points his finger across the room at Peter, and calls out above the hushed murmurs.

Of course, I don't know exactly how it went, but I'm sure that this imaginary scene is close to accurate. This was no jovial toast to welcome the Jerusalem guests to Antioch. Paul proceeded to inflict an all-out verbal whipping on the revered apostle who had literally turned his back on the Gentile believers. Paul's mini-lecture reads like a condensed edition of the book of Romans—heavy on grace, hard on Law, and centered on the atoning death of Jesus Christ. I believe Paul's account of his words to Peter run from Galatians 2:14 through 2:21.[16] We can break Paul's presentation down into several sections:

- Paul's Rebuke of Peter (2:14)
- Paul's Review of Justification by Grace Alone (2:15-16)
- Paul's Rejection of the Charge of License (2:17-18)
- Paul's Reflection on the Exchanged Life (2:19-20)
- Paul's Return to the Central Issue (2:21)

*Paul's Rebuke of Peter (2:14).* When Paul observed the inconsistency between Peter's faith and his practice, he pounced. He began by abruptly pointing out the obvious inconsistency. This must have caused both discomfort and embarrassment for Peter and his companions—and probably anger among the smaller band of fuming Judaizers present among them. Paul pointed out that not long ago Peter had lived like the Gentiles, observing their customs, speaking their language, and eating their foods. Yet now Peter's actions appeared to communicate a lie: In order to have Christian fellowship with the Jerusalem visitors, the Gentiles would have to live like Jews. Once Paul brought the issue out of the gray shadows and into the light, everybody in the room would have noticed the stark contrast . . . and recognized Peter's blatant hypocrisy.

*Paul's Review of Justification by Grace Alone (2:15-16).* Paul then reviews the same gospel that Peter, Barnabas, and the others had already affirmed long ago—the very basis for their "right hand of fellowship" and mutual support of each other's ministries (2:9). Paul's main point in 2:15-16 is summed up by this simple truth: Even those who were born Jewish know they could not be saved by keeping the Law, but only by faith in Jesus Christ. Paul emphasizes several vital theological truths in this restatement of the gospel of salvation by grace alone through faith alone in Christ alone. Let me illustrate these truths by breaking the statement down into a question-and-answer form.

## PAUL'S ARGUMENT IN QUESTION-AND-ANSWER FORM

| Questions Implied | Answers Given | Arguments Affirmed |
|---|---|---|
| Did we Jews become Christians differently than the Gentiles? | "[Even] we . . . Jews by nature and not sinners from among the Gentiles . . . have believed in Christ Jesus" (2:15-16). | There are not two ways of salvation, one for Jews and one for Gentiles. Everybody is saved in the same way: through faith in Jesus Christ. |
| Since we already had the Law, why did we Jews believe in Jesus? | "So that we may be justified by faith in Christ and not by the works of the Law" (2:16). | Faith in Jesus Christ justified us (declared us righteous) before God, something the Law did not do. |
| On what doctrinal truth is this faith based? | "Knowing that a man is not justified by the works of the Law but through faith in Christ Jesus" (2:16). | Any person—Jew or Gentile—is justified through faith in Jesus, not by the works of the Law. |
| Why is a person justified by faith, not works? | "Since by the works of the Law no flesh will be justified" (2:16). | It is literally *impossible* for the Law to justify anybody—Jew or Gentile. |

The bottom line is that sinners are declared righteous (justified) by God through faith in Christ, not by keeping the Law. In fact, it is quite impossible for the Law to save anybody, even the most righteous, Law-loving Jew. Therefore, why capitulate to a group of so-called Christians who separate themselves from genuine believers over keeping the Law?

*Paul's Rejection of the Charge of License (2:17-18).* By exposing Peter's hypocrisy, Paul confirmed the truth of the gospel based on his obvious apostolic authority. But his answer, which emphasized grace and faith apart from works of the Law, led to another question. No doubt the Judaizing false teachers in both Antioch and Galatia were making the same reasonable argument against Paul's insistence on grace: Too much emphasis on grace will make Christ a minister of sin! That is, if a believer in Christ does not need to keep the Law in any fashion, then logically this would mean that justified sinners can continue in sin with no repercussions! In fact, the more we sin, the more "grace" we get to cover those sins. If this is God's way of salvation, then it makes God an advocate of sin.

Paul knew all too well the objections bouncing around in the brains of the Judaizers in Antioch. In fact, as a staunch Pharisee in his pre-Christian days, Paul had likely hurled the same convincing arguments against the "lawless" Christians. Now, though, he asks the question as one saved by grace and placed in union with Jesus Christ. The question: "But if, while seeking to be justified in Christ, we ourselves have also been found sinners, is Christ then a minister of sin?" (2:17). Commentator John Stott provides some insight into the assumptions of this question:

> Paul's critics argued like this: "Your doctrine of justification through faith in Christ only, apart from the works of the law, is a highly dangerous doctrine. It fatally weakens a man's sense of moral responsibility. If he can be accepted through trusting in Christ, without any necessity to do good works, you are actually encouraging him to break the law, which is the vile heresy of 'antinomianism.'" People still argue like this today: "If God justifies bad people, what is the point of being good? Can't we do as we like and live as we please?"[17]

Paul's opponents thought that people who disregarded the Law and its righteous works would be "found sinners." Since Christ is the One who supplies this grace that leads to lawlessness, He would actually be enabling a sinful lifestyle. Is this a valid conclusion to draw from the gospel's message of salvation by grace through faith plus nothing? It seems reasonable, doesn't it? Based on human logic, what else could we conclude? Yet Paul categorically and unequivocally rejects that line of thinking with the strongest negative one can utter in the Greek language: "May it never be!" In fact, Paul turns the argument around on his hearers. Before salvation by grace through faith in Christ, the Law served only to separate Gentiles from the people of God and to condemn us for our sinfulness. None of us can keep the Law perfectly—neither Jew nor Gentile. As the apostle James himself wrote to Jewish believers, "For whoever keeps the whole law and yet stumbles in one point, he has become guilty of all" (Jas. 2:10).

So even James himself, one of the Jerusalem leaders, shows that the Law is a means of condemning, not saving—of demonstrating our sinfulness, not making us more righteous. Why on earth would Paul go back and try to rebuild this legalistic structure around Gentiles? In his mind, it's either the Law or the gospel of Christ; it cannot be both. F. F. Bruce notes this contrast well:

> If the law was still in force, as the Galatians were being urged to believe, then those who sought salvation elsewhere were transgressors by its standard; if it was no longer in force—if Christ occupied the place which was now rightly his in salvation history—then those who sought their justification before God anywhere but in Christ remained unjustified, that is to say, they were still in their sins.[18]

Like the Judaizers of Paul's day, legalists today try to build their assurance of salvation on a life of good works . . . and they judge the genuineness of others' salvation by the same criterion. But what may seem like a sturdy staircase built to lead us into God's favor actually turns out to be a rotten wooden trap that will crumble beneath us. As Paul explains, only the cross of Christ can give us the assurance we need to step out in faith and live a truly grace-filled life.

*Paul's Reflection on the Exchanged Life (2:19-20).* Paul applies the image of death and resurrection to help explain his old relationship to the Law and his new relationship with Christ. Far from being a pathway to life, the Law showed Paul his sinfulness, leading him to the true Way—Jesus Christ. "Through the Law" Paul realized his own unfitness for the kingdom and was driven to the gospel, which is the end of the Law. Having died to his obligation to keep the Law in order to gain righteousness, Paul was not left for dead. Instead, he was made alive to God, enjoying a direct, personal, intimate relationship with the Law-giver Himself (2:19). Paul made the same argument some years later in Romans 3:19-22:

> Now we know that whatever the Law says, it speaks to those who are under the Law, so that every mouth may be closed and all the world may become accountable to God; because by the works of the Law no flesh will be justified in His sight; for through the Law comes the knowledge of sin. But now apart from the Law

the righteousness of God has been manifested, being witnessed by the Law and the Prophets, even the righteousness of God through faith in Jesus Christ for all those who believe; for there is no distinction.

Having stopped trying to please God by keeping the Law, Paul exchanged his damning pursuit of self-righteousness for the life-giving grace of Jesus Christ. The death Christ died was reckoned to him, and he therefore died to the old life and was raised together with Christ to a new life. How can we receive this new life? Ironically, it comes when we die with Christ—when, by faith, we enter into a personal and spiritual relationship with Him that is so intimate that God regards our sinful selves as crucified with Him. Then, just as Christ was raised from the dead, we too are reborn with Christ living in us (Gal. 2:20). In this born-again state, we live the exchanged life on the spiritual level. We give ourselves to Christ and He gives Himself to us, empowering us with His infinite strength so we can live as He desires. This is not lawless living! This is a freedom that transcends the dos and don'ts of legalism and releases us to a life of true love, devotion, and faithfulness.

*Paul's Return to the Central Issue (2:21).* The Christian life is not about working as hard as we can to live right; it's about allowing Christ Himself to live out His life through us. As that happens, Christ's character and glory are displayed in us for all to see. Unlike the Judaizers' anti-grace message, Paul's gospel does not "nullify the grace of God" (2:21). By seeking either to obtain or to maintain righteousness by human effort, the Judaizers rejected the grace of God. For if sinful people can obtain their own salvation by keeping the Law, then "Christ died needlessly" (2:21). His death was a waste, His precious blood spilled in vain!

If anyone insists that our righteousness comes by works or that we earn our salvation through our own efforts, that person is saying, in effect, that Christ died needlessly. Similarly, if anyone believes that we keep our salvation by doing good works, somehow contributing to the work of Christ—meeting Him halfway, so to speak—that individual regards the full and finished work of Christ on the cross as partial and incomplete. No, our justification, sanctification, and future glorification are all results of God's grace alone . . . effected through faith alone . . . in the finished work of Christ alone.

In short, grace is the way to life and the way of life.

# Beyond "Chopsticks"

**GALATIANS 2:20**

Whenever I watch a skilled pianist run his fingers up and down a keyboard, creating beautiful music, I think to myself, I would love to play like that. To be honest, I don't actually get that specific. I just stop with, I would love to play.

You see, my piano repertoire consists of "Chopsticks." You know that one, right? It's so simple that as soon as somebody opens a piano and begins pounding away at "Chopsticks," you can conclude two things off the bat: (1) That guy doesn't know how to play the piano, and (2) he doesn't mind annoying everybody within earshot. That tune lingers with you all day like bad Tex-Mex. Anyway, my piano playing sounds more like an ape banging on a pile of bones than anything resembling music.

But imagine it could be arranged that some piano virtuoso could play the piano through me. What if somebody like the late Vladimir Horowitz or the great Van Cliburn could somehow run his musical genius through my feeble and unskilled fingers? I'll have to be honest—I've actually thought about this from time to time, because at my stage of life, it's the only way I could ever hope to make those ebonies and ivories do anything but torture an audience. So bear with me.

If a great musician were to play through me, the one thing I'd have to do is nothing. Believe me, that part would be hard to pull off! I'd have to consciously let go of my own will and effort, letting the true performer have his way. As long as I consciously sat back and released my own control, I'd be playing Rachmaninoff, Tchaikovsky ... maybe even a little Franz Liszt! But knowing myself, it wouldn't take long for me to think, Hey, this isn't as hard as I thought. I might make a slight modification here, or do a little improvisation in the middle. As soon as those thoughts intruded, it would immediately be back to "Chopsticks."

(continued on next page)

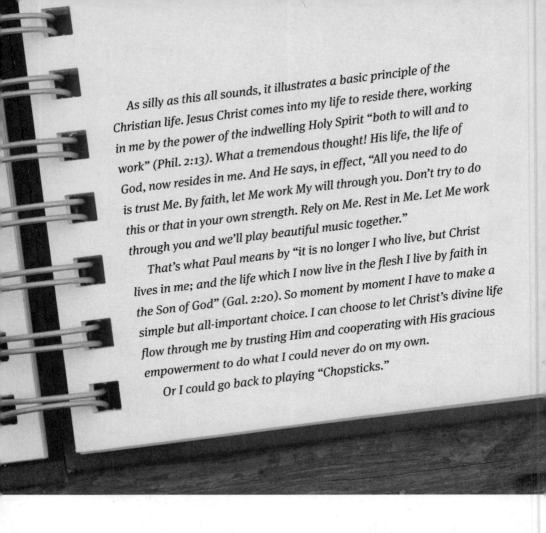

*As silly as this all sounds, it illustrates a basic principle of the Christian life. Jesus Christ comes into my life to reside there, working in me by the power of the indwelling Holy Spirit "both to will and to work" (Phil. 2:13). What a tremendous thought! His life, the life of God, now resides in me. And He says, in effect, "All you need to do is trust Me. By faith, let Me work My will through you. Don't try to do this or that in your own strength. Rely on Me. Rest in Me. Let Me work through you and we'll play beautiful music together."*

*That's what Paul means by "it is no longer I who live, but Christ lives in me; and the life which I now live in the flesh I live by faith in the Son of God" (Gal. 2:20). So moment by moment I have to make a simple but all-important choice. I can choose to let Christ's divine life flow through me by trusting Him and cooperating with His gracious empowerment to do what I could never do on my own.*

*Or I could go back to playing "Chopsticks."*

## APPLICATION: GALATIANS 2:11-21

### Healing Hypocrisy

Without doubt, we've all had bouts with the disease of hypocrisy—claiming to believe one way while living another. Sometimes the infection is temporary, a minor lapse that nobody notices. Other times it's chronic, perhaps even terminal, damaging or destroying our reputations and relationships. In all cases, it's treatable and even preventable. Paul's recounting of his confrontation of Peter's hypocrisy in Galatians 2:11–21 leads us to three practical truths that can help us heal hypocrisy . . . and even vaccinate us against future outbreaks of this dangerous spiritual disease.

First, *Christians are accountable to one another.* We can't live as we please and expect everyone else to look the other way. God's standard of living applies to us all, and we need to help one another maintain it—even if it involves private or public confrontation. But the rebukes we give should be offered with genuine love and concern for those who falter (Ps. 141:5; Prov. 27:6). When we hold others accountable to a life of integrity—and invite others to do the same for us—we can heal hypocrisy.

Second, *Christians impact others.* As Christians, we represent Christ to a watching world—for better or worse. Whether or not people actually model their lives after ours, we are affecting their attitudes toward Christ and influencing their decisions and actions. We need to live lives in conformity with what we believe and teach, knowing that even a whiff of hypocrisy can cause unbelievers to turn away from Christianity in disgust.

Third, *Christians should be committed to the truth.* God is the God of truth (Isa. 65:16). Jesus is the way, the truth, and the life (John 14:6). And the Holy Spirit guides believers into the truth (John 16:13). When we claim to be children of God but live in ways that deny that claim, we're not living in keeping with the truth. In fact, 1 John 3:18 says, "Let us not love with word or with tongue, but in deed and truth." Of all people, Christians should be known for our unwavering commitment to all that is true and right—demonstrated especially in our private and public lives.

Like the common cold, the disease of hypocrisy seems to infect all of us from time to time. But if we remember to keep accountable to one another, reflect on how our lives impact others, and commit ourselves to truthful living, we can cure hypocrisy in our own lives and others'.

# DEFENDING THE SUPERIORITY OF THE GOSPEL (GALATIANS 3:1–4:31)

From Paul's perspective, the Galatians had "Petered out."

They had been delivered from the curse of the Law and its brutal slavery to religious requirements. They had partaken of the glorious grace of God that comes by faith alone in Christ alone. They had started well along the path of the Christian life. But then something had changed all that. Led astray by reasonable words and pressured by the threat of alienation and persecution, the Galatian believers put on a mask of hypocrisy and began playing a role they knew was insincere.

When Paul heard that the Galatian Christians had begun sliding backward into legalism, he saw in them the same spirit he had personally witnessed in the apostle Peter perhaps just weeks earlier in Antioch. Fearing the party of the circumcision, Peter cowered under the cover of the Law (2:12). He and other Jewish believers, failing to walk in line with the gospel of grace, slipped into a brief period of hypocrisy (2:13-14).

In Galatians 2:14-21, Paul recounted the passionate speech he delivered against Peter in the presence of the church in Antioch. But Paul was not merely reporting historical facts. By recounting his rebuke of Peter, Paul was actually addressing the erring Galatians, who had unwittingly followed in Peter's path of fear-induced hypocrisy. Now Paul was ready to set Peter aside and address the Galatians directly.

So Paul draws on all his rhetorical power to defend the superiority of the gospel of grace over the Law of works (3:1–4:31). He points out the foolishness of their detour from the straight path of faith into the impenetrable wilderness of legalism. Having begun by faith, why would the Galatians choose to depend on their own works to please God? Even Abraham, the father of the Hebrews and first beneficiary of the covenant, received the righteousness of God through faith (3:6). The Law, rather than saving us, shows us God's standards and our sin (3:19). It's like a guardrail to keep people from careening off the road. Nobody in their right mind would scrape along the guardrail when they had been fully equipped to drive in the center lane!

## KEY TERMS IN GALATIANS 3:1–4:31

*epangelia* (ἐπαγγελία) [1860] "promise," "guarantee"
This term, often used in covenant contexts (Eph. 2:12; Heb. 6:17; 11:9), generally refers to various guarantees made by God for which believers may hope with confidence. Such promises include the Holy Spirit (Gal. 3:14; Eph. 1:13) and eternal life (2 Tim. 1:1; 1 Jn. 2:25). Paul uses *epangelia* ten times in Galatians, all in chapters 3 and 4. In this context, the word primarily refers to those promises given by God to Abraham, namely, blessings to him and to his offspring (3:16, 18). Paul contrasts the promise with the Law, which can only reveal our flaws, not grant us the righteousness necessary for salvation.

*huiothesia* (υἱοθεσία) [5206] "adoption as sons," "sonship"
It was not uncommon for wealthy men and even emperors in Paul's day to adopt children or even grown men to inherit their fortune or throne. Such heirs were regarded as equal to natural-born children. The family legacy, inheritance, and estate would all go to this heir. Though it only appears once in the letter to the Galatians (4:5), the term *huiothesia* is significant for understanding Paul's argument regarding our position in Christ (see Rom. 8:15, 23; 9:4; Eph. 1:5). We have been adopted and are now given full rights and privileges as sons and daughters of God.

*pistis* (πίστις) [4102] "faith," "confidence," "reliance," "trust"
In both the Old and New Testaments, *pistis*—"faith"—was the means by which a person related to God. In the particular Christian sense, Paul states that faith is the means by which a person becomes a child of God (3:26) and receives the indwelling of the Spirit (3:14). Yet the Old Testament patriarch, Abraham, is the archetype for this New Testament reality, for by his faith he was declared righteous prior to the giving of the Law (3:5-9).

In this deeply doctrinal section, Paul compares the Law to a tutor commissioned to bring us to faith in Christ (3:24). Having grown up and graduated from the Law's elementary school, why would the Galatians want to return to learn the ABCs? Grace, not the Law, had brought the Galatians into the family of God, making them fellow heirs of the kingdom (3:28). In light of these profound theological truths, the Galatians' backsliding into legalism dumbfounded Paul. He found it incredible that they would "turn back again to the weak and worthless elemental things" (4:9). Their retreat to the Law was tantamount to a freed slave returning to the harsh treatment of a brutal master (4:21-31).

Paul's passion for the gospel compelled him to turn his readers back to the freedom of salvation by grace alone through faith alone. In doing so, he argued not only that the sinner is saved by grace but also that the saved sinner lives by grace, reinforcing his central message: Grace is the way to life and the way of life.

# Backsliding into Legalism
## GALATIANS 3:1-14

**NASB**

1a You foolish Galatians, who has bewitched you, before whose eyes Jesus Christ was publicly portrayed *as* crucified? 2 This is the only thing I want to find out from you: did you receive the Spirit by the works of ªthe Law, or by ᵇhearing with faith? 3 Are you so foolish? Having begun ªby the Spirit, are you now ᵇbeing perfected by the flesh? 4 Did you ªsuffer so many things in vain—if indeed it was in vain? 5 So then, does He who provides you with the Spirit and works ªmiracles among you, do it by the works of ᵇthe Law, or by ᶜhearing with faith?

6a Even so Abraham BELIEVED GOD, AND IT WAS RECKONED TO HIM AS RIGHTEOUSNESS. 7 Therefore, ªbe sure that it is those who are of faith who are sons of Abraham. 8 The Scripture, foreseeing that God ªwould justify the ᵇGentiles by faith, preached the gospel beforehand to Abraham, *saying*, "ALL THE NATIONS WILL BE BLESSED IN YOU." 9 So then those who

**NLT**

1 Oh, foolish Galatians! Who has cast an evil spell on you? For the meaning of Jesus Christ's death was made as clear to you as if you had seen a picture of his death on the cross. 2 Let me ask you this one question: Did you receive the Holy Spirit by obeying the law of Moses? Of course not! You received the Spirit because you believed the message you heard about Christ. 3 How foolish can you be? After starting your new lives in the Spirit, why are you now trying to become perfect by your own human effort? 4 Have you experienced* so much for nothing? Surely it was not in vain, was it?

5 I ask you again, does God give you the Holy Spirit and work miracles among you because you obey the law? Of course not! It is because you believe the message you heard about Christ.

6 In the same way, "Abraham believed God, and God counted him as righteous because of his faith."* 7 The real children of Abraham, then, are those who put their faith in God.

8 What's more, the Scriptures looked forward to this time when God would make the Gentiles right in his sight because of their faith. God proclaimed this good news to Abraham long ago when he said, "All nations will be blessed through you."* 9 So all who put their faith in Christ

are of faith are blessed with ªAbraham, the believer.

¹⁰For as many as are of the works of ªthe Law are under a curse; for it is written, "CURSED IS EVERYONE WHO DOES NOT ABIDE BY ALL THINGS WRITTEN IN THE BOOK OF THE LAW, TO PERFORM THEM." ¹¹Now that no one is justified ªby ᵇthe Law before God is evident; for, "ᶜTHE RIGHTEOUS MAN SHALL LIVE BY FAITH." ¹²ªHowever, the Law is not ᵇof faith; on the contrary, "HE WHO PRACTICES THEM SHALL LIVE ᶜBY THEM." ¹³Christ redeemed us from the curse of the Law, having become a curse for us—for it is written, "CURSED IS EVERYONE WHO HANGS ON A ªTREE"— ¹⁴in order that in Christ Jesus the blessing of Abraham might ªcome to the Gentiles, so that we would receive the promise of the Spirit through faith.

3:1 ªLit O   3:2 ªOr law   ᵇLit the hearing of faith
3:3 ªOr with   ᵇOr ending with   3:4 ªOr experience
3:5 ªOr works of power   ᵇOr law   ᶜLit the hearing
of faith   3:6 ªLit Just as   3:7 ªLit know   3:8 ªLit
justifies   ᵇLit nations   3:9 ªLit the believing
Abraham   3:10 ªOr law   3:11 ªOr in   ᵇOr law   ᶜOr
But he who is righteous by faith shall live   3:12 ªOr
And   ᵇOr based on   ᶜOr in   3:13 ªOr cross; lit wood
3:14 ªOr occur

share the same blessing Abraham received because of his faith.

¹⁰But those who depend on the law to make them right with God are under his curse, for the Scriptures say, "Cursed is everyone who does not observe and obey all the commands that are written in God's Book of the Law."* ¹¹So it is clear that no one can be made right with God by trying to keep the law. For the Scriptures say, "It is through faith that a righteous person has life."* ¹²This way of faith is very different from the way of law, which says, "It is through obeying the law that a person has life."*

¹³But Christ has rescued us from the curse pronounced by the law. When he was hung on the cross, he took upon himself the curse for our wrongdoing. For it is written in the Scriptures, "Cursed is everyone who is hung on a tree."* ¹⁴Through Christ Jesus, God has blessed the Gentiles with the same blessing he promised to Abraham, so that we who are believers might receive the promised* Holy Spirit through faith.

3:4 Or Have you suffered.   3:6 Gen 15:6.
3:8 Gen 12:3; 18:18; 22:18.   3:10 Deut 27:26.
3:11 Hab 2:4.   3:12 Lev 18:5.   3:13 Deut 21:23
(Greek version).   3:14 Some manuscripts read
the blessing of the.

How would you feel if your vehicle suddenly lost power on the way up a steep mountain road? With an ache in your stomach, you would pull every lever and push hard on the brake pedal as your car began to roll backward down the hill. Or imagine sitting on a roller coaster as it *click-clack-click-clacks* its way to the top of the first crest, only to stop suddenly at the peak and begin to move backward—*clack-click-clack-click*. Or picture yourself climbing a mountainside, linked to several climbers above you with a nylon rope. Everything goes well as the team slowly advances one hand and one foot at a time. Then, from several yards above, you hear the crunch of gravel, the tumble of rocks, and the word you never want to hear echoing from the side of a mountain: "Fall!"

These frightening scenarios are the stuff of nightmares. Nobody wants to backslide. What a horrible term! I can't imagine a context in which backsliding would be a good thing. The words "backslider" and "backsliding" are found just over a dozen times in the King James Bible, mostly in the book of Jeremiah. The term means "to apostatize," "turn away," "reverse a positive course," or "fall into a slump." Backsliding is not limited to grossly sinful acts. Christians can also backslide into false teaching and the error of extremism—any belief or behavior that deviates from a balanced and healthy Christian life.

The letter to the Galatians is all about this kind of backsliding. The Galatians had not fallen into immorality or defected into paganism. No, their departure from the truth was far more insidious than such obvious apostasies. The Galatian believers willingly and deliberately turned away from the grace of the gospel—an act of spiritual treason dressed in the garb of purity and piety! In short, the Galatians were guilty of backsliding into legalism. Let's take a close look at Paul's response to this betrayal of salvation by grace through faith so we can avoid falling into the same error.

## — 3:1-5 —

In Christian circles, legalism frequently springs from dark alleys like a thief, seeking to rob believers of two priceless doctrines: justification and sanctification. The legalistic assault on justification says, "You need to add to Christ's redemptive work on the cross so God will accept you into His family. You have the ability *in and of yourself* to meet God halfway, to add to His grace, to pull yourself up by your bootstraps!" If the legalistic view of justification were to take over in our churches, it wouldn't be long before we were singing new words to the classic hymn "Amazing Grace":

> Helpful grace plus needed works,
> How rational the sound,
> They help me save my wretched self,
> And lift me from the ground.

The legalistic attack on sanctification is more subtle. Assailants in this camp admit that we are saved by grace through faith, but they claim that once saved we must work hard to please God as we continue in the Christian life. They say, "God did His part to save me; now I need to pick up the baton and run well. When I do good works, God smiles; when I let Him down, He frowns. So my spiritual growth depends on working as hard as I can to please Him." If that view of sanctification were to take control of our churches, instead of "Jesus Paid It All," we'd be singing:

> Jesus paid a lot!
> A lot is left to pay!
> Since the bill is infinite,
> I'll work 'til Judgment Day!

In both legalistic justification and legalistic sanctification, we focus on self. We depend on our own strength rather than God's power either to save us or to mature us in the Christian life. When that happens, we almost always emphasize the outward appearance rather than the inward reality.

The Galatian Christians had become victims of both heresies, so Paul argues that Christians receive the entire salvation package by grace alone through faith alone in Christ alone. The same Holy Spirit who regenerates our inner beings, changing dead sinners into living saints, continues His transforming work as we release our will to His and allow Him to live His life through us. Yet the gift of salvation doesn't stop there. In fact, though we talk about one day dying and going to heaven, even that glorious experience isn't the ultimate end of our salvation. Just as God raised us from spiritual death at the moment of our justification, one day God will raise even our physical bodies from the dead, transforming our mortal bodies into glorious bodies and enabling us to live forever in Christ's kingdom (1 Cor. 15:51-54; 1 Thes. 4:14-17). Every dimension of salvation—past, present, and future—comes to us by grace through faith. We participate by submitting and receiving, not by controlling and completing.

The following chart illustrates this vital truth of the gospel. It may be one of the simplest charts to understand and memorize, but it's also one of the most important. Our salvation, from beginning to end, is the work of the sovereign Father, through the mediating person and work of Jesus Christ, by the finishing work of the Holy Spirit. We are the recipients, the objects of His grace and mercy. Our responsibility? To receive this free gift by faith.

| THREE ASPECTS OF SALVATION BY GRACE THROUGH FAITH | | |
|---|---|---|
| **Justification** | **Sanctification** | **Glorification** |
| By grace through faith, from the Father, through the Son, and by the Holy Spirit | By grace through faith, from the Father, through the Son, and by the Holy Spirit | By grace through faith, from the Father, through the Son, and by the Holy Spirit |

These facts of the gospel are so simple and so vital that only fools would learn the principles only to forget or reject them. This explains why Paul pulls no punches in his sharp rebuke of the Galatians: "You foolish Galatians, who has bewitched you, before whose eyes Jesus Christ was publicly portrayed as crucified?" (Gal. 3:1). The Greek word translated "foolish," *anoētos* [453], describes mindless, thoughtless, or ignorant actions. In other words, the Galatians must be out of their minds to turn away from Christ's once-for-all sacrifice for sin! How insane of them to turn instead to their own self-sacrificial living to compensate for whatever they believed Christ's death was lacking!

What caused the believers to backslide so foolishly into legalism? Paul says they were "bewitched," a term implying the casting of a spell or hex on someone. Paul's point is clear: Only somebody "under the influence" of a spiritual power would abandon the doctrine of salvation by grace through faith. So potent was the legalists' deception that they were able to perform what amounted to an illusion. Like an illusionist who, by sleight of hand, cunningly diverts the eyes of his audience as he replaces one object with another, the legalists had pulled the Galatians' attention away from the true focus of their salvation—Christ's person and work—to something else entirely: the Law and their own works.

After rebuking the Galatians, Paul poses a series of rhetorical questions designed to reveal the utter folly of their legalism. He first reminds them that they did not receive the Spirit by the works of the Law, but by simply hearing the gospel and responding in faith (3:2). All of his readers knew that they had received the gift of the Holy Spirit immediately upon believing the gospel and putting their trust in Christ. Their personal experience of salvation bore this out.

Yet Paul builds on the fact that the Spirit entered their lives by grace through faith alone with its logical implication: If they began their salvation by the Spirit, they cannot be made perfect by the flesh (3:3). Paul's point is that the Spirit came to indwell the Galatians by faith. That same Spirit is working in them, enabling them to grow in the Christian life. Why, then, would they replace the work of the Spirit with living in the power of their own works? Paul couldn't be clearer that the continuation of the Christian life (sanctification) is just as much a result of grace through faith apart from works as the beginning of the Christian life (justification). That is, as we have noted earlier, grace is the way to life and the way of life.

Paul then appeals to yet another aspect of the Galatians' early experience as believers in Christ. After their conversion to Christ, they had endured persecution. We catch a glimpse of this persecution in the book of Acts. As the gospel of grace spread throughout the region around the city of Pisidian Antioch, in the Roman province of Galatia (Acts 13:49), "the Jews incited the devout women of prominence and the leading men of the city, and instigated a persecution against Paul and Barnabas, and drove them out of their district" (Acts 13:50). We can safely assume that once Paul and Barnabas had been driven from the city, the official persecution continued and, perhaps, intensified. This would have made it difficult for the Christians in this region "to continue in the grace of God" as Paul and Barnabas had urged them to do (Acts 13:43).

As the apostles penetrated deeper into the province of Galatia, to Iconium, many Jews and Gentiles believed (Acts 14:1). But "the Jews who disbelieved stirred up the minds of the Gentiles and embittered them against the brethren" (Acts 14:2). As a result, the leaders of the city, both Jews and Gentiles, conspired to persecute Paul and Barnabas (Acts 14:5). No doubt they continued to inflict hardship on the believers in Iconium after the apostles departed. At his next stop, Lystra, Paul was stoned and left for dead (Acts 14:19). Clearly, persecution followed on the heels of the gospel, and the first converts to Christ in Galatia experienced their fair share of hardship. For this reason, Paul and Barnabas retraced their steps through the cities of Galatia, "strengthening the souls of the disciples, encouraging them to continue in the faith, and saying, 'Through many tribulations we must enter the kingdom of God'" (Acts 14:22).

In light of these early days of suffering for the gospel of salvation by grace through faith, Paul demands of his Galatian readers, "Did you suffer so many things in vain?" (Gal. 3:4). The Galatians had endured all their persecutions because they had wholeheartedly embraced Paul's message of grace. If they put themselves back under the Law, the persecution would cease—but at the cost of betraying the gospel!

Paul adds one more plank to his already-sturdy argument against the Galatians' legalistic backsliding. He appeals to the amazing signs and wonders that God had performed at the hands of the apostles of grace when they had preached the gospel to them. Acts 14:3 says, "They spent a long time [in Iconium] speaking boldly with reliance upon the Lord, who was testifying to the word of His grace, granting that signs and wonders be done by their hands." Note that the Lord Himself confirmed the message of the apostles, the "word of His grace." If the Galatians then abandoned this message, they were turning against God's own testimony regarding its truthfulness!

No wonder Paul called the Galatians "foolish"!

## — 3:6-9 —

Even with these powerful appeals, Paul had not yet fired the silver bullet that would slay the monstrous dogma of legalism. In order to break their spell, Paul would have to win the contest on the Law-lovers' own turf—the Old Testament. The Judaizers' mystifying message had so strongly emphasized Moses as the preeminent Jew and the Mosaic Law as the model for religion that Paul's barrage of rapid-fire arguments had to include evidence from the Old Testament. So Paul reaches even further back in Jewish history, before Moses, to Abraham—the first Hebrew patriarch, who received the original promise upon which everything else rested. Paul shows from Abraham's life that the very father of the Jewish nation had himself been saved by grace through faith, not by keeping the Law (3:6).

Paul quotes Genesis 15:6, where Abraham responded to God's promise of an heir and countless descendants. Abraham—old and childless—believed that God would keep His word and do as He promised. In other words, Abraham responded to God's word by simple faith. God then reckoned it to him as righteousness (see Gal. 3:6). This first Hebrew was not justified by keeping the Law but by faith! More than a decade passed before God even instituted circumcision (Gen. 17), and Moses wouldn't receive the Law until some four hundred years later!

So, Abraham did not find favor with God as a result of his personal devotion, public ritual, or hard work. By grace alone through faith alone, apart from anything Abraham had done or would do, God declared him righteous. Expositor Donald Grey Barnhouse describes Abraham's justification this way:

> The day came when, in the accounting of God, ungodly Abraham was suddenly declared righteous. There was nothing in Abraham that caused the action; it began in God and went out to the man in sovereign grace. Upon a sinner the righteousness of God was placed. In the accounting the very righteousness of God was reckoned, credited, imputed. The Lord God Himself, by an act of grace moved by His sovereign love, stooped to the record and blotted out everything that was against Abraham, and then wrote down on the record that He, God, credited this man Abraham to be perfect even at a moment when Abraham was ungodly in himself. That is justification.[1]

Paul then goes on to explain that the Galatians themselves, Jews and Gentiles alike, are the spiritual descendants of Abraham (Gal. 3:7).

"Those who are of faith" are the true "sons of Abraham," just as those who practice wickedness could be called "sons of the devil" or those who follow godliness, "sons of God." Those who are justified—declared righteous—by grace through faith are children of Abraham, the father of faith. In fact, Paul even points out that God had already predicted the Gentiles' future salvation by grace through faith in Genesis 12:3—"All the nations will be blessed in you" (Gal. 3:8). The blessing of Abraham had indeed come to the Gentiles when the gospel of righteousness by grace through faith had been preached to them (3:9).

In essence, Paul's argument ran something like this: "You Galatians want a 'Jewish' Christianity? You want a gospel anchored in the Old Testament? You already have it! You and all people who come to Christ by faith are the spiritual descendants of Abraham, the father of the Jews. Circumcision, the Law, Pharisees, and Judaizers all came later. Faith came first."

In the end, the conclusion is simple: Which is the true gospel that both justifies and sanctifies? The gospel of salvation by grace through faith.

| PAUL'S ARGUMENT: MANY QUESTIONS, ONE ANSWER ||
| --- | --- |
| **QUESTIONS** | **ANSWER** |
| By which gospel did you receive the Holy Spirit? (3:2) → | The gospel of salvation by grace through faith. |
| For which gospel did you suffer persecution? (3:4) → | |
| Which gospel did God confirm through miracles? (3:5) → | |
| By which gospel was Abraham justified? (3:6-9) → | |
| Therefore, which is the true gospel that justifies and sanctifies? → | |

— 3:10-14 —

Some things are black or white. Not all things, but *some* things. For example, you're either married or not married. You can't be both single and married. Similarly, you're either alive or dead; there's no such thing as being both alive and dead. And you've either turned twenty-one or you haven't. You can't be both older and younger than twenty-one.

Some things are just plain black or white. The same is true with the Christian faith. You're either a Christian or you're a non-Christian . . . either saved or unsaved. You can't be *both* a member of God's family *and* not a member of His family. Simply put, you relate to God by grace through faith or you don't relate to Him at all. It's a black-or-white issue.

Another black-or-white issue is the contrast between Law and grace. I've met too many people who think you can gain favor with God by mixing grace and merit, faith and works. Not true! If anybody wants to work for their salvation, they will be required to keep the whole Law perfectly from the moment they take their first breath until the hour of their last. James 2:10 says, "For whoever keeps the whole law and yet stumbles in one point, he has become guilty of all." That's it. Game over. Paradise lost. The moment a person breaks the Law, he or she falls under the judgment of the Law, something Paul calls "the curse of the Law" (Gal. 3:13).

In Galatians 3:10, Paul continues his argument from the Old Testament in order to champion the life of faith. He explains that the Law, rather than adding anything to salvation, actually nullifies righteousness. Why? Because all people, including those who try to live by the Law, inevitably stumble "in many ways" (Jas. 3:2). Even the Old Testament itself declares, "There is not a righteous man on earth who continually does good and who never sins" (Eccl. 7:20). Therefore, instead of establishing their perfect righteousness, the Law places its followers under a penalty, as Paul wrote in Romans: "The wages of sin is death" (Rom. 6:23). Here in Galatians, Paul closely paraphrases a passage from Deuteronomy to demonstrate that the Law itself demands absolute righteousness: "Cursed is he who does not confirm the words of this law by doing them" (Deut. 27:26). Note that Paul applies this curse of condemnation to "as many as are of the works of the Law" (Gal. 3:10). All those who, like the Judaizers, assume they can please God by keeping the Law actually condemn themselves because they fail to keep the entire Law.

I know it has become fashionable today in certain theological circles to divide the Law of Moses into three categories: the moral, the civil (or social), and the ceremonial (or liturgical). The moral Law, it is said, refers primarily to the Ten Commandments and reflects God's unchanging moral principles that all believers must follow as rules for life. The civil or social part of the Law of Moses refers to regulations governing Israel as a nation, that is, laws related to the treatment of slaves, foreigners, and criminals. Finally, the ceremonial or liturgical part of

# Defending against the Hatchets of Legalism

### GALATIANS 3:10-14

Back in 1976, Cynthia and I traveled to Washington, DC, for a United States Bicentennial tour. Along with others in our group, we wandered through the center of the majestic Thomas Jefferson memorial. What a breathtaking sight! Yet more moving than his memorial are the words Thomas Jefferson wrote in a letter to William S. Smith in 1787: "The tree of liberty must be refreshed from time to time with the blood of patriots and tyrants."[2] In other words, maintaining the political freedoms we enjoy requires taking a stand and being willing to sacrifice our own comfort and contentment.

The same is true of spiritual liberty. The tree of Christian liberty must be upheld and defended. The natural fertilizer that refreshes that tree is the Christian patriot who says to the legalist, "That's a lie! That's not the gospel! The gospel is the free gift of God through Jesus Christ. And I will not tolerate any other gospel."

Those peddlers of a false gospel of works have come knocking at my door, their spiritual hatchets and chainsaws in hand, eager to cry "Timber!" after hacking away at the liberty I have in Christ. I don't put up with them for a second. They always appear a bit shocked that somebody will take a strong stand for grace, which makes me wonder what kind of warm reception they received at my Christian neighbors' doors.

Many Christians in Bible-believing churches have lost touch with things worth fighting for. I didn't say we lost the knack for fighting. Oh, we have plenty of fight left in us! It's just that we nag, nitpick, and wrangle over things that aren't even worth the effort. At the same time, though, we succumb to things we ought to stand firmly against. One of those things is the same thing Paul faced in his day: a legalistic gospel.

the Law refers to the details of sacrificial worship described primarily in the book of Leviticus, which govern the functions of the priesthood. Christians who break the Law into three units argue that the civil and ceremonial portions of the Law have been done away with—the civil because the unique theocracy of Israel has been set aside and the ceremonial because temple worship has been superseded by Christ's once-for-all sacrifice for sin. But they say that Christians are still under the moral aspects of the Law as day-to-day rules of life. These constitute the dos and don'ts that govern personal and social ethical issues.

This threefold division of the Law is nowhere explicitly taught in Scripture. Rather, as we have seen, both Paul and James argue that those who keep one part of the Law as a rule for a God-pleasing life are obligated to keep it all. We have no right to pick and choose which rules and regulations to follow. This was, in fact, what the Judaizers were doing—to an extreme! Not only did they see the Law as a rule of life *for sanctification*, but they believed it had to be followed even *for salvation*. As they mixed faith in Christ with the Law, they were selecting some things, like circumcision, and doing away with others, like animal sacrifice. But because the Law is a complete unit of legislation, if we are to have righteousness from the Law we must keep every commandment of the covenant perfectly. If we fail in even the smallest command, we have become Law-breakers and fall under its condemnation (Gal. 3:10; Jas. 2:10-11).

Paul's point, then, is that all people who fail to keep the Law in its entirety live under the shadow of God's impending judgment. How different this is from the Judaizers' deceptive "pick and choose" approach to the Law! They thought their pursuit of certain aspects of the Law would earn God's favor. That teaching, however, is an affront to His grace and mercy, only provoking His judgment.

The Old Testament not only demonstrates the folly of selective obedience to the Law and announces God's judgment for failing to keep it entirely but also points to justification by faith even after the Law was given. In Galatians 3:11, Paul quotes Habakkuk: "Now that no one is justified by the Law before God is evident; for, 'The righteous man shall live by faith.'" In the original context of Habakkuk, God had just revealed that the southern kingdom (Judah) was going to fall to the Babylonians. The news stunned Habakkuk, but God reassured him that Babylon itself would not go unpunished. That cruel kingdom would triumph for a time by its strength, but God would have the ultimate triumph. His people, those who trusted in Him no matter how bleak the circumstances, would be delivered by their sovereign God. Paul's point? Without faith, keeping the external stipulations of the Law was profitless. Even Israel in the Old Testament, living under the Law as a national covenant, was delivered from its curse by faith! Similarly, eternal life comes not to those who proudly seek salvation by keeping the Law but to the humble, who recognize their need for a righteous substitute and put their complete trust in Him.

At this point you can almost picture the Galatians: arms crossed, staring skeptically at Paul. Looking down their noses, they respond, "Okay, Paul. You've made your point. But wouldn't faith plus works be even better than faith alone? Wouldn't grace plus the Law actually improve the Christian life rather than diminish it? After all, the Law came from God, too, just like the gospel!"

Paul makes it clear that the works of the Law cannot blend with the gospel of salvation by grace through faith. The two are mutually exclusive: "The Law is not of faith" (3:12). In contrast to Habakkuk's statement that "the righteous man shall live by faith," the Law declares that "he who practices [the commandments] shall live by them" (3:12; quoting Lev. 18:5). This is one of those black-or-white issues. You're either saved by grace through faith or by the works of the Law. It can't be both. Yet before you opt out of grace and try the Law route, you need to understand something. Because it's impossible for us to perfectly fulfill the requirements of the Law, those who choose that route will end up condemned.

So, those who attempt to be saved—or, really, to save themselves—by any means other than by grace through faith fool themselves. Instead of receiving a blessing as a result of their efforts to obey the Law, they fall under a curse. So how does faith remove us from this curse of the Law? Paul tells us that Christ, who did live a perfect, righteous life without even the slightest sin, nevertheless suffered the curse of the Law (Gal. 3:13). By suffering death "on a tree," that is, a cross of wood, Jesus Christ experienced the kind of death the Law reserves for one who is cursed. To validate this point, Paul alludes to a principle found in Deuteronomy 21:22-23:

> "If a man has committed a sin worthy of death and he is put to death, and you hang him on a tree, his corpse shall not hang all night on the tree, but you shall surely bury him on the same day (for he who is hanged is accursed of God), so that you do not defile your land which the LORD your God gives you as an inheritance."

Though Jesus Christ was the only one ever to fulfill the Law perfectly, He voluntarily submitted to a punishment associated with cursed sinners. Yet He didn't die as a result of His own sin, but as a substitute for those who actually deserved such punishment—you and me. The Greek word translated "redeemed" in Galatians 3:13 is *exagorazō* [1805]. Related to the Greek word *agora* [58], "marketplace," it refers to purchasing or ransoming a person, as a slave might be purchased from the slave market. Though we were once in bondage to the Law and under its constant condemnation, Christ's death in our place has paid the price for our release, freeing us from the curse of the Law and releasing us to serve Christ in a new life of grace.

Barry Beitzel

The *agora,* "marketplace," was the center of commerce in a Greco-Roman city. Here a person could buy anything from apparel to slaves. This photo is of the replica of part of the agora that once stood in Athens, the Stoa of Attalos.

The eternal Son of God—sinless, glorious, holy—slipped out of His perfect heaven and into a sin-infested world. He voluntarily took what we deserved, the judgment of God against sin, and gave us what we could never earn: a right standing before God. Why? Paul closes this section with two reasons for the steep price Christ paid to purchase those who believe. First, He purchased us to bestow upon us the blessing of salvation promised to Abraham in Genesis 12:3. Second, He redeemed us so that He could grant us the gift of the Holy Spirit through faith.

In His plan of salvation, God did not need to relax one letter of His perfect Law to accommodate us wretched sinners who couldn't get through a day without breaking it. Instead, He sent His Son to fulfill every jot and tittle of the Law for us and to suffer the Law's sentence of death for us. Why, then, would anybody once saved by grace through faith in the finished work of Christ seek their own righteousness in the Law—which Christ has already fulfilled? To backslide into legalism would be an affront to the gospel and to the God who alone saves us by His grace.

# APPLICATION: GALATIANS 3:1-14
### Antidotes for Backsliding

Paul's hard-hitting assessment of and argument against backsliding from grace leaves us with three lessons we dare not ignore.

First, *salvation is a free gift; don't try to earn it.* Adding to the gospel of grace only confuses things. Attempting to earn salvation by any degree robs God of His glory. God is graciously holding out His hand and saying, simply, "Take it. It's a gift. You do nothing for it. You owe Me nothing in return." Since that is true, accept it. Accept the gift once and for all through an act of simple faith. Then continue accepting it each day as you stand firmly on the truth that your salvation from first to last—justification, sanctification, and glorification—is yours as a gift from His hand. Rely totally on the finished work of Jesus Christ. He did it all for you.

Second, *legalism is an aggressive enemy; don't make friends with it.* When you spot legalism in any form, get away from it. Whether it's legalistic justification or legalistic sanctification, shun it. Don't give it a hearing. Legalism will make a rational appeal, quoting Bible verses (out of context) that extol the virtues of the Law and the goodness of works. It will also tug at emotions like fear—fear of "anything goes" living or anxiety about pleasing God. We all need to decide that we're going to walk arm in arm with the Spirit of God, keeping legalism at arm's length.

Third, *backsliding is temporary insanity; don't attempt to reason with it.* Paul called the Galatians "foolish" for backsliding from grace and suggested they had been "bewitched" (3:1). Throughout my life I've discovered that there are times when I have to simply confront error and then back off and let the Spirit of God do His work. Why? Because arguing or reasoning with insanity is insane. Only God can give wisdom instead of folly. Only His Spirit can break the spell with clarity. Even your best arguments will not convince a backslidden person who has fallen from grace and gotten stuck in a legalistic way of thinking. The ultimate answer? Pray. Take your stand, point out the truth, then pray that God will do His transforming work.

# A Promise You Can Count On
## GALATIANS 3:15-22

**NASB**

15 Brethren, I speak ªin terms of human relations: even though it is *only* a man's ᵇcovenant, yet when it has been ratified, no one sets it aside or adds ᶜconditions to it. 16 Now the promises were spoken to Abraham and to his seed. He does not say, "And to seeds," as *referring* to many, but *rather* to one, "And to your seed," that is, Christ. 17 What I am saying is this: the Law, which came four hundred and thirty years later, does not invalidate a covenant previously ratified by God, so as to nullify the promise. 18 For if the inheritance is ªbased on law, it is no longer ªbased on a promise; but God has granted it to Abraham by means of a promise.

19 Why the Law then? It was added ªbecause of transgressions, having been ordained through angels by the ᵇagency of a mediator, until the seed would come to whom the promise had been made. 20 Now a mediator is not ªfor one *party only;* whereas God

**NLT**

15 Dear brothers and sisters,* here's an example from everyday life. Just as no one can set aside or amend an irrevocable agreement, so it is in this case. 16 God gave the promises to Abraham and his child.* And notice that the Scripture doesn't say "to his children,*" as if it meant many descendants. Rather, it says "to his child"—and that, of course, means Christ. 17 This is what I am trying to say: The agreement God made with Abraham could not be canceled 430 years later when God gave the law to Moses. God would be breaking his promise. 18 For if the inheritance could be received by keeping the law, then it would not be the result of accepting God's promise. But God graciously gave it to Abraham as a promise.

19 Why, then, was the law given? It was given alongside the promise to show people their sins. But the law was designed to last only until the coming of the child who was promised. God gave his law through angels to Moses, who was the mediator between God and the people. 20 Now a mediator is helpful if more than one party must reach an agreement. But God, who is one, did not use a

is *only* one. [21] Is the Law then contrary to the promises of God? May it never be! For if a law had been given which was able to impart life, then righteousness [a]would indeed have been [b]based on law. [22] But the Scripture has shut up [a]everyone under sin, so that the promise by faith in Jesus Christ might be given to those who believe.

3:15 [a]Lit *according to man* [b]Or *will* or *testament* [c]Or *a codicil* 3:18 [a]Lit *out of, from* 3:19 [a]Or *for the sake of defining* [b]Lit *hand* 3:20 [a]Lit *of one* 3:21 [a]Or *would indeed be* [b]Lit *out of, from* 3:22 [a]Lit *things*

mediator when he gave his promise to Abraham.

[21] Is there a conflict, then, between God's law and God's promises?* Absolutely not! If the law could give us new life, we could be made right with God by obeying it. [22] But the Scriptures declare that we are all prisoners of sin, so we receive God's promise of freedom only by believing in Jesus Christ.

3:15 Greek *Brothers.* 3:16a Greek *seed;* also in 3:16c, 19. See notes on Gen 12:7 and 13:15. 3:16b Greek *seeds.* 3:21 Some manuscripts read *and the promises?*

---

"I promise." Few words can bring more hope or more disappointment than those. You promise your children a summer trip to Disney World, and they hail you for days as the best parent in the world. Then you later inform them it's canceled—and you better have an escape route planned. We all know that people can go from excitement and delight to disappointment and despair in a matter of seconds, all because of how we treat those two words: "I promise."

The reason these words are so packed with emotion is that we live in a world of broken promises. From missed appointments to divorces, from missed payments to bankruptcies, we have all experienced the pain of broken promises. Even though the whole fabric of our society rests on people keeping their word, more and more we see the threads of that fabric wearing thin as broken promises lead to broken relationships and broken lives. Sadly, a person's word is only as good as the person's character and capacity. Only a person with both the integrity and the ability to fulfill a promise can be completely trusted. But if a person is weak in integrity or lacks ability because of his or her circumstances, the promise may be broken.

To see both perfect character and unwavering capacity, we need to turn from faulty and frail humans to a faultless and powerful God. Only God can and will keep all His promises to His people. Nothing, not even our disobedience, can invalidate His unconditional promises. In Galatians 3:15-22, the apostle Paul explains the impact of God's timeless trustworthiness on our salvation and Christian lives. In doing so, he gives yet another reason why we must reject legalism's flawed promise that blessings will come through keeping the Law.

## — 3:15-18 —

So far in his letter, Paul has hammered away at a simple truth: "A man is not justified by the works of the Law but through faith in Christ Jesus" (2:16). He has called opponents of this fundamental doctrine "accursed" (1:8-9) and those who cloud its clarity "foolish" (3:1). How could the Galatians abandon the simple message that had originally given them salvation (3:1-5)? Even Abraham, the father of the Hebrew people, had not been justified by the Law but by faith (3:6-9)!

Of course, the Judaizers had an answer for everything. You can almost hear their response to Paul's appeal to Abraham as the father of faith: "Okay, maybe Abraham was justified by faith. But that was before the Law of Moses was given on Mount Sinai. Once the Law came, it was out with the old and in with the new. The Law superseded everything that came before it. If Abraham's way of salvation had been by faith, then why would God confuse things by adding literally hundreds of rules and regulations?"

To address this inevitable question, Paul turns his attention to the relationship between the gospel of blessing by faith promised to Abraham and the Law given to Moses. In Galatians 3:16, Paul wants to do more than focus on Abraham's salvation experience. He wants to show that just like every believer's justification, Abraham's was and is based on God's unconditional covenant promise, His eternal plan to impart salvation to sinners by grace through faith. The Mosaic Law, which came centuries after Abraham, could never annul God's original plan.

As a master teacher, Paul begins to explain the unconditional nature of God's covenant with Abraham by drawing an analogy between a human covenant and a divine covenant. The term "covenant" has several nuances in Scripture. The Hebrew word *berith* [H1285] could refer to a simple human contract or agreement that was legally binding (Gen. 21:27). Or it could refer to the unconditional promises of God, already seen in His covenant with Noah (Gen. 6:18; 9:9). A covenant could involve two equal parties, like Abraham and Abimelech, in which both were equally responsible to keep their ends of the bargain or suffer the consequences (see Gen. 21:22-34). Or the covenant could involve two unequal parties, like God and humans, in which the granter, God, enters into an agreement knowing the end from the beginning and ultimately takes it upon Himself to fulfill the promises in His own time and by His own means.

A covenant normally held both parties to certain obligations, specifying penalties for breaching the pact. Covenants were often sealed with a solemn ceremony, as they are even today. As bizarre as it may seem to us, in Abraham's day one way of sealing a covenant was by slaughtering an animal, cutting it in half, and having both parties of the agreement walk through the midst of the parts to picture what would happen if either party broke the covenant. We see this ritual observed in the ratifying of God's covenant with Abraham: "So He said to him, 'Bring Me a three year old heifer, and a three year old female goat, and a three year old ram, and a turtledove, and a young pigeon.' Then he brought all these to Him and cut them in two, and laid each

## EXCURSUS: THE COVENANT-KEEPING GOD

### GALATIANS 3:15-18

We don't have to read far into the first pages of the Bible before we discover that God deals with His people through covenants. Bible scholars have often designated the God-ordained covenants as either "conditional" or "unconditional," indicating the degree to which humans were responsible to keep part of the deal. For example, God's promise to Noah never again to destroy the world by water was unconditional—God didn't require anything of Noah for that promise to be kept (Gen. 9:9-11). In contrast, the covenant of the Mosaic Law was explicitly conditional because the people of Israel obligated themselves to keep all of its commands in order to receive blessing from God and avoid curses associated with disobedience (Exod. 24:7). The Abrahamic covenant was unconditional in that God alone obligated Himself to its promises (Gen. 15:17-18). In order to experience the blessings of the covenant, however, Abraham and his descendants were to trust and obey (Gen. 26:4-5).

As we span the history of God's covenants with humanity after the Flood, we see that they all build toward the ultimate fulfillment brought about through Jesus Christ. In His covenant with Noah, God promised never to destroy the world by flood again (Gen. 9:8-17), thus physically preserving humanity in order that God might spiritually redeem His chosen ones. Later God covenanted with Abraham to make his descendants more numerous than the stars, to give him the Promised Land, and to bless all nations through him (Gen. 12:1-3). At Mount Sinai, under Moses' leadership, the Israelites promised to obey God's Law, thus agreeing to the conditional covenantal terms He had stipulated (Exod. 24:3). This temporary institution of the Law would help preserve Israel as a nation until the ultimate fulfillment of God's covenant with Abraham. God's covenant with David expanded on the Abrahamic covenant, specifying that the promise of blessing made to Abraham would be mediated through the royal family of David (2 Sam. 7:12, 16; 22:51). And finally Jesus Christ, the Mediator of the "new covenant," came as the One through whom all of the covenantal promises of God would ultimately be fulfilled (Luke 22:20).

half opposite the other" (Gen. 15:9-10). Yet in the process of ratifying this covenant, something unexpected occurred. Instead of instructing Abraham to walk through the center of the animals to indicate his commitment to keep his end of the bargain, God Himself took form and committed Himself to the covenant alone: "It came about when the sun had set, that it was very dark, and behold, there appeared a smoking oven and a flaming torch which passed between these pieces. On that day the LORD made a covenant with Abram" (Gen. 15:17-18).

Thus, God and God alone obligated Himself unilaterally to fulfilling the various promises of His covenant with Abraham and his descendants. This meant that the promise-keeping God would one day honor His promises regardless of the obedience or disobedience of the recipients of the covenant, the Hebrew people. Each generation after Abraham had to respond in faith and obedience in order to experience the blessings of the covenant. But faithlessness and disobedience could not annul the covenant itself, as Paul says in Romans 3:3-4: "If some did not believe, their unbelief will not nullify the faithfulness of God, will it? May it never be!"

In Paul's day, the Greek word for covenant, *diathēkē* [1242], was also used for a will or testament. When he begins to use a human analogy in Galatians 3:15, Paul points out how strictly a covenant must be kept. Here Paul employs a common Jewish practice of arguing from the lesser to the greater. The argument goes like this: If humans treat properly executed contracts with great respect, how much more will God honor His own contractual obligations! Nobody can set the covenant aside, add new stipulations, or amend it in any way.

Think about this in our own terms. Once you sign your last will and testament before witnesses and a notary, neither you nor anyone else can change it without an equally formal and legal procedure. You can't simply scratch out beneficiaries or scribble in a few new heirs on a whim. The only way to amend a will is to officially revoke and replace it or go through a process with all the same formalities as the original. Contracts, covenants, and agreements remain in full force unless broken or revoked.

In 3:16, Paul moves from the general illustration of a human covenant to the specific promise contained in God's unalterable covenant with Abraham. Remember, the Abrahamic covenant basically promised three things: land, descendants, and blessings. The Promised Land had been given to Abraham and his descendants after him. These descendants, from generation to generation, would receive the covenant and pass it down to their own descendants. And someday this covenant would result in blessings that would extend beyond the Hebrew people to include the Gentile nations.

In his argument, Paul quotes from one of several expressions of God's covenant with Abraham, Genesis 13:15. There, God promised that He would give all the land "to you and to your descendants forever." The word translated "descendants" is the Hebrew term *zera* [H2233]. The word itself, like the English term "offspring," is singular in form but can have either a singular or plural sense. Depending on the context, it could refer to an individual "offspring" or to numerous "offspring." Paul knew that in Abraham's case, the exact fulfillment of the "offspring" promise depended upon which generation after Abraham was being discussed. Immediately after Abraham, his son Isaac was the single offspring of the covenant blessing. Then the promise passed down to Isaac's son Jacob, another individual offspring. After Jacob, the Abrahamic promise fanned out from an individual offspring to multiple offspring—to the twelve sons of Jacob, also called the patriarchs of the twelve tribes of Israel. Thus, the "offspring" promise could refer to an individual descendant or to numerous descendants.

Paul argues that when God referred to the "seed" (offspring) of Abraham, the ultimate fulfillment of His promise pointed into the distant future to Jesus Christ, the "Seed" of Abraham in whom all promises and covenants find their fulfillment. From God's perspective, the Abrahamic covenant went beyond establishing the Hebrews in the Promised Land. It included blessing all the families of the earth, regardless of their national or racial heritage. Therefore, through Jesus Christ alone, the ultimate promised "Seed" of Abraham, everyone can become spiritual heirs of Abraham's promise.

Did you realize that, as a believer in Jesus Christ, you are a spiritual descendant of Abraham? By your spiritual incorporation into Christ by the baptism of the Holy Spirit, you are just as much an heir of the promise as Jesus Christ is. Therefore, you are part of the fulfillment of God's covenant with Abraham. The promise, not the Law, makes you part of God's family.

Paul brings his argument home in Galatians 3:17-18. Though 430 years had elapsed between the Abrahamic covenant and the Mosaic Law, the latter did not supersede or invalidate the former. This was not a new covenant that revoked the old (3:17). God's promise was unconditional; it came with no strings attached. So when the Law was revealed and put in place as a "national constitution" for God's covenant people, it did not annul or change the promise to Abraham. Both existed, as it were, side by side, neither impinging on the other. Let me illustrate this by example.

When a couple adopts a child, they enter into an irrevocable contract—a relationship of parenthood as firm as if the child had been born into their family. In essence, they have signed an unconditional covenant that says, "We're your parents. You're our child. Period." Now, as the infant begins to grow, rules and regulations for the ordering of the family relationships begin to take shape. Don't do this. Don't do that. Clean your room. Take out the trash. Be home by eleven o'clock tonight. Obey the rules, receive an allowance. Disobey, suffer the consequences. Every family has such rules, right? They're a kind of "conditional covenant" relationship—an "if-then" arrangement. Now, imagine if these parents said to their adopted child, "If you don't clean your room today, we're going to tear up the adoption papers! If you come home after eleven o'clock, you will no longer be our child." Those parents would be guilty of a cruel confusion of covenants. The day-to-day arrangement of household rules should have absolutely nothing to do with the underlying covenant that established the family relationship.

That's Paul's point in Galatians 3:18. The inheritance of the blessing was based on promise—an unconditional promise from God to Abraham that established an irrevocable, eternal relationship (Gen. 13:15). The Judaizers, however, were alleging that the inheritance was now based on Law! This represented a complete misunderstanding of the function of the Law of Moses in God's plan and purpose.

## — 3:19-20 —

Paul's conclusion deals with yet another possible objection by the Judaizers: "Paul, your teaching fuses Abraham and Christ so closely that you squeeze out Moses and the Law! In that case, it makes the Law pointless, like a confusing intrusion. Surely God wasn't just wasting His time with us, was He? Why then the Law?"

Here Paul clarifies the true purpose of the Law. The Law was "added" to the already-established relationship of promise for a specific reason: "because of transgressions" (3:19). That's the purpose of the Law. It served both a practical and a theological function. First, it created order out of chaos. It was added to provide regulations for the new nation of Israel after their departure from Egypt to keep them from spiraling into absolute apostasy. Second, the Law provided God's people with a clear expression of His righteous standards, revealing their own sinfulness and driving them to trust in the mercy and grace of God (Rom. 3:19-20;

5:20-21). The Law was never meant to provide a way of salvation but to reveal our need for salvation. In both cases, the Law was a temporary arrangement with an intended point of expiration: "until the seed would come to whom the promise had been made" (Gal. 3:19).

Paul's reference to angels emphasizes that these heavenly beings were somehow involved in the giving of the Law at Sinai along with the "mediator," who was Moses (Exod. 20:18-21; cf. Exod. 23:20-23). Other passages also mention the involvement of angels in the giving of the Law (Deut. 33:2; Acts 7:53; Heb. 2:2). This is yet another reason why Paul's opponents couldn't accuse him of denigrating the Law. He openly acknowledged that it was given not only through Moses, the great servant of God, but through angels. The Law is heavenly in its origin; therefore, it is holy and good. Remember, Paul is not disparaging or rejecting the Law. Rather, he's putting it in its proper place in the outworking of God's plan.

Galatians 3:20 has generated dozens of interpretations. I believe it refers to the conditional nature of the Mosaic Law (evidenced by the use of a mediator between two parties) versus the unconditional nature of the Abrahamic covenant (evidenced by the fact that God alone cut the covenant with Abraham).[3] In any case, Paul is once again emphasizing the priority of the promise over the Law. The promise was unilateral and unconditional; the Law was bilateral and conditional. Why, then, would anybody try to trade in the superior and eternal for the inferior and temporary?

## — 3:21-22 —

Paul has shown the purpose of the Law in God's plan, but the Judaizers probably still objected, accusing the apostle of teaching that the Law was, in fact, evil in that it contradicted the good promise of God. Do the Law and the promise work against each other? Are they at odds? In competition?

Paul says that the Law did its best work on behalf of the promise by convincing people that they were fully and completely disqualified to spend eternity with God. In fact, no Law could have been given that could have imparted life—not because of something wrong with God's righteous standards, but because of something essentially wrong with us! The Law revealed in Scripture "shut up everyone under sin" (3:22). That is, the Law reveals the bad news about us—that we are sinners, separated from a holy God both by nature (Eph. 2:3) and by personal choice (Rom. 3:23).

So the Law shows us our sin, but the gospel shows us the way to escape from sin's penalty and take hold of life. In that sense, the Law and the gospel are complementary, like the two hands of God turning our attention toward Christ. As John Stott once wrote:

> Not until the law has bruised and smitten us will we admit our need of the gospel to bind up our wounds. Not until the law has arrested and imprisoned us will we pine for Christ to set us free. Not until the law has condemned and killed us will we call upon Christ for justification and life. Not until the law has driven us to despair of ourselves will we ever believe in Jesus. Not until the law has humbled us even to hell will we turn to the gospel to raise us to heaven.[4]

Law and gospel are not two ways of salvation, but the two means by which God points us to the one way of salvation—"so that the promise by faith in Jesus Christ might be given to those who believe" (Gal. 3:22).

## APPLICATION: GALATIANS 3:15-22

### Give It Your Best Shot!

Is it really impossible to keep the Law? If we're really disciplined, focused, and committed, aren't we able to fulfill at least the Ten Commandments? How hard is it to keep from murdering, committing adultery, or bearing false witness? Consider your own life. Have you murdered? Been unfaithful in your marriage? Perjured yourself in a court of law? Chances are you come out looking pretty clean, right?

Let's consider, though, what Jesus said is required to keep these commandments perfectly. Thumb over in your Bible and take just a few minutes to read Matthew 5:21-22 and 27-28. What is Jesus saying about the Law? Is keeping it just a matter of outward conformity, or does it require absolute purity of thoughts and motives?

Now turn back to the Old Testament and read the Ten Commandments, listed in Exodus 20:1-17. Using Jesus' explanation of keeping the commandments, how many do you think you've kept? All of them? Most of them? None of them?

Let's be honest. We've broken every one of them. We've not kept *one* of them perfectly in heart and mind. None of us is without idols. We've all put other people, possessions, and priorities ahead of God. We've all lied. Out of discontentment, we've all wanted something someone else has. And those are just the ones we can remember! Imagine all the times we sin in thought and deed and don't even know we're doing it.

Now, at this point you might expect me to list the Ten Commandments, have you grade yourself on your performance, then ask you to start working at improving in the areas where you struggle the most. But that's the furthest thing from my mind. Instead, I want us all to come to finally treat the Law with the respect it deserves—as a standard against which we all fall short. We need to come clean. Face it: *You and I cannot keep the Law!* Not for a week. Not even for a day.

But praise God that someone kept it *for* us! Jesus Christ knew no sin, did no sin, and had no sin. His every thought, motive, and action complied with God's Law. He always honored His earthly parents. He never put anything ahead of His heavenly Father. He kept the Sabbath without fail. He never, ever lied. Jesus Christ earned for us the righteous life that sin keeps us from attaining. Clothed in His perfection, we appear as perfect Law-keepers before the Great Judge. When God looks at us, He sees the flawless obedience of His Son . . . and fully accepts it.

Take time now, before you turn another page, to turn your eyes from the Law to the Lord, from your own attempts at reformation to Christ's work of redemption, from the condemnation of the Law to the salvation that is by grace through faith.

# From Law to Faith:
## Our New Status in Christ
### GALATIANS 3:23–4:11

**NASB**

23 But before faith came, we were kept in custody under the law, being shut up to the faith which was later to be revealed. 24 Therefore the Law has become our tutor *to lead us* to Christ, so that we may be justified by faith. 25 But now that faith has

**NLT**

23 Before the way of faith in Christ was available to us, we were placed under guard by the law. We were kept in protective custody, so to speak, until the way of faith was revealed.

24 Let me put it another way. The law was our guardian until Christ came; it protected us until we could be made right with God through faith. 25 And now that the way of faith

NASB

come, we are no longer under a ᵃtutor. ²⁶For you are all sons of God through faith in Christ Jesus. ²⁷For all of you who were baptized into Christ have clothed yourselves with Christ. ²⁸There is neither Jew nor Greek, there is neither slave nor free man, there is ᵃneither male nor female; for you are all one in Christ Jesus. ²⁹And if you ᵃbelong to Christ, then you are Abraham's ᵇdescendants, heirs according to promise.

⁴:¹Now I say, as long as the heir is a ᵃchild, he does not differ at all from a slave although he is ᵇowner of everything, ²but he is under guardians and ᵃmanagers until the date set by the father. ³So also we, while we were children, were held in bondage under the ᵃelemental things of the world. ⁴But when the fullness of the time came, God sent forth His Son, born of a woman, born under ᵃthe Law, ⁵so that He might redeem those who were under ᵃthe Law, that we might receive the adoption as sons. ⁶Because you are sons, God has sent forth the Spirit of His Son into our hearts, crying, "Abba! Father!" ⁷Therefore you are no longer a slave, but a son; and if a son, then an heir ᵃthrough God.

⁸However at that time, when you did not know God, you were slaves to those which by nature are no gods. ⁹But now that you have come to know God, or rather to be known by God, how is it that you turn back again to the weak and worthless ᵃelemental things, to which you desire to be enslaved all over again? ¹⁰You observe days and months and

NLT

has come, we no longer need the law as our guardian.

²⁶For you are all children* of God through faith in Christ Jesus. ²⁷And all who have been united with Christ in baptism have put on Christ, like putting on new clothes.* ²⁸There is no longer Jew or Gentile,* slave or free, male and female. For you are all one in Christ Jesus. ²⁹And now that you belong to Christ, you are the true children* of Abraham. You are his heirs, and God's promise to Abraham belongs to you.

⁴:¹Think of it this way. If a father dies and leaves an inheritance for his young children, those children are not much better off than slaves until they grow up, even though they actually own everything their father had. ²They have to obey their guardians until they reach whatever age their father set. ³And that's the way it was with us before Christ came. We were like children; we were slaves to the basic spiritual principles* of this world.

⁴But when the right time came, God sent his Son, born of a woman, subject to the law. ⁵God sent him to buy freedom for us who were slaves to the law, so that he could adopt us as his very own children.* ⁶And because we* are his children, God has sent the Spirit of his Son into our hearts, prompting us to call out, "Abba, Father."* ⁷Now you are no longer a slave but God's own child.* And since you are his child, God has made you his heir.

⁸Before you Gentiles knew God, you were slaves to so-called gods that do not even exist. ⁹So now that you know God (or should I say, now that God knows you), why do you want to go back again and become slaves once more to the weak and useless spiritual principles of this world? ¹⁰You are trying to earn

seasons and years. ¹¹I fear for you, that perhaps I have labored ªover you in vain.

**3:25** ªLit *child-conductor* **3:28** ªLit *not male and female* **3:29** ªLit *are Christ's* ᵇLit *seed* **4:1** ªOr *minor* ᵇLit *lord* **4:2** ªOr *stewards* **4:3** ªOr *rudimentary teachings* or *principles* **4:4** ªOr *law* **4:5** ªOr *law* **4:7** ªI.e. through the gracious act of **4:9** ªOr *rudimentary teachings* or *principles* **4:11** ªOr *for*

favor with God by observing certain days or months or seasons or years. ¹¹I fear for you. Perhaps all my hard work with you was for nothing.

**3:26** Greek *sons*. **3:27** Greek *have put on Christ*. **3:28** Greek *Jew or Greek*. **3:29** Greek *seed*. **4:3** Or *powers*; also in 4:9. **4:5** Greek *sons*; also in 4:6. **4:6a** Greek *you*. **4:6b** *Abba* is an Aramaic term for "father." **4:7** Greek *son*; also in 4:7b.

Every one of us was born as a prisoner in a labor camp. Regardless of social status, religious upbringing, race, ethnicity, gender, or intelligence, you and I were reared with shackles on our feet and the gaze of an exacting taskmaster fixed on our backs. That taskmaster is the Law. The shackles are our own sins. And the laborious task is to work ourselves deeper and deeper into death and condemnation.

Galatians 3:22 says that "Scripture has shut up everyone under sin." Leon Morris writes, "The verb *shut up* indicates imprisonment; it is not just that people sometimes do what they should not, but they are the prisoners of sin."⁵ This dilemma affects everyone. Not a single soul can claim exemption from this inescapable bondage to sin. Everyone is born "behind bars," spiritually speaking. In that condition the Law sounds the Judge's gavel, decreeing, "You're a sinner. You're condemned." Any attempts at reforming ourselves according to the standards of the Law end in futility and frustration. The Law's commandments function like a demanding parole board, checking off all of our shortcomings and transgressions any time we try to justify ourselves.

But Galatians 3:22 doesn't leave us abandoned and rotting away in the prison cell of sin. It provides a timely reminder of our liberating hope: salvation by grace through faith in Jesus Christ. It also highlights the true purpose of the Law's unyielding demands—"so that the promise by faith in Jesus Christ might be given to those who believe." In the next several verses Paul builds on this truth by employing three analogies to help us understand the Law's role in bringing a person to faith in Christ. Let's look at this passage more closely.

## — 3:23-24 —

Paul uses two analogies for the Law in these two verses—the jailer and the tutor. Before we received the gracious gift of faith, the Law kept sinners "in custody." The underlying Greek word here, *phroureō* [5432], means "to guard." Now, there are two types of guards—one positive, the other negative. On the positive side, a guard may be positioned to protect us, as a bodyguard might prevent us from being harmed. If this were Paul's meaning, the Law would serve as a rule to keep us from danger. On the negative side, a guard may be positioned to hold us prisoner, as a jailer would prevent us from escaping a dungeon. In that case, the Law would keep us from true freedom. In Galatians 3:23, Paul uses the term in its negative sense, as is made clear by the rest of his statement. Those kept in custody by the Law are "shut up to the faith."

commons.wikimedia.org

Wealthy families could afford a male slave called a *paidagōgos*, or "disciplinarian," who would escort students to and from school, making sure they behaved themselves until they were old enough to be responsible.

Surely we did not need protection from the faith. Rather, the Law served to prevent us from experiencing the freedom that comes from salvation by grace through faith.

The next analogy Paul uses might also be mistaken for a positive image of the Law—that of the "tutor." Some translate the word *paidagōgos* [3807] as "schoolmaster" (KJV), "guardian" (ESV), or "custodian" (RSV). But we should not picture the Law as a teacher merely guiding us to greater knowledge. Paul uses the term in a less positive and constructive sense. One commentator notes, "In Paul's day the pedagogue was distinguished from the teacher (*didaskalos* [1320]). The pedagogue supervised, controlled and disciplined the child; the teacher instructed and educated him."[6] We should have in mind a stern disciplinarian who escorts young children to and from school, often carrying a rod or switch in hand to keep children in line.[7]

Here is Paul's point: Before faith came, we were held in prison by our jailer, the Law. Before faith came, we were held under strict discipline by our custodian, the Law. For us to return to these would be like a freed convict rushing back to the prison cell day after day or a high school graduate asking his strict childhood nanny for permission to go to the bathroom. However, the Law, as both jailer and pedagogue, did its job—to "lead us to Christ" so we would be "justified by faith" (3:24).

## — 3:25-29 —

With the coming of faith—that new relationship with God established on the basis of Christ's atoning sacrifice and effected by God's sovereign grace—we transition from the old life under the Law to our new life in Christ. The harsh, scowling tutor has retired, and we are no longer under his exacting demands (3:25). Rather, we are under the gentle instruction of a gracious Teacher. In these verses Paul sets forth three differences we experience because of our new life in Christ.

First, we have become members of God's family (3:26-27). Through faith we have been adopted as "sons of God." Charles Ryrie defines this adoption as "the act of God that places the believer in His family as an adult."[8] Paul will expand on this concept later, but for now we must realize that our placement into the family of God cancels any previous relationship we may have had, especially to the Law as a tutor.

How are we placed in the family? How do we receive the status of "children of God"? The baptism of the Holy Spirit, which occurred at the moment we trusted Christ as our Savior, placed us in the body of Christ (1 Cor. 12:13). We have been identified with Christ and brought into personal union with Him. Because we have clothed ourselves with Christ (Gal. 3:27), we have also put on His righteousness. Just as Christ is the one and only Son of God by nature, we become sons and daughters of God by grace. Donald Campbell explains Paul's imagery here:

> In the Roman society when a youth came of age he was given a special toga which admitted him to the full rights of the family and state and indicated he was a grown-up son. So the Galatian believers had laid aside the old garments of the Law and had put on Christ's robe of righteousness which grants full acceptance before God. Who would want to don again the old clothing?[9]

Second, we have become one with Christ and all Christians (3:28). Just as the Law levels the playing field and excludes everyone as sinners before God regardless of social position, the gospel welcomes everyone regardless of race, heritage, social standing, or gender. Though Jews had worshiped the one God of the Old Testament Scriptures for much longer than Gentiles, in Christ the Gentile "Johnny-come-latelies" received an equal inheritance with Jewish Christians. Likewise, a believing master held no higher spiritual position than the believing slave he owned; both stood before their common Master, Jesus Christ, in equal submission. Finally, the gospel makes no allowance for men to look down on women as spiritual inferiors; both men and women have equal access to salvation by grace through faith in Christ.

Galatians 3:28 is often quoted but frequently misunderstood. Paul's profound words have been misused in an attempt to level out all distinctions and order in political and civil society, but that goes beyond the intention of the passage. The unity Paul describes is the unity we have "in Christ Jesus" (3:28). He does not say "in society," or "in the family," or "in the business world," or "in government." As John Stott rightly observes, Paul's statement "does not mean that racial, social and sexual distinctions are actually obliterated. . . . When we say that Christ has abolished these distinctions, we mean not that they do not exist, but that they do not matter."[10] It is true that the gospel has inspired positive social and cultural changes such as the abolition of slavery and the rejection of racism and sexism. But Paul's primary emphasis is the spiritual reality, not its social implications. Genuine societal change comes only as Christian spiritual values are reflected in the world by those whose hearts and minds have been transformed by the truth of the gospel.

Finally, we have become heirs of a promise (3:29). The third difference we experience because of our new life in Christ is that we partake of the promise given to Abraham as if we ourselves were his physical descendants. Everything that Christ has inherited by nature, we have co-inherited by our placement in Him. Because Jesus Christ is the "Seed" who inherits the promise of Abraham, we who are baptized into Christ also inherit the promise of Abraham.

This brings us full circle to the argument at hand. The Judaizers were insisting that the Galatians keep the Law in order to be saved or to live the new Christian life. But this was absolutely unnecessary, since the Galatians were already heirs of God's promise to Abraham—the promise of justification by faith made possible by the gift of the Holy Spirit (3:6-9, 14).

## — 4:1-3 —

In Galatians 3:23-29, Paul described the Law as a jailer who guarded us and a disciplinarian who punished us before we placed our faith in Christ—until we became "sons" by faith and "heirs according to promise" (3:26, 29). This idea of inheritance continues in the opening verses of chapter 4, where Paul again expounds the purpose of the Law, but with a slightly different analogy: the transition from slavery to sonship.

Paul pictures a minor child who, though bound to inherit everything from his parents, was still under the authority of "guardians and managers" until his father bestowed upon him the full rights, privileges, and authority of a mature man (4:2).[11] During the child's years as a minor, then, he did not "differ at all from a slave" (4:1).

Similarly, we were once "held in bondage under the elemental things of the world" (4:3). The phrase "elemental things" translates the Greek word *stoicheia* [4747], which is used in Hebrews 5:12 to refer to the "ABCs" of the Christian faith. In Galatians 4:3, however, the word is modified by the phrase "of the world." Therefore, this phrase doesn't refer to the basic doctrines of Christianity or to the Old Testament Law, both of which came from God, not "the world." Paul's use of this phrase in Colossians sheds light on what he means here: He uses the same phrase to refer to "philosophy and empty deception, according to the tradition of men" (Col. 2:8). And in Colossians 2:20, he uses the phrase for man-made, legalistic additions to the Law, not the Law itself. The phrase could also refer to the spiritual forces of wickedness—demons—that hold temporary control over the world, engaging in all sorts of deception (Eph. 2:2; cf. John 12:31; 14:30). While we were unsaved and condemned by the Law, we were in bondage to vain philosophies, man-made codes of ethics, legalistic interpretations of the Law, and demon-inspired religions that brought nothing but hopelessness and despair.

## — 4:4-11 —

God did not leave us under bondage. He sent a savior to rescue us! As we suffered under the bondage of sin, death, and damnation, the Lord of glory exited heaven and entered history. At just the right time, a date set in the plan and purpose of God the Father, the Son of God came forth. He was "born of a woman," God in the flesh come to live among us. He was also "born under the Law," emphasizing not only that He was born a Jew but that He was subject to the Old Testament Law (4:4), which He lived out *perfectly*.

## THE FULLNESS OF TIME

### GALATIANS 4:4

People often scratch their heads and wonder, "If Jesus is so important for salvation, why did He wait so long to come?" That is, why didn't He come while Cain and Abel were still arguing over their offering . . . or before God had to wipe out humanity from the face of the earth with the Flood . . . or when the nation of Israel was just beginning to play fast and loose with the Law?

Others have argued from the opposite direction: "If the message of Jesus' death and resurrection is essential for salvation, why didn't He wait to come until the advent of mass media so His followers could proclaim an undisputable version of His words and works to the maximum number of people?" After all, it would be much more difficult for people to doubt a video of His resurrection than ancient written accounts.

Paul answers both objections about the timing of Christ's coming. The phrase "fullness of the time" in Galatians 4:4 corresponds to the "date set by the father" in 4:2. That is, in God's infinite wisdom and providence over the affairs of history, Jesus Christ came at just the right time—not one day too early, not one day too late. One commentator describes the perfect timing of Jesus' arrival this way:

> This "time" was when the Roman civilization had brought peace and a road system which facilitated travel; when the Grecian civilization provided a language which was adopted as the *lingua franca* of the empire; when the Jews had proclaimed monotheism and the messianic hope in the synagogues of the Mediterranean world.[12]

So, at the perfect crossroads of human history, Jesus Christ became the *center* of human history. At just the right intersection of religion, politics, culture, and economics, Jesus brought about a spiritual revolution that would change the world forever.

The purpose of Christ's coming was to "redeem those who were under the Law" (4:5). To "redeem" means to buy out of slavery. So Jesus, by His perfect life and sacrificial death, purchased us from the slave block of the Law. Now we're no longer slaves but sons and daughters of God.

This new relationship as children of God is more than positional; it is also experiential. Not only did God declare us righteous and, as it were, sign the legal documents to call us His children; He also gave us His Holy Spirit to seal our sonship and to give us the ability to call on Him in prayer as our loving Father (4:6-7). The Aramaic word *Abba* is a term of familiar affection for the head of the household, emphasizing that we have become God's children and enjoy an intimate relationship with Him. Interestingly, the term is used elsewhere in the New Testament when Christ Himself refers to God the Father as His "Abba" (Mark 14:36). By virtue of our being "in Christ" and participating in His relationship of sonship by adoption, we, too, can call God "Abba" and have a personal, familial relationship with Him through the Holy Spirit (Rom. 8:15).

Paul's mention of the Spirit here also confirms that the entire Trinity—Father, Son, and Holy Spirit—is involved in our redemption from slavery and adoption as sons and daughters. God gave fully of Himself to bring us into His family. The Father sent the Son; the Son redeemed us from sin; the Spirit came to dwell with us. All of these blessings of the triune God confirm the reality that we are no longer slaves but heirs (Gal. 4:7).

As God's sons and daughters, of what are we "heirs"? Paul explains in his letter to the Ephesians that God has "blessed us with every spiritual blessing in the heavenly places in Christ" (Eph. 1:3). This would include justification; complete forgiveness of sins; immediate, unlimited, and unconditional access to the Father; membership in Christ's church; the indwelling of the Holy Spirit; the promise of eternal life; and future bodily resurrection (to name only a few).

That's quite an inheritance—and all of it free of charge! None of it is deserved, yet all of it has been bestowed upon us "by grace . . . through faith" (Eph. 2:8). The Galatian Christians had come so far. At one time they were ignorant of God, slaves to idolatry (Gal. 4:8); but by God's grace they had come to know God in a personal, intimate way. Why then, Paul wonders, would they return to the "weak and worthless elemental things," becoming "enslaved all over again" (4:9)?

By following the Judaizers' legalistic prescription for living the Christian life, the Galatians were backsliding into slavery. In addition to circumcision, the Judaizers were trying to impose the strict observance of the Jewish calendar (4:10). In the Law, God had given the Sabbath, festivals, and celebrations to keep the Jewish people focused on Him, but they were never meant to save them—or anyone! By requiring the Gentile Galatian believers to observe these things, the Judaizers were adding works to faith, mixing God's old covenant with His new covenant.

So exasperated was Paul with the Galatians that he wondered if he had expended all his effort in evangelism and discipleship in vain (4:11). This isn't to say that Paul thought the Galatians who had truly trusted Christ were in danger of losing their salvation. Rather, the backsliding of the Galatians into legalism meant that Paul virtually had to start over with their discipleship, teaching them once again the basics of the gospel message—that grace is the way to life and the way of life.

Let's not allow the Galatians' folly to become our own. Let's stop trying to earn the approval of our Father, who has already accepted us—and adopted us—in Christ Jesus. Let us with confidence set aside the distractions of legalism and cry out, "Abba! Father!" as grateful sons and daughters, not fearful, nameless slaves.

# APPLICATION: GALATIANS 3:23-4:11

## Intimacy with the Almighty

Years ago, parenting experts used to talk about the need for parents to spend "quality time" with their kids. The way busy parents sometimes interpreted this was, "Well, I can get away with just ten or fifteen minutes a day with Junior, as long as it's *quality* time." But experts soon supplemented the concept of "quality time" with a related fact: *Quality time comes in the midst of quantity time.*[13]

This fact is not only true when it comes to parents' relationships with their children; it's also true of our Heavenly Father's relationship with His spiritual offspring. Our tendency in this fast-paced world is to step on the throttle—to accelerate, run faster, push our energy to the limits—even in the Christian life. In the process, our walk with God remains shallow and superficial. We spend little time talking to Him, listening to Him, sitting silently in His presence, meditating on the truths of His Word, or enjoying meaningful relationships with other sons and daughters in His family.

Galatians 3:23–4:11 reminds us that we have been adopted as children of God. We're not slaves assigned to a life of devotional drudgery or menial religious tasks on a checklist of divine demands. Rather, we have been called into an intimate relationship with the almighty God. So close are we to our heavenly Father that we are free to call Him "Papa" or "Daddy." Just like our relationship with our natural parents, this kind of heart-to-heart relationship with God requires *time* to season and deepen.

What do you do during this time? Well, if we look to Christ's own personal relationship with His Father, we see several key attitudes and actions that point us toward meaningful intimacy with our almighty Abba. After many years of ministry, I've boiled these down to several essentials for breathing life into our personal relationship with God:[14]

- simplicity—uncluttering our lives and minds from things that distract us from God
- silence and solitude—slowing our pace and making space in our schedules for God
- surrender—releasing our grip on things that take our attention from God
- prayer—calling out to God with our praise, thanksgiving, and petitions
- humility—bowing our entire lives before the will of God
- self-control—holding back our own priorities in favor of God's priorities
- sacrifice—giving up the things God expects us to surrender to Him

These activities don't *cause* us to be children of God. They don't *earn* God's favor or *win* us merit. We must steer clear of a legalistic attitude toward these actions. But if we invest in and cultivate meaningful intimacy with our Father, we will experience quality time as we follow Christ's example. Even in the midst of His earthly ministry, pressed and pushed by people in need, Christ took time for solitude, silence, and prayer.

Take some time right now to reflect upon your own intimacy with God. Answer a few questions: How much time do you spend each day *with* God? Do you talk to Him or just mumble a few meaningless words? Do you pause and listen to Him in your times of silence and solitude, as you thoughtfully read His Word? Or are you so obsessed with your schedule that you rush through your reading to finish your checklist? Do you live a simple life of surrender and self-control, or do you clutter your life with a heap of distractions? These are tough, specific questions that deserve honest answers.

You may walk away from this reflective exercise dissatisfied with your current relationship with God. If so, admit it . . . and make plans to change! I want you to hunger and thirst for a deeper, more meaningful time with your Father. I urge you to walk more closely with Him, to talk more confidently with Him, and to deliberately wait in silence, hanging on His every word. Only when we experience that kind of protracted intimacy with the Almighty will we truly be able to live like heirs of the promise. And as a result, we will delight in calling Him "Abba."

# Caring Enough to Tell the Truth
## GALATIANS 4:12-20

**NASB**

12 I beg of you, brethren, become as I *am,* for I also *have become* as you *are.* You have done me no wrong; 13 but you know that it was because of a ªbodily illness that I preached the gospel to you the ᵇfirst time; 14 and that which was a ªtrial to you in my ᵇbodily condition you did not despise or ᶜloathe, but you received me as an angel of God, as Christ Jesus *Himself.* 15 Where then is ªthat sense of blessing you had? For I bear you witness that, if possible, you would have plucked out your eyes and given them to me. 16 So have I become your enemy by ªtelling you the truth? 17 They eagerly seek you, not commendably, but they wish to shut you out so that you will seek them. 18 But it is good always to be eagerly sought in a commendable ªmanner, and not only when I am present with you. 19 My children, with whom I am again in labor until Christ is formed in you— 20 but I could wish to be present with you now and to change my tone, for I am perplexed about you.

4:13 ªLit *weakness of the flesh* ᵇOr *former*
4:14 ªOr *temptation* ᵇLit *flesh* ᶜLit *spit out at* 4:15 ªLit *the congratulation of yourselves*
4:16 ªOr *dealing truthfully with you* 4:18 ªOr *thing*

**NLT**

12 Dear brothers and sisters,* I plead with you to live as I do in freedom from these things, for I have become like you Gentiles—free from those laws.

You did not mistreat me when I first preached to you. 13 Surely you remember that I was sick when I first brought you the Good News. 14 But even though my condition tempted you to reject me, you did not despise me or turn me away. No, you took me in and cared for me as though I were an angel from God or even Christ Jesus himself. 15 Where is that joyful and grateful spirit you felt then? I am sure you would have taken out your own eyes and given them to me if it had been possible. 16 Have I now become your enemy because I am telling you the truth?

17 Those false teachers are so eager to win your favor, but their intentions are not good. They are trying to shut you off from me so that you will pay attention only to them. 18 If someone is eager to do good things for you, that's all right; but let them do it all the time, not just when I'm with you.

19 Oh, my dear children! I feel as if I'm going through labor pains for you again, and they will continue until Christ is fully developed in your lives. 20 I wish I were with you right now so I could change my tone. But at this distance I don't know how else to help you.

4:12 Greek *brothers;* also in 4:28, 31.

Pastors and teachers who take a firm, uncompromising stand for truth are often criticized as being "all head and no heart"—too intellectual, hard, severe, militant, abrasive, dogmatic, dictatorial. Some might hurl these same labels at the apostle Paul, especially in light of the plea for doctrinal purity we've seen in this letter so far. Such a caricature crumbles, however, when we read the present section of Galatians.

Here we see that Paul was not only a passionate preacher of grace and a firm, uncompromising teacher of truth but also a caring shepherd among the flock. It is easy to lose sight of the deep love and genuine concern Paul had for the Galatians when he called them fools and accused them of backsliding into false teaching. Galatians 4:12-20 helps balance that out. In this part of his letter, Paul's appeal to his readers becomes a heart-to-heart talk rather than a doctrinal discourse. Here the teacher comes across as a warm, tender, transparent, and vulnerable pastor.

These verses wedged in the middle of chapter 4 serve as a reminder to everyone who is passionate about championing the gospel that we're to love people as much as we love the truth. When we communicate the gospel, we are sharing it with people—either those hearing it for the first time or those who have already embraced it:

- people we want to see living free, rescued from the bondage of legalism
- people we want to see enjoying the Christian life to the fullest
- people we love enough to tell them the truth, even if it's hard for them to hear it

Ultimately, championing the gospel isn't about winning or losing arguments. It's about God's people gaining or losing freedom.

## — 4:12 —

In the first three chapters of his letter to the Galatians, Paul mustered his biblical, historical, theological, and experiential arsenal against the Judaizers' false gospel. His goal was to demolish their accusations against his apostleship and expose their false doctrine of justification and sanctification through the Law. In chapter 4, his tone begins to change. He moves from defending to exhorting, from challenging to complimenting, from refuting to remembering. Paul the vigorous apologist becomes Paul the loving and caring pastor. He pleads with the Galatian believers, his spiritual children in the Lord, to return to the truth they had once embraced.

Based on the opening line of this plea, we can almost imagine Paul dropping to his knees, folding his hands, and begging his readers to heed his words. This emotional appeal reveals not only what Paul desired for the Galatians but also how committed to them he was. Given the context of the letter, Paul's entreaty for the Galatians to become "as I am" probably refers to his longing for them to emulate him in Christian freedom. Formerly a zealous Jew, passionate for strict obedience to the Law, the apostle had forsaken all of that fleshly zeal for the passionate pursuit of Christ. Paul describes this transformation poignantly in his letter to the Philippians. Read his words slowly; mentally picture this incredible transformation!

> If anyone else has a mind to put confidence in the flesh, I far more: circumcised the eighth day, of the nation of Israel, of the tribe of Benjamin, a Hebrew of Hebrews; as to the Law, a Pharisee; as to zeal, a persecutor of the church; as to the righteousness which is in the Law, found blameless. But whatever things were gain to me, those things I have counted as loss for the sake of Christ. More than that, I count all things to be loss in view of the surpassing value of knowing Christ Jesus my Lord, for whom I have suffered the loss of all things, and count them but rubbish so that I may gain Christ, and may be found in Him, not having a righteousness of my own derived from the Law, but that which is through faith in Christ, the righteousness which comes from God on the basis of faith. (Phil. 3:4-9)

Paul wanted the Galatians to become like him—delivered from the bondage of the Law and freed to know Christ as Savior. But Paul also said that he had become like the Galatians (Gal. 4:12). In what sense had Paul become like them? Most likely this refers to Paul's practice of becoming "all things to all men" in order to open the door for evangelism (1 Cor. 9:22). To Jews, Paul became like a Jew; to those without the Law, he became like one without the Law; to the weak, he became weak—all for the sake of the gospel (1 Cor. 9:19-23). So, when Paul first came to the Gentile Galatians, he didn't remain aloof as Peter did in Antioch, but he identified with them by adopting many of their customs. He spoke their language, ate their food, respected their culture, and met them where they were. Furthermore, while he was with them, they didn't hassle him. They responded to his loving self-sacrifice in kind, leaving no room for bad memories in Paul's mind. (What a model for all ministers and missionaries to follow!) And the result? Paul didn't change; the Galatians did.

Paul's approach instructs us as we reach the world for Christ. We face two extremes in our churches today. One is distancing ourselves from non-Christians to such an extent that we never have any meaningful contact with them. The other is identifying so closely with unbelievers that we become virtually indistinguishable from them. Paul models the balance we need to seek. When with Jews, he practiced Jewish customs not antithetical to Christianity in order to save as many Jews as he could (Acts 16:1-3; 18:18; 21:20-26; 1 Cor. 9:20). Likewise, when he spent time with Gentiles, he became as they were in matters indifferent to Christianity so he might win more people to the gospel (see 1 Cor. 9:21; Gal. 2:11-21). When we emulate Paul, we become far more effective in our witness. And by His grace, God will use us to bring many new citizens into Christ's eternal kingdom.

## — 4:13-16 —

Having alluded to his early ministry among the Galatians, Paul decides to linger on the past a bit longer. He reminds them of how they had welcomed him and his message. Not only did they not wrong him in any way (4:12) but they actually came to his aid at a time of bodily illness. In fact, Paul says that he originally preached the gospel to them *because* of an infirmity (4:13). This experience was particularly memorable for Paul, who must have been ill either when he first arrived in Galatia or shortly thereafter.

From what was Paul suffering? Various maladies have been suggested.[15] Some believe Paul suffered from malaria in Pamphylia and went up to the higher country of Galatia to recuperate. Others suggest Paul suffered from epilepsy brought on by some kind of wicked spirit (2 Cor. 12:7-10). Some commentators have proposed that Paul was experiencing a disease of the eyes. In light of Paul's statement in Galatians 4:15—"if possible, you would have plucked out your eyes and given them to me"—many conclude that Paul suffered from some affliction of his eyesight. Poor eyesight may also explain why Paul points out the "large letters" he uses to write with his own hand (6:11).

Whatever Paul's condition, it apparently made him disturbing to look at. His illness was a "trial" or test for the Galatians and would normally have caused most people to "despise or loathe" him (4:14). On the contrary, they welcomed Paul, showing him the same respect and kindness they would have shown an angel or even Jesus Himself.

Such was their warm and hospitable reception of Paul at the beginning of his ministry among them. Early on they were open to the gospel and overflowing with the love and mercy characteristic of those who had experienced the power of transforming grace.

But things had changed. They had lost the "sense of blessing" they originally had toward Paul (4:15). The Galatians had turned from treating Paul like an angel to looking on him as an enemy. With the intrusion of the Judaizers' malicious legalism, the Galatians' once sweet relationship with Paul had soured. By telling them the truth about freedom from the Law, Paul had become an opponent of the now Law-leaning Galatians.

Paul's situation is relevant for us today. Teaching the Scriptures often means communicating truth to people who don't want to hear it. In fact, those who once appreciated your teaching may turn on you and hate you for it. G. Walter Hansen draws out the implications of this reality for both pastors and congregations:

> The dramatic shift from the Galatians' warm welcome to their cold rejection of Paul serves as a sober warning to both pastors and their churches. Pastors should not be so naive as to think they will always receive a warm welcome if they consistently teach the truth. In fact, teaching the truth will always run the risk of alienating some people. And people in the church need to be aware that their initial positive response to pastors who teach the truth will be severely tested when the truth cuts like a two-edged sword. During such a time of conviction, people need to maintain their loyalty to their pastors precisely because they have the courage to preach the truth even when it hurts.[16]

## — 4:17-20 —

In contrast to Paul's heartfelt plea on behalf of the truth, the Judaizers had an insidious and insincere agenda. They sought out the young Galatian converts with zeal (4:17). In addition to open attacks on Paul in his absence, the Judaizers also drummed up disingenuous flattery. Although they showered the Galatians with compliments—a practice Paul deemed good when combined with the right motives (4:18)—these legalists were doing it to spotlight themselves and enslave the Galatians under their version of the Law.

So, with the tender heart of a pastor, Paul explained that his motive had always been to serve the Galatian believers until Christ was formed in them (4:19). Like a mother struggling through labor, Paul wanted to endure this agonizing crisis of their faith until the image of Christ could be wrought in their lives. He had been "in labor" once before, when he preached the gospel to them. Now he was enduring again as he struggled to see them grow in Christ and be delivered from the false teachers. The true pastor's work certainly does not cease with evangelism. It continues through a lifelong process of discipleship. As any parent knows, becoming a parent is far easier than being a parent.

Just like any loving parent, Paul would rather have been present with the Galatians than far removed from them (4:20). Perhaps an in-person visit would help resolve some of the perplexity he experienced at the news of their backsliding. Perhaps he could better diagnose their disease, apply a proper salve, and restore them to health. Under these circumstances, Paul could change his tone from one of rebuke to one of loving exhortation. But writing from a distance, Paul had to resort to emergency measures to stop the bleeding—measures that can be painful for the patient. In the case of the Galatians, the truth hurt.

No doubt Paul had heard of the words of Jesus spoken nearly twenty years earlier: "You will know the truth, and the truth will make you free" (John 8:32). If the Galatians needed anything during this great crisis in their Christian lives, it was freedom. Yet the only way to achieve that freedom was to know the truth.

# APPLICATION: GALATIANS 4:12-20
## Truth That Hurts . . . and Heals

Let's face it. Sometimes the truth is the last thing we want to hear, especially if it exposes our spiritual deficiencies. Even when spoken in love by someone who cares deeply about us, the truth can cause us to bristle. The bad news about *us* can make us bitter, angry, and resentful. We tend to lash out at the truth teller to evade the sting of facing the truth itself . . . and changing.

But some of us have been around long enough to appreciate true wisdom. It isn't the know-it-all who holds the key to a better life. It's the man or woman of God who has surrendered himself or herself fully to the truth and is willing to hear it, accept it, live it, and pass it on—even when it hurts. We need to keep in mind that truth can either make us bitter or better.

Truth can help us face our weaknesses and trust in Christ's life-changing power. How do you generally respond to truth? Do you seek out people who are honest in their evaluations or do you avoid them? Have you heard any hard truth about your life lately from someone who cares about you? What was it? Did it sting? Was it helpful? Take a moment to consider what was said, how it was said, and how the God of truth would want you to react to it.

If hearing the truth helped you at all, even if it just caused you to think, why not do something unusual? Take a few minutes to write a note to the person who shared the truth with you. Thank him or her for loving you enough to say the hard thing.

# To Those Who Want to Be under the Law
## GALATIANS 4:21-31

**NASB**

21 Tell me, you who want to be under law, do you not listen to the law? 22 For it is written that Abraham had two sons, one by the bondwoman and one by the free woman. 23 But the son by the bondwoman [a]was born according to the flesh, and the son by the free woman through the promise. 24 [a]This is allegorically speaking, for these *women* are two covenants: one *proceeding* from Mount Sinai bearing children [b]who are to be slaves; [c]she is Hagar. 25 Now this Hagar is Mount Sinai in Arabia and corresponds to the present Jerusalem, for she is in slavery with her children. 26 But the Jerusalem above is free; [a]she is our mother. 27 For it is written,

"REJOICE, BARREN WOMAN WHO
     DOES NOT BEAR;

**NLT**

21 Tell me, you who want to live under the law, do you know what the law actually says? 22 The Scriptures say that Abraham had two sons, one from his slave wife and one from his freeborn wife.* 23 The son of the slave wife was born in a human attempt to bring about the fulfillment of God's promise. But the son of the freeborn wife was born as God's own fulfillment of his promise.

24 These two women serve as an illustration of God's two covenants. The first woman, Hagar, represents Mount Sinai where people received the law that enslaved them. 25 And now Jerusalem is just like Mount Sinai in Arabia,* because she and her children live in slavery to the law. 26 But the other woman, Sarah, represents the heavenly Jerusalem. She is the free woman, and she is our mother. 27 As Isaiah said,

"Rejoice, O childless woman,
     you who have never given birth!

BREAK FORTH AND SHOUT, YOU
WHO ARE NOT IN LABOR;
FOR MORE NUMEROUS ARE THE
CHILDREN OF THE DESOLATE
THAN OF THE ONE WHO HAS A
HUSBAND."

28 And you brethren, like Isaac, are children of promise. 29 But as at that time he who was born according to the flesh persecuted him *who was born* according to the Spirit, so it is now also. 30 But what does the Scripture say?

"CAST OUT THE BONDWOMAN AND
HER SON,
FOR THE SON OF THE BONDWOMAN
SHALL NOT BE AN HEIR
WITH THE SON OF THE FREE
WOMAN."

31 So then, brethren, we are not children of a bondwoman, ᵃbut of the free woman.

4:23 ᵃLit *has been born*   4:24 ᵃLit *Which* ᵇLit *into slavery* ᶜLit *which*   4:26 ᵃLit *which*   4:31 ᵃV 5:1, note 1

Break into a joyful shout,
you who have never been in labor!
For the desolate woman now has more children
than the woman who lives with her husband!"*

28 And you, dear brothers and sisters, are children of the promise, just like Isaac. 29 But you are now being persecuted by those who want you to keep the law, just as Ishmael, the child born by human effort, persecuted Isaac, the child born by the power of the Spirit.

30 But what do the Scriptures say about that? "Get rid of the slave and her son, for the son of the slave woman will not share the inheritance with the free woman's son."* 31 So, dear brothers and sisters, we are not children of the slave woman; we are children of the free woman.

4:22 See Gen 16:15; 21:2-3.   4:25 Greek *And Hagar, which is Mount Sinai in Arabia, is now like Jerusalem;* other manuscripts read *And Mount Sinai in Arabia is now like Jerusalem.* 4:27 Isa 54:1.   4:30 Gen 21:10.

Though we often speak of the "major world religions" as Christianity, Islam, Hinduism, and Buddhism, the truth is that there are literally thousands of religions of various sizes. If you were to take a course on world religions, I can't guarantee that you would walk away much wiser, but I can promise that you would walk away reeling at the enormity and complexity of the subject. Among "scientific" or "sociological" approaches to the study of human religion, two tendencies prevail: (1) to emphasize the things that all religions have in common, seeking the "religious impulse" shared by all humans everywhere; or (2) to emphasize the great diversity of religious traditions throughout the world, differing because of language, culture, and experience.

If you will allow me to cut through the garbled details, however, I would suggest that from one perspective there are really only two religions in the world. The first religion, which comes in countless shapes and sizes, is the religion of human effort and merit. Those who adhere to one of the forms of this religious system believe they gain salvation or blessings through some set of requirements—something they do, fulfill, accomplish, or earn. The second religion is the religion of divine grace and mercy. Adherents of this religion forsake their own merit and rely exclusively on the gracious provision of God, which is not based on what we have done, but on what God has done for us. In this religion, all we can do is believe, accept, trust, and acknowledge.

You might think that the religion of grace and mercy would be swelling with converts. Perhaps you would guess that the religion in which God does it all would be far more popular than religions that say we must do our part. But, ironically, there are many more people who are eager to work for their salvation than there are people who trust God for it. The age-old belief that "there ain't no free lunch" dominates our thinking. We distrust giveaways, turn down gifts, and pay back favors. Our "get what you deserve" culture flies in the face of Christianity's "receive what you don't deserve" theology.

As a pastor, what I find so disturbing about Paul's letter to the Galatians is not that its readers were stuck in a works mentality—most people in the world fit that description—but that although the Galatians had once embraced the message of grace, they decided to shift back to the message of works! In fact, Paul ended the last section with an exasperated exclamation: "I am perplexed about you" (4:20).

In Galatians 4:21-31, Paul presents his closing arguments against the legalistic Judaizers. Like a masterful attorney, he uses the Judaizers' own methods of argument and biblical interpretation to disprove their position. He opens with a question (4:21), provides some historical background from the life of Abraham (4:22-23), then sets forth an allegory in typical Jewish form (4:24-27), ultimately applying the allegory to the Galatians' situation (4:28-31). After this fitting finale against the assailants of Christian freedom, Paul rests his case.

## — 4:21 —

Paul begins with a pointed, perhaps even sarcastic, question: "Tell me, you who want to be under law, do you not listen to the law?" Paul addresses any of his readers who might still be unconvinced. Many were still clutching the Law with white knuckles, unwilling to let go out of principle or pride. In essence, Paul asks, "Okay, you Judaizers and all you Galatians who are listening to them, pay attention! You think that living by the Law is the way to go? Great! Then listen to what the Law itself says!" For the sake of argument, Paul grants his opponents' premise—that we are obligated to follow everything the Law says. Then he turns this premise against them. To put it bluntly, Paul is preparing to rub their noses in it.

Paul took a similar approach in Galatians 3:6-22, building his case on grounds his opponents accepted to prove his own point. In fact, throughout his ministry, Paul presented the gospel beginning where people were. With Jews, he turned to the Old Testament—their primary source for truth (Acts 17:1-3). With pagans, he used their idols, poets, and prophets (Acts 17:22-23, 28; Titus 1:12). Paul practiced an

## ALLEGORICAL INTERPRETATION

### GALATIANS 4:21-31

Throughout history, both Judaism and Christianity have wrestled with the question, "How should we interpret the Bible?" Because the Bible itself contains no preface that sets out specific principles of interpretation, many answers to this question have been offered. Nevertheless, two tendencies of reading the Bible have prevailed throughout history— the literal and the allegorical. John Adair describes two schools of interpretation that began in the early church and have since typified the two groups that have been in tension throughout church history:

> One group, centered at Antioch in Syria, preferred to empha-size a literal approach to reading the Bible. They believed that it was important to bring out the concrete historical realities of the biblical text. And they wanted to teach the events of biblical history as events, with special attention paid to the literary and historical context. The second group tended toward an allegori-cal reading. These believers emphasized the spiritual meaning behind the historical reality, a meaning that points readers to the doctrine of the church.[17]

Allegorical interpretation has been defined as "searching for a hidden or a secret meaning underlying but remote from and unrelated in reality to the more obvious meaning of a text."[18] It became popular among Jewish interpreters who wanted to make the Old Testament relevant for contemporary life or to explain embarrassing stories or even books. So, for example, though the Song of Solomon appears to refer to a romantic relationship between a lover and his beloved, the allegorists reinterpreted it spiritually to refer to God's loving relation-ship with Israel.

When we compare Paul's brief allegory in Galatians 4 with the ex-cessive and even bizarre allegorical interpretations we encounter in some Jewish and Christian writings, Paul's approach seems rather tame. In any case, in the context of his argument, Paul used allegory to catch the attention of his readers and turn the Judaizers' methods of interpretation against them.[19]

evangelistic strategy many Christians today reject—seeking common ground upon which we can construct an uncommon message.

In today's context, this might involve listening to people we utterly disagree with, reading books they've written or read, and taking the time to understand their perspective, as twisted and perplexing as it may be. The late Joe Aldrich's thoughts on this issue are worth pondering:

> Frequently the unsaved are viewed as enemies rather than victims of the Enemy. Spirituality is viewed as separation from the unsaved. The new Christian is told he has nothing in common with his unsaved associates. Frankly, I have a lot in common with them: a mortgage, car payments, kids who misbehave, a lawn to mow, a car to wash, a less-than-perfect marriage, a few too many pounds around my waist, and an interest in sports, hobbies, and other activities they enjoy. It is well to remember that Jesus was called a "friend of sinners."[20]

Paul never compromised his convictions, but he never hesitated to forsake his comfort, to think outside the box, or to reach down (or up!) to the level where people were. So, here in Galatians 4:21-31, Paul engages in a method of argument rarely seen in the New Testament, but which would have been quite familiar to his audience: allegorical interpretation of Scripture.

## — 4:22-27 —

The Jews arrogantly boasted that they were the descendants of Abraham, citing their genealogical pedigree as proof of their high spiritual standing before God. Even the Jews in Jesus' day made this appeal to Jesus: "We are Abraham's descendants and have never yet been enslaved to anyone; how is it that You say, 'You will become free'?" (John 8:33). Like Jesus, Paul argues that true freedom comes not from physical ancestry but by receiving the truth from Jesus Himself (John 8:31-47).

Most Jews in Paul's day believed that their physical relationship with Abraham put them in proper standing before God. Because they were physical products of Abraham's seed, they thought they were heirs to God's promises and blessings. Sadly, I see this same mentality among many Christians who were "born into" or "raised up in" the church. They ride on the coattails of their parents, laud the laurels of their grandparents, or point to a family legacy of faith that has stood strong for generations. They act as though the faith of their ancestors automatically transfers to them. But nothing could be further from the truth. People aren't born Christians—they become Christians.

Paul deals a death blow to the belief in salvation by inheritance by retelling the story of Abraham and the sons he had through Hagar and Sarah (Gal. 4:22-23). One son, Ishmael, was "born according to the flesh," that is, "in the course of nature and requiring no miracle and no promise of God."[21] We see this account in Genesis 16:1-16. Abraham attempted to lend God a helping hand by siring an heir through his servant girl, Hagar. You see, God's simple, straightforward promise that Abraham would have a child through the aged and barren Sarah seemed too steep a mountain to climb. So, reinterpreting the promise as a challenge, Abraham took matters into his own hands and produced Ishmael through natural, or "fleshly," means.

Isaac, on the other hand, was born to the "free woman," Abraham's wife Sarah, "through the promise" (Gal. 4:23). In other words, Isaac was a miracle child, born when Abraham was one hundred years old and Sarah was ninety. God opened Sarah's womb and brought Isaac into the world against all odds—against nature itself! Yet the miraculous birth of Isaac came about just as God had promised (Gen. 15:4; 17:15-16; 18:10; 21:1-3).

Paul plumbs the depths of these historical facts and points out a spiritual analogy that exposes the inherent weakness of the Judaizers' legalistic approach to inheriting the promises of God. The chart below brings out the many contrasts Paul makes between law and grace.

| LAW | GRACE |
| --- | --- |
| Hagar, the bondwoman | Sarah, the free woman |
| Ishmael born "according to the flesh" | Isaac born "according to the Spirit" |
| Old covenant of law given at Mount Sinai | New covenant of grace given by Christ |
| Earthly Jerusalem | Heavenly Jerusalem |
| Slavery to the Law | Freedom in Christ |
| Judaism | Christianity |

In Paul's illustration, Hagar and Sarah represent the two covenants. Hagar represents the old covenant delivered to Moses on Mount Sinai. This agreement bound the nation of Israel—citizens of the earthly Jerusalem—to the Law's statutes and sacrifices, promising that obedience would result in earthly blessings in the Promised Land (Deut. 28:1-14), while disobedience would lead to punishment (Deut. 28:15-68). Life under the old covenant was exacting, precarious, and ultimately disastrous—the people of Israel were eventually exiled as a result of their unfaithfulness to the covenant. Thus Paul likens Hagar and the covenant of the Law with Jerusalem in his day: politically enslaved to Rome and religiously enslaved to a strict pursuit of legalism.

In contrast, the new covenant, symbolized by Sarah, is based on God's promises, not His Law. Christ ratified this agreement on Calvary. He sealed it with His own blood (Heb. 9:11-28). All who enter into the promises of this covenant by faith alone in Christ alone become spiritual children of Abraham and heirs of the heavenly Jerusalem (Gal. 4:26-27). This "Jerusalem above," represented by Sarah, may refer to the heavenly Jerusalem in which the redeemed will one day dwell (Rev. 3:12; 21:2). Or it may refer metaphorically to the universal church—all those truly redeemed in Christ—whose citizenship is in heaven (Phil. 3:20). In either case, this "Jerusalem" represents those saved through faith in Christ, who have been freed from the oppression and curse of the Law.

Paul shores up his argument for the superiority of grace over law by quoting Isaiah 54:1, a joyous hymn declaring the abundant fruitfulness of the woman who was once barren (Gal. 4:27). Isaiah's original words were prophetically directed to the Jewish exiles living in Babylon. With those words Isaiah had assured them that their bondage would not last forever, that they would one day return to their homeland and become more numerous than before. Paul likely quotes this passage to point out that God has always been the champion of the underprivileged, the forsaken, the "barren"—those who appeared to be outside of God's circle of blessing. In the case of the Galatians, this theology directly challenged the Judaizers' claim that only participants in the old covenant of the Law could be blessed by God.

## — 4:28-31 —

If, like the Galatians, you have put your faith in Jesus Christ, you are a child of the free woman, Sarah—a child of promise (4:28). Just as Isaac was supernaturally born as a result of God's promise, so all Christians are "born again" as a result of God's promise that all nations would be blessed through Abraham (Gen. 22:18).

Yet Paul draws a final essential parallel between Isaac and Ishmael that related directly to the Galatian situation—and to our own battle with legalism. Until Christ returns, the children of freedom should expect to be persecuted by their legalistic half brothers. Just as Ishmael ridiculed and scorned Isaac (Gen. 21:8-9), so legalists will persecute believers (Gal. 4:29).

Paul's closing argument climaxes with a coup de grâce (4:30). Quoting Genesis 21:10, 12, Paul notes that Abraham ultimately exiled Hagar and her child Ishmael because of the irreconcilable differences between Ishmael and Isaac. His point is clear: Christians must reject legalism and refute those who teach it. Though Jews would have interpreted this passage as a mandate to reject Gentiles, Paul turns the tables, connecting the Judaizers with the slave woman and all Christians—Jews and Gentiles—with the free woman (4:31). All who have trusted Christ by faith are free!

# APPLICATION: GALATIANS 4:21-31

## Ishmael or Isaac—the Choice Is Yours

To the believers in Galatia, Paul said, "You brethren, like Isaac, are children of promise" (4:28). When we place our trust in Christ alone, we, too, become related to Abraham and Sarah in the only way that makes any spiritual difference. We may not be physically born as Jews in the line of Abraham, Isaac, and Jacob . . . but we are spiritually born again into God's family and made everlasting heirs of heaven's eternal riches. But until we finish our lifelong journey as sojourners and strangers, we need to remember a couple of important principles along the way.

First, *as true members of God's family, we should expect to be persecuted by our half brothers*—religious people who claim to be part of God's family but are not. Just as Ishmael ridiculed his half-brother Isaac (Gen. 21:8-9), legalists will persecute believers (Gal. 4:29). It has been this way throughout history, beginning with Jesus Himself. The religious leaders of His day opposed, mocked, condemned, and executed the true Seed of Abraham. The Judaizers made life and ministry difficult for Paul and all those who, like him, took a stand for the freedom that comes through grace. During the Reformation, popes and kings brutalized Protestants who took a stand on the doctrine of salvation by grace through faith. In our own day, legalistic Christians who have never experienced the sweet liberation of grace can make the Christian life a miserable experience for true believers, overwhelming them with an endless, uncompromising list of dos and don'ts.

This is why when it comes to law and grace, we have to get off the fence. We can't fluctuate between rules and faith, mixing them in our approach to God. He won't allow that. Either we come to Him His way or we don't come at all. C. S. Lewis once wrote, "There are only two kinds of people in the end: those who say to God, 'Thy will be done,' and those to whom God says, in the end, '*Thy* will be done.'"[22] The former are the family of faith and citizens of heaven; the latter are the family of works and slaves of hell. Until we trust in Christ alone, we all belong to the second family. After we're born again, we're members of the first.

Second, *we must recognize the absolute incompatibility of man-made religion and God's gracious provision.* Hagar and Ishmael symbolize human attempts to achieve what only God can do. This humanistic approach to the Lord can't coexist with the way of faith; therefore, just as Hagar and Ishmael were cast out of Abraham's household (Gen. 21:10, 12), so must works-oriented religions and beliefs be removed from God's family (Gal. 4:30).

Once we stop fence straddling, we'll realize how incompatible law and grace really are. The free life can't survive the structured demands of rule-centered living. Conversely, law keeping can't maintain a grip on a truly liberated life. As Christians, we are called to a life of freedom. Let's start living it—today.

# LIVING THE FREEDOM OF THE GOSPEL (GALATIANS 5:1-6:18)

South Africa, January 17, 1934.

An impoverished diamond prospector named Jacobus Jonker, discouraged by his string of bad luck, decides to stay home on this particularly cold and windy day. The night before, torrents of heavy rain washed away loads of silt from his fruitless claim of land, and this morning he's in no mood to sort through the flotsam and jetsam left behind. Instead, he sends his son Gert and some hired hands to work the land.

Later that day, Jacobus hears a ruckus on the road and sees Gert speeding home like a madman, abruptly parking his vehicle and leaping from its seat. Something bad must have happened. Had somebody been hurt? Killed? But rather than a look of panic, Gert wears a smile from ear to ear. As Jacobus opens his mouth to scold his son for his reckless driving, Gert places an egg-sized stone in his hand.

Despite its rough state, the 726-carat diamond glistens in the daylight. Suddenly, Jacobus's legs give out. With tear-filled eyes he falls to his knees, thanking God for the miraculous find that would make him and his seven children wealthy beyond imagination. The diamond would yield well over five million dollars.[1] They were set for life. Or were they?

The true story of the famous Jonker Diamond, however, doesn't end in perpetual fame and fortune. Instead, within a few years Jacobus Jonker again found himself penniless. Having mismanaged his funds, Jonker found himself once again combing the earth, hoping to find another treasure that would restore his fortune.[2]

A fortune lost . . . a treasure squandered . . . a priceless gem wasted. Our world is full of fascinating stories of men and women who suddenly strike it rich, only to lose friends, family, fame, and fortune within months or years. Most people simply can't handle the prosperity or the responsibility that comes with owning a priceless possession.

The Christians in Galatia were no different. When Paul and Barnabas preached the gospel of Jesus Christ to them, they received that price-less gift of salvation by grace through faith with no strings attached. Within weeks, however, they had allowed ruthless bandits and unsavory swindlers to plunder their faith. The legalistic Judaizers sought to rob the Galatians' glorious riches of grace by replacing them with a pitiful religion of works.

In the midst of the Judaizers' pillaging, Paul's letter to the Galatians breaks in with a strong defense. Having taken a stand for both his apostolic authority and the doctrine of justification by faith in the first four chapters of Galatians, Paul has managed to refute the madness of the plundering Judaizers and restore the Galatians' doctrinal diamond to its proper place. Then, like a financial advisor teaching a rich man how to manage his wealth, Paul begins to instruct the Galatians about practical ways to responsibly spend their spiritual prosperity.

One of Paul's goals in the final section of his letter was to respond to the Judaizers' unwarranted claim that living by grace would promote a morally loose lifestyle. Paul clearly teaches that, having been set free by Christ, the Galatians were now expected to "keep standing firm and . . . not be subject again to a yoke of slavery" (5:1). No, if the Galatians either fell back under the Law or turned to lives of sin, they would squander the spiritual wealth provided by the death and resurrection of Christ. Instead, the Galatian believers, like all believers today, had been set free to love and serve one another (5:13-14) and to display true Christlike character (5:22-23). In this way believers truly fulfill the deeper intention behind the written laws. Unlike false teachers who wanted to boast in circumcision instead of the cross (6:12-13), Paul desired to boast only in the "cross of our Lord Jesus Christ" (6:14).

By teaching his readers that the gospel of grace through faith alone provides freedom to live a righteous life, Paul reaffirmed the truth that grace is the way to life and the way of life.

## KEY TERMS IN GALATIANS 5:1–6:18

*eleutheria* (ἐλευθερία) [1657] "freedom," "liberty"
Second Corinthians 3:17 says, "Where the Spirit of the Lord is, there is liberty." This is similar to how Paul explains the concept of freedom in Galatians: Through the Spirit, Christ has freed us from the curse of the Law and our obligation to keep it as part of our covenant with Him. The

freedom to which Paul refers is freedom from slavery to the Law and its stifling prescriptions. This freedom, however, is not to be used as a license for sinful self-indulgence (Gal. 5:13) but employed in the joyous service of the Savior. In Christ believers have freedom from the guilt, shame, and obligation associated with the Mosaic Law—not freedom from living up to the law of love by the power of the Spirit.

### *epithymia sarkos* (ἐπιθυμία σαρκός) [1939, 4561] "desire of the flesh," "lust of the flesh"

"Desire of the flesh" refers to sinful urges for physical pleasures due to one's fallen human nature. The word meaning "flesh" (*sarx*) in this negative context does not mean our material substance, but our sinful tendencies and fallen nature. Though Christ has done away with the consequences of our sin, the effects and temptations remain. Both in Galatians and elsewhere (Rom. 6:1-14), Paul exhorts his readers to put to death the works of the flesh, implying an active process of turning from sin by the Spirit's enablement (see Gal. 5:16-24).

### *peritomē* (περιτομή) [4061] "circumcision," "a circumcised one," "one among the circumcised"

This Greek noun derives from the verb meaning "to cut around" and describes the Hebrew rite in which a male's foreskin is cut away. As instituted by God, the ritual identifies the male as a participant in God's covenant with Abraham. In time, this distinguishing feature became symbolic of the people, the covenant, and the culture. Many Jews thought that the covenant sign of circumcision entitled them to blessings from God and exemption from divine judgment. However, Paul taught that in Christ neither circumcision nor uncircumcision had any significance—only salvation by grace through faith in Christ (6:15). Therefore, in Galatians Paul insisted that the Judaizers who were teaching that Gentiles needed to be circumcised in order to be saved were guilty of preaching a false gospel.

### *stauroō* (σταυρόω) [4717] "to crucify"

As a cruel means of Roman execution, death on a cross was meant to extinguish life in an excruciating, humiliating, and appalling way. In Paul's thinking, "to crucify" can have both this literal meaning as well as a figurative sense. In Galatians, Paul speaks of crucifixion metaphorically to invoke a dramatic image of the change which has occurred in the life of a believer. Early in Galatians Paul mentioned that he had "been crucified with Christ"—he was dead to self, but alive again through Christ living in him (Gal. 2:20). This is true for all believers who have been reborn in Christ: Their old selves have been "crucified," and they now have a new desire—to live for Christ (see 5:24).

# Freedom, Faith, Love, and Truth

## GALATIANS 5:1-12

**NASB**

1a It was for freedom that Christ set us free; therefore keep standing firm and do not be subject again to a yoke of slavery.

2 Behold I, Paul, say to you that if you receive circumcision, Christ will be of no benefit to you. 3 And I testify again to every man who receives circumcision, that he is under obligation to keep the whole Law. 4 You have been severed from Christ, you who a are seeking to be justified by law; you have fallen from grace. 5 For we a through the Spirit, b by faith, are waiting for the hope of righteousness. 6 For in Christ Jesus neither circumcision nor uncircumcision means anything, but faith working through love.

7 You were running well; who hindered you from obeying the truth? 8 This persuasion *did* not *come* from Him who calls you. 9 A little leaven leavens the whole lump *of dough*. 10 I have confidence a in you in the Lord that you will adopt no other view; but the one who is disturbing you will bear his judgment, whoever he is. 11 But I, brethren, if I still preach circumcision, why am I still persecuted? Then the stumbling block of the cross has been abolished. 12 I wish that those who are

**NLT**

1 So Christ has truly set us free. Now make sure that you stay free, and don't get tied up again in slavery to the law.

2 Listen! I, Paul, tell you this: If you are counting on circumcision to make you right with God, then Christ will be of no benefit to you. 3 I'll say it again. If you are trying to find favor with God by being circumcised, you must obey every regulation in the whole law of Moses. 4 For if you are trying to make yourselves right with God by keeping the law, you have been cut off from Christ! You have fallen away from God's grace.

5 But we who live by the Spirit eagerly wait to receive by faith the righteousness God has promised to us. 6 For when we place our faith in Christ Jesus, there is no benefit in being circumcised or being uncircumcised. What is important is faith expressing itself in love.

7 You were running the race so well. Who has held you back from following the truth? 8 It certainly isn't God, for he is the one who called you to freedom. 9 This false teaching is like a little yeast that spreads through the whole batch of dough! 10 I am trusting the Lord to keep you from believing false teachings. God will judge that person, whoever he is, who has been confusing you.

11 Dear brothers and sisters,* if I were still preaching that you must be circumcised—as some say I do— why am I still being persecuted? If I were no longer preaching salvation through the cross of Christ, no one would be offended. 12 I just wish that those troublemakers who want to

troubling you would even ᵃmutilate themselves.

**5:1** ᵃSome authorities prefer to join with 4:31 and render *but with the freedom of the free woman Christ set us free*   **5:4** ᵃOr *would be*   **5:5** ᵃLit *by*   ᵇLit *out of*   **5:10** ᵃLit *toward*   **5:12** ᵃOr *cut themselves off*

mutilate you by circumcision would mutilate themselves.*

**5:11** Greek *Brothers;* similarly in 5:13.   **5:12** Or *castrate themselves,* or *cut themselves off from you;* Greek reads *cut themselves off.*

Scholars call the Galatian letter a "polemic." The term comes from a Greek word that means "warlike" or "hostile." It connotes an aggressive attack in which one whips out all the rhetorical weapons and carries out a no-holds-barred assault on an opposing party. That certainly describes Galatians!

In this letter Paul openly exposes and boldly assails the false teaching of legalism. In the first twelve verses of chapter 5, we find an opening command (5:1) that introduces a contrast developed through 5:12: religion based on the act of circumcision (law) versus new life found in Jesus Christ alone (grace). Because these two ways of life—law and grace—are mutually exclusive, Paul writes with great passion to the Galatians, "Get off the fence!"

## — 5:1 —

Paul begins with an assertion: "It was for freedom that Christ set us free." It sounds redundant, doesn't it? He uses simple, straightforward language to keep his main point clear. In the Greek text, Paul arranges the order of the words to place emphasis on the *object*. We might translate this opening phrase this way: "*To liberty* Christ has liberated us." You see, Christ didn't set us free without purpose or to no end. Nor did He set us free so we could enslave ourselves to the nearest legalist or embark on a wild frenzy of immorality. Christ set us free so we could bask in the benefits of His salvation, living out our freedom in Christ without guilt or condemnation.

This freedom offers us a new lifestyle. Now we have the ability to live by the Spirit's power. We're free to obey God and do His will joyfully. We can love and serve others. We're able to enter into the Lord's presence through prayer, experiencing a close, personal relationship with Him. Before salvation, we couldn't take advantage of any of these benefits. We were penniless, pathetic slaves to sin. But now, as wealthy freedmen and women, we can enjoy them to the fullest. Christ has set us free so that we may enjoy our freedom.

Paul punctuates this declaration of liberty with a command:

"Therefore keep standing firm and do not be subject again to a yoke of slavery." Similar to the yoke used to tie animals to farm equipment or wagons, a "yoke of slavery" was any device used to tie slaves to each other or to limit their movements in some way. The yoke could be made of wood or metal, but either way its function was the same—to force a slave to submit, to remain in prescribed bounds, and to carry out the work assigned to him or her.

The yoke of legalism restricts us by convincing us that an inflexible list of "thou shalts" and "thou shalt nots" is the safest way to remain pure and acceptable to God. Believers caught in the yoke of legalism always search for partners to share the burden with them, recruiting more converts to the cause of slavery. The more legalists attached to the chain gang, the better—that's their mentality. Yet Paul's exhortation breaks the yoke before it catches us by the neck: Don't surrender your freedom; defend it with your life.

## — 5:2-6 —

Paul now turns his attention to those who have begun to embrace legalism. Having been duped by the deceivers, many have let that cruel yoke of slavery slip gently around their necks. Paul exhorts the Galatians to reject its flawed legalism and return to a life of grace before the Judaizers screw the bolts tight and bind them in permanent chains.

Those Galatians who had received circumcision as a sign of their covenant commitment to keep the Law were snubbing the very One who had freed them from the Law: Jesus Christ (5:2). When Paul speaks of circumcision, we need to understand that he's using this Jewish rite to point to the whole of the Judaizers' lifestyle. Just as baptism was the sign of dying to the Law and being raised to a new life of freedom, circumcision was the sign of submission to the Law, essentially reversing and undoing the sign of baptism!

Paul delineates three consequences of entering into the lifestyle of legalism through the sign of circumcision:

- "Christ will be of no benefit to you" (5:2).
- You will be obligated "to keep the whole Law" (5:3).
- You will be alienated from Christ's grace (5:4).

First, by receiving circumcision, the Galatians would have been saying that Jesus' sacrifice on the cross was insufficient either to save them or to sanctify them (5:2). They would have been trying to add to His payment for sin. By accepting the idea of righteousness by their own works, they were rejecting the work of Christ that provides righteousness by faith. From a legalistic point of view, Christ might as well not have come at all. By turning to the Law, they were turning from Christ.

Second, by receiving circumcision, the Galatians placed themselves under a covenant commitment to keep the whole Law (5:3). Just as wedding vows place a person into a covenant relationship as a husband or wife, circumcision obligates people to follow the lifestyle it initiates. The Galatians couldn't choose just one small part of the Law. Once they chose any of it, they had really chosen all of it.

Third, by receiving circumcision, the Galatians severed themselves from the grace of Christ (5:4). Once the Galatians chose the Law as their savior and lord, they cut their ties to Christ as Savior and Lord. Does this mean that the Galatians actually lost the eternal life they had received when they believed? Not at all! Paul is now discussing law and grace as two diametrically opposed rules of life. Notice that Paul doesn't say they had fallen from salvation. When somebody chooses the legalistic lifestyle, they've fallen from the lifestyle of grace and all of its benefits. They are seeking to be justified before God and men by their works done in the power of the flesh—their own abilities, unaided by grace—rather than by grace through faith by the power of the Holy Spirit. In short, when we take up the torch of the flesh, we scorch the work of the Spirit!

What are some differences between living in the flesh and living by faith? First, our approach to personal righteousness is different. When we live according to our own merit, we believe that the burden for holiness rests solely upon our shoulders. As a result, we feel compelled to work by the sweat of our brow to achieve that righteousness. But when we live by faith, we trust that our righteousness is secure in Christ, that the Spirit is working daily to conform us to His image, and that perfect holiness will come only when Christ glorifies us (5:5).

A second major difference between living in the flesh and living by faith is that our lives become characterized not by laws, but by love. The essential fuel for a flesh-oriented life is works; for a Christ-centered life, it's faith expressing itself in love (5:6). James similarly emphasizes that true faith manifests itself through good deeds done out of genuine concern for others (Jas. 1:27; 2:14-17). Though faith and law are mutually exclusive, faith and love are inseparable essentials in a truly grace-based, Spirit-empowered life.

— 5:7-12 —

Paul's intense love and sincere concern for the tripped-up Galatian believers shines in 5:7-12. Here he expresses his optimistic hopes for his hearers while coming down hard on those who have led them astray.

He begins with a word picture taken from the world of athletics. At the start of the marathon of the Christian life, they "were running well" (5:7). But along the way they had been hindered from fully "obeying the truth," that is, living in conformity with the truth of the gospel of grace through faith. Along the path, somebody had interrupted their stride, causing them to stumble. The Judaizers had placed an obstacle in their path, tripped them up, and waylaid their progress.[3] Bruised and battered, they were leaving the track and strapping heavy weights of the Law around their ankles and chests. Paul wanted them to realize the egregious error they were making. Instead of running free toward the crown of life, they were panting laboriously on the treadmill of fruitless endeavor.

God had originally called the Galatians by grace (1:6). So, logically, this new change in direction was not from Him (5:8). Those who had added this alien teaching of legalism to the original pure gospel of grace were in the process of destroying the entire message delivered by Christ's apostles. Paul likens this infection of law to the effects of leaven on a lump of dough (5:9). Just as a speck of leaven will eventually multiply and spread throughout the whole lump, the false teaching threatened to completely undo the faith the Galatians had once received.

But all hope was not lost! Paul expressed his confidence that the Galatians would remove the encumbrances from their path and extract the leaven from their dough, returning to a lifestyle characterized by the priceless grace of God (5:10). He believed that most would shun the legalists after taking his concerns to heart. For those believers who were still unconvinced, Paul's next words about the destiny of the bothersome legalists might finally sway them: The Judaizers would be judged (5:10). Those who live by the Law will be condemned by the Law (Rom. 3:20). Legalism leads to judgment.

We don't know if this is the kind of judgment one experiences in this life or judgment before the throne of Christ. It could be both. If some of the legalists happened to be true believers who had gone astray, they would at least suffer loss of reward at the judgment seat of Christ (1 Cor. 3:15). Why? Because though they presumed to be teachers of the Law, they did not understand what they were teaching (1 Tim. 1:7). James pronounces a sobering warning that should cause any self-proclaimed teacher to pause: "Let not many of you become teachers, my brethren, knowing that as such we will incur a stricter judgment" (Jas. 3:1). In any case, no matter who these false teachers were or what their spiritual state was, God would bring His discipline in His own time and in His own manner.

Finally, Paul answers the hypothetical question, *What if I were to preach circumcision? Me—the apostle who preached grace? Is there any way I could fit that into my gospel of salvation by grace through faith?* We do know that on special occasions Paul allowed for the circumcision of Christians for cultural reasons, as he would grant for Timothy "because of the Jews" (Acts 16:1-3). This fits in with Paul's ministry strategy of becoming "as a Jew" for the Jews, in order to "win Jews" (1 Cor. 9:20). Paul wasn't preaching circumcision but removing a cultural obstacle in order to make way for the preaching of grace. However, it may be that his critics pointed to this as a contradiction between Paul's preaching and practice—or as evidence that Paul did in fact support their position on circumcision.

But Paul makes it clear that even these allowances of circumcision for cultural reasons did not mean that he was "preach[ing] circumcision" (see Gal. 5:11). If this were the case, then why all the controversy? The gospel of grace offends human nature because we stoke our pride by believing we can work for anything we want. Anyone who douses that pride with a message of dependence on Christ will catch a white-hot blast of arrogant rage. The fact that Paul was suffering at the hands of the Judaizers proved that he was not on their side. It proved that his message was indeed a gospel of liberty.

Paul's intense love for the Galatians and zeal for the truth is demonstrated most vividly in 5:12. With an outburst that could offend the squeamish, he announces, "I wish that those who are troubling you would even mutilate themselves." What a statement! Paul says he's so fed up with the legalists' destructive requirement of circumcision that he wishes they would go all the way and emasculate themselves, putting an end to their madness.

This may sound like an extreme—even mean-spirited—reaction to the Judaizers. But if we were as concerned about defending the gospel of grace as Paul was, we too would be guarding it with every rhetorical device we could think of. We would lock our freedom in the deepest bunker of our hearts, vigorously defending it against the attacks of false teachers.

# APPLICATION: GALATIANS 5:1-12

## Checking the Pulse of Our Passion for Freedom

Paul uses some strong, blunt, and even *painful* language in chapter 5. Why? Because he rightly sees that our freedom in Christ is worth fighting for. We dare not let it slip away or allow anybody to snatch it from us. Eugene Peterson aptly writes, "Each day we must take up the stance of freedom again. If we fail to stand deliberately and consciously, the freedom will be lost."[4] In the pursuit of Paul's passion, let's ask ourselves some probing, practical questions that will help us evaluate our own zeal for freedom.

*How highly do I value my freedom in Christ?* Does it mean more to me than money, home, family, friends, job, or reputation? Do I compromise on Christian freedom in order to fit in at church, among my Christian friends, or at my job? Do I succumb to the slavery of legalism, submitting to human rules and regulations?

*How strongly do I resist having my freedom stolen?* Do I submit to rules that strap me down spiritually, stopping or even reversing my Christian growth? Do I actually check the bases for the accepted Christian norms fed to me at church, at home, or from other sources? When was the last time I took a firm stand against legalism?

*How tolerant am I of other Christians and their exercise of freedom?* Do I insist that fellow believers adopt my personal preferences on nonessential matters? Or do I flaunt my freedom in front of those with weaker consciences?

Once we've thoroughly examined our zeal for freedom, we need to exercise it! Every day is a new opportunity to live and breathe the liberty Christ has provided. Don't lose your freedom. Don't give it away like the Galatians did. Don't fall under the influence of legalism. Let grace be your way of life.

# Learning to Walk in Freedom
## GALATIANS 5:13-25

**NASB**

¹³For you were called to freedom, brethren; only *do* not *turn* your freedom into an opportunity for the flesh, but through love serve one another. ¹⁴For the whole Law is fulfilled in one word, in the *statement,* "YOU SHALL LOVE YOUR NEIGHBOR AS YOURSELF." ¹⁵But if you bite and devour one another, take care that you are not consumed by one another.

¹⁶But I say, walk by the Spirit, and you will not carry out the desire of the flesh. ¹⁷For the flesh ᵃsets its desire against the Spirit, and the Spirit against the flesh; for these are in opposition to one another, so that you may not do the things that you ᵇplease. ¹⁸But if you are led by the Spirit, you are not under the Law. ¹⁹Now the deeds of the flesh are evident, which are: ᵃimmorality, impurity, sensuality, ²⁰idolatry, sorcery, enmities, strife, jealousy, outbursts of anger, disputes, dissensions, ᵃfactions, ²¹envying, drunkenness, carousing, and things like these, of which I forewarn you, just as I have forewarned you, that those who practice such things will not inherit the kingdom of God. ²²But the fruit of the Spirit is love, joy, peace, patience, kindness, goodness, faithfulness, ²³gentleness, self-control; against such things there is no law. ²⁴Now those who ᵃbelong to Christ Jesus have crucified the flesh with its passions and desires.

**NLT**

¹³For you have been called to live in freedom, my brothers and sisters. But don't use your freedom to satisfy your sinful nature. Instead, use your freedom to serve one another in love. ¹⁴For the whole law can be summed up in this one command: "Love your neighbor as yourself."* ¹⁵But if you are always biting and devouring one another, watch out! Beware of destroying one another.

¹⁶So I say, let the Holy Spirit guide your lives. Then you won't be doing what your sinful nature craves. ¹⁷The sinful nature wants to do evil, which is just the opposite of what the Spirit wants. And the Spirit gives us desires that are the opposite of what the sinful nature desires. These two forces are constantly fighting each other, so you are not free to carry out your good intentions. ¹⁸But when you are directed by the Spirit, you are not under obligation to the law of Moses.

¹⁹When you follow the desires of your sinful nature, the results are very clear: sexual immorality, impurity, lustful pleasures, ²⁰idolatry, sorcery, hostility, quarreling, jealousy, outbursts of anger, selfish ambition, dissension, division, ²¹envy, drunkenness, wild parties, and other sins like these. Let me tell you again, as I have before, that anyone living that sort of life will not inherit the Kingdom of God.

²²But the Holy Spirit produces this kind of fruit in our lives: love, joy, peace, patience, kindness, goodness, faithfulness, ²³gentleness, and self-control. There is no law against these things!

²⁴Those who belong to Christ Jesus have nailed the passions and desires of their sinful nature to his cross and

NASB

²⁵If we live by the Spirit, let us also ᵃwalk by the Spirit.

5:17 ᵃLit *lusts against* ᵇLit *wish*   5:19 ᵃI.e. sexual immorality   5:20 ᵃOr *heresies*   5:24 ᵃLit *are of Christ Jesus*   5:25 ᵃOr *follow the Spirit*

crucified them there. ²⁵Since we are living by the Spirit, let us follow the Spirit's leading in every part of our lives.

5:14 Lev 19:18.

NLT

The first yellow rays of dawn fan out across the dusky-blue Jerusalem sky. Jesus is already at the temple teaching an eager group of early risers. The daylong cacophony of haggling merchants and buyers has not yet dispelled the cool stillness of the morning. Only the warm, resonant sureness of Jesus' voice, along with the twittering of a few birds in the distance, carry on the air.

Until the scribes and Pharisees barge in.

Shattering the calm with gruff, self-righteous accusations, they manhandle a desperate woman, shoving her to Jesus' feet. Pointing down at her with large, condemning fingers, they bark a well-rehearsed question at the self-made rabbi from Nazareth: "Teacher, this woman has been caught in adultery—in the very act! In the Law, Moses ordered us to stone such a woman. So, what do you say?"

At first, Jesus says nothing. He just bends down and writes something in the dirt, perhaps continuing the lesson He had started prior to this rude intrusion. When it becomes obvious that the murmuring crowd of legal experts will not leave without Jesus' answer, He stands up and responds with penetrating wisdom: "He who is without sin among you, let him be the one to hurl the first stone."

Turning his back on them, Jesus crouches down and resumes writing in the sand.

In silence, one at a time, the whole crowd of frowning accusers slips away. Soon there are two . . . only Jesus and the disheveled woman. Standing up again, Jesus looks around and asks the woman, "Where are they? Did no one stay to condemn you?"

With overflowing tears running down her face, the woman trembles when she answers with a quivering voice: "No one, sir."

Then, very gently, Jesus grants the woman her freedom: "Then I don't condemn you either. Go now. Do whatever you please. Don't let those creepy killjoys judge your lifestyle anymore! You just follow your heart. Believe in yourself and live however you choose. You're free! As long as it doesn't hurt anybody else, do what's right for you. God wants you to be happy! As the Romans say, carpe diem—seize the day! You only have one life to live, so live it to the fullest! Let the good times roll!"

What? Wait a minute! Is that what happened? Is that how this story of Christ's mercy and grace really ended? Did Christ's forgiveness of the woman caught in adultery free her to live however she wanted? Of course not!

Let's rewind that scene and see what Jesus really said.

Then, very gently, Jesus grants the woman her freedom: "Then I don't condemn you, either. Go. From now on sin no more."

• • •

This recasting of the story in John 8:1-11 illustrates a vital point. God's idea of freedom and ours don't necessarily match. We tend to view freedom as something akin to 007's "license to kill": If anything we do is covered by the grace of God, we might as well embrace that liberty and live life to the max! We can cast off all restrictions and go hog wild. And we won't let anybody tell us what to do—ever.

If you think that philosophy of life results in freedom, you haven't spent fifty-plus years in pastoral ministry. Over and over again I've seen that kind of licentious living enslave people in the consequences of their sinful and foolish choices. Sometimes the effects are so extreme that they scar people for life. Trust me. The "just do it" approach to life isn't freedom; it's just another form of bondage.

We've seen Paul react strongly against the error of legalism. Now, in Galatians 5:13-25, he corrects the other extreme—license. As we will see, the balancing act between living under the Law and living lawlessly requires great wisdom, restraint, and, most importantly, the enabling power of the Holy Spirit.

## — 5:13-15 —

Christ's death and resurrection set us free. Most believers understand this, at least to some extent. Far too many, however, have come to terms with what they are freed *from* but not what they are freed *for*. We weren't released like birds from a cage to flutter wherever we want. Nor were we freed from a dungeon to spend the rest of our days in a different jail with a few more amenities. Our freedom in Christ is *true* freedom, but it's freedom with a purpose. Christ has unlocked the prison door, unshackled us, taken us by the hand, and led us to follow Him. He has freed us from condemnation so that we're now able to obey Him.

To help us better understand freedom, let's reflect for a moment on what we are freed from and what we are freed for. The following chart provides a summary.

| WHAT WE ARE FREED FROM | WHAT WE ARE FREED FOR |
| --- | --- |
| God's wrath and condemnation (Rom. 5:9; 8:1) | Righteousness and hope (Rom. 6:18; 15:13; 2 Cor. 5:21) |
| Mastery by temptation and sin (Rom. 6:22; 1 Cor. 10:13) | Rich generosity and concern for others (1 Cor. 12:25; 2 Cor. 9:6-11) |
| Power of Satan and demons (Col. 1:13; 1 Jn. 4:4) | Following God's will (1 Pet. 4:2; 1 Jn. 2:17) |
| Curse of the Law (Gal. 3:13) | Reconciliation with God and others (2 Cor. 5:18-20) |
| Terror and dread before God (Eph. 3:12; Heb. 4:16) | Life in authentic community (Rom. 12:4-5; Eph. 4:16) |
| Tyranny of others' legalistic demands (1 Cor. 10:29, 31) | Transformation into the image of Christ (Rom. 8:29; 12:2) |

God has grand purposes for us when He frees us from our former life of sin and releases us to a new life of righteousness. Too quickly, however, we forget what true freedom is, falling back on worldly ideas of freedom. Because of our tendency to forget what we are freed from and what we are freed for, Paul makes things perfectly clear in Galatians 5:13-15.

Though the Galatians had been "called to freedom" (5:13), it wasn't the kind of freedom of which the Judaizers accused Paul and his fellow preachers of grace. Like legalists today, the Judaizers feared that without the Law as a rule of life, people would become lawless. Paul responds by reminding the Galatians that Christian freedom is not a license to indulge the selfish and sinful desires of the flesh. Commentator John Stott defines Paul's use of "flesh" well: "'The flesh' in the language of the apostle Paul is not what clothes our bony skeleton, but our fallen human nature, . . . which is twisted with self-centeredness and therefore prone to sin."[5] Paul warns his readers against giving our flesh—our natural tendency toward sin—an "opportunity" by abusing our freedom. The Greek word translated "opportunity" is *aphormē* [874], referring to a "pretext." That is, God's grace should never be used as an excuse for sin. I'll repeat that statement so it will never be misunderstood: The grace of God should never be used as an excuse for succumbing to temptation and sin.

Because I believe in and preach grace and freedom, I've occasionally been accused of preaching lawlessness and license. Nothing could be further from the truth. Paul says (and I wholeheartedly agree) that we have been freed from the power of sin. To return to the sinful lifestyle that God has forgiven would be to return to slavery. Instead, having been freed from the dark, shameful oppression of sin, we are to embrace our true calling to serve one another through love (5:13). Liberty should result in love, not legalism or license.

## Legalism, Liberty, License

| "Subject again to a yoke of slavery" (Gal. 5:1) | "You were called to freedom" (Gal. 5:13a) | "An opportunity for the flesh" (Gal. 5:13b) |

Serving others out of love frees us from our own self-centeredness. It humbles our pride. It has the power to transform us into the image of Jesus Christ. Love brings us into the fullness of God's purpose for our lives. In fact, love itself transcends the dos and don'ts of law, rendering them irrelevant. Love also limits our natural tendencies to sin, rendering them impotent. By living a life of service through love, we avoid legalism and license.

This is why Paul can say in 5:14, "For the whole Law is fulfilled in one word, in the statement, 'You shall love your neighbor as yourself.'" So simple, so basic . . . yet so easily forgotten! The idea of loving one's neighbor self-sacrificially is so foundational that this quotation of Leviticus 19:18 shows up all over the New Testament. Jesus says that besides the commandment to love God with all our being, this is the greatest commandment (Mark 12:31). James calls it the "royal law" (Jas. 2:8). Similarly, the apostle John emphasizes the need not only to love God but to love one's brother also (1 Jn. 4:21). In his letter to the Romans, Paul says that every command of the Old Testament Law is "summed up" in this saying (Rom. 13:9). The love Paul has in mind isn't a wishy-washy kind of affection based on fleeting emotions. Nor is it the kind of love that looks for love in return. The love Paul speaks about is the love God demonstrated when He gave His Son for us (John 3:16). This *agapē* [26] love gives and keeps on giving, even when it receives nothing in return.

Finally, Paul warns against living self-indulgent, self-serving, and self-centered lives—lives characterized by the opposite of *agapē* love. If we exploit others and disregard their needs, we will reduce the entire church to clawing competition and cutting criticism (Gal. 5:15). We will consume each other until nothing remains but picked-over bones. What a horrible picture Paul paints of life lived according to the flesh!

## — 5:16-18 —

We have seen that true Christian liberty is a balancing act between legalism and license. The answer to legalism is that the death of Christ set us free from the oppressive and pervasive mandates of the Law. The answer to license is that the Holy Spirit is able to set us free from the oppressive and persuasive desires of the flesh. In Galatians 5:16-18, Paul exposes the gritty warfare that rages between our desperately wicked, sinful tendency toward unrighteousness and the Holy Spirit's work to woo us in the way of obedience and righteousness.

The person we used to be without Christ (the flesh) still tries to gain a foothold in our new life and trip us up. The old nature tempts us to indulge in the old ways or trust in the old means instead of allowing the Holy Spirit to take control. We're free in Christ, but the flesh constantly challenges that freedom. To grow in Christ, then, we must take deliberate action against the relentless demands of the flesh.

The phrase "walk by the Spirit" in 5:16 is another way of saying, "live by the Spirit" or "let your conduct be directed by the Spirit."[6] The issue is control. The solution is surrender. Our sinful desires and the desires of the Holy Spirit are forever at odds with each other. Actually, it's more like an internal war. When we live by the power of the Spirit, we will not indulge the flesh. When we indulge the flesh, we are not living under the control of the Spirit (5:16-17). The great Protestant Reformer John Calvin put this well: "The spiritual life will not be maintained without a struggle. . . . Disobedience and rebellion against the Spirit of God pervade the whole nature of man. If we would obey the Spirit, we must labour, and fight, and apply our utmost energy; and we must begin with self-denial."[7] Small wonder that Jesus, when describing how His followers are to "come after" Him, stated first that we must deny ourselves (Luke 9:23).

The all-out war between the Spirit of God and our sinful flesh is unrelenting in this life. The two are opponents, enemies, unrelenting combatants. So fierce is the battle that the flesh keeps us from doing the things that we genuinely want to do to please God (Gal. 5:17). Many Christians doubt the assurance of their salvation because of this unending struggle with sin. If that's you, stop doubting! The fact that you even care about the struggle is a sign that the Spirit is working in you "both to will and to work for His good pleasure" (Phil. 2:13). If the Spirit of God was not fighting this battle on your behalf, you wouldn't care one bit about struggling against sin.

Paul's words about the war between the Spirit and the flesh are directed against our tendency to slip off balance into license. But he also deals with the other extreme—the Law. How easy it is to respond to the flesh by retreating into legalism! How often we interpret the Spirit working in us to will and to work as our own conscience pushing us to obey external rules and regulations. Paul reminds us that being led by the Spirit means being transformed from the inside out, which results in both attitudes and actions that transcend the Law: "If you are led by the Spirit, you are not under the Law" (Gal. 5:18).

— 5:19-23 —

Paul now sets before us two sharply contrasting pictures, like two military forces on opposite sides of a battlefield. On one side are the "deeds of the flesh" (5:19-21) and on the other, the "fruit of the Spirit" (5:22-23). Let's look at these categories of wickedness and righteousness side by side.

## Deeds of the Flesh vs. Fruit of the Spirit

| DEEDS OF THE FLESH | | FRUIT OF THE SPIRIT |
|---|---|---|
| immorality | angry outbursts | love |
| impurity | disputes | joy |
| sensuality | dissensions | peace |
| idolatry | factions | patience |
| sorcery | envying | kindness |
| enmities | drunkenness | goodness |
| strife | carousing | faithfulness |
| jealousy | | gentleness |
| | | self-control |

At first glance, we notice that the list of the deeds of the flesh is longer than the list of the fruit of the Spirit. Paul gives fifteen concrete examples of the deeds of the flesh, concluding with the phrase "things like these" (5:21). He could easily have listed more. We won't take time to examine each word in the list. That wasn't Paul's intention. His purpose was to paint a dreadful overview of various lifestyles steeped in sin. Four major subjects appear in Paul's sin list:

- *Sexual sin:* This includes things like uncontrolled lust, adultery, fornication, homosexual practice, prostitution, and pornography.
- *Religious sin:* This includes such things as occult involvement, false religions, New Age spirituality, superstition, and idolatrous materialism.
- *Social sin:* This includes things that are destructive to our families, churches, and communities, such as slander, gossip, harboring bitterness, bearing grudges, taking revenge, road rage, refusing to forgive, unjust or unnecessary lawsuits, and physical or verbal abuse.
- *Personal sin:* This includes sins against one's own body, such as drug addiction, workaholism, alcoholism, barhopping, gluttony, and other forms of self-destructive behavior.

Paul says that people who "practice" these deeds of the flesh "will not inherit the kingdom of God" (5:21). Does Paul mean that true believers who get entrapped in some of these sins will lose their salvation? Certainly not! Christ died for all of our sins—past, present, and future. No Christian, not even the most mature, is sinless. Every one of us—including me—struggles on a daily basis with deeds contained in Paul's ugly sin list.

Paul means that those whose lifestyles continually demonstrate indulgence in the deeds of the flesh do not have the Spirit of God.[8] Those who don't have the Spirit of God do not have eternal life. He's not talking about the saint who has a problem with jealousy, or the father who has a temper, or the working mother who becomes hooked on prescription drugs. Paul is talking about people who abandon themselves to a lifestyle habitually dominated by these deeds. Paul didn't mean for his list of dirty deeds to become a checklist for determining whether a person is saved or not. If any of us were to be caught on a bad day, week, or month, we would all fail such a test and be judged by others as outside the kingdom of God.

Rather, Paul's point is that because these lifestyles of sin typify those who do not know Christ, we who do have a relationship with God should be eager to avoid such practices! And we are not just to avoid the bad: those who have the Spirit should display quite a different set of characteristics, the "fruit of the Spirit" (5:22-23).

# The Fruit of the Spirit Is Nuts!

## GALATIANS 5:22-23

As I write these words, I'm at 35,000 feet. It's 5:45 p.m. Saturday. It should be 4:15. The airliner was an hour and a half late. People are grumpy. Some are downright mad. Flight attendants are apologizing, promising extra booze to take off the edge. To complicate matters, a Japanese gentleman across the aisle has a rather severe nosebleed and they're trying to instruct the poor chap . . . but he doesn't speak a word of English!

So, now the meal is late. The lady on my left has a cold and makes an enormous sound when she sneezes (about every ninety seconds—I've timed her). It's something like a dying calf in a hailstorm or a bull moose with one leg in a trap. Oh, one more thing. The sports video just broke down and so did the nervous systems of half the men on board.

It's a flying zoo!

It all started with the delay. "Mechanical trouble," they said. "Inexcusable," responded a couple of passengers. Frankly, I'd rather they fix it before we leave than decide to do something about it at 35,000 feet. But we Americans don't like to wait. Delays are irritating. Aggravating. Nerve jangling. Faced with delay, we are consistently—and, I might add, obnoxiously—demanding. We want what we want when we want it. Nobody finds a delay easy to accept.

In the midst of this kind of situation, Paul's description of the "fruit of the Spirit," seems, well, a little nuts. I can imagine overflowing with those virtues when everything is running smoothly, when the world isn't handing me a raw deal. But when nothing is going right, how can I be expected to live like that? Let me apply this to my onboard chaos:

- Love . . . this lady sneezing on me?
- Joy . . . when they took away our only means of entertainment?

(continued on next page)

- Peace . . . when everybody is in a panic?
- Patience . . . when we've been irreversibly delayed?
- Kindness . . . when we're all on edge and hungry?
- Goodness . . . when all we want to do is lash out?
- Faithfulness . . . when everything in us tells us to take our cue from the majority?
- Gentleness . . . when the flight attendant scowls at me?
- Self-control . . . when I've already lost it inside?

Yes, the rubber of Christianity meets the road of proof at just such intersections in life, whether earthbound or airborne. As the expression goes, our faith gets "fleshed out" at times like these. The best test of my Christian character occurs not in the quietness of my study but in the everyday events of life. Anybody can walk in victory when surrounded by books, silence, a fresh cup of coffee, and warm waves of sunshine splashing through the window. But those late takeoffs, those grocery lines, those busy restaurants, those traffic jams! That's where the fruit of the Spirit faces the rude realities of life.

As we cultivate the fruit of the Spirit, we begin to gain the ability to accept delay or disappointment. The ability to smile back at setbacks and respond with a pleasant, understanding spirit. The ability to cool it while others around you curse it.

For a change, I refused to be hassled by today's delay. I asked God to keep me calm and cheerful, relaxed and refreshed. And you know what? He did. He really did. No pills. No booze. No hocus-pocus. Just relying on and relaxing in the power of the Spirit.

I can't promise you that others will understand. In fact, when the expected response is the "deeds of the flesh," the fruit of the Spirit looks a little weird. You see, I've got another problem now. Ever since takeoff I've been smiling at the flight attendants, hoping to encourage them. But just now I think I overheard one of them say, "Watch that guy wearing glasses. I think he's had too much to drink."

Paul doesn't call these good works the "deeds of the Spirit," but the singular "fruit" of the Spirit. James Boice points out the importance of this distinction: "The singular form stresses that these qualities are a unity, like a bunch of grapes instead of separate pieces of fruit, and also that they are all to be found in all Christians. In this they differ from the 'gifts' of the Spirit, which are given one by one to different people as the church has need."[9] These qualities of the Christian walking by the power of the Holy Spirit flow together from a heart indwelled by the Spirit of God. Life in the Spirit means life controlled by the Spirit in every area, from our innermost attitudes and emotions to our outer-most relationships and responsibilities.

Against the fruit of the Spirit, "there is no law" (5:23). In other words, the Law cannot condemn us when we live by the Spirit. Nor do we need to keep looking up the rules and regulations for every situation when we handle each moment of life with these virtues.

## — 5:24-25 —

All this talk about the fruit of the Spirit leads to a natural question: "How?" How do we walk in the Spirit? How do we keep the flesh from getting a foothold? How do we live a life that consistently reflects the goodness of God? Paul addresses these questions when he reminds us that those who belong to Christ (all believers) have put the flesh to death along with its passions and desires (5:24). This is a past reality. Our old nature was crucified with Christ, nailed to the cross with Him (Rom. 6:6). As Paul said a few chapters earlier, "I have been crucified with Christ; and it is no longer I who live, but Christ lives in me" (Gal. 2:20). That is, the moment we first believed, the Holy Spirit baptized us into the body of Christ, exchanging our sin for Christ's righteousness. The Spirit also came to dwell in us, permanently cleansing us from sin, unit-ing us with Christ, and sealing us with the promise of future redemp-tion. We have been made "alive together with Christ" (Eph. 2:5). So, because we live by the Spirit of God, we should also walk by the Spirit of God (Gal. 5:25). This means choosing to change and continuously following through on that commitment, knowing that the willingness and the ability come not from us, but from Him (Phil. 2:13). So:

- Consciously, consistently, and courageously say no to sin.
- Repeatedly remind yourself of who you are in Christ.
- Pursue His will, His desires, and His calling, no matter the cost.
- Forsake your own weaknesses and depend on His strength.

Having experienced the Savior's liberating touch, we must recall what we were freed from and embrace what we were freed for. Like the woman caught in adultery, freed from condemnation and the curse of the Law, we must heed Christ's exhortation: "Go. From now on sin no more" (John 8:11).

## APPLICATION: GALATIANS 5:13-25

### Putting Out the Trash

In recent years hoarding has come into public consciousness as a disease. Back when I was a kid, it wasn't considered a disease and it wasn't called "hoarding." We thought of hoarders as pack rats, collectors, or just plain cluttered folks who let things pile up. Now we know that some of these people are coping with real obsessive disorders, attachment anxieties, or other kinds of addictions that cause them to keep stacking useless junk upon useless junk until it consumes their lives, leaving them in desperation and despair.

How do hoarders escape from their house-sized piles of trash? *They can't.* At least not on their own. It takes somebody from the outside to enter the midst of their mess, to open the doors, to lift the blinds, and to walk them through the chaos they have built around themselves. Then, piece by piece, small decision by small decision, they begin to make progress, finally putting out the trash that has accumulated throughout the years.

The same can be true of us when it comes to finally letting go of the deeds of the flesh we've been hoarding all our lives. Perhaps we start out by gathering little, harmless complaints. These lead to gripes. Gripes grow into disputes. Disputes result in verbal conflict. Conflict ends in divorce. Or we might begin by collecting meaningless, little glances at a member of the opposite sex. These glances become stares. Stares lead to fantasies. Fantasies grow into hints and suggestions. Before we know it, we've got the A-word attached to our reputations for the rest of our lives.

All of us, without exception, need to open the doors to our lives and let the Holy Spirit blow through, pointing out the trash so we can clean it out. Paul's descriptions of the deeds of the flesh and fruit of the Spirit in Galatians 5:19-23 can serve as a helpful starting point as we let the Holy Spirit begin the process of putting out the trash that has accumulated in our lives.

This is where I'm going to get personal. Or rather, where *you're* going to get personal. You're going to do an inventory of the deeds of the flesh you've been collecting, piling up, or even hoarding over the last several days, months, or years. Then you're going to turn to the fruit of the Spirit and identify those virtues made possible by the Spirit of God that would clean out the garbage that you've allowed to collect in your life.

Carefully read Galatians 5:19-21. What deeds of the flesh seem to be giving you the most trouble? In what rooms of your life have you hoarded and locked away certain sinful patterns? Improper sexual desires and actions? Idolatry—perhaps allowing something or someone to take God's rightful place? How about a hot temper? Arguing with your wife or yelling at the kids? Overeating? Overdrinking? Just pick one and give it a name: "My struggle with _____."

Now read Galatians 5:22-23. Which aspect of the fruit of the Spirit would directly address this struggle? It could be more than one. For example, goodness, faithfulness, and self-control would all go a long way at cleaning out sexual temptation and sin. Virtually every aspect of the fruit of the Spirit would tackle your temper tantrums. Love of God and faithfulness to Him would knock out idolatry. Identify virtues of the Holy Spirit that would help clean out those nasty corners of your life that you've let linger much too long.

Now, get out of the way. Like obsessive hoarders who need to release their white-knuckled grip on their tons of trash, you need to surrender these things to God. It takes both an initial decision and an ongoing recommitment to forsake the deeds of the flesh and allow the Holy Spirit to do His miraculous cleanup work. Resolve anew each morning to walk in the Spirit, surrendering your struggle with _____ to His control. There will be moments of failure. You'll find yourself flat on your face, having wrestled control back from Him only to suffer the consequences of another fall. But keep at it. Seek counsel and help from other Spirit-filled believers. Seek out the supportive prayers of a few close friends. And then hold firmly by faith to Paul's promise in Galatians 5:16: "Walk by the Spirit, and you will not carry out the desire of the flesh."

# Living Together in the Spirit
## GALATIANS 5:26–6:10

**NASB**

26 Let us not become boastful, challenging one another, envying one another.

6:1 Brethren, even if ªanyone is caught in any trespass, you who are spiritual, restore such a one in a spirit of gentleness; *each one* looking to yourself, so that you too will not be tempted. 2 Bear one another's burdens, and thereby fulfill the law of Christ. 3 For if anyone thinks he is something when he is nothing, he deceives himself. 4 But each one must examine his own work, and then he will have *reason for* boasting in regard to himself alone, and not in regard to another. 5 For each one will bear his own load.

6 The one who is taught the word is to share all good things with the one who teaches *him.* 7 Do not be deceived, God is not mocked; for whatever a man sows, this he will also reap. 8 For the one who sows to his own flesh will from the flesh reap corruption, but the one who sows to the Spirit will from the Spirit reap eternal life. 9 Let us not lose heart in doing good, for in due time we will reap if we do not grow weary. 10 So then, ªwhile we have opportunity, let us do good to all people, and especially to those who are of the household of the faith.

6:1 ªGr *anthropos*   6:10 ªOr *as*

**NLT**

26 Let us not become conceited, or provoke one another, or be jealous of one another.

6:1 Dear brothers and sisters, if another believer* is overcome by some sin, you who are godly* should gently and humbly help that person back onto the right path. And be careful not to fall into the same temptation yourself. 2 Share each other's burdens, and in this way obey the law of Christ. 3 If you think you are too important to help someone, you are only fooling yourself. You are not that important.

4 Pay careful attention to your own work, for then you will get the satisfaction of a job well done, and you won't need to compare yourself to anyone else. 5 For we are each responsible for our own conduct.

6 Those who are taught the word of God should provide for their teachers, sharing all good things with them.

7 Don't be misled—you cannot mock the justice of God. You will always harvest what you plant. 8 Those who live only to satisfy their own sinful nature will harvest decay and death from that sinful nature. But those who live to please the Spirit will harvest everlasting life from the Spirit. 9 So let's not get tired of doing what is good. At just the right time we will reap a harvest of blessing if we don't give up. 10 Therefore, whenever we have the opportunity, we should do good to everyone—especially to those in the family of faith.

6:1a Greek *Brothers, if a man.*   6:1b Greek *spiritual.*

One of the greatest commands in the New Testament is "be filled with the Spirit" (Eph. 5:18). This simple yet important command represents a transfer of the control of our lives from ourselves to the living Lord. But being filled with the Spirit does not end in a private realm or some mystical experience. It's not about speaking in strange tongues or performing miraculous signs and wonders. It's not even about having some kind of emotional response or a profound encounter with the Master. Biblically speaking, being filled with the Spirit primarily affects our relationships *with others*. Speaking the truth in love, gently restoring wayward brothers and sisters in Christ, comforting those who grieve, giving assistance and encouragement to those in need—these are the marks of a person who is filled with the Spirit.

Contrary to what our individualistic society promotes, the spiritual life is far more than independent devotion or personal experience. Don't misread me. It's not any less than our personal relationship with Christ. But that is only the starting point. If that's our end point, we've completely missed the point. Our vertical relationship with the Father, which comes through the Son and is energized by the Holy Spirit, is meant to affect our horizontal relationships with those around us—with our nearest loved ones, our church family, our neighbors, and even total strangers.

Still not convinced? Then let the Bible speak for itself. Notice how often Paul and other writers use the phrase "one another" to describe the ways we're supposed to live out the Christian life:

- Love one another (John 15:12; 1 Thes. 4:9; 1 Pet. 1:22).
- Build up one another (Rom. 14:19; 1 Thes. 5:11).
- Accept one another (Rom. 15:7).
- Care for one another (1 Cor. 12:25).
- Serve one another (Gal. 5:13).
- Bear one another's burdens (Gal. 6:2).
- Be kind to one another (Eph. 4:32).
- Comfort one another (1 Thes. 4:18).
- Encourage one another (1 Thes. 5:11; Heb. 3:13).

The list of "one another" commands in the New Testament could go on. For now, let's focus on Paul's "one another" perspective on living together by the power of the Spirit. We'll see that life in the Spirit is a life seasoned with grace—another demonstration that grace is not only the way to life, but the way of life.

## — 5:26 —

Part of relating to others in the Spirit involves knowing what not to do. Galatians 5:26 transitions us from Paul's sharp contrast between the deeds of the flesh and the fruit of the Spirit in 5:19-23, moving to the effects of both lifestyles on our interactions with others. Paul exhorts his readers to avoid boasting, challenging, and envying (5:26). This underscores the reality that fleshly living is always self-centered, self-focused, and self-satisfying. In contrast, living by the Spirit places the emphasis on others.

To "become boastful" means "to boast where there is nothing to boast about."[10] Such a warning would fit well with the Galatians' background of legalism. Legalism always puffs us up and tears down others as it flaunts a person's own accomplishments by his or her own power. The boastful forget that they have been shown grace.

Paul also warns the Galatians to avoid "challenging one another." This verb (*prokaleō* [4292]) means to "call forth" a person in a challenge or to "provoke" a person to anger.[11] It paints the picture of someone with a competitive spirit, a person who can't let things lie. This individual is quick to jump into any disagreement, always ready to pick a fight, and eager to challenge every authority. This is a person who has to be right and must have the last word. Provokers fail to show grace toward others.

Finally, Paul warns about "envying one another," a sin rooted in feelings of inferiority and insecurity. In such a case, possessions, abilities, and accomplishments take center stage. "Keeping up with the Joneses" becomes a way of life, resulting in failure to rest contentedly in our secure and exalted position in Jesus Christ. Those who are envious fail to demonstrate grace deep within themselves by being content with who they are and what they have. It's a miserable way to live!

## — 6:1-6 —

Having provided a snapshot of what it looks like to walk in the flesh, Paul now begins to illustrate how to relate to one another in the Spirit. He sets forth four distinct imperatives for believers that relate to bearing with one another:

- Restore those who stumble, without falling into temptation (6:1).
- Bear one another's burdens according to Christ's law (6:2-3).
- Take personal responsibility with humility (6:4-5).
- Support your teachers with generosity (6:6).

*Restore those who stumble, without falling into temptation (6:1).* Paul begins by describing a grace-oriented, Spirit-filled response to fellow believers who wander from the path of submission to God and obedience to His Word. Legalists, of course, would condemn them. Or they would slap collars around their necks and keep them on short leashes. Or they would say "I told you so" to demonstrate their own spiritual superiority. But this is not the way of the Spirit-filled believer.

Paul says that those who are spiritual should restore the wayward with a spirit of gentleness (6:1). In the body of Christ, believers care about and are therefore responsible for each other. When we see a brother or sister sliding downward into sin, we can't simply turn away, hang our heads, and pretend it's only the pastor's responsibility to confront the wayward. Nor can we shake our fingers, cluck our tongues, and add the person to our blacklist. Neither of these extremes is biblical. Paul explains how true spiritual restoration works.

First, restoration is necessary when a person is "caught" in sin. The language implies that the sinner, through weakness, has gotten himself or herself snared by the lures of the world. He or she is not merely a perpetrator of sin, but a victim of temptation. If you think of it that way, it will give you a new way of looking at the victim with a concern for restoration. This isn't an attempt to downplay sin. Call it what it is: sin. It's not just a mistake or a faux pas. But also realize that any one of us could find ourselves flat on our own face, having stumbled headlong into a trap and needing somebody to help us out. We need to understand this before we begin the restoration process.

Second, Paul limits the intervention to those who are "spiritual." These aren't spiritual giants who have somehow eradicated their sin natures and are living miraculously pure lives. If we had to wait for a perfect saint to implement spiritual restoration, we would be waiting forever. Rather, in this context, the "spiritual" are those who, in a particular situation, have been given the spiritual mindset and relational vantage point to see the situation with moral clarity because they are not clouded by the fog that dulls the consciences of unrepentant sinners.

What does it mean to "restore"? G. Walter Hansen notes that "the verb *restore* calls for spiritual therapy so that a broken member of the body can once again work properly and perform its vital functions for the benefit of the whole body."[12] In the context of restoring fallen believers, Paul links the term with one aspect of the fruit of the Spirit:

gentleness. No wonder Paul says that only those who are spiritual can accomplish the difficult task of restoration!

I remember several times in my life when I have really been in the wrong and have needed to be confronted. Invariably, I have found that those who did that were those who loved me the most and did so with gentleness. Those who took the time to tell me the truth did it with such concern and care that I got the message—without even feeling crushed. They cared enough to help me through it. They didn't leave me alone. To this day I appreciate those men who cared enough to speak "the truth in love" (Eph. 4:15).

You probably know someone who's been tripped up. You probably don't want the job, but God may be calling you to help him or her to get back on track. Don't run from it, but at the same time don't be overly anxious to confront. If you are called to this task, carry it out with gentleness.

Finally, the restorers must look to themselves to avoid falling into temptation (Gal. 6:1). We must walk into every confrontation with our eyes wide open, with a keen sense of our own weaknesses and vulnerabilities. We may not necessarily be tempted to sin in the same way as the person we're hoping to restore, but we may be tempted with pride, harshness, gossip, or legalism.

*Bear one another's burdens according to Christ's law (6:2-3).* No one is meant to "go it alone," and no one is without his or her own burdens. Paul warns against the pride of deceptive self-sufficiency in 6:3: "If anyone thinks he is something when he is nothing, he deceives himself." The truth is that life heaps all kinds of baggage onto everyone's shoulders—job stress, personal loss, struggles with sin, loneliness, physical suffering, sickness, divorce, abuse, addiction. The list could go on and on. In the Christian life, there's no room for "Just leave me alone" or "I'm fine by myself." We all need someone to counsel us, embrace us, and comfort us. And taking the super-spiritual "give it all to the Lord" approach doesn't let us off the hook: We still need to lean on others. Yes, the Spirit is the One who comforts and counsels us, but He most often does this by empowering Spirit-filled people to bear our burdens.

When we bear each other's burdens, we fulfill the law of Christ. That's not a reference to the Old Testament Law or the Ten Commandments. "The law of Christ" refers to the principle of Christlikeness summed up in the Savior's command to love one another (5:14). Jesus said, "A new commandment I give to you, that you love one another, even as I have loved you, that you also love one another. By this all men will know that you are My disciples, if you have love for one another" (John 13:34-35). Paul's words strike at the very heart of the Judaizers' legalistic theology. Christianity does not center on the Law of Moses and its principle of strict justice but on the law of Christ and its principle of mercy and grace. The Spirit-bestowed fruit of love provides the supernatural ability to bear each other's burdens with humility and gentleness.

*Take personal responsibility with humility (6:4-5).* At first glance, Paul's statement about "boasting in regard to himself alone" sounds like a contradiction to his command in 5:26, "Let us not become boastful." And his conclusion in 6:5—"For each one will bear his own load"— seems to fly in the face of his command in 6:2, "Bear one another's burdens." How do we explain this?

F. F. Bruce writes, "What Paul stresses here is personal responsibility. It is not for one Christian to assess or judge the ministry of another; each one is answerable to God for his own."[13] If we allow the whole context to be our guide, Paul means that if we're going to "boast," we should boast in what God is doing through us by the power of the Holy Spirit, not in how much we think we're surpassing other people in our spiritual lives. The issue here is comparison, and Paul once again addresses the problem that originally surfaced in 5:26—"challenging one another, envying one another." In other words, Paul is saying something like this: "Instead of boasting about how much better you are than others—or envying others for how much better they are than you— recognize that you are personally accountable before God and don't worry about everybody else around you."

But what about 6:5? Whose burdens are we supposed to bear? Our own? Somebody else's? If we're supposed to bear our own burdens, then why would anybody be told to bear mine? Commentator G. Walter Hansen points out the difference between two Greek words Paul uses: "burden" (*baros* [922]) in 6:2 and "load" (*phortion* [5413]) in 6:5:

> Though these two words are basically synonymous in other contexts, the change of nouns in this context indicates a change of reference. Verse 2 refers to the need to come to the aid of others who cannot carry the crushing burden of the consequences of their sin. Verse 5 refers to work given to us by our Master, before whom we will have to give an account of how we used the opportunities and talents he gave us to serve him.[14]

*Support your teachers with generosity (6:6).* Most preachers and teachers I know are uneasy talking about, preaching about, and especially asking for money. But finances come up quite frequently in the Bible, so the topic can't be avoided. Most average people, however, don't quite get what paying the pastor has to do with the Spirit-filled life. Paul addresses this question head-on.

In 6:6 he reminds his readers of their responsibility to support those who teach them the Word. This would have been an especially important admonition to the Galatians. In an environment where the Judaizers were trying to snuff out the light of the gospel, any teachers standing for the truth should be supported financially. To neglect this would be to squeeze off the gospel at its source—the appointed teacher or preacher.

Studying and teaching the Word of God takes time and discipline. Staff pastors, whether they preach each Sunday or lead ministries or serve in administrative roles, shouldn't have to work two jobs in order to make ends meet. A seminary professor shouldn't have to stress himself out week to week trying to provide for his family. I'm not saying they should live in the lap of luxury; Paul is not promoting that. But he does say that part of a believer's spiritual responsibility is to share his or her abundance with those who work hard (1 Tim. 5:17-18). As the pastor shares spiritual wealth with his flock, the flock should share material goods with him. In the grace-oriented, Spirit-filled church, pastor and congregation are to look out for one another.

## — 6:7-10 —

"Whatever a man sows, this he will also reap." I would like to suggest that Paul's famous words imply four easy-to-remember principles, which I call "the laws of the harvest":

1.  *We sow and reap in like kind.* If you plant watermelon seeds in the spring, don't expect to harvest grapes in the fall. So, if you dislike watermelons, don't plant them.
2.  *We reap in a different season than the one we sow in.* Gardeners don't plant seeds, pull up a lawn chair, and wait with a basket in hand to harvest. The seeds bear fruit in a different season.
3.  *We reap more than we sow.* I think gardeners would be pretty frustrated if each plant produced only one fruit bearing one seed to grow one new plant. God has created plants for fruitfulness and multiplication.
4.  *We must let go of past harvests and focus on sowing for the future today.* Not every harvest produces a cornucopia of fruits and

vegetables. Some harvests are flat and disappointing; others yield bumper crops. We can't base future returns on past harvests. If we want to reap in the future, we need to plant in the present.

By now you've guessed that I'm not merely talking about farming and gardening. The laws of the harvest apply just as well to the spiritual life as they do to the natural. If we sow sinful thoughts and actions, we will reap the consequences. Those who patiently and faithfully plant seeds of God's Word in their lives will later reap blessings of wisdom, peace, and joy. In other words, those who sow to the flesh shouldn't expect to receive the blessings of the Spirit.

This is Paul's point in Galatians 6:7-10. Having set before his readers the ways of the flesh (5:19-21) and the ways of the Spirit (5:22-23), Paul emphasizes that both of these lifestyles will have their respective judgments or rewards. Though we may fool ourselves into thinking we can somehow escape the laws of the harvest when it comes to sowing to the flesh, God will not be mocked. There will be consequences, even for believers saved by grace through faith and secure in their salvation. In 1 Corinthians 3:13-15, Paul levels this strong warning at those who fail in their responsibility to invest in Christ's kingdom:

Each man's work will become evident; for the day will show it because it is to be revealed with fire, and the fire itself will test the quality of each man's work. If any man's work which he has built on it remains, he will receive a reward. If any man's work is burned up, he will suffer loss; but he himself will be saved, yet so as through fire.

The laws of the harvest work in both directions. If we sow to the flesh, we will reap corruption, but if we sow to the Spirit, allowing Him to manifest His fruit in our lives, we will reap a bountiful harvest (6:8). To grow well, we have to sow well. But what does it mean to sow to the flesh? Quite simply, it means indulging in thoughts and actions that gratify the self. This includes the deeds of the flesh Paul listed in chapter 5. On the other hand, sowing to the Spirit means engaging in thoughts and actions that please Christ. These include expressing our love for God through worship, prayer, and study of His Word. Sowing to the Spirit means living a life of love toward others by caring, meeting needs, encouraging, and confronting. It means actively participating in concrete expressions of the fruit of the Spirit, knowing that God Himself is working in you to grow those seeds so that you may eventually reap an abundant harvest of blessing (6:9-10).

# APPLICATION: GALATIANS 5:26–6:10
## Weed 'Em and Reap

One thing becomes abundantly clear in Galatians 5:26–6:10. The spiritual life is anything but passive. Our lives are like gardens or fields in which we can sow good seed, resulting in bountiful blessings. Or we can sow bad seed, resulting in weeds of corruption. In every Christian's life the tares grow up beside the wheat, the bad plants stunting the development of the good. Envy robs from kindness. Greed restricts generosity. Lust weakens marital faithfulness. Rage drives out gentleness.

One way to keep the fruit of the Spirit growing and to reap its blessings is to continually weed the gardens of our lives. This means constant attention to our attitudes, thoughts, and actions. It means being transparent before fellow believers who love us and will also confront us with the tough questions when we need them. It means plucking and pruning, ridding the field of obstacles and obstructions that come in the form of temptations, sins, and bad habits.

In order to begin the weeding process, it's important to first identify the weeds that happen to have invaded your own personal garden. In the diagram below, you'll find the aspects of the fruit of the Spirit interspersed with "weeds of the flesh." Take time to consider each one of these weeds to determine if it tends to be a perennial problem in your own life. Cross out the weeds you need to focus on plucking, then circle the fruit of the Spirit that will be positively affected if you rid yourself of those parasitic plants. When you're finished, ask the Lord to continue to empower you to labor faithfully as He causes the growth.

## Weeds of the Flesh

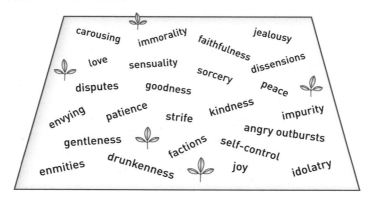

# A Brief Reprise and a Blunt Reproof
## GALATIANS 6:11-18

**NASB**

[11] See with what large letters I [a]am writing to you with my own hand. [12] Those who desire to make a good showing in the flesh try to compel you to be circumcised, simply so that they will not be persecuted [a]for the cross of Christ. [13] For those who [a]are circumcised do not even keep [b]the Law themselves, but they desire to have you circumcised so that they may boast in your flesh. [14] But may it never be that I would boast, except in the cross of our Lord Jesus Christ, through [a]which the world has been crucified to me, and I to the world. [15] For neither is circumcision anything, nor uncircumcision, but a new [a]creation. [16] And those who will [a]walk by this rule, peace and mercy *be* upon them, and upon the Israel of God.

[17] From now on let no one cause trouble for me, for I bear on my body the brand-marks of Jesus.

[18] The grace of our Lord Jesus Christ be with your spirit, brethren. Amen.

**6:11** [a]Or *have written*   **6:12** [a]Or *because of*
**6:13** [a]Two early mss read *have been*   [b]Or *law*
**6:14** [a]Or *whom*   **6:15** [a]Or *creature*   **6:16** [a]Or *follow this rule*

**NLT**

[11] NOTICE WHAT LARGE LETTERS I USE AS I WRITE THESE CLOSING WORDS IN MY OWN HANDWRITING.

[12] Those who are trying to force you to be circumcised want to look good to others. They don't want to be persecuted for teaching that the cross of Christ alone can save. [13] And even those who advocate circumcision don't keep the whole law themselves. They only want you to be circumcised so they can boast about it and claim you as their disciples.

[14] As for me, may I never boast about anything except the cross of our Lord Jesus Christ. Because of that cross,* my interest in this world has been crucified, and the world's interest in me has also died. [15] It doesn't matter whether we have been circumcised or not. What counts is whether we have been transformed into a new creation. [16] May God's peace and mercy be upon all who live by this principle; they are the new people of God.*

[17] From now on, don't let anyone trouble me with these things. For I bear on my body the scars that show I belong to Jesus.

[18] Dear brothers and sisters,* may the grace of our Lord Jesus Christ be with your spirit. Amen.

**6:14** Or *Because of him.*   **6:16** Greek *this principle, and upon the Israel of God.*   **6:18** Greek *Brothers.*

The room is silent. The twilight has retired, giving way to darkness. Countless lamp-lit windows shimmering throughout the city of Antioch mirror the star-studded heavens above. For Paul, whose eyesight wanes in the evening, everything is a dim blur. But he lingers pensively at the window, enjoying the breeze that rolls in from Mount Silpius.

Paul can hear Barnabas reading over the last section of the letter he had been dictating, making sure he didn't leave anything out. The letter would soon make its way on the long trek to the cities of Galatia. The messenger had already been arranged. He would leave in the morning.

Paul sighs and turns to his companion. "Read the last sentence for me again."

Barnabas rolls back the scroll and finds the spot where Paul had left off. Pulling the nearest oil lamp closer to the sheet, he reads the last sentence: "So then, while we have opportunity, let us do good to all people, and especially to those who are of the household of the faith."

"How much space do we have left?" Paul asks.

"Just a little," Barnabas replies.

Paul turns and limps to the table where Barnabas had strewn his writing supplies. He reaches out his hand for the stylus. Barnabas turns it over to him and slides the parchment roll across the writing table. As Paul labors to scan the last column, Barnabas gathers several lamps and candles to illuminate the text.

Paul nods his thanks and begins to write just a thumb-width from the last entry:

"See with what large letters I am writing to you with my own hand."

Thus begin the last words of Paul to the Galatians. In this final section, Paul both summarizes and emphasizes the main points of the entire letter.

Giving this section our concentrated attention will be well worth the effort.

## — 6:11 —

Throughout the Galatian letter, Paul had been dictating his thoughts to an unknown amanuensis (secretary). Though in my creative telling of the story I speculated that Barnabas served in this capacity, in actuality we have no way of knowing who had been taking down Paul's words. We do know, however, that Paul takes pen in hand at 6:11 and conveys his final thoughts with broad, bold strokes.

Undoubtedly, his handwriting toward the end would have verified to the Galatian Christians that this letter was indeed from Paul. Some have suggested he used large letters because of his failing eyesight (cf. 4:15). Or it may have been that Paul's own penmanship differed from the more refined script of his chosen amanuensis. Or, in a manner similar to using ALL CAPS TO ACCENTUATE YOUR POINT, Paul may have intended to draw attention to the abrupt change of writers and

## PICKING UP THE PEN TO MAKE A POINT

**GALATIANS 6:11**

When Paul took up the stylus and began writing a farewell greeting in his own hand, he was actually following a common custom of letter writing in the Roman world.[15] Official correspondence was often composed through a secretary, called an "amanuensis," who was skilled in spelling, grammar, literary style, and a form of handwriting that would conserve space on the expensive parchment while remaining readable. Paul himself used these secretaries on several occasions. Tertius helped write Romans (Rom. 16:22), Silvanus and Timothy are listed not as mere amanuenses but as coauthors for 1 and 2 Thessalonians (1 Thes. 1:1; 2 Thes. 1:1), and several other letters that have a slightly different Greek style may have been composed in similar ways. In some of his letters, including Galatians, Paul made a point of letting his readers know that he himself penned the final greeting with his own hand, taking the pen from his secretary and scratching a message in his own informal script (1 Cor. 16:21; Col. 4:18; 2 Thes. 3:17).

In ancient letters, this final greeting often did more than prove that the letter really was from the purported author. It could also summarize the content of the letter and emphasize its main points.[16] Paul's "large letters" (Gal. 6:11) were intended partly to prove that he had personally begun to write, but mostly to underscore his main point that salvation comes by grace alone through faith alone in Christ alone, not by keeping the Law.

to emphasize his main argument: Salvation is by grace alone through faith alone in Christ alone, not by the works of the Law.

So, pointing to the cross one last time, Paul sends a final rebuke against the rogue band of pirates who were attempting to hijack the faith of the Galatian Christians. As we examine what Paul has emphasized, we will see that it involves not only a succinct reprise of his argument but also a blunt reproof of the Judaizers.

## — 6:12-13 —

Paul begins his reprise by readdressing the issue of inward reality versus outward religion. The Judaizers in Galatia had sneaked in to prey on the hearts and minds of the new believers. They compelled them to be circumcised—undergo the rite of initiation into the old-covenant Law—in order to "make a good showing" in the flesh. Whom were they trying to impress? Paul says they were trying to avoid persecution. At that time, persecution could come from two sources: Jews and Romans.

In both cases, retaining the practice of circumcision would help Christians avoid unwanted wrath. To the Jews, circumcision would mean that the Gentile Christians were not converting to a competing faith but were willing to submit to the old order of things under the rules, regulations, restrictions, and rabbis of the long-standing tradition. To the Romans, who had accepted Judaism as a legal religion in the Roman Empire, Gentiles who were circumcised would fall under the category of Judaism. They would therefore remain under that umbrella of legal toleration. To reject circumcision and take the name "Christian" would mean to sacrifice this protection and potentially face persecution. So, the Judaizers were at least right on that count: Being circumcised would diminish the likelihood of persecution.

To do so, however, not only betrayed Christ, who was the Mediator of a new covenant, but also set up a religion that was all show and no substance. Paul says that those who are circumcised "do not even keep the Law themselves" (6:13). Rather, the Judaizers simply wanted a "get out of persecution free" card and the opportunity to boast about the hard-earned converts to their own distorted, Judaistic Christianity.

Although we're two millennia removed from the original Judaizers, we're still tempted to boast in the flesh. We place a notch in our belts when our baptism numbers swell, demonstrating the grand results of our evangelistic efforts. We keep close tabs on attendance at services, Sunday school, and special events. This numbers game is one of the most fleshly games congregations can play. Another game we play is the glitz-and-glamour game. The bigger and flashier our Sunday morning productions, the more we feel like we've worshiped to the max! But bright lights, loud bands, big budgets, huge crowds, and hyped-up emotional responses mean nothing if they lack real substance. How easy it is to boast in the flesh, focusing on the outward actions rather than the inward reality.

## — 6:14-16 —

In contrast to the Judaizers' boasting in the visible results of their human efforts, Paul returns to the true center of our boasting: the Cross of the Lord Jesus Christ, the only means of justification and sanctification. Christianity isn't about our achievements. It's not about what we can do for God. It's about what God has done for us. In fact, a true understanding of the saving work of Jesus Christ on our behalf excludes all boasting in our own merit. Paul makes this clear elsewhere: "For by grace you have been saved through faith; and that not of yourselves, it is the gift of God; not as a result of works, so that no one may boast" (Eph. 2:8-9).

God chose us (Eph. 1:4). He sent His Son to die for us (Gal. 4:4). He gave us a new life we never could have earned (1 Pet. 1:3). His power and grace alone justified us, sanctify us, and will glorify us. We have nothing to boast about except the person and work of Jesus Christ. Every ounce of credit for who we are and for the hope that we have goes to the Savior who died for us at Calvary.

Besides taking away any basis for personal boasting, the Cross also drew a clear line of division between the believer and the world. This means that the Judaizers' precarious fence sitting has no place in the Christian life. John Stott elaborates on Paul's crucifixion image in 6:14: "Previously we were desperately anxious to be in favour with the world. But now that we have seen ourselves as sinners and Christ crucified as our sin-bearer, we do not care what the world thinks or says of us or does to us."[17] This change in perspective has profound practical implications. The more we focus on Christ and what He accomplished, the less we'll focus on the world and what we accomplish. When the Cross becomes everything to us, the world loses its luster. As the words of a very old chorus go,

> Turn your eyes upon Jesus,
> Look full in His wonderful face,
> And the things of earth will grow strangely dim,
> In the light of His glory and grace.[18]

In fact, all that matters in the Christian life is a "new creation" (6:15). No religious rituals, no acts of devotion, no fleshly merit counts for anything in Christ, who accomplished everything for us. To become children of God, we must become new creatures (2 Cor. 5:17; cf. Rom. 2:29). The only way to do that is to place our trust in Christ, counting on Him to forgive our sins, make us holy, and present us as righteous before God.

Paul then says that "those who will walk by this rule"—the principle that the new life is to be lived in the shadow of the Cross—will be granted peace and mercy. Unlike the Law, which produced anxiety and wrath, God's grace fills a believer's life with a profound, inexplicable peace and a sense of pardon from sin and its penalties. No longer are we trapped in a dark pit of guilt and fear.

Paul extends this blessing of peace and mercy not only to all those who accept this principle of the Cross but also to "the Israel of God." Bible students have interpreted this phrase in numerous ways. Some understand it to be a further description of "those who will walk by this rule," meaning it could be translated, "that is, the Israel of God." In this case, the phrase would refer to all believers in Christ—Jews and Gentiles—as members of "spiritual Israel" in the sense that children of faith are the true children of Abraham (Gal. 3:6-9). Others understand "Israel of God" to refer to unbelieving Israel. Here, Paul would be expressing his earnest desire that even the present enemies of the Cross would one day inherit the blessings of peace and mercy (see Rom. 9:3-4). Still others see the "Israel of God" as the Jewish Christians who, though true physical members of the nation of Israel, overcame the cultural and religious bondage they were in and embraced Jesus as their Messiah, choosing to live according to grace rather than law. Paul himself would fit in this category (Phil. 3:4-11). Because this is the only place in the Bible where we find the phrase "Israel of God," we have no way of determining exactly what Paul meant. Nevertheless, the principle still stands—only those who trust in Christ and His redemptive work will receive the peace and mercy for which every man and woman yearns.

## — 6:17-18 —

As we arrive at the final two verses of Galatians, we find a weary and worn Paul. He writes as if he has exhausted all his energy defending the gospel of grace. Nevertheless, Paul urges the Galatians to no longer allow the legalists to get the upper hand, thus causing him "trouble." Paul had surely suffered agony as he worried over the spiritual health of the churches in Galatia and worked hard at composing a letter to free them from the threat of bondage. If they would heed these words, they would relieve him of his anxiety.

Why should the Galatians listen to Paul rather than the Judaizers? Ultimately it came down to the marks of authenticity Paul bore on his own body. While the Judaizers promoted the physical mark of circumcision, Paul pointed to the "brand-marks of Jesus." The Greek word for these marks, *stigmata* [4742], refers to "signs of ownership such as were branded on slaves and cattle."[19] In 2 Corinthians 11:24-28, Paul catalogs some of the stigmata he received throughout his ministry:

> Five times I received from the Jews thirty-nine lashes. Three times I was beaten with rods, once I was stoned, three times I was shipwrecked, a night and a day I have spent in the deep. I have been on frequent journeys, in dangers from rivers, dangers from robbers, dangers from my countrymen, dangers from the Gentiles, dangers in the city, dangers in the wilderness, dangers on the sea,

dangers among false brethren; I have been in labor and hardship, through many sleepless nights, in hunger and thirst, often without food, in cold and exposure. Apart from such external things, there is the daily pressure on me of concern for all the churches.

Ironically, the very thing the Judaizers were trying to avoid—persecution—Paul regarded as a mark of a true preacher of the gospel. This was in line with Jesus' own words: "Remember the word that I said to you, 'A slave is not greater than his master.' If they persecuted Me, they will also persecute you" (John 15:20).

Having fired that final volley against the legalists, Paul concludes his letter on the same note on which he began and around which the whole letter revolves: grace. "The grace of our Lord Jesus Christ be with your spirit, brethren. Amen." Grace: lavished on the soul by Christ at the moment of salvation. Grace: lived out in service to His glory through the sanctifying work of the Spirit. Grace: the heart and soul of the gospel of Jesus Christ.

Paul's passionate appeal to the foundation of the Christian faith turned his wayward readers back to the path of truth. It can do the same for us when we wander from the liberty of loving service to Christ toward the extremes of legalism or license. Paul argued that not only is the sinner saved by grace, but the saved sinner also lives by grace. His main message is as relevant for us today as it was for the Galatians in their day: Grace and grace alone is the way to life and the way of life.

## APPLICATION: GALATIANS 6:11-18

### Believers Adrift

As we come to the conclusion of Paul's letter to the Galatians, let's step back and consider how we can apply the main truth of the book as a whole. Galatians has confronted us with profound doctrines while challenging us with practical applications. In fact, we dare not conclude the letter without considering how to apply its truths to the Christian life. As we think about the book as a whole, let me suggest a few practical principles to apply.

First, *no one is immune to the temptation of drifting.* If it could happen to people in the first century who lived under the direct teaching of spiritual leaders like Paul and Barnabas, it can certainly happen to us today. Perhaps you're drifting away from the purity of the gospel of grace. Or maybe you're being bullied by legalists and in danger of being carried away by the undercurrents of their manipulative message. The letter of Galatians can serve as a prevailing wind to guide you back into the safe harbor of grace—and as an anchor to keep you in those calm waters. Keep this sobering fact in mind: "If it happened to them, it can happen to me." Read Galatians as if Paul were addressing you *personally*, challenging you with either a rebuke or a warning.

Second, *some things are worth fighting for*. The great news of salvation by grace alone through faith alone in Christ alone is one of those foundation stones of the Christian faith—right up there with the deity and humanity of Christ, the Virgin Birth, the Trinity, and the rest of those doctrines on which the whole Christian church stands or falls. Like Paul, we need to uphold the true gospel, refuting objections and refusing to compromise. Our failure to do this in our own day has allowed for a watered-down gospel that has accommodated and spawned numerous "varieties" of Christianity. The fact stands: A "different" gospel is *not the gospel* (1:6-7). It is heresy. Your family members, neighbors, co-workers, and friends may buy into a teaching at odds with the doctrine of salvation by grace through faith. Or they may be spinning their wheels in a religion of good works meant to win or to keep God's favor. Firmly resist the temptation to fudge on the faith. Refuse to change your clear understanding of grace simply to get along or to keep the peace.

Third, *we all began at the same place, which puts us all on the same level*. We all start out as rebels against God. Through faith in His Son, we become fellow heirs of salvation and inherit the infinite blessings of Christ. In Christ, ethnic, social, and gender distinctions have no bearing on one's standing before God (3:28). It doesn't matter if you were born in a Christian family, have lived a moral life, or have sought to help others in need. If you have never set aside your own attempts to win God's favor or earn His love, do it now. For unbelievers, Galatians makes God's plan of salvation clear. For believers, Galatians reminds us that we have no reason to boast about our own salvation or to take credit for our spiritual growth. As we disembark from this voyage through Galatians, plant your feet firmly on the solid ground of grace. Once and for all set self-help aside and embrace the truth that grace—not law—is both the way to life and the way of life.

# INSIGHTS ON EPHESIANS

*Christ Himself—and Christ alone—is our
peace (Eph. 2:14). . . . What a glorious truth!
Christ alone is peace personified. Centuries
earlier, Isaiah prophesied that the promised
child born of the family of David would be
called "Prince of Peace" (Isa. 9:6). Through
the baptism of the Holy Spirit, every believer
shares a common union of peace with each
other: whether Jew or Gentile; male or female;
black, white, Asian, or Hispanic; rich or poor;
educated or uneducated; strong or weak. The
racial, ethnic, political, social, and economic
dividers that cause so much conflict in our
world fade into insignificance when the
Son of God brings spiritual peace.*

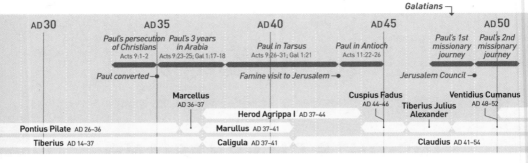

AD 30 | AD 35 | AD 40 | AD 45 | AD 50

Galatians

| AD 30 | AD 35 | AD 40 | AD 45 | AD 50 |

Paul's persecution of Christians
Acts 9:1-2

Paul's 3 years in Arabia
Acts 9:23-25; Gal 1:17-18

Paul in Tarsus
Acts 9:26-31; Gal 1:21

Paul in Antioch
Acts 11:22-26

Paul's 1st missionary journey

Paul's 2nd missionary journey

Paul converted

Famine visit to Jerusalem

Jerusalem Council

Marcellus AD 36-37

Cuspius Fadus AD 44-46

Ventidius Cumanus AD 48-52

Herod Agrippa I AD 37-44

Tiberius Julius Alexander

Pontius Pilate AD 26-36

Marullus AD 37-41

Tiberius AD 14-37

Caligula AD 37-41

Claudius AD 41-54

**Paul's Third Missionary Journey.** After a one-year furlough in Caesarea and Antioch (Acts 18:22), Paul set off on his third missionary journey, passing through the region of Galatia (18:23) and heading again toward Ephesus (19:1). There he spent over two years teaching and preaching to both Jews and Greeks amidst great conflict and controversy (19:1-20:1). After traveling through Macedonia and Greece (20:1-16), he bade farewell to the Ephesian elders in a meeting with them in Miletus (20:17-38). At the end of the third missionary journey, Paul was arrested in the temple in Jerusalem and sent to Rome, where he wrote the book of Ephesians while under house arrest (Acts 21:1-28:30).

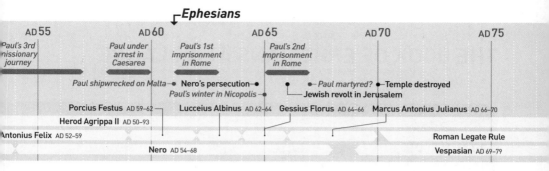

Timeline labels:

┌Ephesians

AD 55 — Paul's 3rd missionary journey

AD 60 — Paul under arrest in Caesarea

AD 65 — Paul's 1st imprisonment in Rome · Paul's 2nd imprisonment in Rome

AD 70

AD 75

Paul shipwrecked on Malta — Nero's persecution — Paul martyred? — Temple destroyed
Paul's winter in Nicopolis — Jewish revolt in Jerusalem

Porcius Festus AD 59–62 · Lucceius Albinus AD 62–64 · Gessius Florus AD 64–66 · Marcus Antonius Julianus AD 66–70
Herod Agrippa II AD 50–93
Antonius Felix AD 52–59

Roman Legate Rule

Nero AD 54–68

Vespasian AD 69–79

# EPHESIANS

## INTRODUCTION

O n March 11, 1942, in the midst of the Pacific War against the Empire of Japan, General Douglas MacArthur left the Philippine Islands, having made a parting vow: "I shall return!" About three years later, MacArthur made good on his promise to rout the enemies from the Philippines, thus making his three-word vow famous.

About nineteen centuries earlier, the apostle Paul made a much more humble version of the same promise in the city of Ephesus: "I will return to you again if God wills" (Acts 18:21). Circumstances prevented him from staying longer in that great city, though Ephesus teemed with "fish" ready to be netted by the gospel. I'm sure the desire to stay on must have been overwhelming, but Paul had boarded a vessel in Corinth on his way back to Antioch, and Ephesus was merely a brief layover on his long journey home.

During his initial stay in Ephesus, Paul entered the synagogue and "reasoned with the Jews" (Acts 18:19). Some of them requested that he stay longer, but that was impossible. He had to return to his home base in Antioch and report back to the church that had sent him on his mission. Paul did, however, leave in Ephesus a Jewish husband-and-wife team whom he had lived and worked with in Corinth (Acts 18:1-3). Priscilla and Aquila, who shared Paul's tent-making trade, stayed on at Ephesus after Paul set sail (Acts 18:18-21).

Following Paul's furlough, during which he reported to the churches in Caesarea and Antioch (Acts 18:22), he soon set off on his third missionary journey, passing through the region of Galatia (Acts 18:23) and heading again toward Ephesus (Acts 19:1). According to the account in Acts 19–20, Paul's ministry in Ephesus was long and fruitful, yet not without controversy and conflict. Consider these major events described in the book of Acts:

# THE BOOK OF EPHESIANS AT A GLANCE

| SECTION | SOVEREIGNTY AND GRACE: THE FOUNDATIONS OF OUR FAITH | RECONCILIATION AND PEACE: THE RESULTS O GOD'S GRACE |
|---|---|---|
| PASSAGE | 1:1–2:10 | 2:11–3:21 |
| THEMES | Salvation by grace alone through faith alone | The mystery of the church revealed |
| | Doctrinal Foundation | |
| KEY TERMS | | Mystery . . .        Love . . . |
| | Predestine | Strangers and aliens |
| | Save | Glory |

| WALKING AND GROWING: THE BELIEVER'S LIFESTYLE | FOLLOWING AND SUBMITTING: THE IMITATOR'S PATH | CLASHING AND CONQUERING: THE WARRIOR'S STRATEGY |
|---|---|---|
| 4:1-32 | 5:1-6:9 | 6:10-24 |
| The new life in the body of Christ | The Spirit-filled life | Victory over Satan with the armor of God |
| Practical Application | | |
| Grace . . .      Body | | |
| Unity<br>Walk | Darkness<br>Submission | Stand<br>Prayer and supplication |

- He encountered followers of John the Baptizer and preached the full gospel of Jesus Christ to them (Acts 19:1-7).
- He spent three months reasoning with Jews in the synagogue of Ephesus, persuading them about the kingdom of God (Acts 19:8).
- He spent two years in the "school of Tyrannus," daily teaching the Word of God to Jews and Gentiles from all over the province of Asia (Acts 19:9-10).
- He performed extraordinary miracles by the power of God, including healing the sick and casting out demons (Acts 19:11-12).
- His reputation as a miracle worker even affected Jewish exorcists, who unsuccessfully attempted to use Paul's methods for casting out demons (Acts 19:13-17).
- His preaching fueled the repentance of former sorcerers, who burned their books of magic valued in the millions of dollars (Acts 19:18-20).
- He incurred the wrath of Demetrius, a silversmith, who had been losing business because people were no longer buying his miniature idols of Artemis, goddess of Ephesus (Acts 19:23-27).
- His preaching stirred up a riot in Ephesus, which culminated in his departure for Macedonia and Greece (Acts 19:28–20:2).

What an amazing ministry! Countless converts were saved through Paul's preaching. They grew in leaps and bounds by his teaching. The few seeds he had planted at the end of his second missionary journey bore abundant fruit in the first two years of his third missionary journey.

Yet that harvest was not without its hardships. A few months later, Paul summoned the elders of the church in Ephesus to him in nearby Miletus, where he said farewell and encouraged them to remain faithful in their ministry (Acts 20:17-38). Through his words to the Ephesian elders, we learn a few details of Paul's ministry in Ephesus:

> "You yourselves know, from the first day that I set foot in Asia, how I was with you the whole time, serving the Lord with all humility and with tears and with trials which came upon me through the plots of the Jews; how I did not shrink from declaring to you anything that was profitable, and teaching you publicly and from house to house, solemnly testifying to both Jews and Greeks of repentance toward God and faith in our Lord Jesus Christ." (Acts 20:18-21)

## KEY TERMS IN EPHESIANS

*agapaō* (ἀγαπάω) [25] "to love"; *agapē* (ἀγαπή) [26]
"love," "benevolence"

The Greek noun *agapē* is rarely found outside the Bible. The Greek culture celebrated *erōs*, an intoxicating, impulsive love between men and women. They also honored *philia* [5373], the warm, noble affection of deep friendship. But *agapē* describes an unconditional, selfless love that expects nothing in return for its affections and benevolence. The related verb *agapaō* perfectly describes God's love toward people as well as Christians' responsibility to reflect that love toward others (2:4; 5:2, 25, 28; 6:24).

*charis* (χάρις) [5485] "grace," "undeserved or unmerited
favor," "cause of delight"

In secular literature, this term is closely associated with the word for "joy"; therefore, *charis* is what brings good will, favor, pleasure, or delight. Paul, however, likely saw in *charis* a new-covenant expression of the Old Testament concept expressed by *hesed*. This term refers to God's spontaneous goodness toward His chosen people and His loyal, abiding love that translates into His covenant faithfulness despite His people's disobedience. As such, "grace" in the New Testament specifically refers to undeserved and superabundant blessings that God bestows on His people.

*mystērion* (μυστήριον) [3466] "mystery," "secret,"
"something unrevealed"

This noun derives from a Greek verb meaning "to mute" and generally refers to a secret. In pagan worship, "mysteries" contained secret knowledge reserved for the few who were willing to sacrifice, perform complex rituals, or even suffer in devotion to a particular god. In Hebrew and Christian writings, however, a "mystery" is a divine truth that had not previously been revealed to humanity. Of the twenty times Paul uses *mystērion* in his writings, six appear in the book of Ephesians (1:9; 3:3, 4, 9; 5:32; 6:19). Here the word describes the gospel message of salvation for both Jews and Gentiles as something newly revealed to lost humanity.

*sōma* (σῶμα) [4983] "physical body," "the corporate
community of the church"

Though elsewhere *sōma* may refer to the physical human body (e.g., Rom. 6:12), Paul's "body language" in Ephesians almost always refers to the "body of Christ," the church, a new corporate community made up of both Jews and Gentiles (Eph. 2:14-16). Christians should properly view themselves not as cogs in a corporate structure but as members of a living and growing organism. The body of Christ is made up of members who each have gifts and functions that work together to accomplish the tasks of making the gospel known in the world and living out its principles.

## EPHESUS IN PAUL'S DAY

### EPHESIANS

Although the impressive ruins of Ephesus are uninhabited today, in the middle of the first century Ephesus was the most important city of western Asia Minor and a major center of political, economic, and religious activity.[1] In the political sphere, the proconsul of Asia conducted most of his affairs in Ephesus.[2] In the economic arena, Ephesus was the region's first port of entry for seafaring vessels and therefore a strategic location for major trade routes. This granted Ephesus a robust market and a large, diverse population.[3] In its religious life, the city boasted a grand temple dedicated to the fertility goddess Artemis, also known as Diana, which was one of the wonders of the ancient world. Besides this, Ephesus had a rigorous imperial cult with several temples dedicated to worship of the emperor.[4]

Barry Beitzel

When Paul was writing his letter to the Ephesians around AD 61, the Roman Empire was ruled by Nero—a maniacal dictator who eventually persecuted Christians with sadistic zeal. A few years after Paul wrote his letter to the Ephesians, Nero would be guilty of setting Rome ablaze in order to fulfill his dream of rebuilding the city in his own style. He blamed the Christians for this fire, igniting a savage persecution in which numerous believers—including Peter and Paul—were killed. Though that powder keg had not yet exploded when Paul ministered in Ephesus and later wrote to the gathering of believers there, the short fuse of imperial intolerance toward the new Christian faith was having numerous flare-ups. The saints in Ephesus would surely have felt the heat of the coming persecutions.

In addition to imperial pressures, the Ephesian believers of Paul's day faced a much more acute and urgent challenge. Ephesus was renowned for its paganism, the crown jewel of which stood proudly in that city—the temple of the goddess Artemis. There was probably no place in Ephesus where a person could stand without falling under the shadow of that temple either physically, spiritually, or economically. The massive shrine drew pilgrims and worshipers—which brought a huge income to local businessmen (see Acts 19:23-30). From the perspective of a first-century Christian living in Ephesus, the city was a hostile environment, to say the least. Paul had experienced it personally during his three years of ministry there. Therefore, he knew that those who remained in this important city needed to be reminded of their position in Christ, as well as of their commitment to walk in a manner worthy of their calling (Eph. 4:1).

Time, tears, trials, teaching, and testifying—these things summed up Paul's ministry in Ephesus. They were the essential ingredients for his fruitful ministry in that great city.

We have no record that Paul ever visited Ephesus again. The long, tear-filled embrace with the elders from the Ephesian church described in Acts 20:36-38 would indeed be the last time they saw their spiritual father in person. Yet those words on the shores of Miletus would not be the last they heard from Paul. A few years later, while he was under house arrest in Rome awaiting an appeal before Caesar, Paul penned the letter to the Ephesians.

## OVERVIEW OF THE LETTER

Paul wrote Ephesians with one basic message in mind: *Because believers have new life through Christ, they ought to live a new life through the Spirit.* The two parts of this message correspond to the two main sections of the letter. Chapters 1–3 show that Christ, through His death, resurrection, and exaltation, has reconciled us to God and united both Jews and Gentiles into "one body," the church (2:16). Having been united to Christ, we are no longer subject to sin and death. Instead, we have been granted forgiveness and new life (1:1–2:10). All obstacles that once separated us from God have been abolished, placing us in a right relationship with God and His people (2:11–3:21). This first section is primarily *doctrinal*, revealing our exalted position in Christ by grace through faith.

The second section, chapters 4–6, instructs believers on how to live in light of the new identity we have in Christ, not walking in our former lifestyle of trespasses and sins, but in a manner worthy of our calling (4:1). The initial sealing of the Holy Spirit received by every believer upon salvation (1:13) must work itself out in the believer's life as the filling of the Spirit (5:18). This results in a life of faithfulness, humility, and good works done through God's enablement. This second section is primarily *practical*, explaining how God accomplishes His work through us.

The whole letter can be divided into five distinct segments: The first two constitute the doctrinal part, and the last three, the practical part.

*Sovereignty and Grace: The Foundations of Our Faith (1:1–2:10)*. This first segment of Ephesians reveals what God has done for us, emphasizing God's sovereignty in showing grace toward those who couldn't even lift a finger to solve their own spiritual plight (1:3-14). Paul punctuates his opening expression of praise with a powerful prayer for spiritual enlightenment for the Ephesians (1:15-23). He also reminds his readers that God granted their spiritual resurrection from death to life solely by His grace through faith in Jesus Christ (2:1-10).

*Reconciliation and Peace: The Results of God's Grace (2:11–3:21)*. In the second segment, Paul vividly describes the reconciliation that has occurred—both reconciliation between Jews and Gentiles and reconciliation between alienated sinners and God (2:11-22). The result of this reconciliation is peace with God and with one another, the basis for unity in the newly formed body of Christ (2:15-16). He then emphasizes the startling uniqueness of the new church age—a profound mystery kept secret in ages past but made known to the New Testament apostles and prophets. In this new era, Gentiles would be saved in the same body through the gospel (3:1-13). As if adding an exclamation point to this doctrinal section, Paul concludes with another magnificent prayer and doxology—praying that his readers would know the love of Christ and be filled with "all the fullness of God" and praising God for the divine power working within us (3:14-21).

*Walking and Growing: The Believer's Lifestyle (4:1-32)*. Having constructed a solid doctrinal foundation in chapters 1–3, Paul sets forth his practical application in chapters 4–6. In light of the believer's new position in Christ, Paul implores his readers to walk in a manner worthy of their calling (4:1). These initial steps of faith include humility, gentleness, patience, tolerance, love, unity, peace, and hope (4:1-6). How does one continue to grow in these and other virtues of the faith? In answer to this question, Paul first describes the ministries of the apostles, prophets, evangelists, pastors, and teachers given by Christ to the church for building up believers in the faith (4:7-16). He goes on to describe the life of spiritual growth, in which believers set aside the "old self" with its wicked ways and put on the "new self," renewed by the Spirit with righteousness and holiness (4:17-32).

*Following and Submitting: The Imitator's Path (5:1–6:9).* The next segment continues to describe the life of the imitator of Christ. Those who once walked in darkness, indulging the flesh, are now urged to walk as children of light, seeking purity, righteousness, truth, and wisdom (5:1-17). How is this transformation accomplished? By yielding to the work of the Holy Spirit in the believer's life (5:18). When the Holy Spirit empowers the believer, His work manifests itself not only through sincere worship (5:19-20) but also through humility and submission in the family (5:21–6:4) and the workplace (6:5-9). By submitting ourselves "to one another" (5:21), we follow in the footsteps of Jesus Christ (5:1-2).

*Clashing and Conquering: The Warrior's Strategy (6:10-20).* Paul concludes his letter to the Ephesians with the vibrant language of spiritual warfare, urging his readers to stand firm against Satan's attacks (6:10-17). He exhorts the Ephesians to prayer and petition as part of their spiritual arsenal (6:18), requesting prayer for himself that he might boldly proclaim the gospel (6:19). Paul ends the letter with some personal greetings and a farewell that mirrors the beginning of the letter: a blessing of peace and grace (6:21-24).

## QUICK FACTS ON EPHESIANS

- *Who wrote it?* Paul the apostle (Eph. 1:1).
- *Where was it written?* From Rome, where Paul was under house arrest (Acts 28:16, 30-31).
- *To whom was it written?* To the saints in the city of Ephesus in western Asia Minor (Eph. 1:1).
- *When was it written?* About AD 61, during Paul's house arrest in Rome while he awaited a hearing before Caesar (Acts 28:16-31).
- *Why was it written?* To strengthen the doctrine and practice of the believers in Ephesus.
- *What is its basic theme?* Because believers have new life through Christ, they ought to live a new life through the Spirit.

# SOVEREIGNTY AND GRACE: THE FOUNDATIONS OF OUR FAITH (EPHESIANS 1:1–2:10)

Sir Francis Bacon once wrote, "Some books are to be tasted, others to be swallowed, and some few to be chewed and digested."[1] Today, most books seek to entertain. They provide minimal mental or spiritual nourishment—only emotional delight. These literary "candies" aren't expected to survive the generation in which they appeared. Of course, a handful of the volumes published each year will make an impression on the academic establishment or on popular culture. These "snacks" of literature have some value, but their influence and memory will fade away with time, as most things do.

Yet every once in a while, a masterpiece is born—a work of literature that may not enter the market with a bang but will outlive all of its lesser siblings and achieve the literary equivalent of immortality. The greatness of these few books is not the result of a clever marketing gimmick or inexplicable popular mania but is entirely due to the incomparable quality of the work. We can probably count on one hand the writings from our generation that will still be read in a thousand years. Clearly, such masterworks are meant to be chewed, digested, pondered, studied, discussed, memorized, recited, and incorporated into one's life.

Without doubt, the books of Scripture are among the few worthy of being fully absorbed by our hearts and minds. They instantly direct us to realities beyond this world, nourishing us with spiritual food from heaven served by the very hand of God. Scripture contains *God's* words, not merely those of the human authors who penned them. Scripture is inspired—"God-breathed"—so that the actual words penned by the human authors of these books come to us from the very mouth of God Himself (2 Tim. 3:16). As such, God gave us Scripture to nourish not only our hearts and minds but also our spirits and souls.

The letter to the Ephesians is no exception. In fact, this letter skips the light hors d'oeuvres of the spiritual banquet and jumps straight into the main course. Within a few verses we discover that this is no dainty lunch for the grazer, but a veritable feast of theological truth served up by a Master Chef.

I've titled this first section "Sovereignty and Grace: The Foundations of Our Faith (Ephesians 1:1–2:10)." In this section, Paul reveals what God has done for us in salvation, emphasizing His sovereign grace toward those who couldn't rescue themselves from the depths of their depravity (1:3-14; 2:1-10). In the midst of this treatise, Paul's powerful prayer for spiritual understanding for the Ephesians reminds us of some of the most foundational theological truths of the Christian faith (1:15-23). Let's begin slowly working through this smorgasbord, taking our time to savor the profound truth it offers.

## KEY TERMS IN EPHESIANS 1:1–2:10

***proorizō* (προορίζω)** [4309] "to predestine," "to decide beforehand"

Though this verb appears only twice in Ephesians (1:5, 11), the concept of predestination is prominent in the opening section of this letter. The term refers to God's sovereign choice of His people in Christ "before the foundation of the world" (1:4). *Proorizō* literally means "to determine before." For the believer, the doctrine of God's predestination should strengthen our trust in the security of our salvation in Christ; it should not excuse complacency or lead to feelings of superiority or privilege.

***sōzō* (σώζω)** [4982] "to save," "to rescue"

The verb *sōzō* can refer to salvation from physical danger (Matt. 8:25), salvation from sin and its effects (Matt. 1:21), or, as in Ephesians, eternal salvation believers receive by grace through faith in Christ (Eph. 2:5, 8). This salvation includes rescue from God's wrath (Rom. 5:9) as well as deliverance into a new life of hope and good works (Rom. 8:24; Eph. 2:10).

# Unloading the Theological Truck
## EPHESIANS 1:1-14

**NASB**

¹Paul, an apostle of Christ Jesus ªby the will of God,
To the ᵇsaints who are ᶜat Ephesus

**NLT**

¹This letter is from Paul, chosen by the will of God to be an apostle of Christ Jesus.
I am writing to God's holy people

**NASB**

and *who are* faithful in Christ Jesus: [2]Grace to you and peace from God our Father and the Lord Jesus Christ.

[3]Blessed *be* the God and Father of our Lord Jesus Christ, who has blessed us with every spiritual blessing in the heavenly *places* in Christ, [4]just as He chose us in Him before the foundation of the world, that we would be holy and blameless before [a]Him. In love [5][a]He predestined us to adoption as sons through Jesus Christ to Himself, according to the [b]kind intention of His will, [6]to the praise of the glory of His grace, which He freely bestowed on us in the Beloved. [7]In [a]Him we have redemption through His blood, the forgiveness of our trespasses, according to the riches of His grace [8]which He [a]lavished on [b]us. In all wisdom and insight [9]He [a]made known to us the mystery of His will, according to His [b]kind intention which He purposed in Him [10]with a view to an administration [a]suitable to the fullness of the times, *that is,* the summing up of all things in Christ, things [b]in the heavens and things on the earth. In Him [11][a]also we [b]have obtained an inheritance, having been predestined according to His purpose who works all things after the counsel of His will, [12]to the end that we who were the first to hope in [a]Christ would be to the praise of His glory. [13]In [a]Him, you also, after listening to the message of truth, the gospel of your salvation—having also [b]believed, you were sealed in [a]Him with the Holy Spirit of promise, [14]who is [a]given as

**NLT**

in Ephesus,* who are faithful followers of Christ Jesus.

[2]May God our Father and the Lord Jesus Christ give you grace and peace.

[3]All praise to God, the Father of our Lord Jesus Christ, who has blessed us with every spiritual blessing in the heavenly realms because we are united with Christ. [4]Even before he made the world, God loved us and chose us in Christ to be holy and without fault in his eyes. [5]God decided in advance to adopt us into his own family by bringing us to himself through Jesus Christ. This is what he wanted to do, and it gave him great pleasure. [6]So we praise God for the glorious grace he has poured out on us who belong to his dear Son.* [7]He is so rich in kindness and grace that he purchased our freedom with the blood of his Son and forgave our sins. [8]He has showered his kindness on us, along with all wisdom and understanding.

[9]God has now revealed to us his mysterious will regarding Christ—which is to fulfill his own good plan. [10]And this is the plan: At the right time he will bring everything together under the authority of Christ—everything in heaven and on earth. [11]Furthermore, because we are united with Christ, we have received an inheritance from God,* for he chose us in advance, and he makes everything work out according to his plan.

[12]God's purpose was that we Jews who were the first to trust in Christ would bring praise and glory to God. [13]And now you Gentiles have also heard the truth, the Good News that God saves you. And when you believed in Christ, he identified you as his own* by giving you the Holy Spirit, whom he promised long ago. [14]The Spirit is God's guarantee that

a pledge of our inheritance, with a view to the redemption of *God's own possession*, to the praise of His glory.

1:1 ᵃLit *through* ᵇOr *holy ones* ᶜThree early mss do not contain *at Ephesus* 1:4 ᵃOr *Him, in love* 1:5 ᵃLit *having predestined* ᵇLit *good pleasure* 1:7 ᵃLit *whom* 1:8 ᵃLit *made abundant toward* ᵇOr *us, in all wisdom and insight* 1:9 ᵃLit *making known* ᵇLit *good pleasure* 1:10 ᵃLit *of* ᵇLit *upon* 1:11 ᵃLit *in whom also* ᵇOr *were made a heritage* 1:12 ᵃI.e. the Messiah 1:13 ᵃLit *whom* ᵇOr *believed in Him, you were sealed* 1:14 ᵃOr *a down payment*

he will give us the inheritance he promised and that he has purchased us to be his own people. He did this so we would praise and glorify him.

1:1 The most ancient manuscripts do not include *in Ephesus.* 1:6 Greek *to us in the beloved.* 1:11 Or *we have become God's inheritance.* 1:13 Or *he put his seal on you.*

It takes a man whose life has been changed to write a life-changing letter. The apostle Paul certainly qualifies.

Saul was a devout Jew from Tarsus, a significant city in the province of Cilicia in southern Asia Minor (Acts 9:11; 21:39; 22:3). Tarsus was "a fusion of civilizations at peace under the rule of Rome," a city we would call "cosmopolitan" or "multicultural" today.[2] Saul was also born a Roman citizen (Acts 22:25-28). Though in most countries today citizenship is a matter of right, in Saul's day it was a privilege, often achieved through distinguished service to the empire or by paying a large fee. Saul's Jewish parents were probably quite wealthy.[3]

Saul of Tarsus grew up in a fundamentalist Jewish household. Circumcised on the eighth day according to the Law of Moses, he lived in strict accordance with that Law up through his young-adult years (Gal. 1:14; Phil. 3:5-6). In fact, when the time came for his schooling, Saul left Tarsus and traveled to Jerusalem in order to study under the most renowned rabbi of the sect of the Pharisees—Gamaliel (Acts 22:3). To use a modern expression, Saul was being groomed for greatness among the powerful and influential Pharisees.

Yet God had other plans for this rising star of Judaism. Saul no doubt intended to utilize his brilliant intellect, stellar reputation, and strong leadership skills to promote the Law. Then Jesus Christ altered his plans, stopping him in his tracks as he sought to persecute the church of God (Acts 9:3-5). At that moment, Saul of Tarsus "died" on the road to Damascus, where he had been sent by the Jewish leaders to destroy the church in that ancient city. Simultaneously, God raised him to a new life, sending him instead to build up the church of Christ worldwide. As Paul the *apostle*—a word that comes from Greek and means "sent one"—this Jewish-Pharisee-turned-Christian-missionary was entrusted with the saving gospel of Jesus Christ for the nations.

So, as Paul the apostle pens the opening lines of his letter to the Ephesians, he reflects on the theological depths of the gospel. He unloads truths about God's sovereignty and grace that he not only knew to be true but also had personally experienced in his own conversion.

## — 1:1-2 —

The opening of Paul's letter to the Ephesians follows the standard epistolary style of Paul's day. He starts by identifying himself as the writer: "Paul, an apostle of Christ Jesus by the will of God" (1:1). This greeting is similar to those of 1 and 2 Corinthians, Colossians, and 2 Timothy, in which Paul points out that he was called as an apostle "by the will of God," strongly emphasizing God's sovereign selection of His hand-picked ambassador.

Next, Paul addresses his recipients, the Ephesians, using two theologically rich terms: "saints" and "faithful" (1:1). In the New Testament, a "saint" is anybody who has been chosen and set apart by God. The great expositor James Boice sums up what it means to be a saint in this original sense:

> Every Christian is a saint, and every saint is a Christian. Moreover, every true Christian is in some sense separated from the world. It does not mean that we are taken out of the world. That is not the way God operates. But it does mean that we are removed from it in the sense of not really belonging to the world any longer. If we are truly Christ's, we have a new nature, a new set of loyalties, and a new agenda.[4]

Not only were the Ephesians members of those "set apart," but since their initial confession of faith in Christ several years earlier the Ephesian saints continued to rely on Christ and to grow in Him. Notice that Paul uses the phrase "in Christ Jesus" to describe the sphere of their faithfulness. This phrase and its equivalents, such as "in Him," "in Christ," or "in the Lord," occur thirty-nine times in Ephesians.[5] They reflect a profound theological truth often unnoticed by readers of the New Testament. By God's grace alone through faith alone in Christ alone, every believer is incorporated "into Christ," that is, "joined to Christ in one spiritual body so that what is true of him is also true for us."[6] John Stott describes this vital theological truth quite clearly:

> To be "in Christ" is to be personally and vitally united to Christ, as branches are to the vine and members to the body, and thereby also to Christ's people. For it is impossible to be part of the Body

## TO THE SAINTS "AT EPHESUS" . . . OR WHEREVER

### EPHESIANS 1:1

Some scholars believe the letter to the Ephesians is wrongly named. Instead of being written to the saints "at Ephesus," some suggest that the letter was actually written as a "cyclical letter" or "open letter" to all the churches in the region of Asia Minor. Why would they say this?

Some ancient Greek manuscripts of Ephesians do not contain the words "at Ephesus" in 1:1. Instead, those copies of the letter say, "to the saints who are faithful." This would mean that the letter was not meant for a particular church in a specific city, but for all saints, as in the case of Peter's letter to "those who have received a faith of the same kind as ours" (2 Pet. 1:1). Also, some scholars point out that Paul's language and style appear to be somewhat impersonal when one considers the deeply personal relationship he had with the saints in Ephesus. Shouldn't we expect to see much more intimate language if Paul were writing to people he had known for several years and with whom he had such close personal ties (Acts 19–20)?

However, the conclusion that Ephesians was originally meant to be a cyclical letter is unlikely for two reasons. First, after comparing all of the ancient Greek manuscripts and weighing the options, the evidence strongly favors including the words "at Ephesus" in 1:1.[7] Second, the apparently impersonal character of the letter is softened by the fact that Paul sent a personal representative, Tychicus, to share his personal greetings, to update the believers in Ephesus on his status, and to encourage them.[8] Though Paul likely expected the letter to be read in other churches in the region (cf. Col. 4:16), its first and primary audience was the famous and influential church in Ephesus.

without being related to both the Head and the members. . . . According to the New Testament—and especially Paul—to be a Christian is in essence to be "in Christ," one with him and with his people.[9]

All of these themes—holiness by being set apart, faithfulness by believing and living in obedience, and unity with God and fellow believers through Jesus Christ—will be fully developed in the rest of Paul's letter.

After identifying himself and his audience, Paul uses his standard greeting of "grace" and "peace" from both God the Father and the Lord Jesus Christ (1:2).[10] In his letter to the Ephesians, Paul will develop these two themes in depth. Grace will be in the spotlight throughout the first three chapters as Paul describes God's favor toward undeserving sinners—the gift of salvation given freely to those who believe. And the reality of peace with God and fellow believers in Jesus Christ will figure prominently in chapter 2.

## — 1:3-6 —

When we hear the word "eulogy," our minds almost instantly picture a close friend or relative of a recently deceased person delivering words of praise for the departed. The English word actually comes from the Greek word *eulogia* [2129], which means "praise," "fine speaking," or "blessing."[11] It fascinates me that Paul uses this Greek term (or its verb form) three times in the Ephesian letter—all in a single verse: "*Blessed* be the God and Father . . . who has *blessed* us with every spiritual *blessing*" (1:3). Thus Paul sets in motion a beautiful and deep litany of praise to his triune God, which extends to the end of 1:14.

Interspersed throughout this concert of praise, three resounding doxologies, or praises of God's glory, emerge. In Paul's mind, everything God does is for His own glory and honor. Theologians call this the "doxological purpose" of God's plan. Note that each of the three doxologies in Ephesians 1:6, 12, and 14 relates to the work of a distinct member of the Godhead—the Father, the Son, or the Holy Spirit.

> *The Father:* "He predestined us to adoption as sons through Jesus Christ to Himself, according to the kind intention of His will, to the praise of the glory of His grace, which He freely bestowed on us in the Beloved" (1:5-6).
> *The Son:* "In [Christ] also we have obtained an inheritance, having been predestined according to His purpose who works all things after the counsel of His will, to the end that we who were the first to hope in Christ would be to the praise of His glory" (1:10-12).
> *The Holy Spirit:* "You were sealed in Him with the Holy Spirit of promise, who is given as a pledge of our inheritance, with a view to the redemption of God's own possession, to the praise of His glory" (1:13-14).

This reminds me of an old doxological anthem tucked away in most hymnals and, sadly, forgotten in most contemporary churches. Many traditional churches with an appreciation for the theologically rich hymns of the faith, however, still sing it often.

> Praise God from whom all blessings flow;
> Praise Him, all creatures here below;

Praise Him above, ye heavenly host;
Praise Father, Son, and Holy Ghost.[12]

One can almost hear the exuberance in Paul's tone in Ephesians 1:3-14 as he focuses all attention upward, blessing the triune God, who has blessed us in so many ways. In fact, in this passage of praise, Paul mentions at least ten reasons to praise the triune God. Let's closely examine each of them.

First, *we praise God because He blessed us with every spiritual blessing* (1:3). God's "good word" of blessing toward us is infinitely more than the mere "bless you" we throw around when somebody sneezes. The word from God's mouth does not return empty, but effects genuine change (Isa. 55:11). In Paul's hymn of praise, he specifically has in mind "spiritual" blessings—benefits already bestowed upon believers because of their intimate association with the Savior, Jesus Christ (Eph. 1:3). Such blessings, sealed by Christ and reserved in heaven, can never be taken away.

Second, *we praise God because He chose us* (1:4). Paul says that God chose us in Jesus Christ "before the foundation of the world." Before anything existed, we were on His mind. Before earth was created, before Adam and Eve were formed, before the fall of humanity occurred, and certainly before you or I took our first breaths, God had already preordained that we would be "holy and blameless" in His presence (1:4).

Entire books have been written on this verse because it does far more than describe divine blessings. It forms the basis for the overarching doctrine of God's sovereign will as it relates to our salvation—the doctrine of election. We need not soften the language here. In fact, before Paul's litany of praise has ended, he will mention election several times. We aren't asked to understand the ins and outs of election, how it fits with free will, or why God chose that person rather than this person. We'll go mad if we try to get our minds around the infinite mind of God, to grapple with His wisdom, to understand His greatness, or to question His goodness. Instead, we're expected to accept the doctrine of election by faith and praise God for it. When was the last time you did that? "Thank you, Lord, for choosing me."

Yet Paul's purpose is not only that we should believe this profound truth and praise God for it but also that we should "walk in a manner worthy of the calling with which you have been called" (4:1). Our response to election should be like Queen Victoria's reaction when she realized she would one day be queen:

When she was young, Victoria was shielded from the fact that she would be the next ruling monarch of England lest this knowledge spoil her. When her teacher finally did let her discover for herself that she would one day be Queen of England, Victoria's response was, "Then I will be good!"[13]

The fact that God has chosen us for salvation in Christ should not cause us to boast; it should drive us to humility. It should not make us live loose lives; it should motivate us to "be good"—that is, to conduct ourselves in holiness and blamelessness before Him (1:4).

Third, *we praise God because He adopted us* (1:5-6). The Greek term *proorizō* [4309], "to predestine," means "to foreordain" or "to determine in advance." To what, though, did God predestine believers? *To adoption as sons through Jesus Christ* (1:5). Under Roman law, which served as a backdrop for Paul's writing, adopted children enjoyed precisely the same rights and privileges as natural children.[14] In the same way, the intimate "Abba" relationship Christ has with the Father by nature is extended to believers by grace. Think of it! Like penniless paupers rescued from the slums and adopted into a king's family, we have been adopted into the family of God.

This brings up a series of questions.

When were we adopted into God's family? The moment we believed. From that point on, we became heirs of all the promises as children of God—eternal life, fellowship with the Father, the promise of resurrection, the reward of reigning with Christ.

Could we have resisted and walked away? Not if we were chosen. God's irresistible working in our lives guaranteed the fulfillment of His sovereign plan for us. Not because we're special or unique, or because we somehow stood out above the crowd of fallen sinners, but by His sheer mercy God chose to save us.

If God chose us, couldn't we be adopted without believing? No, because we're saved through *faith*—our personal, willing response to the gospel message. If we do not believe, the salvation provided by God is not applied to us.

But how do God's sovereign choice and my free-will decision fit together? This answer is easy: *I don't know*. Nor does anyone else! The fact is, we must learn to keep some theological truths in tension. God's sovereign choice in predestination and our personal responsibility to believe are two such truths that run perfectly parallel to each other. Two rails form the same railroad track—two parallel lines that never meet. If we remove one or the other, if we move them closer together, or if we separate them, the train will careen into the ditch. Both rails are essential for the truth to proceed.

From God's limitless, heavenly perspective, everything is planned out. Since we believe in an all-powerful, all-knowing God, how could it be otherwise? From our limited, earthly perspective, however, we don't know who will believe and who won't, so our role is to share the gospel with as many people as we can and then trust God to do His convicting and saving work by His Spirit. Our sharing should be winsome and appealing, but His work is sovereign and irresistible.

## — 1:7-12 —

Ephesians 1:7 makes a seamless transition from the work of God the Father to the work of God the Son, through whom God implemented His plan. Here Paul includes five more reasons to give God our praise.

Fourth, *we praise God because He redeemed us* (1:7). The word *redemption* describes the act of purchasing from bondage by paying a price. The Old Testament term, *geullah* [H1353], refers to a ransom paid to set a person free from his or her obligation of servitude (Lev. 25:47-54). *Apolytrōsis* [629], the Greek equivalent used in Ephesians 1:7, has a similar meaning: purchasing from bondage in order to release one from his or her former compulsions. Paul's use of this term points to the fact that God has redeemed believers, setting them free from the shackles of sin. In order to do so, however, a price had to be paid. How did He do it? Not with silver or gold, but with the precious blood of His own Son, Jesus Christ (1 Pet. 1:18-19).

Fifth, *we praise God because He forgave us* (1:7). Not only have we been redeemed by the blood of Christ, but our debt has been canceled by the infinite riches of His grace. This means that He no longer holds any of our transgressions against us—past, present, or future. As the psalmist says, "As far as the east is from the west, so far has He removed our transgressions from us" (Ps. 103:12). In Ephesians 1:7 Paul uses the term *paraptōma* [3900], "trespass," which indicates taking a false step or "crossing the line"—think of someone walking off the right path and trampling on forbidden land. But even though "all of us like sheep have gone astray, each of us has turned to his own way" (Isa. 53:6), God has placed all of our iniquities upon Christ, by whose death on the cross He forgave us of all our sins.

Sixth, *we praise God because He lavished His grace upon us* (1:7-8). This verse contains two of my favorite words—"grace" and "lavished."

Together they paint a beautiful picture. "Grace" means "unmerited favor," or, more informally, "getting something good that you don't deserve." The truth is, we don't deserve anything from God except condemnation and wrath; but because He has redeemed us and forgiven us, He is now in a position to grant us blessings we haven't earned and could never earn. Yet not only do we receive this priceless grace, but God has "lavished" His blessings upon us, as Christ Himself promised concerning the recipients of His salvation: "I came that they may have life, and have it abundantly" (John 10:10).

Seventh, *we praise God because He made known the mystery of His will to us* (1:8-10). The Greek word *mystērion* [3466] refers to a secret once hidden but now made known. In the New Testament, it refers to truths about God's plan of redemption that had not been clearly revealed in the Old Testament but have now been made manifest. Frankly, God's plan revealed in Jesus Christ caught most religious Jews off guard. They were anticipating a great and mighty military victor who would overthrow Rome, rescue their people from all Gentile oppression, and restore the kingdom to Israel. Though the Jews had a narrow, nationalistic understanding of the scope of redemption through the Messiah, God had planned to sum up "all things in Christ"—not merely things in Israel, or even in the Middle East, but across the entire globe. In fact, God had given to Christ "all authority . . . in heaven and on earth" (Matt. 28:18).

At the present time, however, we do not yet see all things subjected to His universal authority (Heb. 2:8). Rather, the full exercise of Christ's reign will not come about until "the fullness of the times" (Eph. 1:10). Until Christ returns and takes His rightful throne over Israel and all the nations, He is in the process of recruiting into His kingdom joint heirs and co-regents from among both Jews and Gentiles. This "mystery," unrevealed in the Old Testament, broke loose through the gospel of salvation to all. Though such an unexpected move would seem like folly to Jews who cared only for their own national identity, Paul characterizes the mystery as being revealed in "wisdom and insight" (1:8). Simply put, God's timing is perfect, His plan impeccable, and His purposes unimpeachable.

Eighth, *we praise God because He provided an eternal inheritance for us* (1:10-12). God has provided for believers an eternal, irrevocable inheritance grounded in His sovereign choice and predestined according to His will. Due to our position in Christ, we are joint heirs with Him. When He comes into His ultimate inheritance—His universal rule over all creation—we will reign with Him (Rev. 20:6). Those who have trusted in Christ not only receive spiritual blessings of forgiveness, reconciliation, and the indwelling Holy Spirit but also have the promise of heaven with Christ when we die (2 Cor. 5:1-10). But it doesn't end there! For when He returns to this earth to establish His kingdom, we will be raised in new, glorified bodies to share with Him an eternal inheritance of heaven and earth (1 Thes. 4:15-17; Rev. 20:6).

## — 1:13-14 —

Just as the first three reasons to give God praise related to the work of God the Father and the next five related to the blessings we have through God the Son, so the last two reasons relate to the work of God the Holy Spirit.

Ninth, *we praise God because He sealed us by the Spirit* (1:13). By sealing us, God marked us as His own—permanently and irreversibly. The word "seal," *sphragizō* [4972], means "to make something secure,"[15] and the seal itself denotes ownership, approval, or closure.[16] Note the order of the events Paul mentions:

- After listening to the message of truth . . .
- and after believing the gospel of salvation . . .
- then they were sealed with the Holy Spirit of promise.

This means that all those who have heard and believed—those who have placed their trust in Christ alone for salvation—have been permanently sealed. This passage is one reason why I unequivocally believe in the eternal security of the believer. It's impossible for us to trump God's gift, to somehow diminish what God has done. Paul couldn't be clearer: All those who have believed the gospel of salvation have been sealed. The transaction is complete. The Holy Spirit Himself is the promise. Like a wedding band as a symbol of a husband's fidelity to his wife, the Holy Spirit is the seal of God's uncompromising faithfulness to all who believe.

Tenth, *we praise God because He guaranteed our inheritance* (1:14). Harold Hoehner notes that the Greek word *arrabōn* [728], translated "pledge" in 1:14, refers to "the first installment with a guarantee that the rest would follow."[17] In this context, the "pledge," or down payment, refers specifically to the presence of the Holy Spirit, who indwells believers. We have the Spirit now, and He convicts us (John 16:8), comforts us (Acts 9:31), strengthens us to experience Christ's powerful presence (Eph. 3:16), and assures us that we are God's children (Rom. 8:16).

**PAUL'S "TOP TEN" REASONS TO GIVE GOD PRAISE IN EPHESIANS 1:3-14**
1. He blessed us immensely.
2. He chose us unconditionally.
3. He adopted us adoringly.
4. He redeemed us graciously.
5. He forgave us completely.
6. He showed grace to us lavishly.
7. He revealed His mystery wisely.
8. He granted us an inheritance eternally.
9. He sealed us permanently.
10. He guaranteed our salvation personally.

Even so, our current experience of the Spirit is merely a sneak preview of what's coming.

The "redemption of God's own possession" likely refers to the time when believers will receive the fullness of our inheritance as God's children—the resurrection and glorification of our bodies. In Romans 8:23, Paul writes, "We ourselves, having the first fruits of the Spirit, even we ourselves groan within ourselves, waiting eagerly for our adoption as sons, the redemption of our body." And in 2 Corinthians 5:4-5 he states, "For indeed while we are in this tent, we groan, being burdened, because we do not want to be unclothed but to be clothed, so that what is mortal will be swallowed up by life. Now He who prepared us for this very purpose is God, who gave to us the Spirit as a pledge." Paul tells us in 1 Thessalonians 4:15-17 and 1 Corinthians 15:51-54 that when Christ returns, deceased believers will be raised up in new, glorified bodies, and those who are still alive will be transformed. At that time the fullness of salvation will finally come. God will honor His down payment, make good on His promise, and pay in full what He guarantees to us now by the presence of the Holy Spirit in our lives. What a glorious day of celebration that will be!

# APPLICATION: EPHESIANS 1:1-14

## Getting Grace and Giving Glory

Two themes leap from the first half of Ephesians 1: grace and glory. These two pillars provide strong support for Paul's praise to God in 1:3-14. Because believers in Christ have received grace, they glorify God, who gave it. Note that every blessing described in this chapter comes from the Father's eternal will, through Christ's death and resurrection, and by the power of the Holy Spirit. Thus, the almighty, triune God, motivated by unfathomable love, graciously reaches down from heaven and shows us unmerited favor. Salvation from first to last comes to the lost sinner *by grace through faith plus nothing.*

When we begin to realize the breadth and depth of the blessings God has showered upon us, it's easy to dwell so much on the gifts that we lose sight of the Giver. We should remember that Paul describes the gracious work of the Father, the Son, and the Spirit in our lives as part of His doxology—His heartfelt praise to God.

As an exercise of meditating on God's Word, reread Ephesians 1:3-14, preferably in an unmarked Bible. Underline or highlight all of the words that describe the ways in which God has blessed believers. Then pause and reflect on a few of these blessings, noting how they have been meaningful in your own life. How have these truths strengthened or encouraged you? How have they specifically manifested themselves in your life? Though the blessings are common to all Christians, each individual believer experiences these blessings in different ways.

Then, taking your cue from Paul, praise God for the many blessings with which you have been blessed. As the old gospel song instructs us, "count your many blessings, name them one by one."[18] Speak them back to Him. Thank Him for particular expressions of these blessings rather than general provisions.

Let me suggest that you take this a step further. The next time you're preparing for corporate worship, review the blessings you received the previous week. Enter your worship time with these specific works of God at the forefront of your mind. Then use your time of public worship to respond to God in song, prayer, and praise with these specific blessings in your thoughts. When you do, you'll find that your time of worship is far richer, more meaningful, and more sincere than if you walk in without reflecting on the riches God has given you through Jesus Christ.

# Our Prayers and Christ's Position
## EPHESIANS 1:15-23

**NASB**

15 For this reason I too, having heard of the faith in the Lord Jesus which *exists* among you and [a]your love for all the [b]saints, 16 do not cease giving thanks for you, while making

**NLT**

15 Ever since I first heard of your strong faith in the Lord Jesus and your love for God's people everywhere,* 16 I have not stopped thanking God for you. I pray for you

**NASB**

mention *of you* in my prayers; [17] that the God of our Lord Jesus Christ, the Father of glory, may give to you a spirit of wisdom and of revelation in the [a]knowledge of Him. [18] *I pray that* the eyes of your heart [a]may be enlightened, so that you will know what is the hope of His calling, what are the riches of the glory of His inheritance in the [b]saints, [19] and what is the surpassing greatness of His power toward us who believe. *These are* in accordance with the working of the strength of His might [20] which He brought about in Christ, when He raised Him from the dead and seated Him at His right hand in the heavenly *places,* [21] far above all rule and authority and power and dominion, and every name that is named, not only in this age but also in the one to come. [22] And He put all things in subjection under His feet, and gave Him as head over all things to the church, [23] which is His body, the fullness of Him who fills all in all.

1:15 [a]Three early mss do not contain *your love* [b]V 1, note 2   1:17 [a]Or *true knowledge*   1:18 [a]Lit *being* [b]Or *holy ones*

**NLT**

constantly, [17] asking God, the glorious Father of our Lord Jesus Christ, to give you spiritual wisdom* and insight so that you might grow in your knowledge of God. [18] I pray that your hearts will be flooded with light so that you can understand the confident hope he has given to those he called—his holy people who are his rich and glorious inheritance.*

[19] I also pray that you will understand the incredible greatness of God's power for us who believe him. This is the same mighty power [20] that raised Christ from the dead and seated him in the place of honor at God's right hand in the heavenly realms. [21] Now he is far above any ruler or authority or power or leader or anything else—not only in this world but also in the world to come. [22] God has put all things under the authority of Christ and has made him head over all things for the benefit of the church. [23] And the church is his body; it is made full and complete by Christ, who fills all things everywhere with himself.

1:15 Some manuscripts read *your faithfulness to the Lord Jesus and to God's people everywhere.* 1:17 Or *to give you the Spirit of wisdom.* 1:18 Or *called, and the rich and glorious inheritance he has given to his holy people.*

In my experience as a Christian and a pastor, one of the last disciplines we master in the Christian life is prayer. In fact, many Christians live under the dread of being called on to pray in public. I can tell you from having done it for years, *it's hard work!* Yet many more Christians have an even harder time remaining focused on and committed to personal prayer. I've read about heroic saints from church history who would spend three hours a day on their knees. Some of us spend three minutes and feel like it was an hour!

Yes, I know we all say our short, obligatory prayers before meals, a mumbled formula at bedtime, a half-awake drone in the morning, and perhaps an occasional but sincere "Oh dear Lord, please help me out of this mess" during the day. Of course, those of us who go to church listen to prayers from the pulpit, but we aren't sure exactly what our own role is supposed to be on those occasions. For some, "amen" means "I wish I could have said it that way." For others, it's just something you say if you agree with what was prayed. But let's admit it: For a few, it's the signal to wake up and start paying attention to the rest of the worship service.

None of these "prayer-shaped mutterings" come close to true, heartfelt prayer. Praying like we mean it means abandoning the "prayer lingo." It means opening our hearts before the Lord, abandoning pretense, focusing on Him. It means truly believing that we are entering into the very presence of God, who is listening to our words just like any person with whom we have a conversation during the day. Sadly, too few Christians know how to pray, what to pray for, or why they're doing it.

Ephesians, however, was written by a man who really knew how to pray. On the heels of a magnificent flourish of praise (1:3-14), Paul changes gears and continues with purposeful intercession for his readers. He recounts to them the content of his prayers for them, including heartfelt thanksgiving and profound petition to God on their behalf. You can't read about Paul's prayer for the Ephesians and fail to catch his deep passion. Paul prayed like he meant it. In doing so, he gave us a stunning example of genuine prayer.

## — 1:15-16 —

Ephesians 1:15 begins Paul's account of his prayer of thanksgiving and supplication for the Ephesian Christians, which runs all the way to the end of the chapter.[19] Ephesians 1:15-16 includes his thanksgiving. Then 1:17-19 reveals the things Paul prayed for on the Ephesians' behalf. Finally, 1:20-23 refers to the power of Paul's prayer—the resurrected and ascended Lord.

Paul notes that he never ceased to lift up his Ephesian brothers and sisters, mentioning them whenever he prayed (1:16). When we consider the numerous places throughout the empire where Paul had established churches, we can imagine all the regions, cities, and even families that he must have included on his prayer list. Here was a man committed to prayer! Virtually every time he bowed his knees before the Father in prayer, the name "Ephesus" was on his lips. Yet Paul goes deeper than a polite, "Oh, by the way, I just want you to know I'm praying for you." Instead, he reveals specific things that he mentions in his prayers.

Ephesians 1:15 reveals the basis for Paul's thankfulness: the Ephesians' reputation of *faith* in Christ and the *love* they exhibit for the saints. The faith Paul refers to is not their original conversion. Paul himself had spent enough time with the Ephesians to already know the genuineness of their original faith in Christ. Rather, he's referring to the condition of their faith as they grew in Christ. Over the years, the Ephesians' faith had grown steadily stronger. They had built well on the foundation laid by Paul and other ministers (cf. 1 Cor. 3:10), and their reputation for faith had reached Paul's ears. Like a proud father who continually hears news of a famous child's success, Paul expresses his gratitude to God for the spiritual growth of the Ephesians.

Today, many Christians tiptoe gingerly through the Christian life, afraid of stumbling, unsure about whether the path of faith on which they're traveling might lead them into danger. When they hear strange noises, they cower. When darkness sets in, they hesitate. And when obstacles fall in their path, they panic. But not the Ephesians—with the illuminating light of faith, they marched forward, bold and strong, advancing in the Christian life toward spiritual adulthood.

Yet the Ephesians' unwavering trust in Jesus was not the only thing worthy of thanksgiving. Paul also thanked God for the love they had for "all the saints" (Eph. 1:15). Note that Paul doesn't say they loved only their families, their closest friends, their small groups, or even their own fellow Ephesian Christians. Rather, they had demonstrated a generous love toward *all* the saints. How did they do this? Most likely by showing hospitality to travelers, giving shelter to exiles, and providing for the material needs of suffering Christians far away. It's also quite likely that many of the churches that quickly sprang up throughout western Asia Minor began as daughter churches of Ephesus, demonstrating that the Ephesians' faith manifested itself through genuine works of love in evangelism and discipleship.

At this point, I need to emphasize something that is often overlooked. Bible-believing churches need both fidelity to the truth and unconditional love for fellow churches. Without abandoning doctrinal purity on the essentials of the faith, we need to foster unity between churches and between Bible-believing denominations. Our loyalty to Christ—who is the head of the whole body of Christ worldwide (1:22-23)—must work itself out in practical, observable love for one another. A church that has truth but lacks love is not a church; it's a giant Bible class cultivating cliques, leading to a clannish mentality, and producing cult-like attitudes of pride, superiority, and exclusivity. That must stop! We need to pray for other Bible-believing churches, partner with those of genuine faith, and learn from evangelical teachers with backgrounds different than ours. In other words, we need to follow the example of the Ephesians and demonstrate love for "*all* the saints."

## — 1:17-19 —

Think about the last time you earnestly prayed for somebody. What did you ask for? How did you intercede on that person's behalf? Did you pray for God to deliver her from trials? To rescue him from an illness? To help her through a tough financial crisis? To enable him to find a job?

When we contrast our typical prayers on behalf of others with the content of Paul's requests in 1:17-19, most of us can't help but feel ashamed. Paul moves from thanking God for their faith and love to petitioning God for several specific things—though not the typical mundane and materialistic clutter that fills the prayer lists of so many of us. What does Paul ask for? Look at it closely:

### PAUL PRAYS . . .

. . . that God would give them wisdom and revelation related to an intimate knowledge of Him . . .

. . . and that their innermost being would receive divine illumination, so that they would know . . .

1. the hope of His calling,
2. the riches of the glory of His inheritance, and
3. the surpassing greatness of His power toward believers.

The Ephesians obviously knew God, as evidenced by their faith and love. Paul prayed, however, that their knowledge of God would grow even deeper through divine wisdom and insight (1:17). Note that the wisdom and revelation are "in the knowledge of Him," that is, in relation to an intimate, personal, deep knowledge of God. Harold Hoehner notes the following,

> Hence, it is not facts about God that are most important but knowing him personally and intimately. One can know many facts about the leader of a nation through the news media, but that is quite different from personally knowing that leader as his or her family does. Thus, one acquires this knowledge of God not only by facts from the Bible but by the Holy Spirit's giving insight and disclosure in the knowledge of God himself.[20]

In this sense, then, "wisdom" refers to the ability to take profound theological truths *about* God and apply them to everyday situations of life. It means living in the light of God's unfathomable attributes—goodness, grace, mercy, omniscience, omnipresence, omnipotence, love, justice, holiness, patience, and so many more. When God grants wisdom "from above," it manifests itself as "pure, then peaceable, gentle, reasonable, full of mercy and good fruits, unwavering, without hypocrisy" (Jas. 3:17).

A spirit of revelation, then, indicates an unveiling of insight—that is, the ability to grasp the meaning of God's truths so that we comprehend His perspective on life and circumstances. Equipped with this understanding, we see behind the natural world into supernatural meaning. We're able to discern God's providential care for the world and His sovereign hand in our lives.

Through both wisdom and revelation, we enjoy a fuller understanding of our heavenly Father. When that happens, we're no longer "clueless," walking around life as senseless victims of circumstances. Instead, we see through things. We begin to grasp God's perspective on the world. The result? With great eagerness, we submit to His authority and trust in His promises.

Along with this prayer for a deeper knowledge of God through wisdom and revelation, Paul also prays for the ultimate result of that knowledge: an enlightened heart (Eph. 1:18). What does Paul mean by "the eyes of your heart"? One insightful commentator puts it this way: "The 'heart' in Scripture is the seat of thought and moral judgment as well as of feeling. This deep, interior enlightenment provided by the Holy Spirit leads the believer to realize all that God has made available to him."[21]

Paul specifies three things he wanted the Ephesians to know with their innermost being, three spiritual realities that formed the core of their faith. Let's look at each of these in order.

First, Paul wanted the Ephesians to know *the hope of God's calling* (1:18). We tend to think of a calling in individual terms, as referring to someone's ministry position or vocation. The meaning here, however, is much more broad, applying to all Christians. Commentator John Stott writes,

[God] called us to Christ and holiness, to freedom and peace, to suffering and glory. More simply, it was a call to an altogether new life in which we know, love, obey and serve Christ, enjoy fellowship with him and with each other, and look beyond our present suffering to the glory which will one day be revealed.[22]

In this sense, all believers are "called" by God, not just those called into the pastorate or to the mission field.

Second, Paul wanted the Ephesians to know *the riches of the glory of God's inheritance* (1:18). This inheritance includes all God has given to us in salvation through the person and work of Jesus Christ. We've already seen in the last section that believers have received a down payment by the indwelling Spirit. The full payment will be lavished upon us when we meet Christ face-to-face at His second coming. Peter describes this as "an inheritance which is imperishable and undefiled and will not fade away, reserved in heaven for you" (1 Pet. 1:4). At that time, when we stand in glory, basking in our eternal inheritance, all of our human limitations, physical diseases and disabilities, emotional baggage, hardships, and handicaps will be put away forever.

Third, Paul wanted the Ephesians to know *the surpassing greatness of God's power* (1:19). God's abilities are on a completely different plane than anything we might be able to accomplish ourselves. His unimaginable power brings life from death (2:1-5), faith from disbelief (2:8-9), and a good will and works from those who formerly walked in wickedness (2:10; Phil. 2:12-13). As Paul will explain in Ephesians 1:20-23, God's power is able to accomplish so much in our lives because the very same power that raised Christ from the dead and seated Him in heaven is working in believers today (1:19).

## — 1:20-23 —

The last four verses of Ephesians 1 give us evidence of the "surpassing greatness of [God's] power" toward believers (1:19). As we look more closely at this grand finale of Paul's powerful prayer, we observe four proofs upon which we can rest our confidence in God's ability to conform us to the image of Christ—partially in this life, but fully in the life to come. As we tap into this power, it has the potential to radically transform our lives.

First, *God demonstrated His surpassing power when He raised Christ from the dead* (1:20). Far too quickly do we rush through the words of our common confession of faith: "Christ died for our sins and rose from the dead." Stop and think about the strangeness of this claim. Having been beaten, tortured, bound, crowned with thorns, mocked, unfairly tried, nailed to a cross, suspended in the air, and finally stabbed in the side, Jesus of Nazareth was tightly packed in mummy-like wrappings and placed in a tomb. No modern methods of resuscitation would have produced even one blip on a heart monitor. How much less should we expect from any ancient medical treatments of herbs and ointments! Yet a few days later Jesus literally stepped out of the tomb not only restored to health but surpassing His previous mortality with a glorified resurrection body. What an astounding demonstration of the power of God!

Second, *God demonstrated His surpassing power when He seated Christ at His right hand* (1:20). Forty days after being miraculously raised from the dead, the resurrected Messiah had completed His work of teaching and training His disciples to bring the gospel to the nations. Then, as the disciples looked on, God exalted Him to the highest place of honor in the universe—God's own right hand (Acts 1:1-10; 2:33).[23] Before the creation of the world, Christ shared in God the Father's heavenly glory (John 1:1-2; 17:5; Phil. 2:6). Yet He voluntarily surrendered that position of great power and authority, taking on full humanity and humbling Himself as a servant and sacrifice for sin (John 1:14; Phil. 2:7-8). And this wasn't the end of the story. After His resurrection, "God highly exalted Him, and bestowed on Him the name which is above every name" (Phil. 2:9). He returned on high, taking to heaven His full and complete human nature—now glorified and immortal—so that He might be a perfect mediator between God and humanity (1 Tim. 2:5). What an indescribable example of God's awesome power!

Third, *God demonstrated His surpassing power when He put all things in subjection to Christ* (1:21-22). Jesus' position of vast authority over heaven and earth—present and future—was prophesied about by King David long ago in the book of Psalms: "The LORD says to my Lord: 'Sit at My right hand until I make Your enemies a footstool for Your feet'" (Ps. 110:1). Being at the Father's right hand means more than the restoration of the position of glory Christ had prior to His incarnation. It also means having the authority of the fully human heir of David. As the perfect Man who was destined to rule on the throne of David (Luke 1:32), Jesus Christ will "shatter kings in the day of His wrath. He will judge among the nations" (Ps. 110:5-6). Christ is not only exalted above the earthly rulers but is also seated above the heavenly powers—both angelic and demonic (Eph. 1:21; cf. 6:12). What an encouraging picture of God's power granted to our victorious Savior!

Fourth, *God demonstrated His surpassing power when He gave Christ to the church as head over all things* (1:22-23). Christ arose victorious, having conquered sin, death, and the grave. He ascended on high, conquering the limitations of this earthly existence. He took His position in the place of authority over all things in heaven and on earth, things present and future. Yet Paul points out particularly that God placed Christ over the church as its head—governing, shepherding, and leading His mystical body, the fullest manifestation of His work on earth. Think about the amazing benefits this brings to believers, who are incorporated into the church through the baptizing work of the Holy Spirit (1 Cor. 12:12-13)! The ruler who sits on the throne of the universe is also our Brother and our Mediator before the Father (Rom. 8:29; 1 Tim 2:5; Heb. 9:15). Paul's description of the church as the body of Christ is not simply metaphorical imagery. It goes far deeper than that. Because the saints are united to Christ, His work has been applied to them as if they were literally in Him. This is why Paul will later say of believers that God "made us alive together with Christ . . . and raised us up with Him, and seated us with Him in the heavenly places in Christ Jesus" (Eph. 2:5-6). If we are members of His body, we are fully identified with the work of Christ. What an incomprehensible realization of the power of God!

Through praise (1:1-14), thanksgiving (1:15-16), and petition (1:17-23), Paul floods us with wave after wave of profound truths that are difficult to comprehend in full. So vast is the grace of God and so manifold its applications to our lives that we could literally spend a lifetime trying to grasp the depths of these realities.

## APPLICATION: EPHESIANS 1:15-23

### Putting God's Power on Display

We need God's incomparable power. This is an undisputable theological truth. Yet so many Christians live their lives relying on their own wisdom, insight, knowledge, and strength. Though we desperately need God's power given to us through Christ and by the Holy Spirit, we often fail to tap into His infinite might. Why? Because we disconnect ourselves from the one true Source of all things.

We often mistakenly believe we've outgrown the need for God's power. *We can handle these difficult situations on our own, thank you!* We have acquired experience, skill, and training, so we only call upon the Lord when we mess things up and have to awaken to hard, cold reality. To avoid this self-sufficient attitude, we need to remember two things about the power of God, based on Ephesians 1:15-23.

First, *remember that the greatest evidence of power is change.* How can we tell when we're connected to God's power? Even in the physical realm, power produces results. We know something has energy, vitality, and life when we see movement, growth, and development. The same is true in the spiritual realm. When we see the fruit of the Spirit manifested in our lives, we know God is working. God's power works inside our hearts to change us. To better grasp this power, read the following passages and note the power that brings about change in the believer. What is the cause? What are the effects?

Acts 1:8 _____

Romans 15:13 _____

2 Timothy 1:7_____

Second, *remember that God's power is best displayed through our weakness.* Let's face it. Self-made success leads to confidence, confidence breeds pride, and pride ends in a fall. When we begin to believe the lie that we're blessed because we're smarter, stronger, luckier, or more skilled, we will have completely missed the kind of conditions in which God demonstrates His power. Hard as it is to endure it, the most fertile soil for demonstrating God's work in our lives is the thick sod of adversity. Paul himself experienced a nettlesome "thorn in the flesh," a condition that plagued him and weakened him physically (2 Cor. 12:7). Yet this very condition forced him to lean on God's power (2 Cor. 12:9). As a result, the apostle of grace boasted about his weaknesses, knowing that through the cracked and broken vessel of his body, the brilliant light of God's glory could shine through. To connect with God's power, we must admit our own brokenness. Only then is His power able to freely flow through us. To better grasp the concept of God's power made perfect in our weakness, read the following passages and note the effects of God working through human weaknesses.

1 Corinthians 1:26-29 _____

2 Corinthians 12:9 _____

2 Corinthians 13:4 _____

The words of the great preacher Charles Haddon Spurgeon to his congregation sum up the need to seek our strength only in God, who raised Jesus from the dead and seated Him in heaven:

Dear brothers and sisters, go home and never ask the Lord to make you strong in yourselves, never ask Him to make you anybody or anything, but be content to be nothing and nobody. Next ask that His power may have room in you, and that all those who come near you may see what God can do by nothings and nobodies. Live with this desire, to glorify God.[24]

# You Were Dead, but God . . .
## EPHESIANS 2:1-10

**NASB**

[1] And you ªwere dead ᵇin your trespasses and sins, [2] in which you formerly walked according to the ªcourse of this world, according to the prince of the power of the air, of the spirit that is now working in the sons of disobedience. [3] Among them we too all formerly lived in the lusts of our flesh, ªindulging the desires of the flesh and of the ᵇmind, and were by nature children of wrath, even as the rest. [4] But God, being rich in mercy, because of His great love with which He loved us, [5] even when we were dead ªin our transgressions, made us alive together ᵇwith Christ (by grace you have been saved), [6] and raised us up with Him, and seated us with Him in the heavenly *places* in Christ Jesus, [7] so that in the ages to come He might show the surpassing riches of His grace in kindness toward us in Christ Jesus. [8] For by grace you have been saved through faith; and ªthat not of yourselves, *it is* the gift of God; [9] not as a result of works, so that no one may boast.

**NLT**

[1] Once you were dead because of your disobedience and your many sins. [2] You used to live in sin, just like the rest of the world, obeying the devil—the commander of the powers in the unseen world.* He is the spirit at work in the hearts of those who refuse to obey God. [3] All of us used to live that way, following the passionate desires and inclinations of our sinful nature. By our very nature we were subject to God's anger, just like everyone else.

[4] But God is so rich in mercy, and he loved us so much, [5] that even though we were dead because of our sins, he gave us life when he raised Christ from the dead. (It is only by God's grace that you have been saved!) [6] For he raised us from the dead along with Christ and seated us with him in the heavenly realms because we are united with Christ Jesus. [7] So God can point to us in all future ages as examples of the incredible wealth of his grace and kindness toward us, as shown in all he has done for us who are united with Christ Jesus.

[8] God saved you by his grace when you believed. And you can't take credit for this; it is a gift from God. [9] Salvation is not a reward for the good things we have done, so none

NASB

10 For we are His workmanship, created in Christ Jesus for good works, which God prepared beforehand so that we would walk in them.

2:1 ªLit *being*  bOr *by reason of*  2:2 ªLit *age*
2:3 ªLit *doing*  bLit *thoughts*  2:5 ªOr *by reason of*  bTwo early mss read *in Christ*  2:8 ªI.e. that salvation

NLT

of us can boast about it. 10 For we are God's masterpiece. He has created us anew in Christ Jesus, so we can do the good things he planned for us long ago.

2:2 Greek *obeying the commander of the power of the air.*

Some years ago, pastor R. Kent Hughes and a group of high schoolers hiked to the top of Mount Whitney in California, the highest spot in the continental United States at about 14,500 feet. They were all exhilarated by the breathtaking panorama of the Sierra Nevada Mountains and the Mojave Desert below. "What a spot," Hughes exults as he reflects on it today, "with its rarefied crystal-clear air, its indigo and turquoise lakes—vista giving way to vista as far as one could see."[25]

As the group surveyed the world from that pinnacle, one of the teens mentioned that Death Valley, the lowest point in the United States, lay only eighty miles away. Think about that! In fewer than a hundred miles, you could travel from a height of over 14,000 feet to a drop of 282 feet below sea level. Or you could climb from a suffocating 134 degrees in the shade to crisp, cool mountain air in the bright sun. Hughes remarks, "What a contrast! One place is the top of the world, the other the bottom. One place is perpetually cool, the other relentlessly hot. From Mt. Whitney you look down on all of life. From Death Valley you can only look up to the rest of the world."[26]

It's hard to imagine a more extreme contrast, but one does exist—not in the physical world but in the spiritual. In Ephesians 2:1-10, Paul describes the "Death Valley" into which all of us are born (2:1-3), as well as the glorious change of location God has provided through Christ's death and resurrection (2:4-10). Christ has rescued us from the desert of our sinfulness and exalted us to the highest mountain peak of His righteousness!

Get ready to survey this spiritual landscape. Paul's description of the barren state of our souls prior to our salvation will seem overwhelmingly bleak, especially in contrast to the optimistic "I'm okay, you're okay" philosophy that pervades our modern culture. But Paul more than compensates for this dark picture of depravity with the brilliant, majestic image of our salvation by grace through faith.

The content of this crucial passage in Paul's letter to the Ephesians can be outlined by asking four questions:

- What was life like prior to God's gracious intrusion? (2:1-3)
- What did God do for us and why did He do it? (2:4-7)
- How can we receive the gift of salvation? (2:8-9)
- What difference does salvation make in my life? (2:10)

## — 2:1-3 —

Paul first answers the question, "What was life like prior to God's gracious intrusion?" The answer is simple: We were dead, enslaved, and
condemned. Many regard Ephesians 2:1-3 as a classic description of the
doctrine of "total depravity" or "spiritual death." Though outwardly we
looked very much alive, inside we were cut off from true life because
we were severed from God—the Source of life. We were, as it were, buried in our own trespasses and sins (2:1), as a corpse is buried by dirt.
We weren't merely grubby; we were interred! And just like a dead body
resting six feet under, we were completely incapable of extricating ourselves from our grave situation.

Covered by their trespasses and sins, those without Christ found
themselves over their heads in sin. In fact, the unsaved "walked" in
trespasses and sins, following the path set by Satan, the "prince of the
power of the air" (2:2). Where does this zombie-like march through the
valley of death lead them? Into deeper enslavement to the wicked spirit
working among the children characterized by disobedience. So potent
is the power of Satan that he can get people to believe that truth is a lie
and that a lie is the truth. He fills the world with temptations and traps,
and he reigns over his kingdom of darkness like a malevolent dictator
oppressing his powerless victims. Paul includes even himself in this category: "Among [the sons of disobedience] we too all formerly lived" (2:3).
We all lived among the dead, having the exact same nature as they have.

Paul then describes with a triple punch the kind of lifestyle all of us
once experienced (2:3):

- We lived in the lusts of our flesh (emotional depravity).
- We indulged the desires of the flesh (physical depravity).
- We indulged the desires of the mind (rational depravity).

These are not three completely separate things but three aspects of our
human condition as totally depraved, spiritually dead people.

*Emotional Depravity.* When Paul says we once lived in the "lusts of
our flesh," he uses the word *epithymia* [1939], translated "lust," which
is a neutral term that simply means "deep desire" (Mark 4:19; 1 Thes.
2:17). When governed by the flesh, these "deep desires" always lead us

in a downward spiral. Uncontrolled desires and fickle feelings drive those who are wallowing in spiritual death into ever-deeper emotional instability.

*Physical Depravity*. Paul then says that the unsaved sinner had no choice but to indulge the "desires of the flesh." The word "desires" here is the Greek word for "the will"—our decision-making capacity (*thelēma* [2307]). When choices are presented to the lost person, he or she usually makes decisions based on physical, not spiritual, priorities. That's how the old nature thinks. Materialism, physical appearance, external beauty—these things dominate the lives of those walking in spiritual death.

*Rational Depravity*. Finally, Paul mentions the intellectual sphere, the rational capacity of a person. Children of disobedience indulge the desires "of the mind." Not only are their thought lives governed by self-centeredness, but they are also controlled by self-deception, rationalization, confusion, and irrational beliefs. Twisted thinking characterizes those who lack spiritual life from God.

As he continues to describe the horrible condition of fallen humanity, Paul delivers a deathblow to the "we're all fine" philosophy. He sums up the condition of lost people by emphasizing their *nature* and their *end*. They are "by nature children of wrath" (Eph. 2:3). By using the term *physis* [5449], "nature," he refutes anybody who might say, "Well, I'm basically a good person. I just have a few bad habits." He trumps those who claim, "We all have good and bad in us." Rather, all human beings apart from Christ are "essentially and unchangeably bad."[27] Worse than this, our totally corrupt nature results in condemnation. Fallen humans are "children of wrath"—those who are, by default, under the wrath of God (John 3:36; Rom. 1:18).

What a wretched condition! What a tangled knot of heart, body, and mind! What a dreadful, unresolvable destination for all people apart from Christ! If Paul had stopped writing at 2:3, we would have been abandoned to utter despair. The apostle suddenly reverses course, however, with two miraculous words—two of the greatest words in all of Scripture: "But God . . ."

That changes everything!

## — 2:4-7 —

The next question Paul answers for us is, "What did God do for us and why did He do it?" He begins his answer to this question with those two great words: "But God . . ." In the midst of our horrific condition, when we were destined for damnation, already condemned and suffering the effects in our bodies and souls, God accomplished a decisive rescue mission. He sent Jesus Christ—full humanity and undiminished deity—to save sinners from their hopeless plight (John 3:16; Gal. 4:4-5; 1 Tim. 1:15).

While we were dead in our sins—ignorant, unwilling, and unable to change our condition even one degree—God "made us alive together with Christ . . . and raised us up with Him, and seated us with Him in the heavenly places in Christ Jesus" (Eph. 2:5-6)! No wonder this is called the "good news" of Jesus Christ! Grace abounds! His resurrection from the dead and exaltation into heaven have become *ours* by virtue of God's work. No longer are we dead and condemned! Now we're alive and blessed! This is what we call being "born again," made alive in the eyes of God and spiritually incorporated into Christ (John 3:3, 7; 1 Pet. 1:3, 23). Now believers are indwelled by the Holy Spirit, who makes us willing and able to do what was impossible in our spiritually dead state: to believe and to live in a way that's pleasing to God (Phil. 2:12-13).

Note that Paul associates the believer's new position directly with the work of Jesus Christ in His death, resurrection, and exaltation. In fact, what Paul said about Jesus Christ's position in Ephesians 1:20-23, he now applies to believers in a spiritual sense in 2:4-6. Thus, Christ's death to sin, resurrection to righteousness, and exaltation to the right hand of God are *reckoned* to the believer—regarded as applying as fully to the born-again Christian as they do to his or her Savior, Jesus Christ. This reckoning is not simply theoretical. It also anticipates a day "in the ages to come" when all Christians will be resurrected bodily, just as Christ was (2:7).

Charles Wesley's marvelous hymn "And Can It Be" paints a vivid picture of God's miraculous work of spiritual resurrection:

> Long my imprisoned spirit lay
> Fast bound in sin and nature's night.
> Thine eye diffused a quick'ning ray:
> I woke—the dungeon flamed with light!
> My chains fell off, my heart was free,
> I rose, went forth, and followed Thee.[28]

Believers have been made alive together with Christ (2:5). We are no longer spiritually dead; we have been spiritually resurrected, transferred from death to life (John 5:24; Col. 2:13-14). God also raised us up with Christ and seated us in the heavenly places (Eph. 2:6). In anticipation of our future resurrection and glorification, we can already begin to live new lives of righteousness through the work of the Holy Spirit (Gal. 5:16; Phil. 3:20). We are "unchained" . . . our hearts have been freed! Paul is so certain of our future perfection in Christ that he describes this reality as a past event (Eph. 2:6).

This sudden, miraculous turn from death to life brings up the second part of the question answered in these verses: *Why did God do it?* Why would He go to such lengths to rescue dead, condemned, sin-stained, rebellious people? Clearly it had nothing to do with our own merit, worthiness, works, or untapped potential. To answer the "why" question, we need to answer the "who" question.

Ephesians 2:4 begins by describing God as "rich in mercy." The Lord abounds in "great love," which He demonstrated in His saving initiative toward us. His merciful character stayed His hand of justice—getting what we deserve—and exchanged it for grace—getting what we *don't* deserve. Grace is God's unmerited favor unconditionally demonstrated to the undeserving. Notice the parenthetical explanation that puts the entire rescue operation in proper theological perspective: "*by grace* you have been saved" (2:5, emphasis mine). Paul interrupts his normal train of thought from resurrection to exaltation by inserting this clarification, reminding us that none of this comes from ourselves; all of it comes from the merciful, gracious, loving, good hand of God Almighty (2:7).

> We deserved punishment. *By grace* He gave us forgiveness.
> We deserved the consequences of sin. *By grace* He showed us mercy.
> We deserved wrath. *By grace* He gave us relief.
> We deserved hell. *By grace* He has ushered us into heaven.
> We deserved misery. *By grace* He gave us hope.
> We deserved guilt and shame. *By grace* He gave us glory and honor.
> We deserved damnation. *By grace* He gave us deliverance.

I could go on describing the things that we were saved *from* and exulting in the things that we have been saved *to* . . . all of it from start to finish *by God's irresistible grace alone.*

# That Ain't My Job!

## EPHESIANS 2:4-7

There was a time in my early years of ministry when I felt an overwhelming, almost sickening responsibility for a person's response to the gospel. I thought I needed to get out there and beat the bushes—convince, persuade, compel. I needed to arm myself with every apologetic answer to every skeptical question unbelievers could throw at me. I had to be ready to handle every "yeah, but . . ." and every "but what about . . . ?" that came my way. If those things didn't work, I needed to make life miserable for the nonbelievers. Threaten them with hell, remind them of heaven—whatever it took. Then if they still slipped through my tightly woven evangelistic fishnet, I would beat up on myself, replaying the conversation in my mind to see where I went wrong, to figure out what I could have said or could have done better, and to plan a new strategy for next time. I operated somewhere between frustration and exhaustion.

Whew! I was often difficult to be around! I will admit that although my zeal was golden and my goals honorable, my motivation was severely lacking balanced doctrinal knowledge.

You see, as I let Scripture inform my view of God's sovereign grace, the convicting work of the Holy Spirit, and His spiritual resurrection of the "living dead," I came to realize something vital about the new birth in Christ: That ain't my job! I am responsible to proclaim the gospel, share the truth in love, preach the Word, be ready in season and out of season, introduce Christ, give my testimony, and invite unbelievers to accept Christ as their Savior . . . but that's where my responsibility ends. At that point I need to step back and say, "He's all Yours, Lord."

It took awhile for me to learn an important truth about evangelism: Even though I exhaust my miniscule persuasive powers rather quickly, God has never met His match. Just keep praying for your friend who's running wild. Surrender your wayward children

(continued on next page)

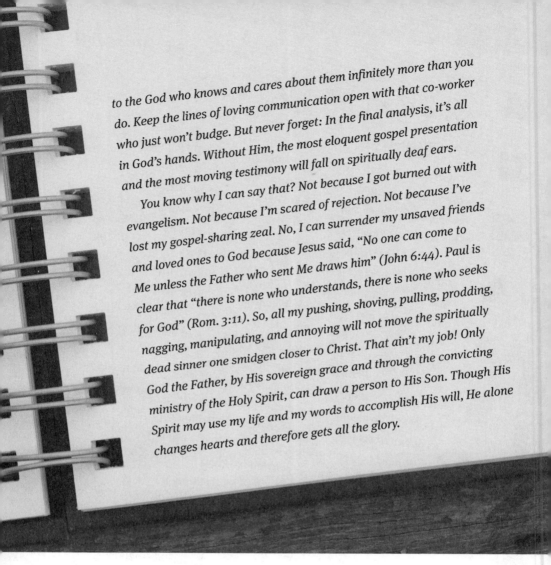

to the God who knows and cares about them infinitely more than you do. Keep the lines of loving communication open with that co-worker who just won't budge. But never forget: In the final analysis, it's all in God's hands. Without Him, the most eloquent gospel presentation and the most moving testimony will fall on spiritually deaf ears.

You know why I can say that? Not because I got burned out with evangelism. Not because I'm scared of rejection. Not because I've lost my gospel-sharing zeal. No, I can surrender my unsaved friends and loved ones to God because Jesus said, "No one can come to Me unless the Father who sent Me draws him" (John 6:44). Paul is clear that "there is none who understands, there is none who seeks for God" (Rom. 3:11). So, all my pushing, shoving, pulling, prodding, nagging, manipulating, and annoying will not move the spiritually dead sinner one smidgen closer to Christ. That ain't my job! Only God the Father, by His sovereign grace and through the convicting ministry of the Holy Spirit, can draw a person to His Son. Though His Spirit may use my life and my words to accomplish His will, He alone changes hearts and therefore gets all the glory.

## — 2:8-9 —

Paul then answers a third important question for his readers: "How can we receive the gift of salvation?" He has painted a vivid picture of the stunning contrasts between darkness and light, damnation and salvation, death and resurrection. Now, in one of the clearest passages on salvation by grace through faith in the entire Bible, Paul describes the *means* by which one receives this incomparable gift of new life.

Paul begins this explanation by repeating—word for word—the parenthetical insertion from 2:5: "By grace you have been saved." Grace is the basis for everything God has done for us. Grace motivated the Father to choose us in Christ before the foundation of the world (1:4-6). Grace provided the one-time payment for eternal redemption—the blood of Christ, who came to earth and died for the forgiveness of our sins (1:7). And by grace alone we receive this forgiveness and salvation—grace apart from any merit of our own (2:8-9).

Though grace is the *objective basis* for our salvation, Paul also mentions an equally important *subjective means* of receiving this grace: faith. We are saved *by grace*, but we appropriate this grace *through faith.* "Faith" simply means trust, reliance, or dependence upon someone or something. In the case of eternal salvation, faith is wholehearted acceptance of the fact that what God says is true, trusting that the gift of salvation will be exactly as He has promised. Of course, faith unto salvation is not simply believing in *anything.* Biblical faith always has specific content—facts we *know* as well as truth we personally *accept.* Paul sums up the truth of the gospel best in 1 Corinthians 15:1-5:

> Now I make known to you, brethren, the gospel which I preached to you, which also you received, in which also you stand, by which also you are saved, if you hold fast the word which I preached to you, unless you believed in vain. For I delivered to you as of first importance what I also received, that Christ died for our sins according to the Scriptures, and that He was buried, and that He was raised on the third day according to the Scriptures, and that He appeared to Cephas, then to the twelve.

The grace of salvation is received when God opens our blind eyes to this gospel, enabling us to understand its claims and to accept its promise of forgiveness for all who believe. When the shroud of death is lifted from our hearts, our minds are illumined to have faith in Christ's death for our sins and His resurrection from the dead. This faith—apart from any works—is then the sole means of entering into an eternal relationship with the Father though Jesus Christ the Son by the regenerating (life-giving) work of the Holy Spirit.

Just to avoid any potential confusion, Paul excludes even a trace of works that could merit or contribute in any way to our salvation. Commentators have often debated what "that" refers to in the phrase "and *that* not of yourselves, it is the gift of God" (Eph. 2:8). Some have suggested that the word refers to "faith," regarding faith itself as the gift that God gives. Others believe "grace" is the gift to which Paul refers.[29] Both of these views, however, run into a serious grammatical problem in the Greek text. Both "faith" and "grace" are feminine nouns, while "that" in 2:8 is a neuter pronoun. In Greek, the pronoun must agree in gender with the noun to which it refers. So, when Paul writes, "and *that* not of yourselves," we can't find a single word as the referent in the text.

New Testament scholar Harold Hoehner solves the problem when he suggests that the pronoun "refers back to the preceding section . . . to 2:4-8a and more specifically 2:8a, the concept of salvation by grace through faith."[30] That is, the entire salvation package is "not of yourselves," but is "the gift of God" (2:8). Paul further specifies what he means by "not of yourselves": This salvation gift is "not as a result of works, so that no one may boast" (2:9). Simply put, God initiated our salvation, He implemented it, and He receives all the glory for it. In contrast, we could do nothing to start it, cannot contribute anything to it, and therefore can take no credit for it.

## — 2:10 —

Finally, Paul ends this first section of his letter by answering the practical question, "What difference does salvation make in my life?" He addresses this in a commonly overlooked verse, Ephesians 2:10. We are God's "workmanship." In other words, we are His masterpiece. But unlike statues or paintings that simply adorn the halls of museums, we're designed for action. God has good works for us to do that He "prepared beforehand"—before we were even born. His plan for our lives does not end when we believe the message of the gospel and receive eternal salvation by grace through faith apart from works. Rather, this experience simply marks the beginning of our Christian life as new creatures "in Christ Jesus" (2:10). His plan extends beyond salvation to sanctification, beyond standing in grace to walking in good deeds.

Therefore, the good works mentioned in 2:10 have nothing to do with earning salvation. Paul clearly ruled that scenario out in 2:9 when he emphasized that we are *not* saved "as a result of works." The Greek word for "works" (*ergon* [2041]) is exactly the same in both verses, so the difference is not in the works, but in what they accomplish and where they come from. In 2:9, Paul refers to works "of yourselves" (2:8), works done in our own strength prior to salvation with the express intention of trying to save ourselves or to contribute something to God's grace. This is absolutely impossible. Ephesians 2:10, on the other hand, refers to the good works of those who are already born-again believers in Christ and who are now empowered by the Spirit to determine and then do things that please God (Phil. 2:13).

Since all of this—from first to last—is God's work, He deserves all the credit. Unfortunately, many Christians want to claim a portion of the responsibility for their salvation. They believe that God makes a free offer, but that we must exercise our own initiative and believe by our own power, or receive it by some action like prayer, repentance, baptism, or joining some local church. Or they believe that once a person has been saved, they must continue to perform up to par in order to *stay* saved. These approaches mirror the world's tendency to exalt human effort. Such thinking resists the truth that in and of ourselves we are utterly helpless; we need a sovereign Savior who can save us in spite of ourselves. Until we finally give up any notion of entitlement, contribution, or partnership in salvation, we will never truly appreciate the work that Christ has done for us—and is doing in us.

# APPLICATION: EPHESIANS 2:1-10
## Giving Credit to the Artist

Museums are filled with room after room of paintings, statues, and other works of creativity and beauty. Usually beside or beneath each work of art, a small sign gives the name of the artist, the title of the piece, its date of production, and the materials used to produce it. Every art connoisseur knows that the most important piece of information on that sign is the name of the artist. Nobody exclaims, "That's on canvas!" or "That's from 1870!" But you'll hear countless voices whispering in awe, "That's a Rembrandt!" or "That's a Picasso!"

Ephesians 2:1-10 describes how the divine Artist took broken materials (2:1-3) and began an ongoing process of producing a glorious work of art (2:4-10). It began with a miraculous resurrection from spiritual death (2:5-6) and will culminate in the ultimate display of the riches of His grace in the coming ages (2:7). In the meantime, God's work of redemption in our lives is meant to bring Him glory and honor through our good works, enabled and motivated by His grace (2:10). In fact, Jesus said, "Let your light shine before men in such a way that they may see your good works, and glorify your Father who is in heaven" (Matt. 5:16).

However, with these good works on display, it's tempting to try to take the credit for them ourselves. But we must resist that temptation. Paul stated that God "made us alive" by His grace (Eph. 2:5) and that we "are His workmanship" (2:10). Having been made alive by Christ,

His life now flows through us by the Holy Spirit and streams out in our good works. By keeping this truth at the forefront of our minds, we will be protected from becoming prideful in our service.

Because our good works are a result of God's work, we are His workmanship. He's the artist; we're the medium through which He displays His glory. Yet our human tendency is to exalt the man or woman who does the good work rather than praise and honor the great Artist who does the good work through us.

To help fend off the temptation of self-exaltation, read, study, meditate on, and memorize the following passages that reinforce this easy-to-forget truth.

\_\_\_\_\_ John 15:5

\_\_\_\_\_ Matthew 5:16

\_\_\_\_\_ 2 Corinthians 3:5

\_\_\_\_\_ 2 Corinthians 4:7

\_\_\_\_\_ Philippians 2:12-13

We are God's workmanship—His masterpiece—and the beauty of the artwork testifies to the skill of the Artist. God's work in us should bring Him thanks, praise, and honor. And it should turn the attention of others to Him, not to us.

# RECONCILIATION AND PEACE: THE RESULTS OF GOD'S GRACE (EPHESIANS 2:11–3:21)

Before we're able to walk or talk, we learn the universal law of cause and effect. When we cry, Mommy feeds us. When we turn that lever, Jack jumps out of the box. If we hit our sister, we get punished. If we make good grades in school, we are rewarded. Eventually, we even learn a fancy articulation of that intuitive principle: "For every action, there is an equal and opposite reaction." Day by day, the rule of cause and effect governs the entire physical universe.

The same holds true in theology. Everything God does in His plan of redemption accomplishes something. God's sovereign grace described in Ephesians 1:1–2:10 involves mighty acts of redemption. Jesus of Nazareth died for the sins of humanity and rose miraculously and bodily from the grave. Having provided everything necessary for salvation, He was taken up to heaven and seated at the right hand of God. By God's grace through faith alone, believers are united to Christ in His death and resurrection. We experience a spiritual rebirth, through which we are empowered to live lives that are pleasing to God (2:8-10). These weighty truths form the solid foundation of the Christian faith.

Paul continues to explain the cause-and-effect relationships of these foundational saving works of the triune God in Ephesians 2:11–3:21. In this section we see more effects of God's grace. So profound are these results that they mark an epochal change in God's plan of redemption— as pronounced as the difference between the Old Testament and the New. I've titled this second section of Ephesians "Reconciliation and Peace: The Results of God's Grace (Ephesians 2:11–3:21)." In this section, Paul describes the reconciliation that has occurred between Jews and Gentiles as well as between sinners and a righteous God (2:11-22). The effect of this reconciliation is peace in the newly constituted body of Christ, the church (2:15-16). This church age—foreseen only mysteriously through hints and images in the Old Testament—has now been fully revealed in the New Testament through the apostles and the prophets (3:1-13). Ultimately, such a surprising and exciting truth leads Paul to jubilant prayer and praise to God (3:14-21).

My hope is that these truths will have the same effect on you and me.

---

## KEY TERMS IN EPHESIANS 2:11–3:21

*doxa* (δόξα) [1391] "glory," "honor"
In the Greek translation of the Old Testament, God's *doxa* sometimes refers to a physical manifestation of His holy, righteous, transcendent essence (Exod. 16:7). It can also refer to His splendor and renown. The prophet Isaiah described a vision in which seraphim proclaimed that God's glory fills the whole world (Isa. 6:3)—that is, His awesome attributes are reflected in the greatness of His creation. For Paul, God's glory is the ultimate goal and end of all things (Eph. 3:21).

*xenoi kai paroikoi* (ξένοι καὶ πάροικοι) [3581, 3941]
   "strangers and aliens"
Paul uses this pair of terms to describe the Gentiles who were separated from God prior to salvation in Christ (2:19). From the term *xenoi* we get the English word "xenophobia," the fear of those who are different from us. The second term, *paroikoi*, refers to those who are noncitizens, foreigners, or nonrelatives of a family. Together the terms serve to emphasize the condition of exclusion the Gentiles experienced when they lived in unbelief.

---

# Destroying the Wall to Build the Temple
## EPHESIANS 2:11-22

**NASB**

11 Therefore remember that formerly you, the Gentiles in the flesh, who are called "Uncircumcision" by the so-called "Circumcision," *which is* performed in the flesh by human hands— 12 *remember* that you were at that time separate from Christ, ªexcluded from the commonwealth of Israel, and strangers to the covenants of promise, having no hope and without God in the world. 13 But

**NLT**

11 Don't forget that you Gentiles used to be outsiders. You were called "uncircumcised heathens" by the Jews, who were proud of their circumcision, even though it affected only their bodies and not their hearts. 12 In those days you were living apart from Christ. You were excluded from citizenship among the people of Israel, and you did not know the covenant promises God had made to them. You lived in this world without God and without hope. 13 But now you

now in Christ Jesus you who formerly were far off [a]have been brought near [b]by the blood of Christ. [14]For He Himself is our peace, who made both *groups into* one and broke down the [a]barrier of the dividing wall, [15][a]by abolishing in His flesh the enmity, *which is* the Law of commandments *contained* in ordinances, so that in Himself He might [b]make the two into one new man, *thus* establishing peace, [16]and might reconcile them both in one body to God through the cross, [a]by it having put to death the enmity. [17]AND HE CAME AND PREACHED PEACE TO YOU WHO WERE FAR AWAY, AND PEACE TO THOSE WHO WERE NEAR; [18]for through Him we both have our access in one Spirit to the Father. [19]So then you are no longer strangers and aliens, but you are fellow citizens with the [a]saints, and are of God's household, [20]having been built on the foundation of the apostles and prophets, Christ Jesus Himself being the corner *stone,* [21]in whom the whole building, being fitted together, is growing into a holy [a]temple in the Lord, [22]in whom you also are being built together into a dwelling of God in the Spirit.

2:12 [a]Or *alienated*  2:13 [a]Lit *became; or were made*  [b]Or *in*  2:14 [a]Lit *the dividing wall of the barrier*  2:15 [a]Or *the enmity, by abolishing in His flesh the Law*  [b]Lit *create*  2:16 [a]Or *in Himself*  2:19 [a]Or *holy ones*  2:21 [a]Or *sanctuary*

have been united with Christ Jesus. Once you were far away from God, but now you have been brought near to him through the blood of Christ.

[14]For Christ himself has brought peace to us. He united Jews and Gentiles into one people when, in his own body on the cross, he broke down the wall of hostility that separated us. [15]He did this by ending the system of law with its commandments and regulations. He made peace between Jews and Gentiles by creating in himself one new people from the two groups. [16]Together as one body, Christ reconciled both groups to God by means of his death on the cross, and our hostility toward each other was put to death.

[17]He brought this Good News of peace to you Gentiles who were far away from him, and peace to the Jews who were near. [18]Now all of us can come to the Father through the same Holy Spirit because of what Christ has done for us.

[19]So now you Gentiles are no longer strangers and foreigners. You are citizens along with all of God's holy people. You are members of God's family. [20]Together, we are his house, built on the foundation of the apostles and the prophets. And the cornerstone is Christ Jesus himself. [21]We are carefully joined together in him, becoming a holy temple for the Lord. [22]Through him you Gentiles are also being made part of this dwelling where God lives by his Spirit.

For nearly half a century, the Iron Curtain split Europe into east and west. The separation was physical, political, and spiritual. Physically, a heavily militarized border cut like an ugly, jagged scar from the Baltic Sea in the north to the Adriatic Sea in the south. Politically, it separated the Communist east from the capitalist west, a division epitomized by the infamous Berlin Wall splitting East Berlin and West Berlin. Spiritually, the Iron Curtain served as a seemingly impenetrable barrier to the gospel, blocking the atheistic Communist nations from the encroaching influence of Christianity.

From 1945 to 1989, the Iron Curtain separated families, friends, nations, and languages, resulting in enmity, animosity, distrust, and fear. Yet in 1989, a minor miracle occurred. Just two years after US president Ronald Reagan stood before the Berlin Wall and challenged his Soviet counterpart, Mikhail Gorbachev, to "tear down this wall," citizens from both East and West Berlin were permitted to demolish the barrier and reunite the once-divided people. Amidst tears of joy and days of celebration, the Iron Curtain was lifted from Germany, marking the beginning of a new era in modern European history.

As much as the fall of the Berlin Wall made an unforgettable mark on the men and women who witnessed it, this historic event can't compare to the epochal moment when Jesus Christ tore down another wall—one that had separated humanity for centuries. Though this wall had been meant to preserve God's Jewish people from moral and spiritual corruption as they represented their God before the nations, it quickly became a divider that alienated the Gentiles, who were meant to receive God's blessing through the Jewish nation (Gen. 26:4). The Law of Moses and the sacrificial system had marked God's path of holy living for the Jews. Yet Gentiles stood outside the gate, aliens to the promises, foreigners to the covenants, and dejected outcasts from the knowledge of God. All of that changed when Christ tore down the wall (Eph. 2:14) and began building a new temple (2:21-22).

In the first part of his letter to the Ephesians, Paul sharply contrasted our former lives as unbelievers, once *dead* in trespasses and sins (2:1), with our new lives as those *made alive* together with Christ (2:4-5). Now Paul turns to another contrast—between the Gentile and the Jew. This time, however, he describes in vivid language how the deep gulf that had once separated these two peoples has been bridged by the finished work of Jesus Christ. Upon this new, level foundation of equality, a new temple, the church, is being built.

## — 2:11-12 —

Paul begins by describing the *common plight* of the "Uncircumcision"—the condition all Gentiles experienced prior to their conversion to Jesus Christ (at least from the perspective of the "Circumcision," those Jews marked by the physical sign of the old covenant). Verses 11 and 12 describe the lives of the Gentiles before the reconciling work of the Cross. Notice the words Paul uses to describe the Gentiles' former relationship to God and His promises: "separate," "excluded," "strangers," "having no hope," "without God." Paul identifies five aspects of the alienation his Gentile readers experienced prior to their salvation.

*Christless.* Gentiles in the first century had no thought of the Messiah. Only the Jews had hoped for a Savior, foreshadowed first in Genesis 3:15. The Jews knew He would come from among their people (2 Sam. 7:13, 16; Isa. 9:1-7), so they looked forward to the coming Son of David who would save them from their sins. The Gentiles, however, had no claim on the coming, anointed King.

*Stateless.* Being "excluded from the commonwealth of Israel" (Eph. 2:12), the Gentiles had no rights of citizenship in God's chosen nation. As the only true theocracy on earth, Israel's ultimate King was God Himself. He ruled His people through His covenants, laws, prophets, priests, and kings. The Gentiles were foreigners to God's nation.

*Friendless.* When God established His covenant with Abraham (Gen. 12:1-3; 15:18-21; 17:1-8), that patriarch of the Hebrew people was called God's "friend" (2 Chr. 20:7; Jas. 2:23). As heirs of God's covenant promises, the descendants of Abraham also enjoyed that special friendship with God. Through the land covenant (Deut. 28–30), the Davidic covenant (2 Sam. 7:8-16; Ps. 89), and the promise of the new covenant (Jer. 31:31-34; Ezek. 36:22-30), God unfolded this special relationship with the Jewish people. Gentiles, strangers to the promises of God, had no part in these covenants.

*Hopeless.* With no Savior, no home, and no promises, the Gentiles had no meaningful future. Because the promises rested with the Jewish Messiah, they couldn't expect their situation to improve—either in this life or in the life to come. They were faced with the same conclusion that Satan faced in Milton's *Paradise Lost*: "Thus repuls'd, our final hope is flat despair."[1]

*Godless.* Though the Gentiles honored and worshiped many gods, none of those lifeless gods could save them from their hopeless condition of spiritual death. Only the living God of Israel could give them what they really needed—life from the dead!

## — 2:13-14 —

Like a tidal wave smashing against an immovable cliff, the unrelenting waves of hopeless despair are broken on the second of Paul's famous contrasts: "But now" (2:13). Having described the Gentiles' common plight before coming to Christ, Paul reveals the *cure*: the Cross of Jesus Christ.

Christ first brought the far-off Gentiles near to Him (2:13). He made it possible for the hopeless and helpless of every age—from the first century to the twenty-first and beyond—to approach Him through faith. By the blood of Jesus Christ—*His death in our place*—God has provided our means of reconciliation. Consider the numerous "but nows" we experience through Christ:

- We were once Christless, but now we are "in Christ Jesus."
- We were once stateless, but now we are full citizens.
- We were once friendless, but now we are members of God's family.
- We were once hopeless, but now we are promised a glorious future.
- We were once godless, but now we can call God our Father.

In short, when Jesus Christ paid the penalty for the sins of all humanity—Jews and Gentiles alike—*the wall of separation crumbled.* As Paul had written to the Galatians, "There is neither Jew nor Greek, there is neither slave nor free man, there is neither male nor female; for you are all one in Christ Jesus" (Gal. 3:28).

Christ Himself—and Christ *alone*—is our peace (Eph. 2:14). The Greek text places a strong emphasis on "Himself," reminding us, as Paul has throughout this letter, that our new life has been given to us as a gracious gift provided *by Christ's work alone*. He has bestowed this gift upon us *by grace alone through faith alone*. What a glorious truth! Christ alone is peace personified. Centuries earlier, Isaiah prophesied that the promised child born of the family of David would be called "Prince of Peace" (Isa. 9:6). Through the baptism of the Holy Spirit, every believer shares a common union of peace with each other: whether Jew or Gentile; male or female; black, white, Asian, or Hispanic; rich or poor; educated or uneducated; strong or weak. The racial, ethnic, political, social, and economic dividers that cause so much conflict in our world fade into insignificance when the Son of God brings spiritual peace.

Paul mentions the "barrier of the dividing wall" broken down by Christ. He likely had in mind the dividing wall that separated Jews from Gentiles in the massive temple complex constructed by Herod in the first century BC. The Gentiles could look at the temple from afar, but prejudicial customs, strict temple laws, thick walls, and stern notices prevented non-Jews from getting any closer. So when Paul said that Christ's death broke down the dividing wall, he meant that the covenant of the Law that formed the basis of such cultural and religious distinctions was no longer in force.

## THE GREAT DIVIDE

### EPHESIANS 2:14

Herod's temple had several courts allowing different levels of access. Only the high priest could enter the innermost Holy of Holies, and this could only happen on the Day of Atonement. Outside that most holy place, the Levites on duty for daily worship operated in "the Holy Place" within the temple. Just outside the temple building, surrounding it, was the Court of Priests, where the altar for burnt offerings stood. Male Jews had access to the adjacent Court of Israel, but Jewish women were limited to the Court of Women. Finally, the Court of the Gentiles was farthest away from the temple, preventing non-Jews from coming close to the temple structure itself. The Gentiles could look up at the temple, but that was as close as they could get. A thick stone barrier called the "wall of separation" represented the great divide between Jews and Gentiles.

In his *The Jewish War*, the first-century Jewish historian Josephus describes the wall separating the Court of the Gentiles from the inner courts of the temple:

> When you go through these [first] cloisters, to the second [court of the] temple, there was a partition made of stone all around, whose height was three cubits: its construction was very elegant; upon it stood pillars, at equal distances from one another, declaring the law of purity, some in Greek, and some in Roman letters, that "no foreigner should go within that sanctuary"; for that second [court of the] temple was called "the Sanctuary."[2]

In fact, in the last century archaeologists discovered two stone inscriptions—warning signs in Greek that once stood prominently in the wall of separation. The text reads, "No foreigner may enter within the barrier and enclosure round the temple. Anyone who is caught doing so will have himself to blame for his ensuing death."[3]

Todd Bolen/BiblePlaces.com

**Warning inscription** from the wall of separation

In Christ, the separation between Jew and Gentile has been rendered obsolete!

## — 2:15-16 —

Christ's sacrificial death on the cross abolished "the enmity." The term *echthra* [2189], "enmity," indicates the opposite of friendship. This is illustrated in Luke 23:12: Herod and Pilate had once been "enemies" (*en echthra*), but during their cooperation in the prosecution of Jesus, they became friends. In Ephesians 2, Paul defines "the enmity" as "the Law of commandments contained in ordinances" (2:15). In fact, the cross of Jesus Christ has put this enmity to death (2:16).

Broken down . . . abolished . . . put to death—these are the terms Paul uses to describe the Old Testament Law of Moses. In his letter to the Colossians, Paul uses similar terms: "canceled out the certificate of debt," "taken it out of the way," "nailed it to the cross" (Col. 2:14). All of the laws, commandments, ordinances, rules, and regulations that had both condemned us before God and separated us from His people have been done away with. No wonder Paul can confidently proclaim in Romans 10:4 that "Christ is the end of the law for righteousness to everyone who believes." I'm constantly amazed at the number of Christians who try to defend the continued validity of the Law as a rule of life today, even in light of such explicit statements as Ephesians 2:14-16. Though we are under the "law of Christ," empowered to live like Him by the Spirit (Gal. 5:16; 6:2), we are not obligated to keep the Law of Moses.

Paul doesn't merely point out what the Cross has negatively accomplished by destroying the old religious system of the Law. He emphasizes what has positively taken place by the reconciling work of Christ. Having broken down the wall that had separated Jews and Gentiles, God now calls members of both groups into the church, which is a new work, completely distinct from Israel. He describes the church, the body of Christ, as "one new man" (Eph. 2:15). Put another way, Jesus didn't "Greekify" Jews or "Jewify" Greeks. Nor did He create a hybrid people called "Grews" or "Jeeks." Rather, Paul explicitly states that God made "one new man" from the two groups, and that one new man is the church, the body of Christ. In this way, unity has been accomplished and peace has been established.

## — 2:17-22 —

Thus far Paul has reminded us of the Gentiles' *common plight* of alienation and enmity (Eph. 2:11-12) and described the *cure* of reconciliation in the body of Christ (2:13-16). Now he concludes this section by explaining the *peace between* Jews and Gentiles based on their shared calling (2:17-19) and describing their *new dwelling* together in one community of the Spirit (2:20-22).

As Paul continues to explain this new unity we have in Christ, he identifies ways in which God's people would change as a result of the demolition of the dividing wall and the building of a new structure. All of these changes center on a profound theological truth called "reconciliation." Having been reconciled to God, both Jews and Gentiles are also reconciled to each other.

How did Jesus reconcile God's chosen community (the Jews) with those outside of it (the Gentiles)? By embodying and proclaiming peace. We have already seen that through His death on the cross, Christ has established the theological basis for peace (2:15). Practically, this peace is made real in our lives through the proclamation of peace (2:17). With the means of salvation in place, the message of salvation can be proclaimed and offered to both Jews and Gentiles.

In 2:17, Paul applies Isaiah 57:19 to the present proclamation of the gospel. Both personally and through His apostles, Christ preached peace both to those who were "far away" (the Gentiles) and those who were "near" (the Jews). Notice that both groups—Jews and Gentiles—must hear and respond to the gospel in order to be reconciled to God and to each other. Though the Jews were "near" in the sense of having heard the prophecies, heeded the Scriptures, and anticipated the fulfillment of the promises, these alone were not enough to save them. Like everybody else, they needed to trust in Christ alone by faith alone for their salvation.

I see in this an important application for us today. Many men and women are raised in Christian homes, exposed to the Scriptures, and surrounded by the gospel. They all fall under the same category as Jews who were "near" to Christ in the sense of being in close proximity to the truth, but they nevertheless must accept the gospel for themselves and enter into the faith—just like the lifelong sinner who has had no exposure to the things of Christ. Even though my four children were raised in the midst of full-time Christian ministry and breathed the air of Christian truth that was constantly taught, preached, and lived, each one of them had to embrace that faith personally. Nobody can be "grandfathered into" the church, and none of us receive the Holy Spirit by passive osmosis. Each of us must trust Christ for himself or herself, thus receiving the Spirit by faith. It's true for my family, it's true for yours, it's true for all.

In addition to being reconciled with God and with each other, all those who believe in Christ have become part of one new humanity at peace with God. What does this peace actually look like on a daily basis? Paul describes four things we all share because of our new relationship with one another.

First, *our new relationship of peace manifests itself in equal and unhindered access to the Father by the Spirit* (2:18). This may not seem like an important development to those of us who have known common access to God for nearly two thousand years. In Paul's day, however, this was an earthshaking change for both Jews and Gentiles. Jews could only access God through their high priest, who entered God's presence once a year on the Day of Atonement (Lev. 16). Gentiles could only have access to God by converting to Judaism, receiving circumcision, and following the Law like the rest of the Jews.

Yet Christ's death tore the curtain in the temple in two from top to bottom (Matt. 27:50-51), demonstrating that in Christ all believers have direct access to God. This is not because of anything we have done or any righteousness on our part, but because of our adoption as God's children and the abiding presence of the Holy Spirit. Again we see the work of the triune God in the plan of reconciliation—we have access to God the Father through the empowerment of the Holy Spirit because of the work of Christ. Now we can come freely and directly to God in prayer for all our needs. No more priests, no more complex rituals, no more fear that we might be consumed by His holy wrath. Rather, we have a common access to God's presence that is free and complete, granted to all who believe.

Second, Paul explains that *the peace we have in Christ confers on us a citizenship among the saints* (2:19). The Gentiles had once been foreigners who had no rights or privileges among the people of God. In Christ, they became "fellow citizens with the saints." Stop and think about that. In some contexts, "the saints" refers to all true believers in Christ (e.g., 1:1). In this context, though, Paul is referring specifically to Old Testament saints—those with whom Gentiles formerly had nothing in common. Now, though, as saints themselves, Gentile believers are on an equal standing with the great patriarchs and prophets of old—Abraham, Moses, Joshua, David, Elijah . . . They're in great company!

Third, Paul tells us that *we now relate to each other as a family, as fellow members of "God's household"* (2:19). In the New Testament, the "household" referred to all those living under the same roof, so to speak. It often included more than what we call the "nuclear family." It might include parents, children, grandparents, grown sons with their

# *Living as an Alien*

**EPHESIANS 2:17-22**

Over the course of my life and ministry, I've had the privilege of traveling to some amazing parts of the world—from New England to California, from the Holy Land to the lands of the European Reformation, from Australia to Austria. All of these places have shown me the common human joys and struggles that transcend borders, languages, and cultures. After many years of traveling, I've learned how to cope with jet lag, how to pack wisely, and how not to offend too many people in the process.

At the beginning of my life, however, when I still thought of my parents' house as "home," traveling to foreign lands posed some interesting challenges. If you've ever traveled or lived overseas, you understand. Those first few steps in a foreign land teach you immediately what it means to be an "alien," a "foreigner." If you happen to wander from the typical tourist path into the authentic trails and towns of a different country, you realize quickly that you are the stranger, often viewed with suspicion, unease, distrust . . . perhaps even dislike.

I'll never forget the day when this reality was drilled into me as a young Marine. Our troopship was several miles from the dock of Yokohama, Japan. We were preparing to go ashore for the first time. Our company commander, in full uniform—which included several rows of medals—stood before us to give this group of young Americans some much-needed advice. Some of us were fresh out of training; the majority had never set foot outside our own borders.

He looked us up and down and probably saw himself standing in the same position decades earlier, needing the same kind of pep talk he was about to give to us. He said, "For the first time in your life, you are the foreigners. You are the strangers. Remember this: You must treat these great people with utmost respect. I don't want to hear

*(continued on next page)*

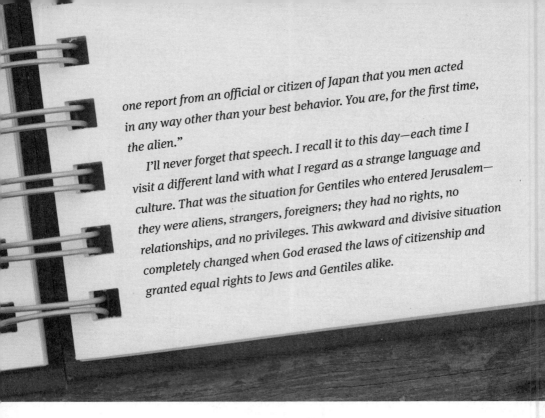

*one report from an official or citizen of Japan that you men acted in any way other than your best behavior. You are, for the first time, the alien."*

*I'll never forget that speech. I recall it to this day—each time I visit a different land with what I regard as a strange language and culture. That was the situation for Gentiles who entered Jerusalem— they were aliens, strangers, foreigners; they had no rights, no relationships, and no privileges. This awkward and divisive situation completely changed when God erased the laws of citizenship and granted equal rights to Jews and Gentiles alike.*

own wives and children, even aunts and uncles. In other words, it included the "extended family." This is a great picture of the new family of God, united under one Father through the person of Jesus Christ and held together by the bond of the Holy Spirit.

Though all of us know that most families deal with some level of dysfunction, the church family should strive to live together as loving brothers and sisters in Christ, regardless of the differences in our racial, social, economic, and cultural backgrounds. This kind of community life brings great benefits to everyone. It provides us with a caring network of support that goes beyond that of friends and neighbors. It gives us a place for mutual accountability and growth. It gives us an opportunity to exercise our spiritual gifts for the benefit of all. And it also provides a beautiful example of love for those outside the Christian faith looking in.

Finally, Paul reveals that *Jews and Gentiles today have a common faith* (2:20-22). Paul uses the image of a temple building to describe the Christian faith community into which both Jews and Gentiles are welcome. The foundation of the building consists of the teachings of the New Testament apostles and prophets, with the person and work of Jesus Christ Himself as the cornerstone of the whole structure. In the

# EXCURSUS: ARE THERE APOSTLES AND PROPHETS TODAY?

## EPHESIANS 2:20

From time to time I come across preachers or teachers who claim to be "apostles" or "prophets." Most often they are using those titles in their most general senses. Missionaries may use the term "apostle" as "one who is sent" or preachers may use "prophet" as either "one who proclaims a message" or "one who stands alone and firm" as the ancient prophets did. Aside from being confused about the Bible's own specific usage of these terms, those "apostles" and "prophets" are harmless. But occasionally the self-styled "apostle" or "prophet" claims to be the same kind of apostle or prophet we see in the New Testament, upon whom the church must be built (2:20).

Is this possible? Can there be genuine apostles and prophets today?

When we submit our understanding to the Word of God and the testimony of the early church, it becomes clear that the foundational offices of apostle and prophet were only for the first-century church period. According to Scripture, "God has appointed in the church, first apostles, second prophets" (1 Cor. 12:28), indicating that these roles came first in sequence as the foundational offices of the church. Also, Paul noted that the marks of an authentic apostle included having "seen Jesus our Lord" (1 Cor. 9:1). In 1 Corinthians 15:6-8, when Paul lists the eyewitnesses of the resurrected Jesus, he indicates that Christ appeared to James and "then to all the apostles," Paul himself being "last of all." As the last apostle to have been personally called by Christ, Paul likened himself to "one untimely born" (1 Cor. 15:8).

Another essential sign of "a true apostle" was the ability to perform authenticating "signs and wonders and miracles" (2 Cor. 12:12). The function of signs and wonders to legitimize the original apostles' message is confirmed in Hebrews 2:3-4, where the author writes, "After [the gospel] was at the first spoken through the Lord, it was confirmed to us by those who heard, God also testifying with them, both by signs and wonders and by various miracles and by gifts of the Holy Spirit according to His own will." Likewise, Mark 16:20 agrees that the disciples of the Lord "went out and preached everywhere, while the Lord worked with them, and confirmed the word by the signs that followed."

But isn't it possible that God continued this foundational apostolic ministry beyond the first century? Wouldn't it make more sense if God continued to call apostles and prophets, confirm His message with signs and wonders, and broaden the foundation of the church in future generations? Interestingly, when we turn to the earliest generation of Christians after the original apostles and prophets, we see that those original disciples of the apostles and prophets referred to those offices as foundational ministries of the church that had ceased.[4] This is especially important when we consider how the early church determined whether a particular Christian writing should be regarded as Scripture. The mid-second-century Muratorian Canon wisely denied the inspiration of a book entitled *The Shepherd of Hermas* based on the fact that it was written *after* the time of the apostles: "It cannot be read publicly to the people in church either among the Prophets *whose number is complete*, or among the Apostles, *for it is after their time*" (emphasis mine).[5]

So, both the Bible and the reliable records of the earliest church after the apostles demonstrate that there was a fixed

(continued on next page)

number of New Testament apostles and prophets, limited to the first generation of the church. Their teachings concerning the crucified and risen Lord, as well as their writings, were foundational for the church. When their lives on earth came to an end, so did their offices. Today their doctrines are preserved in Scripture and taught by their successors—evangelists, pastors, and teachers throughout church history (Eph. 4:11). Therefore, it is safe to say that no one can legitimately claim to be an authoritative apostle or authentic prophet in the church today.

first century, while the New Testament was still being written by those apostles and prophets, the foundation consisted of their teachings from the Old Testament and their eyewitness accounts, not to mention the small but growing number of writings that became part of our New Testament. Today, we have direct access to all of the inspired writings of both the Old and New Testaments, both of which point to Jesus Christ as the center and standard of truth.

As God calls each of us from our various backgrounds, He fits us together as stones in the temple, firmly established on the foundation of the apostles and prophets with Christ as the cornerstone. This living building is no mere gathering of like-minded believers, but a "holy temple," because it is the dwelling place of the Holy Spirit of God (2:21-22). Though he doesn't use the word here, Paul is referring to the

Barry Beitzel

**The Parthenon in Athens.** The ancient buildings of Greece and Rome still stand today because the builders set a stable cornerstone and laid a firm foundation.

church, the body of Christ, which is not a literal building or an earthly corporation, but a living community of faith, resting squarely on the Holy Scriptures and centered intently on Jesus Christ.

# APPLICATION: EPHESIANS 2:11-22
## Three Questions for Members of God's Household

At the end of Ephesians 2, Paul is still in the thick of his dense theological instruction. His descriptions focus primarily on the new standing we enjoy by virtue of being "in Christ"—a new access to God, a new citizenship with the saints, a new family relationship with believers, and a new faith founded on Christ and the teachings of the apostles and the prophets. These spiritual realities are filled with practical implications. We need to ask ourselves three questions in response to the truth of our new position in Christ.

First, *do you really believe this?* I'm not asking, "Do you believe Paul wrote it?" or "Do you acknowledge its theoretical truthfulness as part of the Bible's doctrine of the church?" or "Do you subscribe to a doctrinal statement that affirms the truthfulness of the Bible?" I am asking this: Do you *personally* accept that you have been granted a position in God's household along with its rights, privileges, and responsibilities? When resident aliens go through the long process for US citizenship, it culminates in a ceremony in which they renounce foreign allegiances and pledge their allegiance to their new country of citizenship. They raise their right hands, affirm an oath, and take the pledge, and from that moment on their citizenship is never to be questioned or challenged, either legally or practically.

But what if those same citizens continue to doubt whether the process "stuck"? What if they worry about the genuineness of their oath, the sincerity of their allegiance? They might continue to act as if they are still "strangers" and "aliens," failing to live in the freedom of their new nationality. We, too, must come to terms with the fact that we have genuinely rendered our allegiance to God, and that He has fully accepted us as citizens of His kingdom and members of His family.

Second, *have you actually received it?* The promises of a new standing in Christ apply only to those who have actually placed their faith in Him. Perhaps after trying to answer the first question above, you realized that, no, you don't really believe it. You've been raised in a particular Christian tradition and simply assume you have been grand-fathered in. Or you may have gone through the process of stockpiling the right Christian information, learning to speak "Christianese," and figuring out the best way not to stand out as the black sheep of the Christian family. Yet you've never "raised your right hand" and "taken the oath of allegiance" to the Father through the finished work of the Son and by the life-giving power of the Holy Spirit. If you realize that's you, stop living life as a "resident alien" and accept by faith the free gift of "full citizenship."

Third, *are you living like it?* You say you believe it and have accepted it, but are you actually reflecting your new standing in Christ in your day-to-day life? Are you building on the foundation Christ has laid? Are you doing the hard things, like making peace with people with whom you've had conflicts, providing for the needs of people you may not know, or nourishing the faith of people you may not particularly like? We have the *privilege* of having access to God, enjoying full citizenship in His kingdom, participating as members of His family, and being liv-ing stones in His temple. Yet with this privilege comes enormous *re-sponsibility*. We must resist the temptation to replace the old "dividing wall" with our own man-made walls of division. Rather, we must learn to live in harmony and love with other believers, which includes learn-ing to like the unlikeable and even love the unlovable.

That's what it means to be part of God's household.

# The Mystery, the Ministry, and Me
## EPHESIANS 3:1-13

**NASB**

[1] For this reason I, Paul, the prisoner of Christ Jesus for the sake of you Gentiles— [2] if indeed you have heard of the stewardship of God's grace which was given to me for you; [3] that by revelation there was made known to me the mystery, as I wrote before in brief. [4a] By referring to this, when you read you can understand my insight [b] into the mystery of Christ, [5] which in other generations was not

**NLT**

[1] When I think of all this, I, Paul, a prisoner of Christ Jesus for the ben-efit of you Gentiles* . . . [2] assuming, by the way, that you know God gave me the special responsibility of ex-tending his grace to you Gentiles. [3] As I briefly wrote earlier, God him-self revealed his mysterious plan to me. [4] As you read what I have written, you will understand my insight into this plan regarding Christ. [5] God did

made known to the sons of men, as it has now been revealed to His holy apostles and prophets ªin the Spirit; ⁶*to be specific,* that the Gentiles are fellow heirs and fellow members of the body, and fellow partakers of the promise in Christ Jesus through the gospel, ⁷of which I was made a minister, according to the gift of God's grace which was given to me according to the working of His power. ⁸To me, the very least of all ªsaints, this grace was given, to preach to the Gentiles the unfathomable riches of Christ, ⁹and to ªbring to light what is the administration of the mystery which for ages has been hidden in God who created all things; ¹⁰so that the manifold wisdom of God might now be made known through the church to the rulers and the authorities in the heavenly *places.* ¹¹ *This was* in accordance with the ªeternal purpose which He ᵇcarried out in Christ Jesus our Lord, ¹²in whom we have boldness and ªconfident access through faith ᵇin Him. ¹³Therefore I ask ªyou not to lose heart at my tribulations on your behalf, ᵇfor they are your glory.

3:4 ªLit *To which, when you read* ᵇLit *in*  3:5 ªOr *by*  3:8 ªOr *holy ones*  3:9 ªTwo early mss read *make all know*  3:11 ªLit *purpose of the ages* ᵇOr *formed*  3:12 ªLit *access in confidence* ᵇLit *of Him* 3:13 ªOr *that I may not lose* ᵇLit *which are*

not reveal it to previous generations, but now by his Spirit he has revealed it to his holy apostles and prophets.

⁶And this is God's plan: Both Gentiles and Jews who believe the Good News share equally in the riches inherited by God's children. Both are part of the same body, and both enjoy the promise of blessings because they belong to Christ Jesus.* ⁷By God's grace and mighty power, I have been given the privilege of serving him by spreading this Good News.

⁸Though I am the least deserving of all God's people, he graciously gave me the privilege of telling the Gentiles about the endless treasures available to them in Christ. ⁹I was chosen to explain to everyone* this mysterious plan that God, the Creator of all things, had kept secret from the beginning.

¹⁰God's purpose in all this was to use the church to display his wisdom in its rich variety to all the unseen rulers and authorities in the heavenly places. ¹¹This was his eternal plan, which he carried out through Christ Jesus our Lord.

¹²Because of Christ and our faith in him,* we can now come boldly and confidently into God's presence. ¹³So please don't lose heart because of my trials here. I am suffering for you, so you should feel honored.

3:1 Paul resumes this thought in verse 14: "When I think of all this, I fall to my knees and pray to the Father."  3:6 Or *because they are united with Christ Jesus.*  3:9 Some manuscripts do not include *to everyone.*  3:12 Or *Because of Christ's faithfulness.*

We've all been there. We were clicking along through life, enjoying a season of blessing, growing in the Lord, feeling His hand of protection and abundant provision, and easily overcoming the minor obstacles and distractions that fell in our path. We began to personally experience what people call "the victorious Christian life" or "the abundant life in Christ," and we basked in the glorious peace, love, and joy of the Lord . . .

Until, like a thief crouching in the shadows, ready to pounce when we least expect it, the dark side of life crashed in, clutching at our joy, wrestling away our hope, trying to steal the love we had been experiencing. It may have taken the form of a shocking diagnosis, a tragic loss, or the sudden arrival of horrible news. At times like those, when our world seems to be crumbling and we find ourselves dangling by a thread over a sea of chaos, our theology needs to be rock solid.

We can't easily drum up our confidence in the sovereignty and goodness of God in the storm center of our trials. By then it's too late. There's a better way! Before the tribulations of this fallen world invade our lives in full force, we need to have already built up an impenetrable fortress of truth regarding God's presence with us and His care for us. Before we experience unbearable circumstances and excruciating suffering, we need to have prepared ourselves for such tests.

Some time ago a young theology student at Dallas Theological Seminary asked me, "Of all the things the Lord has taught you over the years, does something stand out more than any other?" After I took a moment to run through more than seventy years of life and fifty years of ministry, my answer came easily: Nothing touches us that hasn't first passed through the fingers of God. Nothing. As we live our lives as children of God, submitting all things to His mighty hand (1 Pet. 5:6), nothing happens to us that He hasn't allowed. And because we know that God is all good, all just, all knowing, and all wise, we can trust that what comes our way is meant for good, not evil—even when we can't understand it.

Besides Jesus, I don't know any other person in the New Testament who rose above his or her circumstances better than the apostle Paul. More than anyone else in his day, he suffered severely for the sake of the gospel (see 2 Cor. 11:24-28). In fact, the hardship he endured frames all of Ephesians 3:1-13. Paul begins by describing himself as a prisoner of Christ for the sake of the Gentiles (3:1). He ends with an exhortation for his readers not to lose heart at his tribulations on their behalf (3:13). Within this framework of suffering for the sake of the Gentiles, Paul paints a theologically rich picture that puts his suffering in proper perspective. How can Paul endure the hardships of his ministry? Because he knows a secret that makes it all worthwhile.

## — 3:1-7 —

You may have noticed that even though 3:1-3 ends with a period, these verses are really a sentence fragment in English. This is because in the Greek text, Ephesians 3:1 and 3:14-21 actually represent Paul's second prayer in the book of Ephesians, while 3:2-13 is one parenthetical run-on sentence explaining the "mystery" of the church. Structurally, the entire chapter looks like this: "For this reason I, Paul, the prisoner of Christ Jesus for the sake of you Gentiles—[parenthetical explanation of the mystery of Paul's ministry to the Gentiles]—for this reason I bow my knees before the Father . . ."

We will pick up the content of Paul's prayer in the next section. In this section let's look more closely at Paul's parenthetical digression. It may be a run-on sentence in Greek, but 3:2-13 is not the idle rambling of a man who had lost his train of thought. It's the key to unlocking the mystery of God that Paul had been divinely commissioned to declare. In fact, Paul's bold stand for the truthfulness of this mystery was the reason he was in prison.

When Paul wrote his letter, he was under house arrest in Rome (Acts 28). Why was he there? The Jews had accused him of being a rabble-rouser, a disturber of the peace, and the promoter of an illegal religion. His big problems began in Jerusalem, where he was falsely accused by Jews from Asia of defiling the temple by bringing Gentiles into the inner courts (Acts 21:27-31). In the midst of the ensuing riot, Roman soldiers actually rescued Paul from his Jewish attackers by arresting and chaining him (Acts 21:32-36)! When given an opportunity to address the crowd of Jews, Paul recounted his conversion experience on the road to Damascus (Acts 22:1-16). He then took his testimony a step further. He shared a vision he had of Jesus, who had explicitly instructed Paul to leave Jerusalem, saying, "Go! For I will send you far away to the Gentiles" (Acts 22:21).

Upon hearing this, the Jewish crowd responded in rage: "Away with such a fellow from the earth, for he should not be allowed to live!" (Acts 22:22). So infuriated were the Jewish religious zealots over Paul's preaching of the Jewish Messiah to the Gentiles that several Jews swore not to eat or drink until they had killed him (Acts 23:12-15). Clearly, the Jews were unimpressed by Paul's God-given mission to the Gentile church. Eventually, after several years of being shuffled around in the custody of the Roman government, Paul ended up under house arrest in Rome, having exercised his right as a Roman citizen to appeal his case to Caesar (Acts 25:11). To the chagrin of Paul's Jewish opponents, his message to the Gentiles never let up. While detained in Rome, he wrote four letters that continue to shape our lives to this day: Ephesians, Philippians, Colossians, and Philemon.

When Paul explores the heart of the new mystery for which he was in chains, we ought to pay close attention. He begins by calling his ministry to the Gentiles "the stewardship of God's grace" (Eph. 3:2). Paul had already explained in great detail the grace that saved believers, uniting them in Christ. This truth about the person and work of Jesus Christ had been made known to Paul by a revelation (3:3). He calls it "the mystery" (Greek *mystērion* [3466]; cf. 1:9). John Stott gives some insight into the meaning of this term:

> We need to realize that the English and Greek words do not have the same meaning. In English a "mystery" is something dark, obscure, secret, puzzling. What is "mysterious" is inexplicable, even incomprehensible. The Greek word *mystērion* is different, however. Although still a "secret," it is no longer closely guarded but open. . . . The Christian "mysteries" are truth which, although beyond human discovery, have been revealed by God and so now belong openly to the whole church.[6]

Paul had been granted special insight into this "mystery of Christ" (3:4). In fact, the revelation of this mystery was completely new, unheard of prior to its unveiling to the New Testament apostles and prophets (3:5)—recipients of those foundational ministries established by Christ through the power of the Holy Spirit for the first generation of the church (2:20). Previous generations had been told of a coming Messiah, but they had assumed He would be a Messiah for the Jews only. They had no idea that the salvation promised through their Davidic King would cross the boundaries of Israel to be offered to the Gentiles. What's worse, the mystery involved a union of Jews and Gentiles in one body, rendering the Gentiles "fellow heirs," "fellow members," and "fellow partakers of the promise in Christ Jesus" (3:6).

Imagine yourself in the place of a proud first-century Jew. You expected the Messiah to come, raise up an army, wage the righteous wars of the Lord, drive out the Roman oppressors and any other foreign powers and pagan influences, and restore temple worship to what God intended. Only then, during the messianic age, would the Gentiles stream to the mountain of the Lord to learn His Law—submitting to the Davidic King, the Law of Moses, and the people of Israel as God's chosen nation of kings and priests (Isa. 2:1-4; cf. Exod. 19:5-6).

When Paul came along preaching the gospel of God's unconditional acceptance of Gentiles through the Jewish Messiah, you would have been not only surprised and offended, but downright disgusted! Paul preached that through Christ the Gentiles wouldn't simply admire the

Lord and His people from a distance. *They would be His people too!* In fact, only in that one body—made up of Jews *and* Gentiles—could the nationalistic Jews find their own salvation.

Of this gospel—in all its glory for the Gentiles and controversy for the Jews—Paul was made a minister (*diakonos* [1249]; Eph. 3:7). Notice that Paul didn't make himself a minister. He didn't choose to be an apostle, a missionary, and a martyr as his lifelong career goal. Rather, God's grace marked Paul as a minister. The Greek word *diakonos*, sometimes translated "deacon," refers most generally to "a person who renders service."[7] It often refers to an official administrative position, like that of a king's servant functioning in a ministerial capacity.[8] Paul viewed himself as having been given a sacred, even royal, trust. Through a miraculous encounter with Jesus Christ Himself, Paul had been transformed from a zealous Pharisee bent on destroying the church to a willing minister of the gospel to the Gentiles. Talk about an about-face!

## — 3:8-10 —

Why would Paul call himself "the very least of all saints" (3:8)? Having just acknowledged that his role as a minister of Christ came to him only by God's grace, he reflects on his own past and recognizes his complete unworthiness. Paul expresses this in 1 Corinthians 15:9: "I am the least of the apostles, and not fit to be called an apostle, because I persecuted the church of God." Yet he puts things in perspective when he adds, "But by the grace of God I am what I am, and His grace toward me did not prove vain; but I labored even more than all of them, yet not I, but the grace of God with me" (1 Cor. 15:10).

God chose Paul to be a minister of the mystery, tasked with two important missions: (1) to preach the good news of the "unfathomable riches of Christ" to the Gentiles; and (2) to bring the formerly hidden mystery of the church to light (Eph. 3:8-9). This mystery, hidden for ages in the mind of God, was now being made known to all creation, including rulers and authorities in the heavenly realms (3:10).

As if proclaiming the good news to the world wasn't enough, Paul's ministry of reconciliation through Christ also impacted another world—the invisible spiritual world. What does this mean? New Testament scholar Max Turner explains, "The rulers in question are probably the whole host of heavenly beings; not merely God's angels or merely the evil powers of 6:12 but both. They are the assembled witnesses before whom God vindicates his wisdom. He does this through a church which brings his wisdom to expression."[9]

The apostle Peter expressed this same truth when he wrote, "It was revealed to [the Old Testament prophets] that they were not serving themselves, but you, in these things which now have been announced to you through those who preached the gospel to you by the Holy Spirit sent from heaven—things into which angels long to look" (1 Pet. 1:12). That refers to the "good angels," who themselves had to catch up to understand what God had planned to do through Christ in the church. If angels of God had a steep learning curve to master, surely the wicked spirits were left in the dust! In fact, Paul says that if the rulers of this world—likely the demonic powers working through human earthly powers—had understood the plan of God in advance, "they would not have crucified the Lord of glory" (1 Cor. 2:8).

## — 3:11-13 —

The secret that had been hidden in God's eternal purpose was now proclaimed in the open. Paul emphasizes that the message of the gospel has eternal roots. Before the events of Genesis 1:1 put the universe of time and space in motion, God had planned to bring about salvation and unity through Christ in the church. The Father decreed it, the Son implemented it, and the Spirit empowered it. The triune God purposed before time began to proclaim this message of Jesus Christ through the church (3:11). In short, although we can date the coming of Christ, His death, and His resurrection in the first century, *the message of the church has eternal roots in the purpose and plan of God.*

Because of this eternal rootedness of the gospel message in Christ— who is both eternal God and temporal man, before time and in time— *we have a secure relationship with God* (3:12). Boldness and confidence characterize our relationship with God. If you wake up at 1:05 in the morning in a cold sweat because of some family crisis, the Father is there, ready to listen to your pleas, to ease your burdens, and to give you peace. As the old song goes, "He's got the whole world in His hands." And you, as a child of God, can approach Him with boldness and confidence.

Finally, *this unalterable relationship with God can guard us from discouragement* (3:13). Paul was under arrest, unsure of his future on earth and wondering if he would be freed, imprisoned indefinitely, exiled, or simply put to death. His outlook may have been bleak, but his "uplook" was clear. God wasn't biting His nails, wondering what would happen next. Paul knew that even though it may have appeared that God was waiting around, unwilling to intervene on his behalf, the reality was that the Almighty had a plan. Just as He had a plan for bringing the gospel to the Gentiles, when the time was right He would reveal His will for Paul. Paul's responsibility was simply to trust and obey as he rested in God's enabling grace.

And what a grace it was! By grace, Paul had been called into his ministry. By grace he had been equipped to reveal God's mystery to the Gentiles. By grace God incorporated both Jew and Gentile into one church. By grace we, the church, proclaim the riches of God's salvation to each new generation. In the next section we'll see the expected response to such good news—to fall to our knees in a prayer of thanksgiving and worship.

# APPLICATION: EPHESIANS 3:1-13

## Drafted into God's Army

Obviously, I have a heart for those conscripted into the ministry. Notice I didn't use the word "called." There's nothing wrong with that word, but I'm not talking about those who have a choice in the matter. I'm talking about people like Paul who were heading in one direction and found themselves *drafted* into the special service of Christ. In my experience, those are the people who end up really impacting their realms of influence for the gospel—those who were drafted into God's army.

So, I have a few thoughts about those conscripted into Christian service. First, *they're in the ministry because God placed them there, not because others pushed them there*. Not because Mommy wanted her little boy to be a preacher. Not because Grandpa had a dream that his granddaughter would lead the children's ministry. Not because Daddy was a seminary professor and Junior needed to follow in his footsteps. Those kinds of "callings" don't have the staying power to get ministers through college, seminary, internships, the first few rocky years, and the inevitable major crises involved in real ministry. Most people conscripted into God's army disappoint their parents or loved ones, who had "higher" hopes for their children.

Second, *most people involved in fruitful, productive ministry weren't really looking for it*. It wasn't a long-awaited dream. In fact, most of the time it was a shocking surprise. Trust me—when people heard that Chuck Swindoll was going into the ministry, disbelief followed.

As my high school band director said (with tongue in cheek) when I went back after twenty-five years, "Swindoll, you're supposed to be in prison!" God, in His grace, reaches into the rank and file of humanity and picks out a few who are to be His spokesmen and women. We didn't look for it. We hadn't prayed for it. We weren't longing for it. Chances are good we didn't even want it. But the Lord says, "Fight it if you want . . . you are Mine!" When wide-eyed young people ask me how they can know if they're being called into the ministry, I often respond, "If you can imagine yourself doing anything else in life, do *that* instead."

Third, *those of us in ministry don't deserve it.* I know I certainly don't! Believe me, I know what I deserve, and it probably looks more like prison than where God has brought me. Yet God has provided me with grace upon grace during my journey through ministry. And I've needed it. I am utterly incompetent in and of myself to accomplish what God has had in mind for me. The road has been long, arduous, and treacherous, often marked with twists and turns I could never have anticipated. Many others would say the same thing. But, as Paul testifies, "I was made a minister, according to the gift of God's grace which was given to me according to the working of His power" (3:7).

As citizens of God's kingdom, all of us are gifted and called into Christian service. If that's you, deepen your roots and grow where you're planted. Bear fruit for Him. Contribute to the edification of the body. Yet some of us are drafted into God's army to spend our lives focusing on building up His kingdom. Is that you? If so, never look back. Instead, recognize the seriousness of this call, expect hardship, arm yourself for battle, and press on!

# Paul on His Knees . . . Again
## EPHESIANS 3:14-21

**NASB**

14 For this reason I bow my knees before the Father, 15 from whom ªevery family in heaven and on earth derives its name, 16 that He would grant you, according to the riches of His glory, to be strengthened with power through His Spirit in the inner man,

**NLT**

14 When I think of all this, I fall to my knees and pray to the Father,* 15 the Creator of everything in heaven and on earth.* 16 I pray that from his glorious, unlimited resources he will empower you with inner strength

17 so that Christ may dwell in your hearts through faith; *and* that you, being rooted and grounded in love, 18 may be able to comprehend with all the ªsaints what is the breadth and length and height and depth, 19 and to know the love of Christ which surpasses knowledge, that you may be filled up to all the fullness of God.

20 Now to Him who is able to do far more abundantly beyond all that we ask or think, according to the power that works within us, 21 to Him *be* the glory in the church and in Christ Jesus to all generations ªforever and ever. Amen.

3:15 ªOr *the whole*  3:18 ªV 8, note 1  3:21 ªLit *of the age of the ages*

through his Spirit. 17 Then Christ will make his home in your hearts as you trust in him. Your roots will grow down into God's love and keep you strong. 18 And may you have the power to understand, as all God's people should, how wide, how long, how high, and how deep his love is. 19 May you experience the love of Christ, though it is too great to understand fully. Then you will be made complete with all the fullness of life and power that comes from God.

20 Now all glory to God, who is able, through his mighty power at work within us, to accomplish infinitely more than we might ask or think. 21 Glory to him in the church and in Christ Jesus through all generations forever and ever! Amen.

3:14 Some manuscripts read *the Father of our Lord Jesus Christ.*  3:15 Or *from whom every family in heaven and on earth takes its name.*

In his last moments in person with the elders of Ephesus, the apostle Paul dropped to his knees and prayed with them (Acts 20:36). Knowing that they would never see him again in this life, they wept loudly, embracing and kissing him (Acts 20:37). Though they escorted him to the ship as he left Miletus, the leaders from the church in Ephesus would always have the image of Paul kneeling with them in prayer riveted in their memories.

When Paul begins the last segment of the doctrinal part of his letter with the words, "I bow my knees before the Father" (Eph. 3:14), several of the older recipients of the letter likely recalled that last emotional meeting with the great apostle. There he knelt, bowing before God, interceding on behalf of the elders of the church in Ephesus. Now, for the second time in his letter to that same church, Paul engages in warfare on his knees. For a few moments, let's kneel beside him as he offers up his second prayer for his beloved Christian friends in Ephesus.

## — 3:14-15 —

Before we examine the content of Paul's prayer, however, we need to ask, "What prompted this prayer, which had been lingering in his heart for some time?" Remember that he almost burst into the prayer in 3:1 when he wrote, "For this reason, I, Paul, the prisoner of Christ Jesus for the sake of you Gentiles . . ." Yet at that point Paul interjected a parenthetical description of the mystery of the gospel, of which he had been made a minister (3:2-12). He followed this with an exhortation for the Ephesians "not to lose heart" at his tribulations on their behalf (3:13).

So, when Paul says a second time, "For this reason" (3:14), he is transitioning from the profound theological truth of the mystery of the church to the vital reality that Paul and his readers have become partakers of this mystery. He moves from the general truth to the particular. By 3:14 he has given his readers a reason to avoid discouragement—the mystery once kept hidden has now been revealed . . . *to them*! Through Paul's unwavering commitment to preaching the gospel, the Ephesians had become partakers of this new inheritance in Christ, joint heirs with the Jews in the church of Jesus Christ (3:6). In light of these truths expressed in Ephesians 2 and 3, Paul drops to his knees and prays for the Ephesians.

It seems appropriate to make a couple of brief comments about our posture in prayer before we go any further. Our posture in prayer is not as important as the act of prayer itself. Whether you pray standing, kneeling, sitting, or lying on your face, the important point is to pray fervently, consistently, and repeatedly. I frequently pray while driving. I always pray before difficult encounters with individuals. On occasions of intense need, I'll kneel before the Lord. I've prayed holding hands with others. I've prayed while laying hands on another. I've prayed with my eyes open, my eyes closed, my hands folded, and my hands raised. Again, the attitude of the heart is what counts. There's nothing magical about our posture. In Paul's day, however, most people prayed while standing, usually with their hands open in front of them as an act of openness and surrender (Mark 11:25; Luke 18:11; 1 Tim. 2:8). When first-century Christians dropped to their knees in prayer, they did so to show deep adoration, submissiveness, and urgency.[10]

Now, back to Paul's prayer. Notice first that he addresses God the Father (Eph. 3:14). There's a simple formula Christians should keep in mind when praying. Though the Father, Son, and Holy Spirit are each fully God, they are not the same person, but three distinct, inseparable, coeternal, coequal persons. They are the same in divinity, but each has a distinct role or function in relation to creation and redemption. When it comes to proper Christian prayer, we ought to pray *to* the Father, *through* the Son, and *by* the Holy Spirit. Just as Jesus instructed, when we pray we should address the Father: "Our Father who is in heaven" (Matt. 6:9). In fact, the examples of prayer in the New Testament over-whelmingly address God the Father, presenting requests and petitions to Him.

"God the Father" is properly the eternal Father of God the Son, the Lord Jesus Christ, who for eternity past was ever present with the Father and the Holy Spirit. Paul, however, refers to God simply as "Father," which may indicate that he has in mind God's fatherly attitude toward creation. This understanding is confirmed by the fact that Paul further describes "the Father" as the One "from whom the whole family in heaven and earth is named" (Eph. 3:15, NKJV). Although the Greek text of 3:15 could be translated either "from whom every family" or "from whom the whole family," I think the second best fits the context. Paul is referring to the whole family of God—Jews and Gentiles alike—who are all related to Him through Jesus Christ by the unifying work of the Holy Spirit. This has been the whole point of the letter up until now, so this mysterious union of all believers in Christ becomes the basis for Paul's prayer.

## — 3:16-19 —

In the prayer itself, Paul petitions God for four things for the Ephesians:

1. that they would be strengthened through the Spirit (3:16);
2. that they would be rooted and grounded in love (3:17);
3. that they would comprehend the immensity of Christ's love (3:18-19); and
4. that they would be filled to God's own fullness (3:19).

In these four requests, I see Paul covering four dimensions of human need: psychological, emotional, mental, and spiritual. Let's examine each more closely.

First, *Paul prays that they would be strengthened through the Spirit* (3:16-17). Psychologically, we are all in constant danger of becoming discouraged by a loss of inner motivation (3:13). The solution is not found in the latest motivational gimmick or by attending the next "feel good about yourself" seminar. We must turn to the Spirit's strengthen-ing power. From His treasure trove of riches, God will bestow on us a strength that wells up from the depths of our being, which Paul calls "the inner man" (3:16). When the Holy Spirit dwells in us, He mediates to us the real presence of Jesus Christ (3:17). How is this accomplished? By attempting to reform our own lives? By making ourselves more holy?

By cleansing our temple so the Spirit will dwell in a clean vessel? No! Paul says Christ dwells in our hearts "through faith"—the same means by which all of God's grace is mediated to believers.

I can't exaggerate the psychological impact of this confidence that God the Spirit is dwelling in us. The more we keep Christ at the center of our lives, letting Him shape our attitudes, values, choices, decisions, and actions, the more we will be like Him. This transformation from deep within will then affect every other segment of our lives—physical, emotional, mental, and spiritual. Yet it begins in the heart of our being, and it grows by faith alone.

Second, *Paul prays that they would be rooted and grounded in love* (3:17). Psalm 1 likens a righteous person who delights in the Law of the Lord to "a tree firmly planted by streams of water" (Ps. 1:3). It produces fruit in its season, and it cannot be easily shaken. Like that tree, the life rooted in Christ's love produces bountiful fruit. Whereas "rooted" paints an agricultural image, "grounded" comes from the world of construction. Like a building resting on a firm foundation, those whose lives rest on love cannot be shaken (Matt. 7:25). As believers tap into and rest upon the unconditional love of God flowing in and through them, they find themselves *emotionally* balanced and stable.

I need to clear something up, though. When Paul talks about "love," he uses the term *agapē* [26]. It includes emotion, but it's not primarily referring to how we feel about somebody or something. Quite frankly, whether I *feel* loved has nothing to do with whether I actually *am* loved. One commentator defines *agapē* as "seeking the highest good in the one loved."[11] Yes, there's emotion felt toward somebody, but the emphasis is on the unconditional commitment. Paul knew that when believers are not simply skipping along the surface of love, they will be able to handle the emotional ups and downs of life. That is, when they are *rooted* and *grounded* in unconditional love, they will be agents of peace, unity, and reconciliation rather than strife, discord, and conflict.

Third, *Paul prays that they would comprehend the immensity of Christ's love* (3:18-19). A wonderful old hymn begins:

> O the deep, deep love of Jesus,
> Vast, unmeasured, boundless, free![12]

Whereas the "love" mentioned in 3:17 referred to the unconditional love flowing from us because of our relationship with Christ, the "love of Christ" in 3:19 refers to Christ's love shown toward us.[13] So confounding, so unexpected, and so infinite is the love of the One who gave His life for our sins that Paul runs out of images with which to express it. In fact, Paul prays that the Ephesians would know something that's beyond knowledge! Paul uses a spatial image to convey the inexpressible and incomprehensible nature of the love of Christ. Its breadth, length, height, and depth are immeasurable. His love extends boundlessly in every direction, like an infinite universe whose end can never be reached.

I can't help but think of the Cross when I read those words:

- *Broad* enough to cover anybody!
- *Long* enough to go beyond any barrier!
- *High* enough to take us all the way to glory and beyond!
- *Deep* enough to touch any need, any sin, or any hurt!

So, addressing the mental dimension of his readers' being, Paul prays that the believers would grow deeper in their knowledge of God, whose greatness can never be fully grasped, whose love can never be fully understood, and whose glory can never be fully experienced. Paul is not talking here about "head knowledge." Anybody can believe and confess that God's love is beyond anything we can imagine. But to experience it—to know it as the recipient of His mercy and grace—*that's* something that can't be understood in a merely intellectual sense.

It reminds me of the response by jazz great Louis Armstrong when he was asked to explain what jazz is: "Man, if you gotta ask, you'll never know." Jazz isn't something that's dissected, measured, described, and explained. It's something that's heard, felt, and experienced. The same is true of the love of Christ but in an infinitely greater sense. Paul prays for the Ephesians' comprehension because apart from the illuminating work of the Spirit, this kind of supernatural knowledge is impossible.

Finally, *Paul prays that they would be filled to God's own fullness* (3:19). Paul continues to set forth one impossibility after another. Unconditional love . . . unknowable knowledge . . . and now being filled by an infinite God. Clearly, we finite beings cannot contain the infinite God (2 Chr. 6:18). So what does Paul mean? He prays that to the fullest extent of our human capacities, we would overflow with God's strength, love, and knowledge. We will never be God, nor will we be little "gods." Those are impossibilities. We can, however, be greater humans than we are—conformed more and more to the image of Jesus Christ as the Spirit floods us with His fullness and we become "partakers of the divine nature" (2 Pet. 1:4).

My family and I used to live about forty-five minutes from the Pacific Ocean. On occasion, we would vacation at a friend's apartment at Laguna Beach, one of our favorite places to relax in Southern California. What a great place to kick back and watch the kids play in the surf and make sand castles—to enjoy the sights, smells, and sounds of the beautiful, roaring ocean! I remember on one occasion when our daughter Colleen was about six, she brought back to our home a jar of seawater. When I tucked her into bed that night, I noticed it was sitting there on her dresser. I asked, "Sweetheart, what's this?"

She answered, "Well, Daddy . . . I just wanted to bring the ocean home with me." She was exactly right. That quart jar was filled to the brim with the Pacific Ocean. Not all of it, of course, but as much as it could hold. The essence of the *real* Pacific Ocean—though not all its quantity—filled that jar.

In the same way, Paul prayed that the essence or nature of God would fill the Ephesians. When this happens, the spiritual dimension of our being is engaged as we enjoy an intimate fellowship with our great God. That's a level of intimacy that transcends anything we experience in human relationships.

## — 3:20-21 —

A great prayer like this deserves a grand benediction—a magnificent conclusion. God's greatness overwhelmed Paul, just as it overwhelms you and me today. So he turned all of our attention from what we need to *become* to who God is and what God can do. Compared to what God is able to do for us, our thoughts and prayers appear to be mere musings and ramblings (3:20). Yet the inexhaustible power of the Holy Spirit works within us, as He mediates His miraculous abilities to us through the church. Such a God—and only such a God—is worthy of all glory and honor forever and ever (3:21).

Paul's prayer began with bowing his knee before the Father of all (3:14). It ends with his looking upward and giving all glory to the Father (3:20-21). In between we are encouraged to claim the Spirit's strength . . . to remember Christ's love . . . and to seek the Father's fullness. Only upon this proper theological foundation concerning the nature of God can we build a stable, practical Christian life worthy of the One who has made us a part of His eternal family.

# APPLICATION: EPHESIANS 3:14-21

## Following on Our Knees

Paul's flourish of prayer for the Ephesians was meant to encourage and strengthen them in the face of the trials and tribulations they would inevitably face in this life. Whether we're downtrodden, depressed, disappointed, or just discouraged, we should never hesitate to follow Paul's lead and fall on our knees before God. Based on Ephesians 3:14-21, let me give you three suggestions for how to follow Paul on our knees.

First, *we need to claim Christ's strength* (3:16). When we've lost our inner energy and motivation in our walk with Christ, we can remember that He wants to empower us. On our own, we're weak. When we wait on Him, relying on His provision through prayer, our strength is renewed and our spirits refreshed. Isaiah 40:29-31 puts it beautifully:

> He gives strength to the weary,
> And to him who lacks might He increases power.
> Though youths grow weary and tired,
> And vigorous young men stumble badly,
> Yet those who wait for the LORD
> Will gain new strength;
> They will mount up with wings like eagles,
> They will run and not get tired,
> They will walk and not become weary.

When we're on our knees, we can claim His strength.

Second, *we need to remember that we're loved* (3:17). When we come before the Lord in prayer, we should never forget that His love for us is perfect. With this confidence, we can pray with the kind of expectation that a beloved child has before a loving father (see Matt. 7:11). With the love of God ever present in our minds, we can accept unanswered prayers knowing that God's desire is not to ruin us, but to work out His plan in our lives for His glory and our good (Rom. 8:28). From our knees, we can say to Him, "Lord, You love me. You know all these rotten things about me, You know all the things that fill my mind, You know the depths of my depravity, and You still love me. You know all my needs better than I do, and You love me." When our minds are foggy and we don't remember what we once knew so well, we need to recall His all-embracing love (Eph. 3:18-19).

Finally, *we need to rest entirely on Him, not on ourselves* (3:20-21). When we're weakest, His power works through us (2 Cor. 12:9-10). In fact, our weak, helpless position gives God an opportunity to strengthen us and come to our aid. When we've fallen to our knees, with literally nowhere else to go, we need to lean on His strength alone. Let Him fight and win our battles. Let Him give us the strength to go on, to face our fears, to endure our suffering, and to conquer our sin. Remember the One "who is able, through his mighty power at work within us, to accomplish infinitely more than we might ask or think" (Eph. 3:20, NLT).

Prayer turns our attention from ourselves to God, from earthly things to heavenly things, from life lived in the horizontal to life lived in the vertical. When we find ourselves mentally, emotionally, or spiritually drained, we need make prayer our first response—not the thing we try as a last resort when all else fails.

# WALKING AND GROWING: THE BELIEVER'S LIFESTYLE (EPHESIANS 4:1-32)

Like a doorway from the classroom of knowledge to the laboratory of experience, most of Paul's letters contain a "hinge"—a point where they shift from principle to practical, from doctrine to duty, from orthodoxy to orthopraxy. For example, in Romans 12:1 Paul begins his practical section with, "Therefore I urge you, brethren, by the mercies of God . . ." In Galatians 5:1 he writes, "It was for freedom that Christ set us free; therefore keep standing firm and do not be subject again to a yoke of slavery." Similarly, in Colossians 3:1 Paul says, "Therefore if you have been raised up with Christ, keep seeking the things above, where Christ is, seated at the right hand of God." Notice that all of these hinges contain the word "therefore." It's a word that prompts us to look back before pressing on. In other words, Paul pauses to say, "In light of all the great theological truths I've just shared, act in the following way."

Ephesians 4:1 represents the literary hinge of Paul's letter. Think of the profound doctrinal principles he has been developing so far in the letter:

- our adoption as God's children (1:4-5)
- the hope of our inheritance (1:11, 18)
- the truth of Christ's glorious rule (1:20-23)
- the riches of God's lavish grace (2:1-10)
- our unity with God and each other (2:11–3:13)
- the glory of the Lord's incomprehensible love (3:14-21)

I've named this first section of Ephesians' practical half "Walking and Growing: The Believer's Lifestyle (Ephesians 4:1-32)." In light of the believer's calling and position in Christ, Paul exhorts the Ephesians to walk in a manner worthy of that calling (4:1), taking steps marked by humility, gentleness, patience, tolerance, love, unity, peace, and hope (4:2-6). He also emphasizes the unity of the body in the process of spiritual growth, noting that Christ has given to the church gifted apostles, prophets, evangelists, pastors, and teachers to build up believers in their faith (4:7-16). Through this process of corporate spiritual growth, believers can set aside the "old self" and put on the "new self," empowered by the Spirit to live lives pleasing to God (4:17-32).

Having been grounded in profound theology, let's follow Paul through the gateway into the practical arena of everyday life.

## KEY TERMS IN EPHESIANS 4:1-32

***henotēs* (ἐνότης)** [1775] "oneness," "unity"
In light of Paul's rhythmic hymn of unity in 4:4-6, we can conclude that *henotēs,* "unity," is a virtue that Christians should constantly strive for. In a world of countless "gods," many "lords," and competing "truths," Ephesians emphasizes the oneness of the Father, Son, and Spirit, the unity of the Christian faith, and the continuity of its practices from church to church. Paul's exhortation to preserve the oneness of the Christian faith is also a call to recognize the exclusive statements inherent in the Christian faith, which should never be compromised in a world of religious pluralism.

***peripateō* (περιπατέω)** [4043] "to walk," "to behave," "to conduct oneself"
Though literally *peripateō* means "to walk around" (see Matt. 4:18), it has a common idiomatic usage referring to one's lifestyle or pattern of behavior (Rom. 6:4; 1 Jn. 1:6). In Ephesians 4:1, Paul begins the practical section of his letter with the general exhortation "to walk in a manner worthy of the calling with which you have been called." This new lifestyle, or Christian "walk," is therefore the overarching theme of the second half of Ephesians.

# A Worthy Walk
## EPHESIANS 4:1-6

**NASB**
¹ Therefore I, the prisoner of the Lord, implore you to walk in a manner worthy of the calling with which you have been called, ²with all humility and gentleness, with patience, showing tolerance for one another in love, ³being diligent to preserve

**NLT**
¹ Therefore I, a prisoner for serving the Lord, beg you to lead a life worthy of your calling, for you have been called by God. ²Always be humble and gentle. Be patient with each other, making allowance for each other's faults because of your love. ³Make every effort to keep

the unity of the Spirit in the bond of peace. *There is* one body and one Spirit, just as also you were called in one hope of your calling; ⁵one Lord, one faith, one baptism, ⁶one God and Father of all who is over all and through all and in all.

yourselves united in the Spirit, binding yourselves together with peace. ⁴For there is one body and one Spirit, just as you have been called to one glorious hope for the future.

⁵ There is one Lord, one faith, one baptism,
⁶ one God and Father of all, who is over all, in all, and living through all.

Several years ago I had the privilege of leading and speaking at the memorial service for the late, great Dallas Cowboys coach Tom Landry. I had the chance to talk with and listen to one ballplayer after another who had played on Coach Landry's teams down through his many years as head coach. What a pleasure it was to hear their estimation of that godly Christian man, who even without words impressed both his team and his rivals with his depth of character. A common theme kept rising to the surface, a theme summed up by the words of a former player, Randy White: "The thing that I admire most about Coach Landry was the example that he set, not so much as a football coach, but for the person that he was. He didn't just talk the talk. He walked the walk. I always respected that in him."[1]

We hear a lot about people who believe one thing and do another, who "talk the talk" but don't "walk the walk." So when a man with such a large public image as Tom Landry backs up his confession of faith with a consistently Christian way of life, it generates enormous respect. Sadly, however, many Christians never seem to put the two together, to move from the talk to the walk, from faith to life, from calling to commitment.

As we study the first six verses of Ephesians 4, let's do so with a dedication to rise above mere head knowledge and put feet to our faith so that we walk in a manner worthy of our calling in Christ.

## — 4:1-3 —

For three chapters Paul has been emphasizing the *calling*. We have been called *by God the Father*, who decreed His plan of salvation in eternity past. We have been called *by Jesus Christ*, who implemented the plan through His incarnation, life, death, resurrection, and ascension. We have been called *by the Holy Spirit*, who regenerated us, sealed us, and empowers us to do His will. Having set the stage in chapters 1–3, it's as if Paul raised a megaphone to his mouth, pointed a finger our way, and shouted, "And . . . action!"

The time has come to apply the truth of our calling to our lives.

This is why Paul begins with the verb meaning "I implore." It's the Greek word *parakaleō* [3870], which could also be translated "urge" or "exhort." There is passionate urgency in Paul's tone. He earnestly exhorts his readers not merely as an apostle with prophetic authority but as "the prisoner of the Lord." As one who has been incarcerated for the sake of the gospel, his life has become an example to follow of living a life worthy of the calling.

What does Paul urge them to do? To "walk." I love that word; it says it all, since it refers to a person's "conduct or lifestyle."[2] I like it that Paul didn't say "fly" or "sprint" or "run" or "charge." Walk. It almost sounds manageable, doesn't it? Just put one foot in front of the other. Small ones if you have to, big ones if you can. Just walk. Walk in the right direction, walk in the right way, and walk with the power of the Spirit . . . but *walk*.

Now, *how* should we walk? In a way consistent with our calling, which Paul described in chapters 1–3. The word for "worthy" is *axiōs* [516], which means "being fitting or proper in corresponding to what should be expected."[3] Paul calls his readers to live lives equal to the reality of their calling. What does this actually look like? For the next few verses, Paul paints a very clear picture of the kind of lifestyle that is worthy of the calling.

He begins in 4:2 by laying down five stepping-stones for a worthy walk, which we can summarize with five words:

Where do these stepping-stones lead? Ephesians 4:3 shows the destination: "the unity of the Spirit in the bond of peace." That's the goal of these deliberate steps in the Christian walk. To avoid any missteps, let's examine each step more carefully.

## Stepping Stones from Humility to Love

*Humility.* The Greek word *tapeinophrosynē* [5012] means "lowliness of mind." The same word is used in Philippians 2:3: "With *humility of mind* regard one another as more important than yourselves" (emphasis mine). Quite simply, for the Christian it means putting Christ first, others second, and self last. Not a popular formula, is it? It was no more popular in the first century than it is today. The word painted the picture of a crouching slave—abject, servile, in complete subjection to his master.[4] Yet this is exactly the kind of attitude that accompanied Christ's incarnation and earthly ministry (Phil. 2:5-8). In fact, he described Himself as "gentle and humble in heart" (Matt. 11:29) and said that He came not to be served "but to serve" (Mark 10:45).

*Gentleness.* As we see in Christ's own self-description, humility and gentleness go hand in hand. Whereas humility is an attitude of mind, gentleness refers to the outward manifestation of a person's humble demeanor. Gentle people are not harsh with others, don't fight to get their way, and don't turn everything into a winner-takes-all competition. Instead, they demonstrate consideration for the needs and feelings of others. Like humility, gentleness is a vital step toward unity because it softens our sharp edges and keeps us from scraping, cutting, and bruising those who get close to us. If all of us in the church balanced our strength with humility and gentleness, as Jesus did, then virtually all our conflicts would disappear.

*Patience.* The third stepping-stone of the worthy walk is patience. Of the three virtues we have considered so far, the step of patience is the most difficult because it comes to us in the hardest way. It means exercising humility and gentleness in the company of disappointing, frustrating, and downright offensive people. It means sticking to something when everything within you and outside of you is pushing you to give in. Patience takes time to nurture, especially in our impatient world. We pace the room if the microwave takes thirty seconds. We zip through traffic if one lane is moving too slowly. We stare at our watches if the worship service runs three or four minutes over. Yet patience is essential if the church is to arrive at true unity. It allows all of us to learn at different paces, to make mistakes, and to hunker down for the lengthy, arduous process of steady spiritual growth.

*Tolerance.* Just as humility and gentleness form a firm footing in our worthy walk, patience and tolerance also work together. Patience predisposes us to endure all kinds of circumstances; tolerance helps us endure all kinds of people. Tolerant people reach out with forgiveness, understanding, and sympathy. They treat others with grace—letting them grow with Christ in different ways and at different paces. Tolerant people welcome others with a warm embrace because their hearts have been embraced by Christ (1 Jn. 4:19). Paul obviously isn't talking about tolerating sin, wickedness, immorality, and evil. That's far from his mind, and it should be far from ours as well (1 Cor. 5:9-13; Rev. 2:20). Rather, Paul refers to showing mercy and grace to others, letting others live their Christian lives in ways that may not be exactly how we think they should. This means allowing people to develop their unique abilities without fear of being judged.

*Love.* The final stepping-stone on the path to unity is love—once again, *agapē* [26], or unconditional love that expects nothing in return. In many ways, the previous four virtues describe what real love looks like, which is why Paul says we must have humility, gentleness, patience, and tolerance "in love." Love looks out not for one's own interests but for the interests of others (Phil. 2:4). All of these stepping-stones together point the way to true unity.

Like a quiet clearing at the end of a garden path, "the unity of the Spirit in the bond of peace" marks a point of progress in the walk worthy of our calling (Eph. 4:3). Yet having arrived, we must work diligently to preserve it. We need to safeguard it from those vices that stand in direct contrast to the five virtues just mentioned: a prideful ego, a severe demeanor, an irritable spirit, a judgmental heart, and a hateful attitude.

Unity needs to be a persistent and consistent goal of every member of the body of Christ. Because Christ has called us in peace (2:14-15), we must nurture the "bond of peace" in our daily walk (4:3). In a divisive, warring, hurtful world, the most powerful testimony the church can give is genuine unity prompted by true love and shown in the example of peace.

Sadly, however, there's not a more divided church on any continent or in any era of church history than there is in the United States today. It's nothing short of tragic. Every city has its own stories of church splits—some of them are legendary. Towns and villages have pastors that won't talk to each other, much less support or encourage one another. As believers committed to walking in a manner worthy of our calling, we should all cry out, "What a shame!" Because when unbelievers observe our disregard for unity, they think, "What a sham!"

We twenty-first-century believers need to read Paul's words as if they were written directly to us. He's imploring both ministers and church members, both men and women, both young and old, to lay down our arms and to pick up the banner of peace.

## — 4:4-6 —

So fundamental is unity to the Christian walk that Paul shines a light on seven of its facets. These are seven things that all believers share, regardless of denomination, location, age, worship preference, or any other things that might divide orthodox, Bible-believing, evangelical churches. In this list, note that these are *present* realities—they don't just exist in some ideal future when God finally breaks down the barriers to church unity. Rather, these are seven pillars upon which practical unity can be built. Let's briefly survey them.

*One body.* Jew and Gentile, slave and free, male and female, rich and poor, young and old—all of these otherwise conflicting types of people have been placed in "one body," the church. There was never meant to be "the old people's church" and "the young people's church." God didn't establish a "rich people's church" and a "poor people's church." He didn't have in mind a "black church" and a "white church" . . . or a "traditional church" and a "contemporary church." There is *one body*.

*One Spirit.* The same Spirit of God gives life to and dwells in every believer. He calls us through various means. He gifts us in various ways. Yet He indwells all of us equally. There are not different Holy Spirits for different people and different groups (1 Cor. 12:4-11). One Holy Spirit gives all of us new life.

*One hope of our calling.* All Christians share the hope of eternal life (Titus 1:2), which is centered on Jesus Christ, who *is* our hope (1 Tim. 1:1). That's a common vision of the future all Christians are expected to share. One of the great divides among Bible-believing Christians, however, relates to end-times events. Will there be a Millennium? A Rapture before the Tribulation? How will it all pan out? Yet even in the midst of these great differences, *all of us share a common hope*—eternal, sinless, painless, deathless joy in the presence of God (Rev. 21:4-7, 22-27). We should emphasize these grand truths that unite us rather than the minor issues that divide us.

*One Lord.* Paul already mentioned that all believers share in "one Spirit," commonly called the third person of the Trinity. Paul then refers to the second person of the Trinity: the "one Lord," Jesus Christ (see 1 Cor. 8:6; 12:3). All true Christians have been saved by grace through faith in the person and work of the one Lord.

*One faith.* All Christians are united by one faith. In this instance, the word "faith" probably means the body of essential Christian truths, as used in Jude 1:3—"the faith which was once for all handed down to the saints." That is, the basic Christian doctrines concerning the

Father, Son, and Holy Spirit; the person and work of Jesus Christ, the God-man died who for our sins and rose from the dead; and other core teachings that unite all Christians in the same revealed faith. Simply put, there are not many legitimate "Christianities" but only one true "Christianity." Even though different churches, denominations, and believers may have unique perspectives and interpretations regarding nonessential matters, all orthodox evangelicals agree on the essential truths revealed in Scripture.

*One baptism.* Regardless of the various methods of baptizing, the age of a person when he or she is baptized, or what words are used in the observance, all Christians believe that baptism is the rite of initiation into the Christian faith. Through baptism we publicly proclaim our identification with Christ—an outward sign of an inward reality. The methods may vary, but every true Christian church practices this essential ordinance.

*One God and Father of all.* As the last of his seven facets of unity, Paul mentions the first person of the Godhead: God the Father. As those saved through faith in His Son and the regenerating work of the Spirit, all Christians look to one Father. If anybody would still doubt that all believers are truly united with one another, Paul makes it crystal clear that the one God is "over all and through all and in all" (Eph. 4:6). As the Spirit, the Son, and the Father are one, so we are also one, we who were created in God's image and re-created to be conformed to the image of Christ (Rom. 8:29; 2 Cor. 3:18).

What wonderful reasons to walk in a manner worthy of the calling with which we have been called!

# APPLICATION: EPHESIANS 4:1-6

## A Wake-Up Call for the Called

It doesn't take a psychologist or sociologist to make us aware that each of us is unique. We have different temperaments, different gifts, different experiences, different convictions, different interests, different blessings, and different pains and scars. Yes, one of the things we all have in common is that each of us is completely different!

But surely people with so many different backgrounds can't live together in peace, can they? Don't we live in a dog-eat-dog world where Paul's seven theoretical facets of oneness just can't translate into lasting unity? Besides, in order to maintain purity of doctrine and practice, we need to break away from believers who aren't living up to our standards, don't we? I'm sure God cheers us on with great delight when churches split over incidentals and a Christian shuns another believer over a difference of opinion, right?

Wrong! Brothers and sisters, we need to repent of these ways of thinking and deliberately stop these ways of acting! None of these things reflect a walk worthy of our calling. None of them flow from a life of humility, gentleness, patience, tolerance, and love.

This is a good place to pause and probe. Let me ask you a few deeply personal questions. Better yet, ask yourself these questions and don't rush to your answers too quickly. Are you a gossip? Do you spread rumors? Do you sow discord within the family of God? Do you ignore the major truths that unite you with other believers and instead focus on the minor issues that divide you? Do you quickly lose patience with others? Do you only give to others when you know you'll get something in return? Do you hold grudges? Harbor bitterness? Foster resentment?

If you find yourself guilty of any of these charges, ask yourself, "Why do I do these things?" Where did you learn this? You didn't learn it from Christ. You weren't moved toward disunity and discord by the work of the Spirit. You didn't become a part of the church's problem by pursuing obedience to God the Father. Where did this come from? It came from one or more of three sources: the world, the flesh, and the devil. When I find myself guilty of these things, I need to renounce them. I need to turn my back on them, make amends with those I've hurt and harmed, and throw myself upon God's mercy and claim His forgiveness.

Can you join with me right now and commit yourself to diligently preserving "the unity of the Spirit in the bond of peace" (4:3)? What an important commitment! Only when we take this step of commitment will we begin a walk worthy of the calling with which we have been called.

# Embracing a Full-Bodied Ministry
## EPHESIANS 4:7-16

| NASB | NLT |
|---|---|
| 7 But to each one of us grace was given according to the measure of Christ's gift. 8 Therefore ªit says, | 7 However, he has given each one of us a special gift* through the generosity of Christ. 8 That is why the Scriptures say, |

**NASB**

"WHEN HE ASCENDED ON HIGH,
HE LED CAPTIVE A HOST OF
   CAPTIVES,
AND HE GAVE GIFTS TO MEN."

9 (Now this *expression,* "He ascended," what [a]does it mean except that He also [b]had descended into the lower parts of the earth? 10 He who descended is Himself also He who ascended far above all the heavens, so that He might fill all things.) 11 And He gave some *as* apostles, and some *as* prophets, and some *as* evangelists, and some *as* pastors and teachers, 12 for the equipping of the [a]saints for the work of service, to the building up of the body of Christ; 13 until we all attain to the unity of the faith, and of the [a]knowledge of the Son of God, to a mature man, to the measure of the stature [b]which belongs to the fullness of Christ. 14[a]As a result, we are no longer to be children, tossed here and there by waves and carried about by every wind of doctrine, by the trickery of men, by craftiness [b]in deceitful scheming; 15 but [a]speaking the truth in love, [b]we are to grow up in all *aspects* into Him who is the head, *even* Christ, 16 from whom the whole body, being fitted and held together [a]by what every joint supplies, according to the [b]proper working of each individual part, causes the growth of the body for the building up of itself in love.

4:8 [a]Or *He* 4:9 [a]Lit *is it except* [b]One early ms reads *had first descended* 4:12 [a]Or *holy ones* 4:13 [a]Or *true knowledge* [b]Lit *of the fullness* 4:14 [a]Lit *So that we will no longer be* [b]Lit *with regard to the scheming of deceit* 4:15 [a]Or *holding to* or *being truthful in* [b]Or *let us grow up* 4:16 [a]Lit *through every joint of the supply* [b]Lit *working in measure*

**NLT**

"When he ascended to the
   heights,
he led a crowd of captives
and gave gifts to his people."*

9 Notice that it says "he ascended." This clearly means that Christ also descended to our lowly world.* 10 And the same one who descended is the one who ascended higher than all the heavens, so that he might fill the entire universe with himself.

11 Now these are the gifts Christ gave to the church: the apostles, the prophets, the evangelists, and the pastors and teachers. 12 Their responsibility is to equip God's people to do his work and build up the church, the body of Christ. 13 This will continue until we all come to such unity in our faith and knowledge of God's Son that we will be mature in the Lord, measuring up to the full and complete standard of Christ.

14 Then we will no longer be immature like children. We won't be tossed and blown about by every wind of new teaching. We will not be influenced when people try to trick us with lies so clever they sound like the truth. 15 Instead, we will speak the truth in love, growing in every way more and more like Christ, who is the head of his body, the church. 16 He makes the whole body fit together perfectly. As each part does its own special work, it helps the other parts grow, so that the whole body is healthy and growing and full of love.

4:7 Greek *a grace.* 4:8 Ps 68:18. 4:9 Some manuscripts read *to the lower parts of the earth.*

Over the many years I have been in ministry, I've seen interest in spiritual gifts wax and wane. Sometimes a church in desperate need of renewal would suddenly rediscover that the Spirit had enabled its leaders and members to do something beyond the Sunday-to-Sunday grind that had kept them in a rut. Instead, each member of the church discovered his or her spiritual gifts and together they put them into practice and witnessed a long-needed revival. On the other hand, I've also seen healthy churches become obsessed with spiritual gifts—concerned about which gifts are for today's church, which should be used when, and whose gifts are most important. The results? Churches split, unity crumbles, ministries collapse.

The topic of spiritual giftedness is clearly important for an understanding of the Christian life. Paul directly addresses this issue in a number of places, most specifically in Romans 12, 1 Corinthians 12–14, and here in Ephesians 4. In each of these passages, Paul not only describes various gifts given to individual believers but also explains the purpose of the gifts—*to build up the body of Christ*. In Ephesians 4:7-16, we'll see that Paul expected a great deal of diversity in the church as different people exercised their gifts. At the same time, Paul points us to God's ultimate reason for giving spiritual gifts to His people—so that we might "attain to the unity of the faith, and of the knowledge of the Son of God" (4:13).

To use our spiritual gifts effectively, we first need to understand their source of power, how Christ made that power available to us, and why He did so.

## — 4:7-8 —

Paul begins 4:7 with a mild contrast—"But to each one of us." What is Paul contrasting his statement with here? In 4:4-6, he set out his "oneness" litany—one body, one Spirit, one hope, one Lord, one faith, one baptism, one God and Father of all. Yet unity is only part of the picture. Paul also insists that unity is not the same as uniformity. Harmony is not monotony. Instead, the perfect picture of the church is diversity in unity—each person working in his or her unique capacity toward a common goal.

When Paul says, "to each one of us," we can personalize that. He means *you!* To you, grace has been given according to the measure of Christ's gift (4:7). That is, you have been called by God, saved by the death and resurrection of Christ, and sealed by the Holy Spirit. The immeasurable grace of God has been extended to you personally. Too many Christians, however, settle for the grace of salvation—*saving grace*—and never realize that God has also given them the grace of sanctification—*enabling grace*. Though we have been given "Christ's gift," which places us in the body of Christ (4:7), many Christians fail to receive Christ's "gifts," which equip us to minister in and to the body of Christ (4:8).

In 4:8 Paul paraphrases Psalm 68:18, applying an important Old Testament image to his New Testament context. In that psalm, David called for God to rescue His people and vindicate them as He had in the past. The Lord had led His people in triumph during the Exodus (Ps. 68:7). Mount Sinai quaked (Ps. 68:8), and the kings of the earth were scattered (Ps. 68:11-14). Then He set Himself upon His holy mountain (Ps. 68:15-17) and received gifts from men (Ps. 68:18). Paul applied this picture to Christ's ascension because he saw it as a potent representation of God's triumph.

After His crucifixion and resurrection, Christ led His people to freedom and ascended in victory. He "led captive a host of captives" (Eph. 4:8), seating believers with Him spiritually in the heavens (2:6). Though we were once enemies of God (2:12), we have been brought into His family through the reconciliation of Christ (2:19). Once bound by sin and subject to the kingdom of Satan, we have been taken captive by Christ and are joint heirs in the kingdom of heaven.

Whereas Psalm 68 spoke simply of God receiving spoils of war from His vanquished enemies, Paul indicates that Christ's conquest of sin, death, and the devil resulted in the distribution of the wealth He received through His victory. Upon whom did Christ shower these gifts? What were they? Paul answers these questions in 4:11 after a brief parenthesis.

## — 4:9-10 —

The mention of Christ's ascension leads Paul into a short parenthetical thought, in which he gives his readers a brief insight into some facts surrounding that victorious event. Paul states that the phrase "He ascended" emphasizes the fact that Christ must have also "descended" (4:9-10). But from where did He descend and how far down did He go? This question has irked Bible scholars for centuries. Three major interpretations are common:

1. Perhaps the descent refers to the Incarnation, in which the divine Son of God descended from heaven to take on a human nature. Paul's words here would then be parallel to his similar thought in Philippians 2:6-8. In this case, the phrase "into the lower parts of the earth" could be translated "into the lower parts, namely, the earth."[5] As a subset of this view, some say Paul could have had in mind the lowest part of the earth, namely, the tomb in which Christ was buried.[6] In any case, the earthly, physical sphere would be what Paul had in view.

2. Perhaps the descent refers to events following Christ's ascension, when the Holy Spirit descended upon the church at Pentecost and bestowed gifts on the body of Christ (Acts 2). This would be similar to Christ's promise to send the Holy Spirit after He had ascended to the Father, coming to them in the spiritual sense through the Spirit's presence in the church (John 14:16-18).[7]

3. Perhaps the descent refers to the time between Christ's death and resurrection.[8] Many Christians believe that after His death on the cross, Christ descended into the place of departed spirits, proclaiming victory over wicked spirits in bondage and leading Old Testament saints on a victorious ascent to paradise (see 1 Pet. 3:18-20).[9]

I lean toward the third interpretation. I say "lean" because I'm the first to admit when a text isn't perfectly clear. The other views also fit the language of Ephesians 4:9-10 and have parallel passages to support their interpretations. This isn't a doctrine I'd fight for or split a church over, but the view of Christ's descent to the spiritual realm known as "Sheol" or "Hades" between His death and resurrection is extremely ancient and enduring in the history of the church. In fact, the Apostles'

## The Descent and Ascent in the Work of Christ

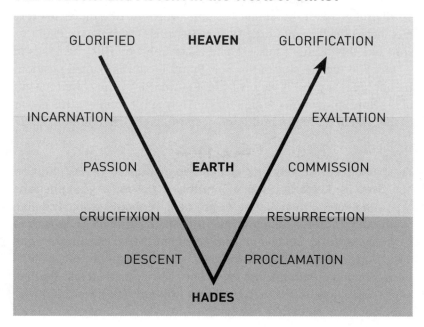

Creed, recited by countless churches worldwide, states that Christ "was crucified, dead, and buried; He descended into Hades."[10]

Nevertheless, whatever disagreements scholars may have over Ephesians 4:9, they all agree on the essential meaning of 4:10. Christ ascended to the Father "so that He might fill all things." This last phrase tells us that Christ did not ascend simply to leave the world behind Him. Rather, He ascended so that he might expand His presence and influence in the world. How, exactly, could He accomplish such a task from the right hand of the Father in heaven? In John 16:7, Jesus said, "I tell you the truth, it is to your advantage that I go away; for if I do not go away, the Helper will not come to you; but if I go, I will send Him to you." Earlier Jesus had said that through the presence of the Holy Spirit in the church, He Himself would come to dwell among His people (John 14:16-18). In Colossians, Paul calls this the "mystery . . . which is Christ in you" (Col. 1:27). Though Jesus has ascended to heaven bodily and is seated at the right hand of the Father, He can be truly present with us through the work of the Holy Spirit, whose presence bridges the distance between heaven and earth. This made it possible for Christ to promise His disciples that in the day when the Holy Spirit comes, "you will know that I am in My Father, and you in Me, and I in you" (John 14:20).

When Christ sent the gift of the Holy Spirit from heaven, the Holy Spirit brought with Him numerous gifts, which He distributes to every member of the body of Christ "just as He wills" (1 Cor. 12:11). Paul reasons like this: Christ's descent and ascension won Him the spoils of victory and the blessing of the Holy Spirit. From His exalted position, He has led many in His victory train. In turn, He has bestowed the gift of the Holy Spirit upon the church. The Holy Spirit manifests His power in the church through a multitude of spiritual gifts that differ in kind.

## — 4:11 —

Five passages in the New Testament list approximately twenty gifts God has given us: Romans 12:6-8; 1 Corinthians 12:8-10, 28-30; Ephesians 4:11; and 1 Peter 4:10-11. Before we proceed, we should probably define "spiritual gift." It is *a God-given ability or skill that enables a believer to perform a specific function in the body of Christ with effectiveness and ease.* Note that spiritual gifts are given by the Lord, not by other Christians. Teaching, training, and experience can strengthen and sharpen your spiritual gifts, but they can't bestow them. They are "spiritual" gifts, not because they're mystical, impractical, or subjective things,

## SPIRITUAL GIFTS LISTED IN SCRIPTURE

Ephesians 4:11 mentions four personal ministries of gifted leaders in the church, but several other passages in Scripture list the kinds of spiritual gifts that have been distributed among all believers.

| ROMANS 12:6-8 | 1 CORINTHIANS 12:4-11 | EPHESIANS 4:11 | 1 PETER 4:10-11 |
|---|---|---|---|
| Prophecy | Word of wisdom | Apostles | Speaking |
| Service | Word of knowledge | Prophets | Serving |
| Teaching | Faith | Evangelists | |
| Exhortation | Healing | Pastor-Teachers | |
| Giving | Miracles | | |
| Leading | Prophecy | | |
| Mercy | Distinguishing of spirits | | |
| | Speaking in tongues | | |
| | Interpreting tongues | | |

but because their power comes from the Holy Spirit, and they bring about real spiritual change.

Here are a few other vital facts about spiritual gifts:

- Every believer has at least one spiritual gift; some have more than one (see 1 Cor. 12:7; 14:1).
- Spiritual gifts are given with our salvation and are used to fulfill God's calling for us (1 Cor. 14:26; Eph. 4:12; 1 Pet. 4:11).
- The gifts are varied and fill different roles. Some are more visible than others, but all are equally important (1 Cor. 12:12-25).
- All the gifts derive their power from the same source—the triune God (1 Cor. 12:4-6).
- Spiritual gifts are given not for one's own edification but for the common good (1 Cor. 12:7).
- All the gifts are meant to give glory to the one who so lavishly bestows them (1 Pet. 4:11).

I know that a lot of pastors, teachers, and ministries try to help believers "discover" their spiritual gifts. Meaning well, they use tests, forms, books, and creative projects, all of which tend to circumvent the best and only foolproof way to learn and sharpen your spiritual gifts: *ministry experience.* Do you desire to discover and develop your spiritual gifts? Then roll up your sleeves and get to work in a ministry! Find an opportunity and volunteer. See a need and step in . . . give it a try. As you take steps toward fulfilling the great commission, you'll quickly discover the areas in which the Holy Spirit has uniquely gifted you for ministry.

In Ephesians, Paul focuses on four types of gifted people given to the church: apostles, prophets, evangelists, and pastor-teachers. Let's take a closer look at each of these roles and see how they function together to equip the church.

*Apostles.* Apostleship in a general sense refers to people who are sent in an official capacity. In the New Testament it often has a more technical meaning. Apostles had seen the risen Lord (1 Cor. 9:1; 15:7-9). They had been endowed by God with the ability to do amazing signs and wonders to confirm their gospel message (2 Cor. 12:12; Heb. 2:3-4). Their labor produced fruit among unreached peoples, establishing churches far and wide (1 Cor. 9:1; 15:9-10). Moreover, they were gifted by the Holy Spirit with unparalleled wisdom, which rendered their message absolutely authoritative (1 Cor. 2:12-13; 2 Pet. 3:15). The apostles were among the foundational ministers of the original church who revealed sound doctrine and wrote the New Testament texts, which would carry the church into the future (1 Cor. 3:10; 2 Thes. 2:15). Because of the uniqueness of this ministry, there are no "official" apostles today.[11]

*Prophets.* Like the gift of apostleship, the gift of prophecy was also regarded in Scripture as a foundational ministry of the church and therefore historically temporary (Eph. 2:20). Prophets were the unique mouthpieces of God. Like Old Testament prophets, the prophets of the early church foretold the future (Acts 11:28; 21:9-11) and exhorted, encouraged, and strengthened God's people (Acts 15:32; 1 Cor. 14:29-31). More importantly, though, they revealed the Word of God when the New Testament Scriptures had not yet been completed and collected. Their authoritative and inspired messages came by direct revelation from the Holy Spirit.

After the completion of the New Testament, the gifts of both apostles and prophets wound down. Of course, Christians today can be specially gifted to carry the message to unbelievers, penetrate unreached parts of the world, and proclaim God's Word effectively to believers. But these kinds of gifts for ministry should not be categorized as apostolic and prophetic gifts but as those of the next two categories: evangelists and pastor-teachers.

*Evangelists.* As traveling ministers similar to itinerant preachers or missionaries today, evangelists brought the gospel to non-Christian regions (Acts 8:5-13; cf. 21:8). They often started churches or further developed those established by apostles. A gifted evangelist possesses a special ability to communicate the gospel, to make it particularly plain and relevant to unbelievers, and to help hesitant people take the step of faith. The results of their efforts are often numerically impressive.

Just a note here. Each of us, whether we have this specific gift or not, have the privilege of sharing Christ's gospel with others. While those gifted in evangelism are to lead the way in proclaiming the gospel, we must all share in carrying out the great commission (Matt. 28:18-20). We should never be tempted to "leave evangelism to the experts." Christ wants to use each of us to spread His message in our own unique networks or circles of influence (2 Tim. 4:5).

*Pastor-Teachers.* The two terms "pastors" and "teachers" are linked grammatically in the Greek text. Paul uses one article for the two terms, indicating a close relationship between them. Though they can be distinguished, Paul likely had in mind a close association between pastors and teachers. It's quite likely that "pastors" and "teachers" referred to roles of the "elders" in the churches, whose responsibility it was to "pastor" (shepherd) and to "teach" (1 Tim. 3:2; 5:17; 1 Pet. 5:1-3). This single gift had two distinct dimensions. On one hand, it empowered its possessors to shepherd their flocks by meeting the day-to-day needs of the congregation—counseling, confronting, comforting, and guiding. On the other hand, it enabled them to feed their sheep through the teaching and preaching of the Word. This gift has not changed over time. Leaders functioning as pastors and teachers do the same work in the churches today that their predecessors did centuries ago.

These brief descriptions of apostles, prophets, evangelists, and pastor-teachers exemplify the care God has for His church. He didn't leave the church orphaned, with nobody to teach, comfort, shepherd, or nurture them in their fledgling faith. Instead, He sent His Spirit, whose grace so transformed the lives of believers that they would be used by God to build up the body of Christ—both the local churches and the universal church throughout the world.

## — 4:12-16 —

I'm more convinced than ever that if there's a message the church of the twenty-first century needs to hear, it's the message of Ephesians 4:12-16. We have come on hard times, in which the church is treated more like a corporation or an institution than a body of believers or family of the faithful. Pastors today act more like CEOs than like shepherds—some even prefer that title. Many church-growth methods and leadership techniques are modeled after corporate America. We must allow Ephesians 4 to remind us that *the church is not a corporation*. The church is a family. The church is a body. Listen to the words of Pastor Ray Stedman, one of the men who mentored me early in my ministry:

> We easily forget that the church is a body. We have tried to operate the church as an institution, a corporation, a business. But the reality Paul wants us to grasp in Ephesians is that the church is a body, made up of "cells"—and the cells are individual believers, you and me and our other brothers and sisters in Christ. Each cell has a unique role to play in keeping the entire body healthy.[12]

I started this section by mentioning both positive and negative effects of the modern interest in spiritual gifts. Let me point out what is perhaps the greatest benefit of concern about spiritual gifts that I've had the privilege of seeing over the course of my ministry: the promotion, under the gifted leadership of evangelists and shepherding teachers, of a full-bodied ministry. That is, when the ministry model outlined in Ephesians 4:11-16 becomes a reality in our churches, people begin to grow by leaps and bounds. I'm not talking about numerical growth—an explosion of warm bodies suddenly flocking to hear the latest gifted preacher or to respond to the newest fad. I mean deep spiritual growth resulting in changed lives, love for fellow believers, and an uncontrollable drive for evangelism and missions. Yet this kind of growth *does* result in numerical growth as unbelievers are saved and floundering believers find their way to a vibrant ministry centered on actually making disciples.

Following his rapid-fire list of leaders given to the church in 4:11, Paul answers the "why" and the "how" questions in 4:12-16. *Why* has the Lord gifted the body with these leadership gifts? And *how* do these relate to the spiritual gifts distributed throughout the entire body of Christ? He gives three reasons for God's gifts to the church (4:12) and emphasizes four results of a healthy, full-bodied ministry of the Spirit (4:13-16). In the process Paul reveals three purposes for the gifted ministries of leadership in the church: an immediate purpose (4:12), an intermediate purpose (4:13-15), and an ultimate purpose (4:16). I've outlined these reasons in the following chart.

The immediate purpose of God's gifts of leadership in a local church is to equip every believer in the congregation to work toward building

## Three Purposes for God's Gifts

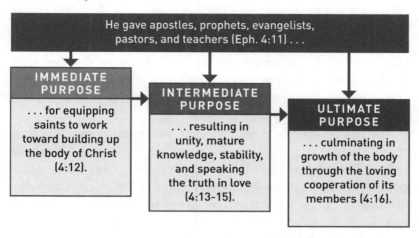

up the body of Christ (4:12). These three steps Paul lists—equipping . . . serving . . . building up—should not be thought of as independent of one another. In fact, they are logically and practically related. The first (equipping saints) leads to the second (serving), which results in the third (building up the church).

God gave the leadership of the church "for the equipping of the saints" (4:12). With this brief statement the emphasis shifts entirely from church leadership to the church body. Did you notice that? Like a baton passed between relay runners, the responsibility for everything in 4:12-16 now rests on the whole body of Christ, not just a few paid professionals! God gave the called, trained, and ordained leadership to the church for "equipping the saints." As a result of this equipping, members of the body learn to function in new ways, exercising their individual gifts for the benefit of the whole body under the direction and encouragement of their leaders.

The members of a congregation are equipped "for the work of service" (4:12). Unfortunately, the way we often do ministry in our churches is to hire staff people to do all the real work. The congregation sits back, arms folded, and observes or supervises while the hired hands do the heavy lifting related to the ministry. Then if something isn't getting done, they hire more professional heavy lifters! What a betrayal of Ephesians 4:12! The "professionals" aren't paid to do the work of the ministry; they're paid to train *others* to do the work of the ministry! Just imagine what churches would have to strike out from their pastor's job description if they took that mandate seriously!

One of my more colorful mentors, Dr. Howard Hendricks, used to say, "The church is too much like a football game—fifty thousand people in the stands, desperately in need of exercise, watching twenty-two people on the field desperately in need of rest." Yes, the Bible speaks of paid ministers who are expected to lead, preach, and teach (1 Tim. 5:17). Yet their primary purpose is to equip the rest of the church to engage in meeting the needs of the flock, exercising their individual spiritual gifts for the benefit of all.

The goal of equipping and serving is "the building up of the body of Christ" (Eph. 4:12). Paul uses the noun for "building up," *oikodomē* [3619], several times in his writings to refer to God's body-building program.[13] Though the word alone might conjure up the image of an elaborate building project—such as a temple—being constructed stone by stone (2:21), in 4:12 and 16, Paul uses the image of an infant being "built up" as the individual parts grow together in proportion with the whole. When the mature body functions as it ought, good health is maintained, needs are met, and we no longer look and live like children.

Having described the immediate purpose of gifted leadership in the church (4:12), Paul then presents the intermediate purpose: promoting unity, mature knowledge, doctrinal stability, and authentic, loving speech (4:13-15). The first sign of a grown-up congregation is that the believers possess "the unity of the faith." "The faith" refers to that body of essential truths shared by all true Christians, which Jude calls "the faith which was once for all handed down to the saints" (Jude 1:3). Though it would be foolish (perhaps even cultish) to expect every person in a church to agree on every minor point of doctrine, there are basic truths of the Christian faith that all believers agree upon, regardless of denomination. These include major doctrinal issues like the Trinity, the full deity and full humanity of Christ, the Virgin Birth, the atoning death of Christ to pay for our sins, the miraculous bodily resurrection of Christ, the promise of His future return, salvation by grace alone through faith alone in Christ alone, the inspiration and inerrancy of Scripture, and similar orthodox, nonnegotiable truths. We should strive to maintain this kind of doctrinal unity while promoting tolerance of differing opinions on less crucial matters.

This doctrinal unity requires a strong "knowledge of the Son of God" (Eph. 4:13). In fact, the core doctrines of the Christian faith center upon the person and work of Jesus Christ in His first and second coming. Helping believers know Him both factually and relationally, both theologically and intimately, is a goal of the preaching and teaching ministries of the church. Paul himself desired this kind of ever-increasing knowledge of Christ: "that I may know Him and the power of His resurrection and the fellowship of His sufferings, being conformed to His death" (Phil. 3:10). This true knowledge touches not only the head but also the heart, resulting in a life of devotion and dedication.

Maturity expressed through unity of the faith and knowledge of Christ leads to doctrinal stability (Eph. 4:14). How could it not? The opposite trait—immaturity—leads to spiritual malnutrition and doctrinal gullibility. As a proud grandfather who has watched his own children and his children's children go through the growth process, I know there's nothing cuter than little children who are clueless. They believe almost anything without question, live their lives in a fog of ignorance, and happily don't know what they don't know. Those small, impressionable, and oblivious little minds are nothing but fun to be around. But I can't think of anything more tragic than adults who live clueless lives, especially those longtime believers who "ought to be teachers" but need somebody to teach them "the elementary principles" of the Christian faith (Heb. 5:12). I've seen it countless times. Along comes some slick, capable spokesman for a cult, and the childish believer, like a reed in the wind, bends in that direction, inviting false doctrine into his or her life. They buy a twisted message because they have been deceived by the trickery and craftiness of deceitful scheming.

Paul frequently warned congregations against false teachers, and the Ephesian church was no exception. He first warned the Ephesian elders to guard their flock against subtle heresies around AD 57 (Acts 20:26-31). In his letter to the Ephesians he again cautioned them about false teaching (Eph. 4:14). A few years later he even more strongly admonished Timothy, who was leading the church in Ephesus, to take a stand against false doctrine (1 Tim. 1:3-6; 4:1-2; 6:20-21; 2 Tim. 1:13-14; 2:14-26). Even after Paul, the congregation was still fighting heretics well into the 80s and 90s (1 Jn. 2:18-19; 4:1-3; Rev. 2:1-7). Yet false doctrine is not a thing of the past. In fact, throughout the centuries Satan and his followers have continued to fabricate deceitful philosophies, false religions, and twisted versions of Christianity. These false teachings employ "trickery," "craftiness," and "deceitful scheming" (Eph. 4:14). Only an unwavering commitment to the truth can help us maintain stability in the hurricane of heresy that constantly swirls around God's people.

If one kind of immature believer is like a child who can't tell truth from error, another kind is like a lopsided scale, unable to balance a passion for truth with a love for others. True maturity gives us another sign of a built-up body: "speaking the truth in love" (4:15). The English phrase "speaking the truth" translates one Greek verb, *alētheuō* [226], which means "being truthful," or, to use a made-to-order term, "truthing." It refers not only to what we say but also to everything we think and do.

The balance between truth and love is often difficult to maintain. Some of us are good at truth. We can spot the smallest inaccuracy in a person's theological expression and have no fear of pointing it out. In our zeal for preserving the integrity of the Scriptures, however, we can easily hurt others by failing to show them love in the process of correcting them. Others of us have the opposite problem. Desiring to keep peace, we let false teaching go uncontested or allow lies to go uncorrected. We just can't bring ourselves to rock anyone's boat for fear that we'll cause too many waves in the church. But God wants us to be neither abrasive nor timid. He wants us to show both strength and love. Commentator John Stott sums up this balance beautifully: "Truth becomes hard if it is not softened by love; love becomes soft if it is not strengthened by truth. The apostle calls us to hold the two together."[14]

Paul presented the immediate purpose of gifted leadership in the church in 4:12—equipping the saints to work toward building up the body of Christ. He described the intermediate purpose in 4:13-15—developing unity, knowledge, stability, and truthfulness. Finally, he reveals the ultimate purpose in 4:16—the growth of the whole body through the loving cooperation of all of its members.

A human body is healthy when all of its parts are operating properly and working in harmony. Similarly, a church body is healthy when all of its members submit to the headship of Christ, walk in the Spirit, contribute to the community with their gifts and talents, and live in cooperation with each other. The body grows as the individual members grow, and the members grow as they feed on the Word and minister to one another.

The church doesn't become mature overnight. It takes time and patience and love. As God works through each individual's exercise of spiritual gifts for the sake of others, He builds us up as a healthy, productive, wholesome body. We need to trust the growth process as we individually contribute to the project. Only then will we learn to embrace a full-bodied ministry as God designed it.

# APPLICATION: EPHESIANS 4:7-16

## Body Life at Its Best

Unity of the faith . . . knowledge of Christ . . . doctrinal stability . . . a balance of truth and love—these qualities mark a healthy, growing church. They also describe a spiritually mature believer. Let's take a few moments to explore these particular virtues as they appear in the life of our church as well as in our personal lives.

*Unity of the faith.* Is your church conscious of the core doctrines of the Christian faith, which all true believers hold as central? Could you personally articulate these doctrines? Or do you pride yourself on your distinctive teachings or practices unique only to you or your church tradition? Read the following passages and consider what attitudes and actions need to change in your own life in order to promote the unity of the faith: Ephesians 4:3; Philippians 2:1-4; Colossians 3:14-15.

*Knowledge of Christ.* Paul called the good news concerning the person and work of Christ "of first importance" (1 Cor. 15:3). And he determined to know nothing among the Corinthians except "Jesus Christ, and Him crucified" (1 Cor. 2:2). Clearly, the identity of Jesus as the God-man who died for our sins and rose from the dead stands at the center of our knowledge of Him. Knowing God through Christ renews our minds, directs our hearts toward Him, and produces lasting fruit in our lives. Read the following passages and consider ways in which you can refocus attention on Christ in your thoughts and devotion: Romans 12:1-2; 2 Corinthians 10:5-6; 2 Peter 1:5-8.

*Doctrinal stability.* Stability of doctrine is impossible without a strong knowledge of God's Word. In fact, Peter emphasized that we need proper instruction in Scripture to avoid becoming unstable Scripture twisters (2 Pet. 3:16). This means not only personal Bible study but also community Bible teaching by the ordained "pastors and teachers" (Eph. 4:11; 1 Tim. 4:13; 5:17). It also involves attention to sound doctrine—both theological and practical teachings conformed to Christian truth. Study 2 Timothy 2:2; 3:16-17; Titus 1:9; and Hebrews 5:12-14. How can you contribute to the doctrinal stability of your church community? In what ways are you engaged in being equipped in sound biblical teaching? How are you passing this sound doctrine on to others (including the members of your family)?

*Balance of truth and love.* When it comes to living and speaking the truth in a spirit of love, do you tend to overlook untruths for the sake of keeping the peace? Or do you attack falsehood with a vengeance, ignoring love in the process? Think of specific situations in which you may have tended toward one extreme or the other. Read the following passages and note how they balance truth and love, then consider how you might achieve that balance in your own life: Proverbs 15:1; 2 Timothy 2:24-26; 4:2; 1 Peter 3:15.

As you address these facets of both personal and corporate maturity, remember that only Christ, through the power of the Spirit, can bring about authentic and lasting change in our lives. Only when we focus on and trust in Him moment by moment will He conform us to His image. Only then will we experience body life at its best.

# Off with the Old, On with the New
## EPHESIANS 4:17-32

**NASB**

17 So this I say, and affirm together with the Lord, that you walk no longer just as the Gentiles also walk, in the futility of their mind, 18 being darkened in their understanding, ªexcluded from the life of God because of the ignorance that is in them, because of the hardness of their heart; 19 and they, having become callous, have given themselves over to sensuality ªfor the practice of every kind of impurity with greediness. 20 But you did not learn ªChrist in this way, 21 if indeed you have heard Him and have been taught in Him, just as truth is in Jesus, 22 that, in reference to your former manner of life, you lay aside the old ªself, which is being corrupted in accordance with the lusts of deceit, 23 and that you be renewed in the spirit of your mind, 24 and put on the new ªself, which ᵇin the likeness of God has been created in righteousness and holiness of the truth.

25 Therefore, laying aside falsehood, SPEAK TRUTH EACH ONE of you WITH

**NLT**

17 With the Lord's authority I say this: Live no longer as the Gentiles do, for they are hopelessly confused. 18 Their minds are full of darkness; they wander far from the life God gives because they have closed their minds and hardened their hearts against him. 19 They have no sense of shame. They live for lustful pleasure and eagerly practice every kind of impurity.

20 But that isn't what you learned about Christ. 21 Since you have heard about Jesus and have learned the truth that comes from him, 22 throw off your old sinful nature and your former way of life, which is corrupted by lust and deception. 23 Instead, let the Spirit renew your thoughts and attitudes. 24 Put on your new nature, created to be like God—truly righteous and holy.

25 So stop telling lies. Let us tell our neighbors the truth, for we are all

HIS NEIGHBOR, for we are members of one another. 26 BE ANGRY, AND *yet* DO NOT SIN; do not let the sun go down on your anger, 27 and do not give the devil <sup>a</sup>an opportunity. 28 He who steals must steal no longer; but rather he must labor, performing with his own hands what is good, so that he will have *something* to share with <sup>a</sup>one who has need. 29 Let no <sup>a</sup>unwholesome word proceed from your mouth, but only such *a word* as is good for edification <sup>b</sup>according to the need *of the moment,* so that it will give grace to those who hear. 30 Do not grieve the Holy Spirit of God, <sup>a</sup>by whom you were sealed for the day of redemption. 31 Let all bitterness and wrath and anger and clamor and slander be put away from you, along with all malice. 32 Be kind to one another, tender-hearted, forgiving each other, just as God in Christ also has forgiven <sup>a</sup>you.

4:18 <sup>a</sup>Or *alienated* 4:19 <sup>a</sup>Or *greedy for the practice of every kind of impurity* 4:20 <sup>a</sup>I.e. the Messiah 4:22 <sup>a</sup>Lit *man* 4:24 <sup>a</sup>Lit *man* <sup>b</sup>Lit *according to God* 4:27 <sup>a</sup>Lit *a place* 4:28 <sup>a</sup>Lit *the one* 4:29 <sup>a</sup>Lit *rotten* <sup>b</sup>Lit *of the need* 4:30 <sup>a</sup>Lit *in* 4:32 <sup>a</sup>Two early mss read *us*

parts of the same body. 26 And "don't sin by letting anger control you."* Don't let the sun go down while you are still angry, 27 for anger gives a foothold to the devil.

28 If you are a thief, quit stealing. Instead, use your hands for good hard work, and then give generously to others in need. 29 Don't use foul or abusive language. Let everything you say be good and helpful, so that your words will be an encouragement to those who hear them.

30 And do not bring sorrow to God's Holy Spirit by the way you live. Remember, he has identified you as his own,* guaranteeing that you will be saved on the day of redemption.

31 Get rid of all bitterness, rage, anger, harsh words, and slander, as well as all types of evil behavior. 32 Instead, be kind to each other, tenderhearted, forgiving one another, just as God through Christ has forgiven you.

4:26 Ps 4:4. 4:30 Or *has put his seal on you.*

When it comes to how we dress, the occasion determines the wardrobe. If we want to ratchet up the level of formality, we might don sharp tuxedoes or elegant evening gowns. If we're headed to the office, a coat and tie or "business casual" outfit might do the trick. A day at the beach means flip-flops and swim gear. Let's face it—the way you dress does impact how people perceive you. Of course, clothing doesn't change who you are inside; but who you are inside does affect your choice of clothing.

The Christian life is no different. Ephesians tells us that we must wear the right "clothes" to match the new life we have in Christ. Before we can put on our new clothes, however, we first need to take off our old ones. Thankfully, in Ephesians 4:17-32, Paul tells us how to do both and gives us two contrasting pictures—the old, raggedy person we once were . . . and the new, radiant person we're meant to be. The believer's change of clothes is an important piece of the overall message of Ephesians: *Because believers have new life through Christ, they ought to live a new life through the Spirit.*

## — 4:17-19 —

Remember the tattered, soiled rags of sin you wore before you came to Christ? Maybe you were saved a little later in life, and those memories haven't faded as quickly as you had hoped. But chances are that all of us keep a set of old clothes in the closet so we can slip back into familiar, comfortable patterns of sin every now and then. That's why Paul told us to make a clean break with the past, to throw out *all* of our filthy rags for good.

In 4:17, Paul returns to the same thought with which he began chapter 4, his exhortation to "walk in a manner worthy of the calling with which you have been called" (4:1). Yet in 4:17 he expresses it by negating its opposite: "that you walk no longer just as the Gentiles also walk." This also alludes to Paul's description of the spiritually dead unbeliever mentioned in chapter 2: "And you were dead in your trespasses and sins, in which you formerly walked according to the course of this world" (2:1-2). The idea of "walking like the Gentiles" refers to the old sinful lives the Ephesians lived before placing their trust in Christ (cf. 1 Thes. 4:5). Back then, their thoughts were futile—foolish. They had no goal, purpose, or consideration for God. In order to help the Ephesians discard their grubby garments, Paul clearly defined what those articles of stained clothing really were: a dark mind (Eph. 4:17-18), a hard heart (4:18-19), and a sin-filled life (4:19).

*A dark mind.* The first piece of grubby garb that needs to be tossed out of the believer's wardrobe is the "futility of . . . mind," a "darkened . . . understanding," and the "ignorance" of God (4:17-18). This doesn't mean that an unsaved person lacks intelligence or reason, but that he or she has no spiritual perception. Unbelievers are simply incapable of accepting the things of God, which are "spiritually appraised" (1 Cor. 2:14). This begins to explain how a greatly intelligent, sophisticated, and well-educated person can be totally lost with regard to God, Christ, and spiritual things.

*A hard heart.* The second article of mucky clothing is a "hardness of . . . heart" and a "callous" condition (Eph. 4:18-19), which Paul describes as the root cause of the futility, darkness, and ignorance of their minds. The Greek word translated "hardness" is *pōrōsis* [4457], which indicates a stony, petrified condition, like that of a once living, growing tree that has been petrified over the course of centuries. Applied to the heart in 4:18, it emphasizes the impenetrable nature of a person's cold, calloused heart. New Testament scholar Max Turner suggests that "hardness of heart" in the Bible "means sheer rebelliousness, not emotional insensitivity. . . . This leads to further darkened under-standing as God is displaced from the central position he should oc-cupy. This in turn leads to failure of the human conscience and the downward spiral in sin."[15]

ALCE/Dollar Photo Club

**Petrified Wood.** Paul describes the heart of an unbeliever as "petrified," hardened against the things of God.

*A sin-filled life.* A dark mind and hard heart aren't exactly ideal con-ditions for cultivating a garden of nourishing spiritual delights. Instead of the fruit of the Spirit, such conditions bring forth the weeds of sen-suality, impurity, and greed (4:19). These terms picture a lifestyle that has sunk to a moral low. Having become utterly insensitive to right and wrong, the man or woman in this condition lives a wild life without decency, shame, or thought of repercussions. That vividly describes our contemporary Christless culture—unhindered lust, unbridled promis-cuity, and uncontrolled self-indulgence. Author Kent Hughes describes it well: "Our culture is hell-bent in its cavalier, reckless pursuit of sin, and it makes psychopaths its martyrs and drag queens its models."[16]

Though Paul's words refer primarily to unbelievers, the fact that he urges his readers to "walk no longer" as the Gentiles do (4:17) indicates that even Christians can backslide into these conditions. Having re-turned to their old wardrobe of sin, they will find their minds shrouded in moral haze, their hearts increasingly hardened to the work of the Spirit, and their lives careening into a tangled jungle of immorality from which it is difficult to escape. Filth is filth, regardless of who wears the dirty garments.

## — 4:20-24 —

Paul uses word order to place additional emphasis on the word "you" in 4:20. It's as if he were pointing his finger directly at his readers and calling them out of a vast crowd: "You there!" Those who have come to know Jesus Christ have no business mucking it up with the Gentiles, whose minds are darkened, whose hearts are hardened, and whose lives are spinning out of control. Having heard His voice, believers have been called out of their former lives of darkness into the resplendent light of Christ (4:21). Having received a Christ-focused teaching, believers have sanctified Christ as Lord in their hearts (1 Pet. 3:15). Receiving Jesus as the Truth (John 14:6), they are now able to walk in the truth, forsaking a wild life of sin (2 Jn. 1:4).

In light of this radical change, Paul urges his readers to utterly abandon any trappings of their former way of life. Paul exhorts them to remove their old, ragged, deteriorating clothes and throw them away (Eph. 4:22) and by the renewal of their minds (4:23) to "put on the new self," tailored after the pattern of Jesus Christ Himself (4:24). Just as God created Adam from the dust of the ground, He formed our new selves from the raw material of Christ's righteousness, holiness, and truth.

Notice what Paul focuses on in this passage: the renewed mind (4:23). That's the polar opposite of the mind mired in futility. How do we renew our minds? We immerse ourselves in Jesus Christ (4:20-21). We learn more than mere information *about* Him; we learn *Him* (4:20)— His life, death, resurrection, and lordship. We continue to hear Christ as our Teacher, and we remain intimately associated with Him.[17] This means leaving behind our values and choices that reject God and His ways. It means replacing them with a new worldview—one that eagerly cooperates with God's will and Christ's way. Renewal goes deeper than changing outer habits; it's an inside work of the Spirit that works itself out in a new will and actions (Phil. 2:12-13). It's like taking a shower every day that cleanses us and readies us to put on the Christlike clothes of our new wardrobe.

## — 4:25-32 —

After *describing* the concept of putting off the old self and putting on the new (4:22-24), Paul spends several verses *prescribing* how this can be done practically in day-to-day life (4:25-32). In keeping with his "setting aside" and "taking up" image, he visits several realms of life, encouraging his readers to rid themselves of their filthy old habits and to replace them with new virtues. Let me present a brief overview of the contents of 4:25-32 in the form of a chart, and then we'll spend some time digging into these important examples of "putting off" and "putting on." In these verses Paul presents several bad attitudes or actions that have to go . . . and the positive attitudes or actions that must replace them. In each case, he presents a reason for doing so—either the basis for the change or a benefit reaped.

## PUTTING OFF AND PUTTING ON IN EPHESIANS 4:25-32

| VERSES | PUT OFF | PUT ON | REASON |
| --- | --- | --- | --- |
| 4:25 | Falsehood | Truthful Speech | Because we are members of one another |
| 4:26-27 | Sinful Rage | Controlled Indignation | Because it will take away from Satan an opportunity for temptation |
| 4:28 | Dishonest Gain | Honest Labor | Because we will have something to share with the needy |
| 4:29 | Unwholesome Speech | Edifying Speech | Because it will impart grace to those who hear |
| 4:30-32 | Hateful Attitudes and Actions | Loving Attitudes and Actions | Because we should not grieve the Holy Spirit, but rather imitate Christ |

Let me begin with a couple of observations about all of these negative and positive traits. First, they affect not only our relationship with God but also our relationships with others. Second, Paul balances negative commands with positive ones, explaining his reason for each command and demonstrating that our behavior should be connected to our beliefs. Finally, at the end of the list he clusters several vices and contrasts them with several virtues, implying that he could have continued his list of "putting off" and "putting on" for several pages. In other words, these specific examples are merely the beginning of an ongoing practice of replacing our old habits with new ones.

*From falsehood to truthful speech* (4:25). The word for "falsehood," *pseudos* [5579] in Greek, includes all forms of lying, from out-and-out contradictions of known facts to carefully couched nuances intended to deceive and mislead. It includes everything from white lies to unbelievable whoppers. Because the Ephesians had renounced the supreme falsehood of paganism, Paul urged them to take that decision even further by forsaking all "lesser" lies.[18] Likewise, for us to grow as Christians, we also must uproot falsehood and cultivate truthfulness.

Why does Paul exhort his readers to truthful speech? He does so because lying is a heinous sin against the body of Christ. It undermines trust and results in conflicts and confusion. Jesus reminded us that Satan is the father of lies (John 8:44), but the Lord is the God of truth (Isa. 65:16). As members of His body, eternally joined and related in love, truth is our new birthright and a mark of those who belong to God.

Think of the different forms of lying that surround us every day. Consider whether any of them characterize your own life and need to be put off like a worn-out garment:

- deception
- diplomatic hedging
- exaggerating the facts
- half-truths
- plagiarism
- flattery
- hypocrisy
- habitual promise breaking

We're immersed in a culture that feeds on deception and oozes with falsehood. That doesn't make our truth-telling mandate easy, does it? Some members of the media make their living stretching, shaping, spinning, and tweaking stories that might not have been quite as interesting without those little misleading or exaggerated tidbits inserted here and there to make you come back for more. Advertisements are known for lies. This is why there are consumer advocacy groups to do "fact checks" and government agencies to step in and say "Enough is enough!" And we are constantly bombarded by contradictory truth claims from cults and religious charlatans. In this tempest of falsehood, we Christians need to be tellers of the truth. Start at home. Carry it to work. Practice it with your neighbors. Make it part of your code of conduct.

*From sinful rage to controlled indignation* (4:26-27). Echoing Psalm 4:4, Paul allows for properly expressed anger in the life of a believer. What a relief! I think we'd all be in a heap of trouble if Scripture excluded *all* forms of indignation. In fact, Christ Himself exhibited righteous anger at sin (Matt. 21:12-13). When Paul commands, "Be angry," however, he didn't have in mind temper tantrums, uncontrolled fits of rage, or lingering bitterness. Rather, biblical, righteous indignation directs its anger at the appropriate object—sinful behavior, moral corruption, and unjust circumstances. Frankly, we could use more of this kind of anger today. Too often we remain silent and apathetic while sin and injustice run roughshod over people.

Sinful anger, on the other hand, lingers. It holds a grudge. It seeks retaliation, revenge, and harm toward those who anger us. Paul is quite clear about this kind of expression of anger: *Don't do it!* In fact, to keep us from coddling our angry attitudes and actions, he sets a limit: "Do not let the sun go down on your anger" (Eph. 4:26). In other words, don't brood over it. Don't go to bed mad and allow it to simmer overnight. Understandably, not all conflicts can be quickly resolved before bedtime. Sometimes it may take days or even weeks to work out full reconciliation. We can, however, personally resolve not to let our anger fester into the next day. The longer you let a broken relationship go without reconciliation, the easier it will be for Satan to drive a wedge into the relationship, creating division and disunity in the body of Christ (4:27).

Paul puts this in even more explicit terms in Romans 12:17-19. He writes,

> Never pay back evil for evil to anyone. Respect what is right in the sight of all men. If possible, so far as it depends on you, be at peace with all men. Never take your own revenge, beloved, but leave room for the wrath of God, for it is written, "VENGEANCE IS MINE, I WILL REPAY," says the Lord.

*From dishonest gain to honest labor* (4:28). Stealing encompasses a whole array of activities, from obvious acts like shoplifting, embezzling, fraud, and robbing banks to the subtle "borrowing" of office supplies, wasting time at work, reneging on a debt, or failing to pay a fair wage. All of these are forms of dishonesty for the sake of personal gain—some blatant, some subtle . . . all sinful.

Instead of stealing, Paul directs us to work. Through the work of our hands we not only provide for ourselves and our families but also contribute to the good of others. When we are able to provide for our own needs, we relieve the church or community from having to burden themselves with supporting us. This allows such resources to be used for those who are truly in need. At the same time, our own honest labor can produce an excess, giving us an opportunity to share from the abundance of our prosperity with those in need.

*From unwholesome speech to edifying speech* (4:29). The Greek word *sapros* [4550], translated "unwholesome," was used to describe rotten fruit or putrid fish in the ancient world—in other words, the kind of stinking things that would make you say "Yuck!" Applied to language, it can refer to several kinds of speech—cursing, vulgar phrases, crude jokes, and even sarcastic, unkind, or mean-spirited remarks. Plenty of the material shared online nowadays also falls into this category.

To give a better idea of the broad scope of "unwholesome" speech, Paul contrasts it with its opposite: words that are good for edification and appropriate to the situation, which impart grace to those who hear (4:29). The emphasis should not be on entertaining others but on edifying them. We should avoid tearing people down and focus on building them up. As Thumper said in the Disney classic *Bambi*, "If you can't say somethin' nice . . . don't say nothin' at all." Not bad advice from an animated rabbit! If we could only learn to live by this simple rule, we'd save our families, friends, and churches from a world of pain.

*From hateful attitudes and actions to loving ones* (4:30-32). Paul next inserts a thought that could be inserted after any of his five examples: "Do not grieve the Holy Spirit of God, by whom you were sealed for the day of redemption" (4:30). Paul has already mentioned the work of the Holy Spirit in sealing us at the moment of salvation (1:13). Yet his statement in 4:30 gives us insight into the fact that though the sealing is permanent, our sin can cause the Holy Spirit pain and distress. The word translated "grieve" (*lypeō* [3076]) is the same word used to describe Jesus' agonizing distress in the garden of Gethsemane on the night of His betrayal (Matt. 26:37). When we lie, lash out in anger, steal, refuse to forgive, or insult or curse another, we literally cause the Spirit sorrow. But when we walk in freedom, loving as Christ loved, caring as Christ cared, forgiving as Christ forgave, we delight the Spirit. What powerful motivation for putting off the old and putting on the new!

With this reminder of the presence of the Holy Spirit, Paul lists a number of attitudes and actions that reflect an unkind, unforgiving, and hateful heart (Eph. 4:31):

- *bitterness*: an attitude that harbors resentment and rejects reconciliation
- *wrath*: a deep-seated rage that fails to subside
- *anger*: an uncontrollable temper with explosive outbursts
- *clamor*: loud outcries that disrupt peace and cause confusion
- *slander*: destroying the reputation of another through gossip
- *malice*: harming others through intentional acts of wickedness

Consistent with his theme of "off with the old, on with the new," Paul exhorts the Ephesians to replace these six hateful vices with three loving virtues (4:32):

- *kindness*: acting graciously and mercifully toward others, just as God has with us (2:4-5)
- *tender-heartedness*: offering care and comfort to those in need, just as the Holy Spirit has come alongside us as our Helper (John 14:16)
- *forgiveness*: extending reconciliation to those who have offended or harmed us, just as Christ has forgiven us (Eph. 1:7)

Paul exhorts the Ephesians—and us—to rid our closets of the stained, tattered, and filthy garments of our past and to replace them with the clean, fresh wardrobe custom-tailored by the Spirit. When we do, we reflect the holiness of God, follow the example of Christ, and avoid grieving the Holy Spirit of promise. Of course, every one of us will inevitably fail on occasion, slipping into our old habits, reviving old vices, and repeating past sins. Yet 1 John 1:9 provides an immediate means of restoring our righteous garments when we've stained them with sin: "If we confess our sins, He is faithful and righteous to forgive us our sins and to cleanse us from all unrighteousness." One of my mentors referred to this verse as "the Christian's bar of soap."

When your new clothing gets a smudge, stain, or tear, don't ignore it! Turn to Christ quickly; deal immediately and openly with your sin. Confess it—all of it—and experience His merciful restoration. Continually lay your life before Him as a living sacrifice (Rom. 12:1-2), and learn to walk tall and clean, clothed in the splendid righteousness provided to us free of charge. Make it your aim to exemplify the truth that those who have new life through Christ should live a new life through the Spirit.

## APPLICATION: EPHESIANS 4:17-32

### Renewing Our Wardrobe

When it comes to clothing, we've come a long way since Adam and Eve's scratchy fig-leaf coverings. When we open our wardrobes today, we have countless options: Coat and tie or shorts and T-shirt? High heels or sandals? Button-up or tank top? Skirt or dress pants?

Sadly, all of us have been born with an ugly suit of sin—a fallen nature that falls infinitely short from the radiant glory in which God desired us to be clothed. Throughout our lives we add to this natural tendency toward wickedness, resulting in a massive wardrobe of ragged wretchedness. Our thoughts, attitudes, and actions are so stained and polluted with sin that "all our righteous deeds are like a filthy garment" (Isa. 64:6).

In Ephesians 4:17-32, Paul provides a number of contrasts between the old and new—the dirty wardrobe of our natural fallen condition and the new wardrobe of our redeemed life in Christ. However, until we're clothed with our glorified, sinless, immortal bodies (2 Cor. 5:4), we must make constant choices to "lay aside the old self" and "be renewed" in the spirit of our mind (Eph. 4:22-23).

To help reflect on this, consider which of the following "old clothes" need to be "put off" from your life . . . and which "new clothes" need to be "put on." These are drawn from Paul's contrasts in Ephesians 4:17-32. Consult the explanations in the commentary above if some of these characteristics are unfamiliar to you. Try to identify at least three negative vices to take off and three positive virtues to put on.

| OLD CLOTHES TO TAKE OFF | NEW CLOTHES TO PUT ON |
| --- | --- |
| Sensuality and impurity (4:19) | Righteousness and holiness (4:24) |
| Greediness and stealing (4:19, 28) | Speaking truth (4:25) |
| Falsehood (4:25) | Forgiveness (4:26, 32) |
| Wrathful anger (4:26, 31) | Productive labor (4:28) |
| Unwholesome speech and slander (4:29, 31) | Generosity (4:28) |
| Bitterness (4:31) | Timely words of encouragement (4:29) |
| Clamor (4:31) | Kindness (4:32) |
| Malice (4:31) | Tender-heartedness (4:32) |

Once you've identified the areas that need a wardrobe renewal, take these to God in prayer, asking in the name of Jesus Christ, by the power of the Spirit, that you may be transformed "by the renewing of your mind" (Rom. 12:2). Unlike wardrobe changes, this swapping of actions can't begin and end merely with changes in external behavior. It needs to begin with repentance and a change of attitude through the inner working of the Spirit, or, as Paul describes it, by a renewal "in the spirit of your mind" (Eph. 4:23). Your actions, habits, and lifestyle will follow.

# FOLLOWING AND SUBMITTING: THE IMITATOR'S PATH (EPHESIANS 5:1–6:9)

The best-selling Christian devotional book of all time, *The Imitation of Christ*, was written around 1418 by Thomas à Kempis. He was a member of the Dutch monastic community known as the Brethren of the Common Life. Some church historians regard their movement as a forerunner of the Protestant Reformation. Indeed, the great Protestant preachers John Wesley and John Newton considered *The Imitation of Christ* as highly influential in their own devotional lives. Even today Christians from all over the world find encouragement in its words. That classic devotional begins with the following words:

> "He who follows Me, walks not in darkness," says the Lord (John 8:12). By these words of Christ we are advised to imitate His life and habits, if we wish to be truly enlightened and free from all blindness of heart. Let our chief effort, therefore, be to study the life of Jesus Christ.
>
> The teaching of Christ is more excellent than all the advice of the saints, and he who has His spirit will find in it a hidden manna. Now, there are many who hear the Gospel often but care little for it because they have not the spirit of Christ. Yet whoever wishes to understand fully the words of Christ must try to pattern his whole life on that of Christ.[1]

The themes of imitating Christ, following His example, and walking by His Spirit are found throughout the New Testament (Matt. 10:38; 1 Cor. 11:1; Phil. 2:5; 1 Pet. 2:21). In fact, following Christ in humble submission is the essence of true discipleship. The mandate for living in imitation of Christ is clear. Yet we can't accomplish this imitation of Christ on our own. We need something more than a shallow "monkey see, monkey do" approach to spirituality in which we try hard to copy Jesus' actions. What we need is a real Spirit-empowered *transformation* in order to be "conformed to the image of His Son" (Rom. 8:29). Because believers really do have an eternal and irrevocable new life through

Christ, they should live out that new life daily in every sphere of their lives through the power of the Spirit. This simple truth of Ephesians takes on concrete form in this next section of Paul's letter.

I've titled this section of Ephesians "Following and Submitting: The Imitator's Path (Ephesians 5:1–6:9)." In this section Paul continues to describe the life of the believer in extremely practical terms. Those who once walked in darkness, indulging the flesh, are now urged to walk as children of light, seeking purity, righteousness, truth, and wisdom (5:1-17). This spiritual makeover can only be accomplished by yielding to the work and enablement of the Holy Spirit (5:18). When the Spirit of Christ empowers the believer by His transforming grace, His work manifests itself not only through sincere worship (5:19-20) but also through humility and submission in the family (5:21–6:4) and the workplace (6:5-9). By submitting ourselves "to one another" (5:21), we will walk in the footsteps of Jesus Christ (5:1-2). Then, and only then, will we live in the imitation of Christ.

## KEY TERMS IN EPHESIANS 5:1–6:9

*skotos* (σκότος) [4655] "darkness"
In the ancient world, once the sun set in the evening, most people relied on either moonlight or small lamps to light their way. Often, darkness meant the coming of an unseen and unknown world in which hazards lingered and dangers lurked. Paul portrays those who are apart from Christ as actually *being* "darkness" in contrast to being "Light in the Lord" (5:8). Christ Himself is the Light who reveals truth and removes moral and spiritual darkness (2 Cor. 4:6; 2 Tim. 1:10). Paul associates several specific practices with the darkness (Eph. 5:3-4, 11), and he directs believers to steer clear of such works.

*hypotassō* (ὑποτάσσω) [5293] "to place under,"
"to subject"; passive "to submit"
Though mutual submission is a major theme in the latter half of Paul's letter to the Ephesians (5:21), in his letter to the Philippians Paul presents the perfect model of humility and submission in Jesus Christ (Phil. 2:5-8), who fulfilled the will of the Father throughout His life. In the active voice, the term means "to place something under submission." In the passive voice, as used by Paul in Ephesians 5, it describes a person yielding to the leadership or authority of another.

# From Walking in Darkness to Living in Light
## EPHESIANS 5:1-14

**NASB**

¹ Therefore be imitators of God, as beloved children; ²and walk in love, just as Christ also loved ªyou and gave Himself up for us, an offering and a sacrifice to God ᵇas a fragrant aroma.

³ But immorality ªor any impurity or greed must not even be named among you, as is proper among ᵇsaints; ⁴and *there must be no* filthiness and silly talk, or coarse jesting, which are not fitting, but rather giving of thanks. ⁵ For this you know with certainty, that no ªimmoral or impure person or covetous man, who is an idolater, has an inheritance in the kingdom of Christ and God.

⁶ Let no one deceive you with empty words, for because of these things the wrath of God comes upon the sons of disobedience. ⁷Therefore do not be partakers with them; ⁸for you were formerly darkness, but now you are Light in the Lord; walk as children of Light ⁹(for the fruit of the Light *consists* in all goodness and righteousness and truth), ¹⁰ªtrying to learn what is pleasing to the Lord. ¹¹Do not participate in the unfruitful deeds of darkness, but instead even ªexpose them; ¹²for it is disgraceful even to speak of the things which are done by them in secret. ¹³But all things become visible when they are ªexposed by the light, for everything that becomes visible is light. ¹⁴For this reason ªit says,

"Awake, sleeper,
And arise from the dead,
And Christ will shine on you."

5:2 ªOne early ms reads *us* ᵇLit *for an odor of fragrance* 5:3 ªLit *and all* ᵇOr *holy ones* 5:5 ªI.e. one who commits sexual immorality 5:10 ªLit *proving what* 5:11 ªOr *reprove* 5:13 ªOr *reproved* 5:14 ªOr *He*

**NLT**

¹ Imitate God, therefore, in everything you do, because you are his dear children. ² Live a life filled with love, following the example of Christ. He loved us* and offered himself as a sacrifice for us, a pleasing aroma to God.

³ Let there be no sexual immorality, impurity, or greed among you. Such sins have no place among God's people. ⁴ Obscene stories, foolish talk, and coarse jokes—these are not for you. Instead, let there be thankfulness to God. ⁵ You can be sure that no immoral, impure, or greedy person will inherit the Kingdom of Christ and of God. For a greedy person is an idolater, worshiping the things of this world.

⁶ Don't be fooled by those who try to excuse these sins, for the anger of God will fall on all who disobey him. ⁷ Don't participate in the things these people do. ⁸ For once you were full of darkness, but now you have light from the Lord. So live as people of light! ⁹ For this light within you produces only what is good and right and true.

¹⁰ Carefully determine what pleases the Lord. ¹¹ Take no part in the worthless deeds of evil and darkness; instead, expose them. ¹²It is shameful even to talk about the things that ungodly people do in secret. ¹³ But their evil intentions will be exposed when the light shines on them, ¹⁴ for the light makes everything visible. This is why it is said,

"Awake, O sleeper,
rise up from the dead,
and Christ will give you light."

5:2 Some manuscripts read *loved you.*

Far off in the dark, foggy night, the captain of a massive battleship spotted a faint light. Immediately he ordered his signalman to send this message: "Alter your course ten degrees south."

Promptly the captain received a response: "Alter your course ten degrees north."

The indignant captain stiffened. Obviously not used to having his orders rejected, he repeated the message, this time with greater force and an added punch: "Alter your course ten degrees south. *I am the captain of this vessel!*"

Almost instantly another message was received—calm, to the point: "I am Seaman Third Class Jones. Alter your course ten degrees north."

The captain fumed. What was a low-ranking seaman doing giving orders to a ship captain? This had to stop. He responded pointedly, "Young man, I repeat: Alter your course ten degrees south. *This is a battleship!*"

Then came the terse reply as the light pierced the darkness: "Captain, I repeat: Alter your course ten degrees north. *This is a lighthouse.*"[2]

Though this humorous story is fictional, it illustrates an important point: *Lighthouses should never be ignored.* They're not placed on islands and shorelines to distract or frustrate us. Their beacon lights are there to protect us. To ignore or defy a light in the darkness is to jettison reason in favor of folly.

God's light is like that too. All too often men and women shrink back from it in fear, defy it with arrogance, or ignore it to their peril. Yet believers guided by the Spirit of truth recognize God's light as their saving grace.

Ephesians 5:1-14 contrasts the life of light with the life of darkness, exhorting believers to maintain their walk as children of the light (5:8) and to expose the deeds of darkness (5:11). But like a stubborn, self-confident captain unwilling to change the course of his proud ship, our sinful flesh will seek to resist the obvious course of action: Heed God's warnings and walk in His ways. To do anything else would mean to run headlong into moral disaster.

## — 5:1-2 —

Paul returns to the familiar theme of "walking," an image that launched his practical section in Ephesians 4:1, where he wrote, "Therefore I, the prisoner of the Lord, implore you to walk in a manner worthy of the calling with which you have been called." In 5:2, he exhorts his readers to "walk in love." In fact, Paul tells them to "be imitators of God" (5:1).

The Greek word translated "imitators" is *mimētēs* [3402], from which we derive our English word "mimic." When we mimic somebody, we act out what they're doing; we follow their lead, trying to copy their actions. But how can we possibly mimic God's actions? This would be an incredibly daunting challenge if it were not for Paul's next phrase: "as beloved children." In other words, as members of His spiritual family, we should take after our heavenly Father.

This is where Christ comes in—the true Son of God who took on full, sinless humanity. As God's Son, after whose image we are being renewed by the Holy Spirit, Christ becomes the exemplar—the template for what it looks like to be a true human mimicking God. Like an older brother, Christ is the perfect model for us to follow. It stands to reason that, as beloved children, we are to carry on our lives with the characteristics that are true of the Son. He's good; we should be good. He's kind; we must be kind. He's just; we should be fair. He's holy; we are to be pure. He's full of grace; we ought to demonstrate grace toward one another. The list could go on and on.

Paul also illustrates the extent of our imitation. We are to walk in "love"—unconditional *agapē* love. The example? Christ's self-sacrificial love by which He gave Himself up for us, thus pleasing God as "a fragrant aroma" (5:2). Paul presents us with the greatest standard of selfless love, just as Jesus Himself taught: "Greater love has no one than this, that one lay down his life for his friends" (John 15:13). As one commentator notes, "He is telling us to love our neighbors in the sense of being willing to work for their well-being even if it means sacrificing our own well-being to that end."[3]

Like a gloomy, stormy sea, however, the world around us opposes Christ's way of love at every turn and tries with all its might to crash us into a rocky shoreline. This is why Paul issues a strong summons to purity in the next several verses, which are an urgent warning against the world's destructive, self-serving ways—and a clear beacon of light to pierce the darkness.

## — 5:3-6 —

Like a searchlight scanning the shadowy niches of life, Paul focuses on several sins that can dim the witness of the Christian community. Though we are called to be "lights in the world" (Phil. 2:15), certain behaviors can dim our witness and render us indistinct and ineffective. In fact, the dimmer the light, the more we look like those who are cut off from God's kingdom—the children of disobedience upon whom the wrath of God is coming (Eph. 5:5-6). By associating these deeds of darkness with unbelievers, Paul's exhortation packs a powerful punch: If you're children of the light, don't live like children of darkness! Let's shine some light on the dark deeds that Paul mentions in 5:3-4: immorality, impurity, greed, filthiness, silly talk, and coarse jesting.

Paul begins with two deeds that relate to sexual sin. The first, "immorality," translates the Greek word *porneia* [4202], which shares a common root with our word "pornography." It includes all kinds of sexual sin outside of marriage, including fornication, adultery, homosexuality, and prostitution. While these outward actions should all be avoided, in the Sermon on the Mount Christ focused attention even more pointedly at their inward source—the lust that He said was tantamount to committing adultery in the heart (Matt. 5:28). Paul also refers to "impurity," using the Greek word *akatharsia* [167], which is related to our English word "catharsis" but formed as a negative. Just as something cathartic cleanses us, something "akathartic" pollutes us. Thus, *akatharsia* refers to the effects of immorality on our hearts, minds, and bodies—moral uncleanness that leads to guilt, shame, habitual sin, obsessions, addictions, and a life that spirals out of control.

What a tragedy that our dark modern world actually champions immorality and impurity! Almost any kind of sexual expression is encouraged on television, in films, and especially online. Many believe that the free expression of sexuality is harmless or even healthy, wrongly assuming that nobody gets hurt. Yet Paul warns us not to be deceived by these "empty words" that rationalize sin (Eph. 5:6). Sexual immorality only degrades our humanity; it never enhances it. It turns humans created in the image of God into objects created for gratifying our own selfish desires. God has so much more to give us than what we chase after in the dark.

The next sin in Paul's list is greed. The word translated "greed," *pleonexia* [4124], could also be translated "covetousness" (2 Cor. 9:5), and in fact Paul uses a related word in Ephesians 5:5 to refer to a "covetous man" (*pleonektēs* [4123]). Colossians 3:5 relates it closely to the sinful deeds of the earthly body, including immorality, impurity, passion, and evil desire. So "greed" includes an insatiable appetite for sex, but it also involves a hunger for more material possessions.[4] Both Ephesians 5:5 and Colossians 3:5 link greed and covetousness to idolatry, because greed "makes a god of what it seeks to possess."[5]

From immoral *works* that indulge fleshly desires which should "not even be named" among the saints (Eph. 5:3), Paul turns to immoral *words* that are "not fitting" among believers (5:4). "Filthiness" refers to shameful, disgraceful talk, including degrading obscenities that rob people of their dignity.[6] This would also include innuendos and lewd or suggestive speech.

The phrase "silly talk" is one compound word in Greek: *mōrologia* [3473]. From its root we derive the English word "moron," which means "fool." It's not a stretch to translate this colloquially as "talking like a moron." In Scripture, *fool* doesn't primarily refer to a person lacking intellectual ability but to somebody who denies the reality of God. David wrote, "The fool has said in his heart, 'There is no God'" (Ps. 14:1). Historically, *mōros* [3474] pointed to "a practical denial of God as the Judge of good and evil."[7] *Mōrologia* refers to pointless, empty, and foolish talk—unnecessary verbiage that's neither profitable nor edifying. It reminds me of this proverb nestled in the book of Ecclesiastes: "For as the crackling of thorn bushes under a pot, so is the laughter of the fool" (Eccl. 7:6). In other words, the flame from such scraps is noisy but short-lived, leaving nothing but ashes and a pot of cold food—useless!

"Coarse jesting" also comes from a single Greek word, *eutrapelia* [2160], which probably points out forms of humor that depend on twisting words into double entendres in order to make something innocent seem suggestive, sensual, or immoral.[8] You know that kind of humor. You've probably been around people who get their kicks contorting language into indecent, degrading insinuations. This kind of coarse jesting is typical of people whose minds are always in the gutter, feeding on mental sewage.

At this point, a clarification is in order. Paul's condemnation of filthiness, silly talk, and coarse jesting has nothing to do with a healthy sense of humor. In fact, I firmly believe that God gave us laughter as a gift. Think about it. We humans, created in the image of God (Gen. 1:26-27), are the only creatures He made with a genuine sense of humor. In other words, we have the mental and emotional capacity to be delighted by humor and laugh out loud at irony. Simply put, one thing that distinguishes animals from humans is that *animals never get the joke!*

Paul's condemnations are not about a robust sense of humor, even though we acknowledge that there is "a time to weep and a time to laugh" (Eccl. 3:4). Paul's rebuke addresses the problem of *inappropriate* jesting . . . or joking at an inappropriate *time*. Sensual talk and gutter humor provide no benefit. In fact, they tear people down. Instead, we should use our tongues for "giving of thanks" (Eph. 5:4).

We know better than to think that sexual indulgence, materialistic madness, and degrading speech are "no big deal." Yet it is easy to become so numb to these pandemics of modern society that Paul's unflinching directness in Ephesians 5:5-6 comes as a shock to us. Paul says quite bluntly that people engaged in a blatantly and perpetually sinful lifestyle—immoral, impure, and covetous—have no share in the kingdom of God (5:5). In fact, God's wrath will come upon them (5:6).

Now, Paul doesn't mean that our salvation is forfeited if, in a moment of weakness, we fall into some form of immorality or covetousness. God knows that we're human and that we will sin (1 Jn. 1:8). The difference is whether we deliberately persist in a lifestyle that resists the Lord or whether the general tenor of our lives reflects a Godward direction. In Ephesians 5:5-6 Paul is talking about shameless continuation in a sinful lifestyle—unchanging and unchangeable, even in the face of exhortation, confrontation, and discipline. This kind of unresponsiveness to the things of God may very well indicate that people are, in fact, "dead in . . . trespasses and sins" and still "by nature children of wrath" (2:1, 3). In short, like creatures of the night that cower from the light, those who claim to be believers but constantly turn away from the light of righteousness, purity, and holiness demonstrate that they are actually people of darkness.

## — 5:7-10 —

Having described the lifestyles of those who walk in darkness, Paul urges his readers to "not be partakers with them" (5:7). The implication is that true believers can, at least for a season, get caught up in some of the practices just described. Why would those who have been made "partakers of the promise in Christ Jesus through the gospel" (3:6) ever want to lock arms with those whose end is destruction? The "sons of disobedience" (5:6) wander all their days in a cavern of sin and its treacherous darkness. Why would we want to follow their blind lead when we've been called out of darkness into Christ's marvelous light (1 Pet. 2:9)?

Paul doesn't merely say that believers in Christ once lived in darkness. His language is much stronger. In our life before Christ as unbelievers, we "were formerly darkness" (Eph. 5:8). Do you see the difference? Living in darkness might allow for the possibility that we have at least a pilot light or a faint glow allowing us to get by with a few good works. But when Paul says that we *were* darkness, he means we were actually part of the problem itself. The doctrinal statement at the seminary where I studied and later served for several years puts it bluntly:

# A Light in the Darkness

**EPHESIANS 5:7-10**

Shortly after I graduated from high school, my family and I took a trip to Carlsbad Caverns in New Mexico. There were no theme parks back then, so this natural phenomenon would've been the next best thing. I'll never forget that long, winding, narrow path leading us ever downward through those majestic subterranean halls. My sister and I were having a great time. We climbed around rock formations, descended stairs, and crossed tiny bridges as we wound our way through those labyrinthine tunnels. The lighting in that place cast eerie shadows through the forest of stalagmites and stalactites.

Finally, we reached the heart of the cavern. It was cold, damp, and dark—even with the few incandescent bulbs glowing here and there. Our guide then did something we didn't expect. CLICK! She turned out all the lights! At that moment I knew what people meant by "thick darkness." I couldn't see anybody sitting around me. I put my hand in front of my face, so close I could feel the heat from my palm . . . but I couldn't see my fingers. It was the kind of darkness that would cause grown men to revert back to childhood phobias!

Then suddenly, without warning, the tour guide lit a tiny match with a gentle snap. In that pitch blackness, it took only a small spark of fire to illuminate the whole room. Instantly, I could see all the faces around me. Like me, they had been looking around, gawking into the darkness, desperate for something to catch their gaze. When the match's light pierced the darkness, every face instinctively turned toward that match like members of an orchestra fixing their attention on the conductor. That light not only drove out the darkness; it also attracted attention. We couldn't help but stare at it.

Travel back with me two thousand years. Not to a cavern, but to a hillside. Not in a place of physical darkness, but to a land of spiritual darkness. Sitting on that hillside was a revolutionary Teacher who was just getting underway in His ministry. The religious officials who

(continued on next page)

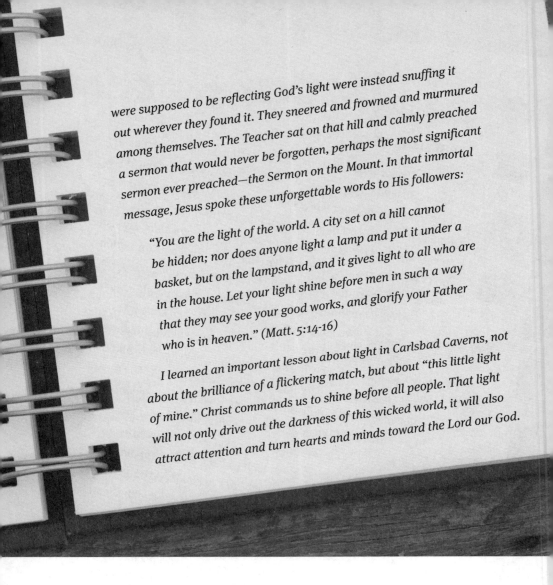

were supposed to be reflecting God's light were instead snuffing it out wherever they found it. They sneered and frowned and murmured among themselves. The Teacher sat on that hill and calmly preached a sermon that would never be forgotten, perhaps the most significant sermon ever preached—the Sermon on the Mount. In that immortal message, Jesus spoke these unforgettable words to His followers:

"You are the light of the world. A city set on a hill cannot be hidden; nor does anyone light a lamp and put it under a basket, but on the lampstand, and it gives light to all who are in the house. Let your light shine before men in such a way that they may see your good works, and glorify your Father who is in heaven." (Matt. 5:14-16)

I learned an important lesson about light in Carlsbad Caverns, not about the brilliance of a flickering match, but about "this little light of mine." Christ commands us to shine before all people. That light will not only drive out the darkness of this wicked world, it will also attract attention and turn hearts and minds toward the Lord our God.

We also believe that this spiritual death, or total depravity of human nature, has been transmitted to the entire human race of man, the Man Christ Jesus alone being excepted; and hence that every child of Adam is born into the world with a nature which not only possesses no spark of divine life, but is essentially and unchangeably bad apart from divine grace.[9]

We don't even have a "spark of divine life." What a hopeless plight! "Apart from divine grace," we were stumbling around in the darkness, trapped in the dungeon of our sin, unable to find the way out. We were shallow, superficial, and selfish. Both in secret and in public we did things we're ashamed of today . . . but we had no power to change. No matter how many New Year's resolutions we vowed, it didn't take any of us but a few hours before we broke them. We didn't change. We *couldn't* change. We were powerless, helpless, hopeless, and lost.

But then Christ came and pierced the darkness of our souls. Remember that line in Charles Wesley's moving hymn "And Can It Be?"

> Long my imprisoned spirit lay
> Fast bound in sin and nature's night
> Thine eye diffused a quick'ning ray:
> I woke—the dungeon flamed with light![10]

Formerly darkness, now light—that's the new identity for all believers in Christ from the moment they place their faith in Him. As light-bearers who reflect God's perfect light of holiness, truth, love, and hope, we are urged to point the way for others to escape the darkness. To do this, we need to "walk as children of Light" (5:8). What does this look like? Paul describes it as producing goodness, righteousness, and truth (5:9). We depart from the former ways described in 5:3-5. Instead, pleasing the Lord becomes our life ambition (5:10). Paul describes here a complete reorienting of our lives, a turning away from the path of darkness and advancing on the path of life—all set in motion and empowered by the grace of God through the power of the Holy Spirit.

## — 5:11-14 —

In contrast to the wonderful effects of the luminous grace of God reflected in the lives of His children of light, the "deeds of darkness" have a devastating impact on everyone (5:11). Participating in darkness not only hurts fellow Christians but also brings harm to nonbelievers. When we claim to have the light of truth but then lie, defraud, abuse, slander, or gossip, we alienate and confuse non-Christians. Many dismiss us as hypocrites. Others see the gospel itself as a sham. They may turn away from God completely because of our soiled, inconsistent testimony, seeking their own light in self-help programs or false religions. When we fail to reflect the light of goodness, righteousness, and truth, we leave people wandering in wickedness, unrighteousness, and deception.

Rather than participating in the evil and barren deeds of darkness, we are to "expose them" (5:11). How do we do this? To be sure, Paul didn't intend that we parade other people's sins before a self-appointed moral court. Remember, the light we're called to reflect isn't a high-powered laser beam designed to target and incinerate wickedness wherever it's found. Rather, our light is meant to reveal what's there by way of contrast. By simply engaging in deeds of light, you and I expose the deeds of darkness. When we live honestly, we expose dishonesty. When we live with integrity, we shock the person who pads his or her expense account or wastes time at the office. We don't walk around wearing a big sandwich board that announces, "I'm the only honest person in the company!" Nor do we pass around little tracts that talk about how pious and great we are. We expose the darkness by shining the light. At times we need to speak up against evil or stand up against injustice, but that's not Paul's focus in 5:11-13. Just live like you ought, and "your light [will] shine before men in such a way that they may see your good works, and glorify your Father who is in heaven" (Matt. 5:16). These words of Jesus lead to the most important effect of shining our light. When we do, the light that exposes, warns, and attracts becomes a means God uses to ignite His flame in the lives of others.

The final words of this section reflect this vital message. Paul understood the great influence believers can have for good, so he issues a challenge by quoting lines from what was probably a common "hymn of repentance and encouragement sung regularly by earlier believers."[11] With this brief snippet of a chorus, Paul reminds his readers that the dawn of redemption has pushed back the thick cloak of night. A glorious morning has risen in which believers now bask in the brilliant rays of Christ's glory:

> Awake, sleeper,
> And arise from the dead;
> And Christ will shine on you. (Eph. 5:14)

# APPLICATION: EPHESIANS 5:1-14

## Let It Shine, Let It Shine, Let It Shine!

Far back at the dawn of time, the first rays of God's light burst into the darkness. With the words "Let there be light," God's six-day work of creation began (Gen. 1:2-4). Since that time, light and darkness have been separated, unable to dwell in the same place. Where darkness reigns, light is absent; where light shines, darkness flees. Let's reflect on the effects of God's light of truth and righteousness, drawing principles for us to practice as we do:

- *Light dispels the darkness of the world.* Read Psalm 119:105; and John 8:12; and John 12:46. Whether the light is the Word of God written (the Bible) or the Word of God incarnate (Jesus Christ), God's light illuminates our path and allows us to find our way in a dark world. When we live lives in conformity with God's Word and follow Christ's example, we become righteous agents of light that expose and drive out the darkness of wickedness.
- *Light attracts attention.* Read Matthew 5:14. Lives aglow with God's light serve as beacons of hope for weary travelers seeking rest. Or they serve as searchlights, seeking lost men, women, and children to call out of the kingdom of darkness. Or they may even serve as warning lights, drawing attention to their own dark deeds. In any case, the light of our good works should attract people to the gospel, inviting them into the light.

Dispelling darkness . . . attracting attention. Let's bring these purposes of light closer to home. How well is God's light shining through the lamp of your life? How often is it accomplishing its purposes? Does your presence in this world make a difference in your home, your school, or your occupation? Do you have a vibrant witness that draws people to your Savior, or do you hide your light under a basket and save it just for church on Sunday (Matt. 5:15)? Does your integrity prick the consciences of those who are sliding ever deeper into darkness? One final, penetrating question: Would you have to admit that sin has crept in and begun to extinguish whatever light remains in your witness?

The Lord genuinely desires to use you. So, if sin has dimmed His light in your life, take time *now* to confess it to Him and seek His cleansing and forgiveness. But don't stop there. Ask Him to kindle anew His flame within you so your light will shine brilliantly and consistently.

# Christian Living 101
## EPHESIANS 5:15-21

**NASB**

15 Therefore ªbe careful how you walk, not as unwise men but as wise, 16ªmaking the most of your time, because the days are evil. 17 So then do not be foolish, but understand what

**NLT**

15 So be careful how you live. Don't live like fools, but like those who are wise. 16 Make the most of every opportunity in these evil days. 17 Don't act thoughtlessly, but understand

NASB

the will of the Lord is. [18] And do not get drunk with wine, [a] for that is dissipation, but be filled with the Spirit, [19] speaking to [a] one another in psalms and hymns and spiritual songs, singing and making melody with your heart to the Lord; [20] always giving thanks for all things in the name of our Lord Jesus Christ to [a] God, even the Father; [21a] and be subject to one another in the [b] fear of Christ.

5:15 [a] Lit *look carefully*  5:16 [a] Lit *redeeming the time*  5:18 [a] Lit *in which is*  5:19 [a] Or *yourselves*  5:20 [a] Lit *the God and Father*  5:21 [a] Lit *being subject*  [b] Or *reverence*

NLT

what the Lord wants you to do. [18] Don't be drunk with wine, because that will ruin your life. Instead, be filled with the Holy Spirit, [19] singing psalms and hymns and spiritual songs among yourselves, and making music to the Lord in your hearts. [20] And give thanks for everything to God the Father in the name of our Lord Jesus Christ.

[21] And further, submit to one another out of reverence for Christ.

At times it helps to return to the very basics. Life gets complicated, things get convoluted, and we get confused. When that happens, it helps to distinguish the essentials from the nonessentials as we return to the fundamental building blocks of Christian living. This is exactly what we find in Ephesians 5:15-21. Let's consider it "Christian Living 101."

For most of us, these five basic principles are nothing new. They're reminders of essential truths. For others, however, they serve as an introductory course for the Christian life—a primer on how to live out our faith in a faithless world. In the previous section we saw that Christians are commanded to be light in the dark world. In this section, beginning with "therefore," Paul again emphasizes the walk of the believer as he or she is led and empowered by the Holy Spirit.

The truths in this section are as foundational for seasoned saints as they are for baby believers. So let's take Paul's hand as he leads us through five primary principles of the Christian life:

1. The Conduct Principle (5:15)
2. The Time Principle (5:16)
3. The Decision-Making Principle (5:17)
4. The Control Principle (5:18-20)
5. The Submission Principle (5:21)

## — 5:15 —

The first of Paul's five basics of Christian Living 101 is the *conduct principle*. Paul says believers must walk with care and wisdom. He's not talking about where you're walking or how fast, but the *manner* in which you walk. This is the principle of right conduct in the everyday

Christian life. As in tightrope walking, the main concern is the quality of the walk—maintaining balance and avoiding a fall.

In Scripture, lacking wisdom means living as if God didn't exist (Ps. 14:1). It means conducting everyday affairs with no concern for God . . . as if His perspective on the mundane matters of life were not relevant. Walking with care and wisdom, however, means acknowledging the Lord in all of our ways (Prov. 3:6). It means being ever conscious of His concern for us and His desire to see us conducting our lives in a manner worthy of our calling in Christ (Eph. 4:1).

## — 5:16 —

Paul's second basic foundation stone of Christian living is the *time principle*. Grammatically, the word translated "making the most of" (*exagorazō* [1805]) is a participle indicating a way in which one accomplishes the first action. That is, in order to walk with care and wisdom (5:15), we must work at "redeeming the time" (KJV). The word translated "time" is *kairos* [2540], which suggests the idea of "opportunities." The participle itself refers to purchasing, buying back, or even rescuing. Theologian Charles Hodge translates this phrase as "rescuing [opportunity] from waste or abuse."[12] Just as Christ redeemed us, rescuing us from a futile existence enslaved to sin and empowering us to live lives of purity and purpose, we ought to buy back our time from futility and sin, turning our everyday opportunities toward His purposes. In another place Paul covers all the bases: "Whether, then, you eat or drink or whatever you do, do all to the glory of God" (1 Cor. 10:31).

As frail and fallen humans, each of us is subject to extremes. At times we either waste our time or become borderline neurotic about it. We're either procrastinators or workaholics. The first extreme passively resists God's purposes for our lives; the second disregards the joy of peace and rest. What can we do to counter these extremes? We can overcome procrastination with *discipline*—directing our energies into what really matters. Discipline means prioritizing and planning, staying focused on the goal, and not losing sight of God's purpose. We overcome the extreme of restless workaholism with *discernment*— recognizing that we were not created as machines to accomplish endless tasks but as works of art molded by God's own hands to serve and glorify Him (Gen. 1:26-27; 2:7). He made us to experience meaningful relationships with Him and with others, all the while appreciating His beautiful creation. We must remind ourselves that the work of God's kingdom consists of more than just *labor*.

Paul gives a straightforward reason for making the most of every opportunity without procrastination or overambitiousness: "because the days are evil" (Eph. 5:16). This can be understood in two ways. It may be that we need to use our time wisely and carefully in order to counter the evil in this world. Or it may refer to the way the evil world tempts us toward wasting our time on frivolous entertainment, fruitless pursuits, or fragmented activities. In either case, the solution is the same: Redeem the time!

## — 5:17 —

Paul's third lesson for Christian Living 101 is the *decision-making principle*. Building upon the principles of living with cautious wisdom (5:15) and using time wisely (5:16), Paul introduces this principle with a reminder: "Do not be foolish" (5:17). Remember, the quintessential fool is the person who says, "There is no God" (Ps. 53:1), then lives his or her life accordingly. Therefore, to the degree that we live as if God were not present in our lives, not interested in our decisions, and not worthy of our attention, we're living as fools.

Instead of living foolishly, we must "understand what the will of the Lord is" (Eph. 5:17). Few things in the Christian life are more basic or important than this—discerning God's will for our lives. Numerous books have been written by people offering an oversimplified combination to unlock the secret safe of God's will. Many people make it sound like God's will for our lives is some kind of fixed path that we can know and follow with certainty.[13] Others have suggested that God's will is—and always remains—a complete mystery, so we should just make our decisions, do whatever we want, and hope for the best. But both the *absolutely fixed* and *absolutely free* approaches to God's will lack balance. The truth is, Scripture gives us a number of clear indications of God's expressed, revealed will for our lives. Look at this sampling:

> And do not be conformed to this world, but be transformed by the renewing of your mind, so that you may prove what the will of God is, that which is good and acceptable and perfect. (Rom. 12:2)

> For the sorrow that is according to the will of God produces a repentance without regret, leading to salvation, but the sorrow of the world produces death. (2 Cor. 7:10)

> For this is the will of God, your sanctification; that is, that you abstain from sexual immorality. (1 Thes. 4:3)

Submit yourselves for the Lord's sake to every human institution, whether to a king as the one in authority, or to governors as sent by him for the punishment of evildoers and the praise of those who do right. For such is the will of God that by doing right you may silence the ignorance of foolish men. (1 Pet. 2:13-15)

Reject the pattern of this world. Be transformed. Renew your mind. Endure sorrow unto repentance. Be sanctified. Abstain from sexual immorality. Submit to human authorities. Do what's right. These are just a few simple, straightforward, clear, and objective expressions of the will of God for our lives. I am convinced that if we spend our time pursuing the things that God *explicitly* wills for us in Scripture, we won't do the things that are against His will. Moreover, when we pursue these things the Spirit of God creates in us character and virtues that help us more easily discern the will of God in areas that are *not* clearly revealed.

I've noticed two tendencies regarding our response to God's will: Either we run ahead of Him or we resist Him. The first is caused by a lack of patience and prudence. We jump to conclusions, rush into decisions, or tumble headlong into every opportunity that presents itself. When it comes to God's specific, personal, and often subjective will for our lives, such as choosing a career, a mate, a home, or a church, we get rather creative in the ways we run ahead of God. Some of us employ the "plop and point" method, letting our Bible fall open and randomly pointing our finger at a verse to guide the day's choices. Or we decide that a string of green or red traffic signals is a divine sign. We need to stop this kind of superstitious hocus-pocus. Don't look for the face of Jesus in an enchilada or lie awake, listening for sounds in the night—three clicks and a bump! That's "voodoo theology." Though popular, that kind of nonsense is far removed from how God would have us perceive His will.

The second extreme—resisting God's will—comes as a result of pride. We dichotomize between "sacred" and "secular," banishing God from the latter. We stubbornly ignore the clear mandates of Scripture, finding all kinds of reasons why they don't apply to us.

Following God's lead involves a simple, though by no means quick-and-slick, method. Pray. Seek Him humbly, sincerely, and patiently with an open, willing heart. If you don't have a willing heart, start there: Pray for one. Go to His Word prayerfully and intelligently, thinking through all your decisions in light of biblical principles and in line with His clearly revealed will for everyone. Seek the counsel of wise and seasoned Christians, ideally those who have gone through the process of making similar decisions. Listen most closely to those who are objective, who personally have nothing to gain or to lose by your decision. Then, when you become convinced of His illuminating light, step forward in humble faith and trusting obedience. We may not always perceive every facet of God's will—it often includes some surprises—but what matters most is walking as best we can in His revealed light.

## — 5:18-20 —

This now brings us to the *control principle*—the fourth basic teaching of the Christian life. Paul begins this exhortation with a contrast—being drunk and out of control versus being under the Spirit's control. This is the difference between having our minds depressed and our senses numbed versus having them invigorated and stimulated. People who are controlled by too much alcohol waste their time, squander their resources, and make fools of themselves. When people are drunk, the things they say usually profit no one. Their words are either garbled and slurred nonsense or full of coarse vulgarities.

Contrast that with people who are controlled by the Spirit. Their minds are clear to see all that Christ has done and is doing. Their hearts are filled with joy as their lips overflow with praise. The Spirit of God fills their hearts with gratitude as their mouths speak in "psalms and hymns and spiritual songs" (5:19). In fact, their entire lives are directed to God the Father through the Lord Jesus Christ (5:20) and by the power of the Holy Spirit.

How are we filled with the Spirit? We see His effects in Ephesians 5:19-20, but is there anything we can do to *promote* these? In the Greek text, "be filled with the Spirit" (5:18) is a passive imperative. That is, it's a *passive command*, meaning we are to allow the Spirit to fill us with all of His blessings, empower us with His enablement, and lead us in His ways. Our whole lives, yielded to God, are to overflow with the work of the Holy Spirit. New Testament scholar Harold Hoehner sums up Paul's thought this way: "With the indwelling each Christian has all of the Spirit, but the command to be filled by the Spirit enables the Spirit to have all of the believer."[14]

## — 5:21 —

Finally, Paul's fifth foundation of the Christian life is the *submission principle*. This reminds us of a vital yet frequently forgotten fact of the Christian life: We're not meant to live it alone. We're meant to subject ourselves to one another, "bear[ing] one another's burdens" (Gal. 6:2), encouraging one another in love and good works (Heb. 10:24-25), and looking out for one another's interests (Phil. 2:3-4).

Let me be frank. If your Christianity is making you more of a recluse, it's not true Christianity; it's selfishness. If what you are calling the Christian life is pulling you further and further away from others, you need to go back to the basics of Christian Living 101. We are to be subject to one another "in the fear of Christ" (Eph. 5:21). Because we love, respect, and honor Christ, we are to love, respect, and honor others. It's that simple. In the final analysis, if our Christian walk doesn't lead us into deeper and more meaningful relationships with fellow believers, we've missed the mark.

So important is this principle of submissive service to one another that Paul spends much of the rest of his letter dealing with how this principle is supposed to work in specific areas of our lives. These include the realms of marriage, parenting, and even employment (5:22–6:9). Because Paul goes into such depth on those topics, we'll deal with them separately. For now, let's review the five lessons of Christian Living 101 by taking a final exam to test ourselves on these vital principles.

# APPLICATION: EPHESIANS 5:15-21
## A Final Exam for Christian Living 101

Having completed Christian Living 101, we're now in a position to give ourselves a comprehensive exam. Think through the following questions and rate how well you're doing on a scale of 1 to 10, with 1 showing the need for the most growth and 10 indicating maturity.

1. Are you careful and wise in your behavior?

   1    2    3    4    5    6    7    8    9    10

2. Are you disciplined and discerning in the way you spend your time?

   1    2    3    4    5    6    7    8    9    10

3. Are you actively and correctly pursuing the Father's will?

   1    2    3    4    5    6    7    8    9    10

4. Are you living under the influence and control of the Holy Spirit?

1    2    3    4    5    6    7    8    9    10

5. Are you deliberately and frequently finding ways to honor and serve others?

1    2    3    4    5    6    7    8    9    10

If you're not doing so well in some of these areas of basic Christian living, there's good news for you—you're not alone! The truth is, Christian Living 101 isn't something you simply learn and get a passing grade on before moving on to other subjects. Rather, it's something you spend a lifetime developing, refining, and improving. Like many skills, if you don't keep growing in these areas, you'll slide backward.

How encouraging it is to know that we have an excellent Tutor! Paul says that we can obey with consistency and confidence because "it is God who is at work in you, both to will and to work for His good pleasure," and that "He who began a good work in you will perfect it until the day of Christ Jesus" (Phil. 2:13; 1:6). Christian Living 101 isn't an independent study or a self-guided course. By yielding to the Holy Spirit, we receive divine enablement to grow spiritually.

Select one of the specific questions above and ask God to begin working in you both to will and to work. Remember, God is not your enemy when you're in need. On the contrary, He is your Advocate, your Shepherd, and your Teacher. He's always eager to help. In fact, Jesus called the Spirit the "Helper" (John 14:16, 26; 15:26; 16:7). In the same way, He encourages us with these words from the author of Hebrews: "Let us draw near with confidence to the throne of grace, so that we may receive mercy and find grace to help in time of need" (Heb. 4:16).

# Solving the Mystery of Marriage
## EPHESIANS 5:22-33

**NASB**

22 Wives, *be subject* to your own husbands, as to the Lord. 23 For the husband is the head of the wife, as Christ also is the head of the church, He Himself *being* the Savior of the body. 24 But as the church is subject

**NLT**

22 For wives, this means submit to your husbands as to the Lord. 23 For a husband is the head of his wife as Christ is the head of the church. He is the Savior of his body, the church. 24 As the church submits to Christ,

to Christ, so also the wives *ought to be* to their husbands in everything.

²⁵Husbands, love your wives, just as Christ also loved the church and gave Himself up for her, ²⁶so that He might sanctify her, having cleansed her by the washing of water with the word, ²⁷that He might present to Himself the church ᵃin all her glory, having no spot or wrinkle or any such thing; but that she would be holy and blameless. ²⁸So husbands ought also to love their own wives as their own bodies. He who loves his own wife loves himself; ²⁹for no one ever hated his own flesh, but nourishes and cherishes it, just as Christ also *does* the church, ³⁰because we are members of His body. ³¹FOR THIS REASON A MAN SHALL LEAVE HIS FATHER AND MOTHER AND SHALL BE JOINED TO HIS WIFE, AND THE TWO SHALL BECOME ONE FLESH. ³²This mystery is great; but I am speaking with reference to Christ and the church. ³³Nevertheless, each individual among you also is to love his own wife even as himself, and the wife must *see to it* that she ᵃrespects her husband.

5:27 ᵃLit *glorious*   5:33 ᵃLit *fear*

so you wives should submit to your husbands in everything.

²⁵For husbands, this means love your wives, just as Christ loved the church. He gave up his life for her ²⁶to make her holy and clean, washed by the cleansing of God's word.* ²⁷He did this to present her to himself as a glorious church without a spot or wrinkle or any other blemish. Instead, she will be holy and without fault. ²⁸In the same way, husbands ought to love their wives as they love their own bodies. For a man who loves his wife actually shows love for himself. ²⁹No one hates his own body but feeds and cares for it, just as Christ cares for the church. ³⁰And we are members of his body.

³¹As the Scriptures say, "A man leaves his father and mother and is joined to his wife, and the two are united into one."* ³²This is a great mystery, but it is an illustration of the way Christ and the church are one. ³³So again I say, each man must love his wife as he loves himself, and the wife must respect her husband.

5:26 Greek *washed by water with the word.*
5:31 Gen 2:24.

Some sections of Scripture resemble minefields full of explosives rather than treasure chests full of truth. You find yourself reading through a powerful chapter like Ephesians 5, and suddenly you come across several topics that can ignite explosive responses—husbands and wives (5:22-33), parents and children (6:1-4), and masters and slaves (6:5-9). When read in light of progressive twenty-first-century norms, some of the ideas in these sections sound old-fashioned to some, quaint to others, and downright ridiculous (or even dangerous) to a few.

Frankly, when it comes to Ephesians 5:22–6:9, I feel like I'm sailing into precarious waters—like those unnamed seas on ancient, faded maps, marked only with a bold, three-word warning: HERE BE DRAGONS! Why is this area so dangerous? Because here Paul deals with some of the most challenging of all relationships on earth:

husband-wife, parent-child, and employer-employee. Each is filled with conflict and a wide range of emotions. But the truth is that those alleged "dragons" infesting Ephesians 5:22–6:9 live only in our imaginations. When we interpret these passages in their biblical and historical contexts, we'll find that their truths transcend culture, personal preference, and human wisdom.

Before diving into Ephesians 5:22-33, we first need to remind ourselves of the context in which we find these verses. First, Paul's practical section of Ephesians (chapters 4–6) begins with an exhortation for all believers to "walk in a manner worthy of the calling with which you have been called, with all humility and gentleness, with patience, showing tolerance for one another in love" (4:1-2). These words set the tone for the rest of the letter, including Paul's treatment of family and other interpersonal relationships. Second, chapter 5 itself begins with an equally powerful command: "Be imitators of God, as beloved children; and walk in love, just as Christ also loved you and gave Himself up for us" (5:1-2). Third, Paul's specific admonitions for husbands, wives, parents, children, masters, and slaves flow out of his primary exhortation to "be subject to one another in the fear of Christ" (5:21).

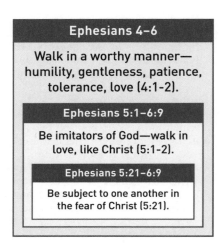

**Ephesians 4–6**

Walk in a worthy manner—humility, gentleness, patience, tolerance, love (4:1-2).

**Ephesians 5:1–6:9**

Be imitators of God—walk in love, like Christ (5:1-2).

**Ephesians 5:21–6:9**

Be subject to one another in the fear of Christ (5:21).

This whole overarching context informs us that everything we do in the Christian life is to be governed by godly, Christlike behavior: humility, gentleness, patience, tolerance, love, and mutual submission. This means that the submission Paul has in mind isn't a one-way street. Rather, it's both people seeking the other's best *and* Christ's honor. Submission gently but firmly displaces selfishness and conceit, competition and pulling rank, and domination and dishonor. When we hear the word *submission* in the biblical sense, we should never picture a gruff commander and his soldiers, a CEO and his managers, or a king and his subjects. We should rather look to the one perfect example of humility and submission—Jesus Christ, who submitted perfectly to God the Father.

This means that wives should treat their husbands with respect, children should cooperate with their parents, and employees should work for their bosses with sincerity and integrity. Husbands, parents, and employers should display the same humble leadership Christ modeled for us: "The Son of Man did not come to be served, but to serve, and to give His life a ransom for many" (Matt. 20:28). Together we work for Christ's glory, recognizing that we're living testimonies of His undeserved grace, life-giving love, and unifying headship over all.

## — 5:22-24 —

After urging all of us to be subject to one another, Paul brings this teaching into the most intimate kind of relationship: that of husband and wife. He begins by applying the submission principle of 5:21 to wives in 5:22-24. He will then spend 5:25-33 applying the principle to husbands.

Paul says wives are to "be subject to [their] own husbands, as to the Lord" (5:22). In the New American Standard translation, the words "be subject" are in italics. This indicates that the original Greek text does not include these words. But the Greek grammar makes it clear that Paul is simply continuing the thought introduced in 5:21—"be subject to one another in the fear of Christ." The Greek text then says, literally, "The wives to their own husbands" (5:22). Note that Paul is speaking here only about the marriage relationship (wives and husbands), not about the general relationship between men and women. He makes this clear with the Greek word *idios* [2398]—"your own." Wives are not told to be in submission to *every* man but to their own husbands. Finally, the phrase "as to the Lord" introduces an analogy, which Paul will unpack in the following verses.

At this point we need to emphasize that in Christ we all have equal dignity, so Paul's statement has nothing to do with inferiority. In Galatians 3:28, Paul says, "There is neither Jew nor Greek, there is neither slave nor free man, there is neither male nor female; for you are all one in Christ Jesus." Such a statement was a profoundly countercultural claim in Paul's day. It was a time when many Jews felt superior to Gentiles, while Gentiles frequently disrespected Jews. Sometimes slave traders considered their wares to be pieces of property, like cattle, whose value was directly linked to their strengths, skills, or abilities. And men often believed that women, who were typically less physically strong than them, were therefore essentially inferior. Not so, says Paul! Men and women, masters and slaves, Jews and Gentiles—all are equal in the eyes of God. Different groups of people do, however, play different and complementary roles in an orderly society.

The Lord has designed husbands to provide leadership in the home and wives to support their husbands. He has chosen to order life this way, and we need to trust that He who knows all also knows best. In our culture, though, feminists balk at the idea of roles and block their ears at any mention of willing submission. There are a couple of reasons for this. First, people often misunderstand that Paul's exhortation for women is balanced with an even stronger mandate for men in Ephesians 5:25-33. Contrary to today's opinion, Paul is no chauvinist! Second, they also fail to realize another important fact. Understood in its whole biblical context, Christian marriage is meant to be a partnership, an intimate relationship, and a deep, mutually gratifying friendship—not a dictatorship! By appealing to the relationship between Christ and the church as a model for marriage (5:23-24), Paul taps into a beautiful picture of the intimate, personal, and loving relationship between the Savior and His people. Yes, Christ is our head (5:23), but we are also "fellow heirs" with Him (Rom. 8:17). He is our Master (Jude 1:4), but He is also our friend (John 15:15).

Christ—our Provider, Protector, Head, Master, and Savior—is our supreme role model. If a husband loves his wife and sacrifices himself for her sake, as Christ did for His church, then his wife will joyfully love him and sacrifice herself for him in return, as the church does for Christ (Eph. 5:23-24). Now, some of us may have cast a wary glance at the words "in everything." Frankly, some men have co-opted this phrase to justify taking unfair advantage of their wives and neglecting the responsibility of self-sacrificial, loving servant leadership. Commentator John Stott sets us straight on this account:

> We have to be very careful not to overstate this biblical teaching on authority. It does not mean that the authority of husbands, parents and masters is unlimited, or that wives, children and workers are required to give unconditional obedience. No, the submission required is to God's authority delegated to human beings. If, therefore, they misuse their God-given authority (*e.g.* by commanding what God forbids or forbidding what God commands), then our duty is no longer conscientiously to submit, but conscientiously to refuse to do so.[15]

Now that we have looked at Paul's words to wives, let's move on to the next several verses, where we'll see that husbands also have a high calling in Christ.

## — 5:25-27 —

Though all believers are to "be subject to one another in the fear of Christ" (5:21), this mutual submission takes different forms. The wife is to support and honor her husband through genuine respect (5:22-24). And the husband is to cherish and honor his wife through true love (5:25-27).

*Love.* It seems so basic, doesn't it? At first glance it could appear that husbands have the easier role. Yet when Paul describes the *quality* of love for which the husband must strive, we realize what a heavy burden of responsibility is placed on him in his leadership role. Make no mistake: Paul refers to *agapē* [26] love—the kind of love that seeks the highest good of the other, even at the price of one's own comfort, safety, and benefit. It's not the word for sexual intimacy, the Greek word *erōs*, which can be a self-seeking, passionate love. Nor is it the word *philia* [5373], the affection and closeness one feels in two-way love, as in a friendship or partnership. Husbands are called to unconditional, self-sacrificial love: *agapē*. No wonder Paul points to Jesus Christ as the perfect example of the kind of love expected of godly husbands!

Authentic Christlike love has several dimensions: surrendering, sanctifying, forgiving, and honoring (5:25-27). Christ surrendered Himself to death on the cross for our eternal good. He cleansed us and freed us from sin so that we would be set apart for Him. He perfects and beautifies us with His own radiant glory, readying us to be with Him always when He returns. Let's look more closely at these actions associated with Christlike love.

Following Christ's example of self-sacrificial love for the church, a husband's love will move him to *surrender* his preferences and let go of his self-seeking desires in order to meet his wife's needs. Think about the extent of Christ's own self-sacrificial love for the church (5:25). Paul explains this love beautifully and succinctly in Philippians:

> Do not merely look out for your own personal interests, but also for the interests of others. Have this attitude in yourselves which was also in Christ Jesus, who, although He existed in the form of God, did not regard equality with God a thing to be grasped, but emptied Himself, taking the form of a bond-servant, and being made in the likeness of men. Being found in appearance as a man, He humbled Himself by becoming obedient to the point of death, even death on a cross. (Phil. 2:4-8)

In submission to God, every husband must exercise extreme humility and be willing to give up whatever is needed for the sake of his wife. Husbands, if your love isn't sacrificial, your wife knows it. If you are selfish in your relationship with her, it will have a negative impact on your entire marriage. If you're unwilling to give up whatever is necessary for her, she can tell. It makes her responsibility of submission that much more difficult. This can make the whole relationship begin a downward spiral. The solution? *Husbands, love your wives as Christ loved the church!*

This love will also cause a husband to have a *sanctifying* influence on his wife (Eph. 5:26). He will encourage her growth—intellectually, emotionally, and spiritually. Just as Christ's relationship with His church promotes spiritual growth, so husbands are expected to nurture positive growth in their wives. This might mean freeing up time for your wife to exercise her own gifts, talents, and interests. It certainly means helping her through her hurts, caring about her wounds, being at her side when she needs someone to lean on—anything that contributes to her wholeness and well-being.

Loving like Christ loves the church also means *forgiving* (5:26). A Christlike husband will embrace grace rather than hold grudges. He will extend compassion rather than blame and shame. He will accept and value his wife for who she is rather than demand perfection. Just as Christ cleansed us in order to present the church to Himself spotless and blameless (5:26-27), so also husbands must extend grace and mercy to their wives.

Finally, husbands must *honor* their wives, recognizing them as precious gifts from God (5:27). Just as Christ seeks to display the church in all her glory, a husband should also seek to honor his wife in a way that demonstrates his love for her. The apostle Peter puts it plainly when he writes that a husband must "show her honor as a fellow heir of the grace of life" (1 Pet. 3:7).

## — 5:28-33 —

In addition to the analogy of Christ's love for the church, Paul presents another manner in which a husband is to love his wife: A man is to love his wife as he would love his own body (5:28). The way a man treats his wife reflects a lot about his own character, integrity, and self-respect.

A loving husband will nourish and cherish his wife, just as he takes care of his own body. A godly husband will help his wife feel fulfilled, grow toward maturity, and deepen her love for the Lord. He will tenderly and warmly affirm her through both emotional reassurance and physical affection. He will wrap his arms of protection around her when she is fearful and extend his hands of provision toward her when she has needs. In other words, nothing a husband does should reflect a greater love for himself than that which he has for her. When a husband models these things, his wife will have no trouble submitting to him. How could she?

Paul returns to his original analogy of Christ and the church, pointing out an even deeper and more profound purpose for the marriage relationship. Not only is the love of Christ for the church a model for marriage, but the husband-and-wife relationship is meant to be lived in such a way that it points people to Christ!

Christ tenderly cares for us as He does His own body—because we *are* His body (1 Cor. 12:27). Because He saved us and made us a new creation in Him (2 Cor. 5:17; Eph. 2:15), we are as much one with Him as a husband and wife are "one flesh" through the beauty of their intimate physical union and shared emotional lives. Our bond with Christ cannot be dissolved. And because the marriage relationship represents our permanent union with Christ, God does not want it dissolved either. He created marriage to be a powerful witness to His work of reconciliation and unity. This is why Paul refers back to Genesis 2:24, which speaks of the unity and permanence of marriage: "For this reason a man shall leave his father and his mother, and be joined to his wife; and they shall become one flesh." This intimate relationship, Paul tells us, is meant to point to Christ and His church (Eph. 5:31-32). That is, the more our marriages reflect the ideal of mutual submission—the wife respecting and helping her husband and the husband loving and honoring his wife—the more we reflect to others the mysterious relationship between Christ and believers.

In 5:33, Paul summarizes his essential message to husbands and wives regarding how to exercise mutual submission toward one another: "Each individual among you also is to love his own wife even as himself, and the wife must see to it that she respects her husband." *Love* and *respect*—these are the essential ingredients in a God-honoring, Christlike, Spirit-filled marriage. Again I ask, what wife wouldn't support a husband who loved her as much as he loved himself—and as sacrificially, tenderly, and purely as Christ loves His bride? What wife wouldn't respect and submit to a husband who followed Christ's gentle model of servant leadership? All of us long to be loved and respected, nourished and cherished. Let's bring these attitudes and actions into our marriages and watch Christ transform them into a mirror of His wondrous grace!

# APPLICATION: EPHESIANS 5:22-33

## The Most Challenging of All Relationships

Like a precious and expensive handcrafted rug, a good marriage can't be stitched together in a hurry. In fact, weaving a beautiful tapestry of love, surrender, sacrifice, respect, honor, forgiveness, intimacy, nurture, and affection is the task of a lifetime. If you don't cultivate these essentials every day, however, whatever work has been done can begin to fray at the edges, unravel at its loose ends, and wear away at its center. A healthy marriage must be nurtured and cultivated over the long haul as both partners apply diligence and selfless commitment. Like weaving an intricate tapestry, marriage takes patience and constant checking against the pattern—Jesus Christ.

When it comes together, though, matching the divine design, marriage takes on sacred depths. It becomes an interlocking of souls so profoundly connected that only the word "mystery" can describe it. Marriage is most certainly worth the effort, and its value is beyond any price. So, husbands, wives—are you ready to take up the challenge? Are you ready to ask yourself some probing questions and to commit to taking steps toward a close-knit relationship with your spouse? How are the threads of your marriage holding up? Are they woven together in a beautiful tapestry that pictures Christ's relationship with His church? Or is your relationship unraveling? Take some time to evaluate your marriage in light of what you've learned in this section.

### Reflective Questions for Wives

- What is your attitude toward submitting to your husband? Have you been resistant? Why?
- Do you support and encourage your husband? Do you treat him with respect, even when you disagree with him?
- In what ways do you seek your husband's highest good? If your husband were to answer this question, would he agree with your answer?
- What specific attitudes and actions do you need to cease in order to apply the principles of Ephesians 5:21-24, 33? What specific attitudes and actions do you need to cultivate in order to model your relationship after the relationship between Christ and His church?

*Reflective Questions for Husbands*

- Are you loving your wife as Christ loves the church? How? Consider specific examples of Christlike love you have expressed through surrendering, sanctifying, forgiving, honoring, nourishing, and cherishing. Would your wife agree with your answer?
- How have you viewed the husband's role of leadership in the home? What model or mentor have you followed who might not exactly align with Christ's example (a father, grandfather, or friend)? What were some of the shortcomings of that human example that may have influenced your approach to marriage?
- Have you tended more toward the extreme of tyranny, being "the boss" rather than the gentle shepherd of the family? Or have you tended toward the extreme of passivity, failing to take seriously your leadership responsibilities?
- What specific attitudes and actions do you need to give up in order to apply the principles of Ephesians 5:25-33? What specific attitudes and actions do you need to cultivate in order to model your relationship after that of Christ and His church?

# Who's the Boss? Honoring God at Home and at Work
## EPHESIANS 6:1-9

**NASB**

[1] Children, obey your parents in the Lord, for this is right. [2] HONOR YOUR FATHER AND MOTHER (which is the first commandment with a promise), [3] SO THAT IT MAY BE WELL WITH YOU, AND THAT YOU MAY LIVE LONG ON THE EARTH.

[4] Fathers, do not provoke your children to anger, but bring them up in the discipline and instruction of the Lord.

[5] Slaves, be obedient to those who are your ᵃmasters according to the flesh, with fear and trembling, in the sincerity of your heart, as to Christ; [6] not ᵃby way of eyeservice, as

**NLT**

[1] Children, obey your parents because you belong to the Lord,* for this is the right thing to do. [2] "Honor your father and mother." This is the first commandment with a promise: [3] If you honor your father and mother, "things will go well for you, and you will have a long life on the earth."*

[4] Fathers,* do not provoke your children to anger by the way you treat them. Rather, bring them up with the discipline and instruction that comes from the Lord.

[5] Slaves, obey your earthly masters with deep respect and fear. Serve them sincerely as you would serve Christ. [6] Try to please them all the time, not just when they are

**NASB**

men-pleasers, but as slaves of Christ, doing the will of God from the [b]heart. [7]With good will [a]render service, as to the Lord, and not to men, [8]knowing that whatever good thing each one does, this he will receive back from the Lord, whether slave or free.

[9]And masters, do the same things to them, and give up threatening, knowing that both their Master and yours is in heaven, and there is no partiality with Him.

6:5 [a]I.e. earthly masters, with fear  6:6 [a]Lit according to  [b]Lit soul  6:7 [a]Lit rendering

**NLT**

watching you. As slaves of Christ, do the will of God with all your heart. [7]Work with enthusiasm, as though you were working for the Lord rather than for people. [8]Remember that the Lord will reward each one of us for the good we do, whether we are slaves or free.

[9]Masters, treat your slaves in the same way. Don't threaten them; remember, you both have the same Master in heaven, and he has no favorites.

6:1 Or *Children, obey your parents who belong to the Lord;* some manuscripts read simply *Children, obey your parents.*  6:2-3 Exod 20:12; Deut 5:16.  6:4 Or *Parents.*

From the intricate and priceless tapestry of marriage, Paul moves on to apply his principles of Spirit-filled submission to two other challenging relationships: parenthood (6:1-4) and employment (6:5-9). Though these two relationships exist in different realms of life, the principles of submission and responsible leadership are the same as those Paul dealt with in the previous section on marriage. In fact, we can apply these principles of harmony to all kinds of relationships—in the church, in society, in government, and in any relationship that may need attention. Humility and grace always seem to be in short supply.

## — 6:1-4 —

Paul begins by addressing children who are responsible for obeying their parents "in the Lord" (6:1). On the surface, it may appear that Paul is limiting the scope of children's obedience, either (1) to parents who are Christians (that is, "in the Lord") or (2) to parents who are behaving in a godly manner (that is, walking "in the Lord"). The parallel passage in Colossians 3:20, however, helps us better understand Paul's thought here: "Children, be obedient to your parents in all things, for this is well-pleasing to the Lord." So in Ephesians 6:1 the phrase "in the Lord" qualifies the verb "obey," explaining that children must be subject to their parents as their way of being subject to the Lord.[16]

Jesus Himself, the very Son of God, through whom the Father created all things (John 1:1-3), "continued in subjection" to His earthly parents, Joseph and Mary (Luke 2:51). Therefore, nobody can say that submission and obedience imply inequality or inferiority. Rather, voluntarily accepting a role of subjection leads to harmony and blessing. Paul says as much when he reiterates the fifth commandment God gave Moses in the Law (Exod. 20:12; Deut. 5:16)—the first of the Ten Commandments with a specific promise (Eph. 6:2). In his quotation, though, Paul makes a minor change to apply the text more generally to his readers' new situation. The original commandment offered blessing in the Promised Land (Israel) for children who honored their parents: "Honor your father and your mother, as the LORD your God has commanded you, that your days may be prolonged and that it may go well with you on the land which the LORD your God gives you" (Deut. 5:16). But Paul's readers—mostly Gentile believers in Ephesus—were not the recipients of the Law of Moses, were not obligated to its numerous mandates, and were not the intended beneficiaries of its promises. So Paul leaves out the final clause of the commandment, generalizing the theological principle that applies even to Christians today: Obedience to parents brings with it a blessing in this world, just as it brought with it a blessing to the Israelite children. Paul says that submission to parents will lead to wellness and long life (Eph. 6:3).

Of course, this isn't a guarantee that those who honor their fathers and mothers will never get sick and will live to be a hundred! Rather, Paul is presenting proverbial wisdom: Children who learn from the wisdom of their parents will avoid all sorts of destructive hardships and even deadly consequences. In fact, the same kind of promise is described in Proverbs 1 for those who heed the call of wisdom: They will "live securely and will be at ease from the dread of evil" (Prov. 1:33).

Paul's practical point is clear. In God's ordering of the family, He has placed parents in authority over children because the young need the wisdom, guidance, and protection only loving fathers and mothers can provide. The Christian home is meant to be a school for life lessons. Parents are meant to be teachers of truth and trainers in righteousness. They are to live the gospel of Christ and walk in grace. Children must therefore honor and obey their parents, not grudgingly, not merely outwardly, but with respect and love.

Yet in order to have a harmonious family characterized by mutual submission (Eph. 5:21), parents have a vital responsibility too. The command that children obey their parents does not give mom and dad divine sanction for harsh, unloving, tyrannical, ironfisted rule. Rather, Paul turns to the head of the home, the father, and warns him, "Do not provoke your children to anger" (6:4). The New English Bible begins this verse, "You fathers . . . must not goad your children to resentment."

The NIV says, "Do not exasperate your children." The idea is that through his overbearing actions a father can push a child over the edge, not only failing to impart wisdom but actually pushing a child away from wisdom! What are some of the things that "goad" children toward anger, resentment, and bitterness?

- unreasonable demands for perfection
- constant nagging over minor infractions
- not leaving room for freedom of expression and personal growth
- lack of encouragement and affirmation
- harsh, unloving rebukes or cruelty
- public embarrassment
- verbal or physical abuse
- inconsistent discipline
- showing favoritism for one child over another
- unfair or extreme discipline that doesn't match the offense
- overprotective hovering that stifles growth

Instead of provoking, which brings children down, Paul says, "bring them up in the discipline and instruction of the Lord" (6:4). The Greek word for "bringing up," *ektrephō* [1625], also appears in 5:29, referring to the nourishment of one's own flesh. So, just as husbands are to nourish their wives as they would their own bodies, fathers are to nurture their children. This includes providing for their physical, mental, emotional, and spiritual needs. It means providing proper, balanced, loving discipline when the child goes astray . . . and it means instructing the child positively in the right way. Speaking of which, a good sense of humor can add great joy in the home. Happiness is often a sign of healthy relationships. Wise are those parents who bring laughter and fun into their family work projects, mealtime discussions, and everyday conversations!

## — 6:5-9 —

Paul now moves from the proper functioning of the home into another realm of the social order, slaves and masters. Before we apply Paul's principles to our modern context, let me dispel a few misconceptions about Paul's original historical context.

First, when Paul brings up the issue of slaves and masters, he is not departing far from his discussion of family relationships. In the first century, many slaves were akin to "domestic servants"—actual members of a household; therefore, the master-and-slave relationship was logically associated with Paul's discussion of marriage and parenting.

To leave this relationship out of his discussion would be to ignore a common feature of the first-century household.

Second, by describing how Christian masters and slaves were to relate to one another, Paul was not, in fact, explicitly supporting the institution of slavery. In 1 Corinthians 7:21, he writes, "Were you called while a slave? Do not worry about it; but if you are able also to become free, rather do that." Two verses later, Paul even says, "You were bought with a price; do not become slaves of men" (1 Cor. 7:23). What a remarkable statement! Paul clearly notes that if a slave can gain freedom, this is to be preferred . . . and those who are free should not submit themselves to slavery. We see here the principle that slavery is a tolerable—but not ideal—situation. So why doesn't Paul challenge the institution of slavery directly? John MacArthur explains,

> New Testament teaching does not focus on reforming and restructuring human systems, which are never the root cause of human problems. The issue is always the heart of man—which when wicked will corrupt the best of systems and when righteous will improve the worst. If men's sinful hearts are not changed, they will find ways to oppress others regardless of whether or not there is actual slavery.[17]

Third, slavery in Paul's world was not the same kind of institution that it was in the nineteenth century. Slaves in the first century were more a socioeconomic class than a racial class of imprisoned forced labor. Though slavery was riddled with inequalities and injustices that needed to be overcome, in some homes slaves enjoyed considerable freedoms, rights, and responsibilities. In some cases they would have looked more like contract employees or domestic servants. They sometimes worked as tutors, nannies, cooks, or gardeners. In other words, the reason most Christians could tolerate the institution of slavery in the first century was because in many cases it was tolerable. Unlike the brutal race-based slavery in later history, first-century slavery did not necessarily strip humans of their dignity or reduce them to mere pieces of disposable property. See "Slavery in Paul's Day" (on next page) for more details.

Today, thankfully, most societies have banned slavery and diligently seek to avoid slave-like conditions. So for us, Paul's words to slaves and masters can be best applied to those in permanent employee-employer relationships. While the institutions of ancient slavery and modern employment do have fundamental differences, the practical principles governing both institutions are similar. Whether you are a contract worker,

## SLAVERY IN PAUL'S DAY

**EPHESIANS 6:5-9**

When we think of slavery, chances are we picture men and women in chains forced into menial labor and treated like property to be bought and sold. Or we might imagine modern-day examples of virtual slavery in sweatshops where small children and exploited women labor around the clock for pennies. Or perhaps we're reminded of the victims of human trafficking—kidnapped, treated like objects, and stripped of their freedom, dignity, and self-respect.

Though these images reflect the kind of slavery known in the nineteenth, twentieth, and twenty-first centuries, we would be mistaken to project them back onto the institution of slavery in Paul's day. While they were certainly not free, slaves in the ancient world should be regarded more as a social class than as victims of racism, injustice, or exploitation. Historians believe that slaves in Roman society may have constituted between twenty-five and forty percent of the population.[18] It is true that prior to the time of Paul, the Roman Empire acquired the majority of its slaves from among their vanquished foes as spoils of war, but men and women could become slaves in a number of ways. Children of slaves were automatically owned by their masters. Abandoned children could be brought up as slaves. People could even sell themselves into short- or long-term slavery to fulfill debts or other obligations. Slavery in the ancient world was thus based more on social, economic, and political status than on race or ethnicity.

The actual daily tasks of slaves varied depending on their skills, the status of their masters, and the city or region in which they lived. Duties could be as menial as cleaning or as brutal as mining. But slaves could also be cooks, teachers, or even physicians. Although slaves were sometimes abused or taken advantage of, their treatment depended on the temperament of their masters or mistresses. Because good slaves were a valuable investment, masters gained more from treating them well and keeping them healthy than from neglecting or harming them.

Masters could set their slaves free at any time. When freed, a slave took his master's name and was typically granted the same social status as the master.[19] Since Roman law allowed for the possibility of granting rights to such slaves, the composition of the slave population began to change over time, especially in regard to an increase in ethnic diversity. Whereas at one time only non-Roman peoples were slaves, by the time of Paul the population of slaves included both Romans and non-Romans.[20]

an hourly employee, a manager, or a business owner, Paul's principle of submission applies to you (see Eph. 5:21). Paul talked to the slaves and masters of his day in the same way he would address employees and employers today. The way we conduct ourselves during the dozens of hours we spend at work each week is just as important for the promotion of the gospel as the few hours we spend each week at church.

When Paul first addresses masters in Ephesians 6:5, we see the first element of a godly work ethic—obedience. It's the same responsibility children have toward their parents (6:1). As workers obligated to carry out the instructions of our bosses, we owe them the same honor, respect, and submission that we owed to our parents when they were raising us. In fact, our submission should be "with fear and trembling," with a sincere heart, and with the same kind of service we would show toward the Lord Himself. "Fear and trembling" refers to respect and humility, and laboring with a sincere heart "suggests that the employee should not hold back from his best but should actually pour himself out liberally in honest service."[21] Yes, the Lord Jesus is our heavenly Master, and we ultimately worship and serve Him alone; yet by giving one hundred percent to our "masters according to the flesh" (6:5), we are actually serving the Lord. Why? Because Paul said elsewhere, "whatever you do, do all to the glory of God" (1 Cor. 10:31).

Basically, then, we're to carry out our assignments with honor, humility, and honesty. We're to work hard at our jobs and treat our employers with respect. But what about those times when your boss seems underserving of respect? Or when your task seems unnecessary, ill-planned, or even pointless? How about when you believe you could do a better job running the organization? The answer is the same. *Obey. Submit. Show respect.* Unless an employer tells us to do something illegal, unethical, or contrary to Christ's explicit commands, we are responsible for carrying out the assignments given to us.

Paul describes this perspective in Ephesians 6:6-7. We are to avoid "eyeservice," which means serving "with a view to impressing others."[22] That is, "putting on appearances" or doing things "just for show." This kind of work ethic leads to the old adage, "When the cat's away, the mice will play." Paul unequivocally excludes this kind of behavior for Christians. We must not strive to be "men-pleasers," focusing on appearances only, but authentic servants of Christ even in the realm of secular work. When the earthly boss is gone, we must never forget that our heavenly Master is always with us, and it is to *Him*, not to other human beings, that we must ultimately give account for our lives.

As employees, we receive a paycheck for the work we do. But that reward is temporary and soon spent. Paul promises, however, that God will reward us eternally for our faithful service to our earthly bosses (6:8). Your employer may not appreciate most things you do. He or she may not even know your name. But God knows you better than you know yourself, and He will never forget your diligent, wholehearted efforts in service of Him (Heb. 6:10).

Just as Paul addressed husbands and fathers as those responsible for leadership in marriage and the family, he also addresses masters—equivalent to our modern employers—as leaders of their households (Eph. 6:9). Note that Paul begins by saying, "Do the same things to them." That is, bosses are to treat their employees with the same spirit with which workers are to treat their bosses, namely, with honor and respect, as ministering to the Lord. They are to hold them in high regard, not threatening, not showing partiality. What a revolutionary concept! It was completely at odds with the cultural expectations of masters and slaves in the first century . . . and it still doesn't square with our typical models of leadership and management in the twenty-first!

Why is it so important to treat employees with respect? Because with God "there is no partiality" (6:9). Employers and employees are equal in God's eyes. Both will someday stand before God to account for their attitudes and actions. Never forget: The world doesn't watch our behavior at church on Sundays or in Bible studies on weeknights. They watch us at home. They see us at work. They notice how we treat our parents. They pay attention to how we raise our children. They notice when we labor at our occupations with integrity. And they appreciate the qualities of a thoughtful, fair, and generous boss. In all of these realms—marriage, family, and work—we are to be subject to one another in the fear of Christ (5:21). In this way we will demonstrate to all people that not only are we saved by the blood of Jesus Christ, but we are also living lives under the control of the Holy Spirit.

# APPLICATION: EPHESIANS 6:1-9

## Tips for Those in (and under) Authority

Whether you're a parent or a child, an employer or an employee, Paul's profoundly practical principles in Ephesians 6:1-9 are for you. Depending on your particular situation—either in or under authority—your response to Paul's teachings will differ. Chances are good, though, that you're like the centurion in Matthew 8:9, who was a man under authority with soldiers under him. In other words, all of the following tips will probably apply to you one way or another.

First, *we must commit all our relationships to the Lord.* For Christians, whose entire lives have been bought by the blood of Christ (1 Cor. 6:19-20), there should be no family relationship, no occupation, and no hobby that doesn't belong to Him. This is especially true of our relationships with our children, our parents, our employees, and our employers. They all belong to Him. So we should approach all of these realms of life as holy callings. In light of this, take a moment to commit both family and vocational relationships to God's service, "for from Him and through Him and to Him are all things" (Rom. 11:36).

Second, to those in authority as parents or employers, *we need to treat those under our authority with kindness.* Employers and parents alike stand in positions of influence and authority, but none of us are free from submitting to Christ's authority in our lives. We who are fathers, mothers, managers, or bosses serve our heavenly Master through our positions of responsibility and leadership. Doesn't it make good, practical sense to treat those under our supervision with kindness, patience, respect, and generosity? After all, the attitudes we model to children or employees are likely to be the ones reflected back to us. We should use our influence and authority not to control and manipulate but to nurture, guide, and empower.

Third, to those under the authority of parents or employers, *we need to treat those in authority over us with respect.* We are to honor our fathers and mothers (Eph. 6:2). When we're minors living at home, we do this by obeying them. But when we get older, leave home, and have families of our own, does this excuse us from honoring our parents? Not at all! Though we may no longer be under their immediate, everyday authority, we should still honor and respect them. This can take such practical form as helping them when they have needs, continuing to seek out their wisdom and insight, and simply keeping in touch beyond just family gatherings and holidays. When it comes to our relationships with employers, the principle is similar. We need to submit to them, not only when they're around to see but when they're not looking. It means giving them our "all" when on the job, as if we were working for the Lord Himself (6:6-7).

Whether you're an ordained minister, a high schooler, a single mom, a plumber, a grandfather, or a solder in the army, you're working for the Lord. We need to take our tasks of leadership and followership sincerely, "with fear and trembling, in the sincerity of [our hearts], as to Christ" (6:5).

# CLASHING AND CONQUERING: THE WARRIOR'S STRATEGY (EPHESIANS 6:10-24)

In my opinion, a great film should end with an epic battle against a seemingly insurmountable foe whose power is overcome by virtues like courage, fortitude, goodness, and determination. The bigger the actual battle, the better. Of course, I appreciate a good mystery now and then. And I can choke back tears over a heart-wrenching tragedy as much as the next guy. I've even sat through my share of romances and feel-good films with my wife, in which the good guy gets the girl or the final scene fades out on an impossibly happy ending. But in my mind, nothing beats a military victory in a final battle . . . or a duel between a villain and a hero . . . or an action sequence that sets the forces of evil to flight. Maybe it's just that I'm a typical, predictable American male, but I'd like to think my fondness for a heroic climax reflects my wonderment at God's own great epic battle—the conflict between death and life, Satan and God's people—which God will one day bring to a dramatic and astonishing end.

Interestingly, Paul's great drama of Christian living comes to a close with a brief but unforgettable glimpse at the great ongoing battle between the powers of darkness and the kingdom of light. In fact, at the risk of sounding overly dramatic, I call this final section, Ephesians 6:10-24, "Clashing and Conquering: The Warrior's Strategy." Paul concludes his letter to the Ephesians with the intense language of spiritual warfare, urging his readers to stand firm against the strategy of the devil (6:10-17). He strongly exhorts the Ephesians to arm themselves with prayers and petitions as pieces of their spiritual arsenal essential for advancing the gospel (6:18-20). In his closing thoughts, the imprisoned and impassioned apostle wraps up the letter with personal greetings and a warm farewell that mirrors the beginning of the letter: a blessing of peace and grace (6:21-24). Here, at the end of this great letter to the Ephesians, Paul buttresses his overarching theme: *Because believers have new life through Christ, they ought to live a new life through the Spirit.*

## KEY TERMS IN EPHESIANS 6:10-20

***histēmi* (ἵστημι)** [2476] "to stand"

With a call to arm oneself with the armor and weapons of God, Paul exhorts believers to "stand firm" (6:13-14). In a world filled with earth-shaking trials and life-altering storms, simply standing can feel like quite a challenge. In Paul's thinking, standing implies strength that comes from divine truth, righteousness, peace, faith, and assurance of salvation. The result is a stability of character and confidence that can weather all storms.

***proseuchē kai deēsis* (προσευχὴ καὶ δέησις)** [4335, 1162] "prayer and supplication"

These two words, frequently coupled in both the Old Testament and the New (1 Kgs. 8:54; 2 Chr. 6:29; Phil. 4:6; 1 Tim. 2:1), refer to general addresses to God (*proseuchē*) and specific requests for particular needs (*deēsis*). In Ephesians, Paul associates prayer with the armor of God as one of the believer's defenses against spiritual attack (Eph. 6:18).

# Standing Strong against Satanic Schemes
## EPHESIANS 6:10-13

**NASB**

10 Finally, be strong in the Lord and in the strength of His might. 11 Put on the full armor of God, so that you will be able to stand firm against the schemes of the devil. 12 For our struggle is not against aflesh and blood, but against the rulers, against the powers, against the world forces of this darkness, against the spiritual *forces* of wickedness in the heavenly *places.* 13 Therefore, take up the full armor of God, so that you will be able to resist in the evil day, and having done everything, to stand firm.

6:12 aLit *blood and flesh*

**NLT**

10 A final word: Be strong in the Lord and in his mighty power. 11 Put on all of God's armor so that you will be able to stand firm against all strategies of the devil. 12 For we* are not fighting against flesh-and-blood enemies, but against evil rulers and authorities of the unseen world, against mighty powers in this dark world, and against evil spirits in the heavenly places.
13 Therefore, put on every piece of God's armor so you will be able to resist the enemy in the time of evil. Then after the battle you will still be standing firm.

6:12 Some manuscripts read *you.*

A mighty fortress is our God,
A bulwark never failing;
Our helper He amid the flood
Of mortal ills prevailing.
For still our ancient foe
Doth seek to work us woe—
His craft and power are great,
And, armed with cruel hate,
On earth is not his equal.[1]

When Martin Luther penned the powerful lyrics of "A Mighty Fortress Is Our God" in the midst of the Reformation, Ephesians 6:10-13 likely inspired him. Paul's words in this ominous passage remind us of a fact we often forget: When we began the Christian life, we didn't stroll onto a happy playground . . . we stepped onto a harsh battleground. Though we don't hear bombs bursting in the distance or bullets whizzing past our ears, we live every day of our lives on a spiritual battlefield. And make no mistake: Satan's snipers have us in their crosshairs. They know us intimately. Having studied us for years, they are familiar with our strengths and fully aware of our weaknesses. They're masters of psychology and experts on human nature. They know their prey far better than we know our devilish predators.

Whether you're a young believer or an old saint, spiritually strong or weak, well trained or just a novice, Satan and his emissaries have one goal for you: *destruction*. Their one great hope is not simply to cripple you but to decimate you. Though their own ultimate doom is certain, they intend to bring down as many with them as they can. Paul writes what he does because he wants to keep us standing firm in our faith to the very end. He assures his readers that, even in the hail of artillery fire that continually rains down upon us, we can be safe from Satan's schemes.

But we can't do it on our own. We who have received new life through Christ must live that new life by the power of the Spirit.

## — 6:10-11 —

Paul's spiritual battle cry rings out in 6:10. Think of it as his call to arms—a bugle blast meant to awaken us from passivity and alert us to the realities of the conflict. He urges us to "be strong in the Lord." Only through His strength will we be able to stand and fight in this ongoing spiritual conflict.

Satan would like nothing better than for us to picture him as the little red imp on our shoulder, whispering naughty ideas into our ears. As long as we think of him as a pesky little pest that we can brush away like a mosquito, we won't realize just how insidious he is. Pay attention to the nature of the arsenal with which we believers have been supplied: "the strength of His might" (6:10). The reality is that in our own strength, we are no match for Satan or any of his wicked minions. Only when we rely on Christ's strength can we hope to defeat such a deceptive and destructive foe.

This doesn't mean that God the Son and Satan are equal and opposite beings. Far from it! The Bible teaches that Satan is an angelic creature of God (Ezek. 28:12-16) who can do nothing apart from God's control or permission (Job 1:6-12; Luke 22:31). He's not the counterpart of God but of the archangel Michael (Jude 1:9; Rev. 12:7). Satan is also the enemy and accuser of humans (Zech. 3:1-2; 1 Pet. 5:8). While we must not deny that Satan has the power to attack and ensnare us (Eph. 4:27; 6:11; 1 Tim. 3:7), we also must not attribute to Satan more power than he actually has.

The second verse of Martin Luther's hymn "A Mighty Fortress Is Our God" powerfully illustrates this truth:

> Did we in our own strength confide,
> Our striving would be losing,
> Were not the right man on our side,
> The man of God's own choosing.
> Dost ask who that may be?
> Christ Jesus, it is He—
> Lord Sabaoth His name,
> From age to age the same,
> And He must win the battle.[2]

Do you remember Paul's prayer at the beginning of this letter? He asked that believers might know "the surpassing greatness of His power" which is "in accordance with the working of the strength of His might" (Eph. 1:19). Now we see why. This is no mere head knowledge. In fact, it even goes beyond what people call "heart knowledge." The knowledge Paul had in mind was *personal* and *practical* knowledge—a learned awareness of God's strength, a knowledge gained by spiritual victory in the midst of battle. Our enemy is strong, and his attacks are relentless, but the power of Christ can defend us against any assault of Satan.

Continuing his summons to battle, Paul instructs the Ephesians on

Lagui/Dollar Photo Club

A **Roman soldier** armed for battle.

how to employ God's strength: "Put on the full armor of God, so that you will be able to stand firm against the schemes of the devil" (6:11). Because we fight a spiritual battle, only spiritual armor can protect us. Observe that this isn't *your* armor—it's *God's* armor. You can't provide it for yourself. You can't muster up enough mental, emotional, or physical strength to fight a spiritual battle. It's utterly impossible. Since the enemy is spiritual, you and I need spiritual armor.

We'll discuss the details of this armor in the next section. For now it's sufficient to point out that Paul is not referring to literal armor that a believer places on his or her body. He's likening God's spiritual power and protection of His people to a common sight of his day—the full protective gear and offensive weaponry of a Roman soldier. Remember, Paul wrote Ephesians while under house arrest, guarded by a Roman soldier (Acts 28:16, 20). For an illustration of God's protection, Paul could have simply looked out his window.

In the rest of this section, let's take a closer look at two facets related to the armor of God: (1) *the reasons we need the armor* (Eph. 6:12) and (2) *the effects of wearing the armor* (6:11, 13).

## — 6:12-13 —

*The reasons we need the armor* (6:12). Paul paints a dark and foreboding picture of the world in which we live, highlighting three reasons we desperately need God's supernatural protection. First, Satan and his demons are not "flesh and blood" (6:12); they are spiritual beings. As such, their presence and power cannot be detected through our five senses. Rather, they must be discerned spiritually. This puts us at a distinct disadvantage from the start. Ever since the Fall, we have been creatures pulled toward this physical world, focused on what we can see, feel, hear, taste, and smell. To do battle with Satan, we need to set aside our worldly wisdom and empirical approach to life. Instead of relying on that, we must open our eyes and ears of faith, trusting that what God says about the spiritual realm is more real than the ever-changing "realities" of this present tangible world.

Second, we struggle against an organized hierarchy of demonic rulers, powers, and forces of wickedness. Think of this as the spiritual Mafia. But let's be sensible here. Some have made Paul's ranking of demons in Ephesians 6:12 walk on all fours. They concoct complex descriptions of specific kinds of demons who rule over precise areas of the world. It's best, however, to see Paul as referring to some kind of ordered evil ambition in the demonic ranks without feeling obligated to create an organizational chart of the demonic realm. Not only is such a tight organization impossible to discern in Scripture—it's not necessary. God can win His war against Satan regardless of how well organized he and his demons might be.

Third, this force of evil is characterized by unparalleled wickedness. Kent Hughes has said it best in two sentences from his book on Ephesians: "Satan has no conscience, no compassion, no remorse, no morals. He feeds on pain and anguish and filth."[3] Few villains in Hollywood adequately portray the depths of pure evil that exist in Satan and his demonic mob. Frankly, human beings can't fully relate to the total wickedness that motivates the devil. It seems like every bad guy in literature, television, or film has some kind of potential for redemption, a limit to his or her wickedness, or at least a reasonable explanation for his or her evil behavior that can almost prompt pity. Yet when it comes to Satan, there is no possibility of redemption, no limit to his evil except what is placed on him by God's sovereign restraint, and no rational explanation or motivation for what he seeks to do. Perhaps the villain known simply as the Joker in Christopher Nolan's 2008 Batman sequel, *The Dark Knight*, reflects to some degree the kind of senseless depravity that characterizes our satanic foes: "Some men aren't looking for anything logical. . . . They can't be bought, bullied, reasoned, or negotiated with. Some men just want to watch the world burn."[4]

We see proof of this depravity in our world every day. Violent crime, devastating wars, religious deception, moral deterioration, political corruption—the list has no end. We don't even have to turn on the television or surf the Internet to see the results of satanic wickedness. We merely need to look within and around as we observe the sin—the disharmony, selfishness, and corruption—in our own marriages, families, neighborhoods, and churches. Taking advantage of humanity's fallen nature (2:1-3), the forces of evil can lead the unwary and unprotected believer away from the right path and into a path of destruction. John Stott writes,

> Wobbly Christians who have no firm foothold in Christ are an easy prey for the devil. And Christians who shake like reeds and rushes cannot resist the wind when the principalities and powers begin to blow. Paul wants to see Christians so strong and stable that they remain firm even against the devil's wiles (verse 11) and even *in the evil day*, that is, in a time of special pressure. For such stability, both of character and in crisis, the armour of God is essential.[5]

*The effects of wearing the armor* (6:11, 13). We've seen the reason we need the armor of God (6:12). Now let's consider the results of having God's supernatural protection. For this, let's step back one verse and look at 6:11 and 6:13 together; they complement each other. In 6:11, Paul instructs the Ephesians to "put on the full armor of God." In 6:13, he picks up this same idea after explaining why this armor is essential: "Take up the full armor of God." The effects of wearing this armor are also described in both verses: "so that you will be able to stand firm against the schemes of the devil. . . . so that you will be able to resist in the evil day, and having done everything, to stand firm" (6:11, 13).

God's armor enables us "to stand firm." We have a fearsome enemy, but because we're protected by God's power, we have no reason to tremble at his temptations or quake at his threats. We don't need to cower in terror or run in panic. In Christ, our victory is certain. The outcome of the battle has been determined. It is true that our "adversary, the devil, prowls around like a roaring lion, seeking someone to devour" (1 Pet. 5:8), but when we resist him with God's strength, he flees our presence like a frightened cockroach scurrying from the light (see Jas. 4:7).

So, one obvious effect of wearing God's armor is the ability to stand firm in spiritual victory (6:11, 13). Another effect is the ability to discern the devil's schemes. The Greek word translated "schemes" in 6:11 is *methodeia* [3180], a word used in Ephesians 4:14 with reference to "craftiness in deceitful scheming." The word is plural, indicating that Satan has numerous—no doubt *countless*—devices in his arsenal for undermining our spiritual progress. Though the devil is damned and depraved, he is no dummy. He can identify, target, and exploit your weaknesses and the chinks in your man-made defenses before you're even aware of them yourself. Having *God's* armor can help protect us from these devastating assaults.

A third effect of the armor of God is that we will be ready for anything that comes. Paul says we will be able to "resist in the evil day" (6:13). The phrase "the evil day" probably refers to both general spiritual oppression in our present time and special attacks by wicked spirits against us. Harold Hoehner writes, "The believers should be aware that they must be prepared, not only for everyday evils but for the times of heightened and unexpected spiritual battles. For example, when the devil failed to tempt Jesus to sin, he left Jesus until an opportune time (Luke 4:13)."[6] If Satan tempted the unimpeachable Son of God at "opportune" times, we can be sure his gang of demonic thugs will do the same to us. But when we stand firm in the provision of strength and promise of protection we have through Jesus Christ, Satan will slink away in defeat.

Again, the stirring words of Luther's hymn reinforce this fundamental truth:

> And tho this world, with devils filled,
> Should threaten to undo us,
> We will not fear, for God hath willed
> His truth to triumph thru us.
> The prince of darkness grim,
> We tremble not for him—
> His rage we can endure,
> For lo, his doom is sure:
> One little word shall fell him.[7]

# APPLICATION: EPHESIANS 6:10-13

## Three Principles to Stand On

We have glimpsed Satan's diabolical plan and learned of God's indispensable protection. Let's now consider three principles concerning spiritual warfare that we can apply personally to our lives.

First, *no satanic assault is stronger than God*. Satan's forces are indeed powerful. But if you can't go to sleep tonight because you're afraid, or if you suddenly wake up in a cold sweat for fear of Satan's schemes, then you've missed the message. This is not about being afraid. This is about standing strong in the provision of Jesus Christ. Nothing is stronger than the Spirit of God living within us, empowering us to avoid deception, overcome temptation, and stand firm through satanic or demonic attacks. First John 4:4 promises, "Greater is He who is in you than he who is in the world." So let me ask you this probing and very personal question, a question only you can answer: Do you have the Spirit of God dwelling within you? Have you experienced the new birth by grace alone through faith alone in Christ alone? Only those who have been born anew into His family can stand on the side of the One who is stronger than all spiritual enemies.

Second, *no satanic scheme can penetrate God's armor*. Without that protection, we're exposed to every assault, every arrow, every bombardment by the enemy. Yet when we are "born again to a living hope," we are also "protected by the power of God through faith" (1 Pet. 1:3, 5). A grand old gospel hymn puts it well:

> Leaning, leaning
> Safe and secure from all alarms;
> Leaning, leaning,
> Leaning on the everlasting arms.[8]

If you're a believer, are you leaning on your own temporal defenses? Or have you fully thrown yourself into the protective arms of the Savior? Have you been trying to unravel Satan's schemes and repel his attacks by your own wisdom, methods, and righteous works? Or have you taken the step that only a believer in Christ can take: surrendering yourself to Him and allowing Christ alone to be your Advocate and Defender?

Third, *no satanic evil can prevail over God's church*. Around AD 110, in a letter to the very same church in Ephesus as Paul's prison epistle, the famous preacher, teacher, and martyr Ignatius of Antioch described quite dramatically the corporate aspect of spiritual warfare. No doubt aware of Paul's own rousing passage on spiritual warfare, Ignatius wrote to the church in Ephesus, "Make every effort to come together more frequently to give thanks and glory to God. For when you meet together frequently, the powers of Satan are overthrown and his destructiveness is nullified by the unanimity of your faith."[9]

One thing is clear in Paul's letter to the Ephesians: We can't "go it alone." We weren't meant to. Just as the Holy Spirit dwells within each of us individually (1 Cor. 6:19), He also dwells within the gathered community—the body (1 Cor. 3:16-17; Eph. 2:21-22). So, do you want to be prepared for spiritual attack and to stand firm in the protection of God? Then stay close to God's people. Draw strength from their presence and encouragement (Heb. 10:23-25).

# Ample Armor for Weak Warriors
## EPHESIANS 6:14-20

**NASB**

¹⁴ Stand firm therefore, HAVING GIRDED YOUR LOINS WITH TRUTH, and HAVING PUT ON THE BREASTPLATE OF RIGHTEOUSNESS, ¹⁵ and having shod YOUR FEET WITH THE PREPARATION OF THE GOSPEL OF PEACE; ¹⁶ᵃin addition to all, taking up the shield of faith with which you will be able to extinguish all the flaming arrows of the evil *one*. ¹⁷ And take THE HELMET OF SALVATION, and the sword of the Spirit, which is the word of God.

¹⁸ᵃWith all prayer and petition ᵇpray at all times in the Spirit, and with this in view, ᶜbe on the alert with all perseverance and petition for all the saints, ¹⁹ and *pray* on my behalf, that utterance may be given to me in the opening of my mouth, to make known with boldness the mystery of the gospel, ²⁰ for which I am an ambassador in ᵃchains; that ᵇin *proclaiming* it I may speak boldly, as I ought to speak.

**6:16** ᵃLit *in all*   **6:18** ᵃLit *Through* ᵇLit *praying* ᶜLit *being*   **6:20** ᵃLit *a chain* ᵇTwo early mss read *I may speak it boldly*

**NLT**

¹⁴ Stand your ground, putting on the belt of truth and the body armor of God's righteousness. ¹⁵ For shoes, put on the peace that comes from the Good News so that you will be fully prepared.* ¹⁶ In addition to all of these, hold up the shield of faith to stop the fiery arrows of the devil.* ¹⁷ Put on salvation as your helmet, and take the sword of the Spirit, which is the word of God.

¹⁸ Pray in the Spirit at all times and on every occasion. Stay alert and be persistent in your prayers for all believers everywhere.*

¹⁹ And pray for me, too. Ask God to give me the right words so I can boldly explain God's mysterious plan that the Good News is for Jews and Gentiles alike.* ²⁰ I am in chains now, still preaching this message as God's ambassador. So pray that I will keep on speaking boldly for him, as I should.

**6:15** Or *For shoes, put on the readiness to preach the Good News of peace with God.*   **6:16** Greek *the evil one.*   **6:18** Greek *all of God's holy people.* **6:19** Greek *explain the mystery of the Good News;* some manuscripts read simply *explain the mystery.*

In Ephesians 6:10-13, Paul described the spiritual battle that rages around Christians every day. He gave us verbal snapshots of our enemy and his forces of darkness. He encouraged us to stand against the wiles of the devil by resting on God's strength alone. And he used a powerful metaphor for God's provision of protection and power for His saints— the "armor of God." A diabolical battle requires divine weapons and a satanic attack demands spiritual defenses. In 2 Corinthians 10:3-5, Paul refers to the potency of this God-given arsenal. These words are worth a careful reading:

> For though we walk in the flesh, we do not war according to the flesh, for the weapons of our warfare are not of the flesh, but

divinely powerful for the destruction of fortresses. We are destroying speculations and every lofty thing raised up against the knowledge of God, and we are taking every thought captive to the obedience of Christ.

If this passage powerfully describes the spiritual war in which we are engaged, Paul's poignant words in Romans 8:37-39 remind us of the guaranteed spiritual victory we have in Christ:

But in all these things we overwhelmingly conquer through Him who loved us. For I am convinced that neither death, nor life, nor angels, nor principalities, nor things present, nor things to come, nor powers, nor height, nor depth, nor any other created thing, will be able to separate us from the love of God, which is in Christ Jesus our Lord.

Because of the battle we're in, and because God has given us "everything pertaining to life and godliness" in Christ (2 Pet. 1:3), Paul exhorts us to "take up the full armor of God" (Eph. 6:13). So what, specifically, is the armor of God? Is it simply a general image of His divine protection? Actually, Paul spends the next several verses detailing a number of specific elements of this armor—the believer's spiritual articles of defense and offensive weapon. As we'll see, we are called to put on the whole armor of God, but each of these items equips us in a unique way. Let's try on each piece Paul presents and learn to utilize them all with precision and mastery.

In 6:14-17, Paul describes the individual pieces of armor:

- the belt of truth
- the breastplate of righteousness
- the boots of peace
- the shield of faith
- the helmet of salvation
- the sword of the Spirit

Then, in 6:18-20, Paul shifts from the meaningful metaphors to a concrete exhortation that puts the armor to full use in spiritual warfare: Pray as if your spiritual life depends on it, *because it does!*

## — 6:14-17 —

Before we briefly examine each item of spiritual armor, we need to remind ourselves once again that Paul is speaking metaphorically. He is using the image of a standard military uniform common in his day and combining this with his extensive knowledge of the Old Testament to paint an unforgettable picture of the specific means of protection granted by God to every believer.

The Old Testament images Paul had in mind likely came from the book of Isaiah. Isaiah 11:5 mentions the Messiah coming with a belt of righteousness and faithfulness. Isaiah 59:17 refers to the Lord donning "righteousness like a breastplate" and putting "a helmet of salvation on His head." And Isaiah 52:7 describes the beauty of the feet of those who pronounce good news of happiness, salvation, and the kingdom of God. No wonder Paul calls these gifts bestowed upon God's people by grace through faith "the armor of God." Such armor calls for close inspection.

*The belt of truth* (6:14). Most of us today don't "gird our loins," do we? Today we buckle belts around our waists. The belt of a Roman soldier's uniform, however, did more than hold his pants up or add a bit of stylish flare to otherwise outmoded attire. This heavy, six-inch-wide leather belt secured the soldier's tunic so that the material wouldn't hamper his movement. It also helped hold in place his breastplate and the sheath for his weapon. The belt thus had the important function of keeping him free, protected, and agile enough to attack or defend, whichever the situation in battle required.

In Paul's image, the belt is composed of truth—the truth of God, revealed in His written Word (John 17:17). It also includes truth of character, or integrity—practical living that conforms to the instruction of God's Word (2 Jn. 1:4). In the heat of battle, when the flaming arrows of deception are flying around us and unjust accusations explode close enough to impact us, we need truth of doctrine and truth of character to keep us from falling apart. This is why Paul urges us to keep that belt pulled tight: to keep the truth of God's Word close to us, to keep His incarnate Truth—Jesus Himself (John 14:6)—at the center of our lives, and to maintain our strength with unquestioned integrity. As members of Christ's army, we're to stay true to what the Bible says is right. Doing so will keep us safe from countless dangers.

*The breastplate of righteousness* (6:14). The Roman breastplate was a large piece of leather, bronze, or chain mail that covered both the front and back of a soldier from his neck to his thighs. Its purpose? To protect the warrior's vital organs—the core of his physical life, without which he would die in minutes. As such, the breastplate was an essential piece of armor. No soldier would consider stepping into battle without it.

For Paul, this was a perfect image of the righteousness that comes from God alone, righteousness we could never earn by our own merit or maintain in our own strength. Paul describes this as "the righteousness of God through faith in Jesus Christ for all those who believe" (Rom. 3:22). Theologians call this righteousness "justification," which is the sovereign act of God whereby He declares righteous the believing sinner while he or she is still in a sinning state. This is a declaration of innocence granted freely to believers the moment they are saved. Not based on good works but on Christ's finished work on the cross, this positional righteousness can never be forfeited, lost, diminished, or taken away. The Bible also describes practical righteousness that flows from our positional righteousness by the work of the Holy Spirit (Eph. 2:10; 5:9). Though these two must be distinguished—the righteousness by faith alone and the right living that is a result of faith—they are never meant to be separated. Authentic faith always leads to authenticating works (Jas. 2:22, 26).

The breastplate of righteousness is as essential to us as the Roman soldier's breastplate was to him. Our enemy, the accuser of believers (Rev. 12:10), loves to direct his arrows at the heart of our faith. He tries desperately to convince us that God can't bridge the gap our sins have created. He hopes to plant seeds of doubt of God's infinite grace. He lobs missiles of guilt and shame and condemnation toward us, tempting us to believe that the love and forgiveness of God must be conditional. But when we stand firm in the knowledge that God has declared us righteous based solely on the blood of Christ and empowers us to live holy lives by the Holy Spirit alone, the devil and his wicked workers must retreat in defeat.

*The boots of peace* (6:15). I'm sure Paul had spent many long hours looking at his jailer's boots, called *caligae*. New Testament scholar Harold Hoehner clearly describes the *caligae*: "The Roman legionaries wore heavy sandals . . . with soles made of several layers of leather averaging 2 centimeters (¾ inch) thick, studded with hollow-headed hobnails. They were tied by leather thongs half-way up the shin and were stuffed with wool or fur in the cold weather."[10] These shoes were ideal for fast-moving hand-to-hand combat. Like today's football and soccer cleats, they were meant to give maximum footing and traction to prevent sliding. They were designed to function in any terrain and were adaptable to any climate.

Our "footing" against Satan is our peace with God. Christ has secured this peace for us (Eph. 2)—peace not only with God but also with one another and within ourselves. As a result of this peace, our Lord will never condemn us (Rom. 8:1). Satan may pressure us all he wants, trying to convince us that God will reject and judge us when we falter. But if we know that our peace with God is secure, then we won't slip and fall. We'll stand stable and firm against the devil's taunts. Moreover, we'll gain ground against his opposition so that we can spread the good news of peace with God through Christ to the troubled world around us.

*The shield of faith* (6:16). The shield Paul had in mind was the Roman *scutum*, a four-and-a-half-foot oval or rectangle of hide-covered wood framed with iron.[11] Often the leather was soaked in water prior to battle in order to put out the enemy's dangerous incendiary missiles—arrows dipped in pitch and set on fire. Max Turner notes, "In battle this [shield] could be locked together with others to form a wall in front, and a roof overhead."[12]

The barrage of "flaming arrows of the evil one" we experience in the Christian life can take many forms. Let me name a few: temptation, doubt, anger, frustration, pride, despair, fear, guilt, shame, confusion, deception, discouragement, depression, hopelessness, greed, lust, presumption, stubbornness, laziness, suspicion, jealousy, hate, wrath, discord, conflict . . . the list continues on and on. In short, the kinds of fiery attacks at the devil's fingertips are virtually innumerable. The shield of faith, however, provides an impenetrable protection from these things.

Through faith we see our circumstances from God's perspective. We trust in Him to carry us through all trials and temptations. We stand firm and resolute, confident that our almighty Commander in Chief will see us through. In the midst of Satan's rain of fire, we can take up the shield of faith as we pray, "Lord, I trust You today in spite of these attacks. I trust You even though these things are coming my way. In spite of my nature, regardless of the habits I have formed, today, Lord, I walk in trust with You, and I use the shield of trust to repel all those arrows. I pray that You will start early this morning in protecting me with this shield, because I can't protect myself. I need Your shield and I trust You, Father, when I'm afraid. I trust You when it gets dark. I trust You when I'm in a situation that tempts me to the core. I trust You to guard my tongue, my eyes, my hands, my feet, my mind, my heart, and my soul."

*The helmet of salvation* (6:17). In the first century, Roman soldiers' helmets were "made of bronze fitted over an iron skull cap lined with leather or cloth."[13] By Paul's day, they often had a band to protect the forehead and plates to protect the nose and cheeks. Little of the head was exposed to danger, but a soldier could still see clearly so as not to be caught off guard by swift-moving enemies or unexpected objects.

The Christian's helmet in Paul's illustration is salvation. When Paul tells the Ephesians to "take the helmet of salvation," he's referring to one of the last actions of a soldier about to engage in battle—slipping on his helmet and grabbing his sword. But this doesn't imply that the believer's salvation comes last. That is, we don't earn salvation only after putting on truth, righteousness, peace, and faith. Rather, all of these things come to us the instant we are saved by grace through faith. What Paul is saying is that we must constantly remind ourselves of our salvation. We need to have *assurance* of our position with Christ. Why? Because Satan would like nothing better than to aim his arrows at our minds, convincing us that we don't really belong to Christ, that we aren't eternally saved. He would love to rob us of the hope of our resurrection, our glorification, and our eternal home in heaven.

It pains me to hear of the countless Christians who struggle with assurance of their salvation. Too many believers wonder if they believe the right things . . . in the right way . . . and with the right amount of conviction. Or they wonder if they should have prayed a certain kind of prayer, gone forward at a certain meeting, or met some other traditional qualification. Or they struggle with assurance because they see imperfection in their lives and can't seem to break free from certain temptations. What a tragedy! We're saved by God's sovereign grace alone, through our simple faith alone, in the person and work of Jesus Christ alone. Don't dissect your faith, either overly intellectualizing or overly psychologizing it. Don't try to add conditions to your salvation like an altar call, a raised hand, water baptism, a public confession of sins, or other things that may accompany or follow saving faith but are not replacements for it. Keep short accounts before God with regard to sin . . . but don't let your imperfection in this life rob you of your assurance. The more you look into your own heart, the worse it will appear. Instead, stay focused on Christ's saving work on the cross. Look to Scripture's promises of eternal, irrevocable salvation (John 10:28; Rom. 8:37-39; 1 Jn. 1:8-10).

The assurance of your salvation is one of the most strategic parts of your equipment. Take it! You are saved. You came to Christ. You will never be unsaved. You never need to lack assurance. The assurance that came when you were born again is still yours to claim today. One of Satan's favorite and most disturbing tactics is to weaken your confidence in your eternal security. You have the helmet of salvation. Paul says, "Wear it!"

*The sword of the Spirit* (6:17). You may have noticed that so far all of God's armor for spiritual warfare has been defensive in nature. The final article God has provided, however, is offensive: "the sword of the Spirit, which is the word of God." The sword Paul referred to was the Roman short sword used in hand-to-hand combat (Greek *machaira* [3162]). Its two-sided blade was light and razor sharp. It was a highly effective weapon in the Roman army's arsenal.

The Christian's sword is the Word of God. However, the Greek word translated "word" here, *rhēma* [4487], is a reference to the spoken Word—the Word verbalized. Though its meaning overlaps with *logos* [3056] (a term for "message" or "word"), the focus of *logos* is the content of the message, while the focus of *rhēma* is the expression of that message. Thus, Paul's emphasis here is not simply reading Scripture but actually using God's revealed Word against Satan and his insidious spirits of darkness. That's what Jesus did when He was tempted by Satan in the wilderness of Judea. After Jesus fasted forty days and forty nights, the devil tempted Him to turn some stones into bread to eat. Jesus quoted Deuteronomy 8:3, saying, "Man shall not live on bread alone, but on every word [*rhēma*] that proceeds out of the mouth of God" (Matt. 4:4).

It's no wonder, then, that Paul likens the spoken Word of God to a sharp sword. Just like an earthly sword—or any deadly weapon, for that matter—the sword of the Spirit is not something we can pick up as novices and immediately wield like pros. Rather, it takes many years to grow in the Word of God, sharpening our skills, enhancing our knowledge, and applying it to our lives. Then, with God's Word in our heads through memorization, in our hearts through meditation, and in our hands through application, we have the power to effect change by speaking, sharing, and living out that Word.

## — 6:18-20 —

Finally, Paul adds one last element to the Christian's battle strategy. This tactic reminds us that we do battle in God's strength, not our own. In 6:14-17 he described the pieces of armor given to us by God—each piece dependent on the others, all of them essential to win a victory over the wiles of the devil. Now, in 6:18-20, Paul turns our attention to our practical response. Having suited up for battle, what do we do now? Stand around and wait? Crouch in a corner, ready to pounce? Paul's exhortation is actually much simpler and more effective. We are to *pray*, making constant petitions with perseverance (6:18). Above all else, prayer expresses our reliance on God.

Our enemy, Satan, studies our weaknesses and plots his attacks accordingly. We need to be just as precise in the requests we take to the Father on behalf of our fellow soldiers in Christ. We bring before Him "all prayer and petition" (6:18). But even at this point, when we are doing battle against the forces of wickedness on our knees, don't believe for one second that it's all on our shoulders. Rather, in our pleas to God, the Spirit Himself comes to our aid. To pray "in the Spirit" means to pray by His power, according to His ability, not ours, and in accordance with His will. Elsewhere Paul wrote, "In the same way the Spirit also helps our weakness; for we do not know how to pray as we should, but the Spirit Himself intercedes for us with groanings too deep for words" (Rom. 8:26).

As we pray, we must "be on the alert" (Eph. 6:18), having our hearts trained to detect oncoming assaults from the enemy. No matter what, we must keep on praying, never becoming discouraged if victory takes longer than we expected. Remember, too, that we're all targets of the same brutal, relentless force of wickedness, so we must continually lift each other up in prayer. This is why Paul urges us to pray "for all the saints"—from the least to the greatest, from the baby Christian still stumbling over the tiny obstacles Satan tosses in his path to the mature missionary trudging through spiritual jungles as Satan attempts to derail her lifelong endeavors. From first to last, the battle cry of the Christians is "Pray!"

Even the apostle Paul acknowledged his desperate need for prayer support. In 6:19, he asked for prayer that God would give him supernatural ability to proclaim the gospel with boldness. We usually assume that Paul was fearless, impervious to discouragement, and unstoppable in the pursuit of his calling to preach wherever, whenever, and to whomever. But Paul was a frail, fallen human being like the rest of us. And remember, he was under house arrest, "an ambassador in chains" (6:20), the victim of the frustrating effects of Satan's warfare against the saints. Paul needed prayer from his fellow believers, fearing that the mystery of the gospel might get stuck in his throat, muffled by apprehension about what might happen to him or his loved ones if he spoke with too much zeal.

Paul was human, just like you and me. Yet he was humble and honest enough to admit his need and to ask for help both from God, his Defender, and from the people of God, his support. Are you willing to do the same?

# APPLICATION: EPHESIANS 6:14-20

### Suiting Up and Shipping Out

When Paul wrote his letter to the Ephesians, he was lingering under house arrest, waiting to appear before Caesar. We can read about his two-year wait in the last few verses of Acts, but in the last chapter of Ephesians we can also see that though his body was imprisoned, his mind remained free and active. Guarded by Caesar's soldiers day after day, Paul closely observed their armor. Studying the helmet, breastplate, belt, boots, shield, and sword, he began to think about warfare. In physical battle, the soldiers would be well protected. But in a spiritual battle against invisible foes, all that equipment would be utterly useless.

In the face of the spiritual forces of wickedness in the heavenly places, our only hope for victory comes from Christ. Our only provision of protection comes from the Father's glorious throne. The only effective weapon against the inevitable attacks of the enemy is the razor-sharp double-edged sword of the Spirit, the Word of God. As believers caught in the midst of ongoing spiritual conflict with periodic explosive battles that brink on total warfare, how can we risk being caught unprepared? Isn't it time to take our spiritual lives seriously? It's time to stop being content with simply *having* a new life through Christ . . . we need to *live* the new life by the power of the Spirit.

Have you put on God's full armor? How prepared are you to stand strong when the next wave of Satan's attacks tries to knock you to the ground? Think through the pieces of armor Paul listed and evaluate the state of your readiness today.

*The belt of truth.* How well are you living the truth of God's Word? Are there any areas of your life where your integrity could be called into question? Secrets you're hiding? Sins you're concealing? Ongoing deceptions or half-truths you just can't live with anymore? Take steps today to tighten the belt of truth before you lose control.

*The breastplate of righteousness.* Have you been content merely to receive the grace of justification—being *declared* righteous by God— but reluctant to yield to the grace of sanctification—being *made* more righteous by the work of the Spirit? Are there clear areas in your life in which personal morality and holiness have been compromised? Are there chinks in your armor that could easily become primary targets for

Satan's precision archers? What can you do to strengthen these weak places?

*The boots of peace.* Do you have trouble resting in the peace Christ has secured for you? Do you fret, worry, and linger over things beyond your control? Or do you fail at extending peace toward others? Do you constantly stir the pot, bringing disquiet and chaos into peoples' lives? To have a life characterized by peace you must turn to the Prince of Peace, who alone can restrain the prince of darkness.

*The shield of faith.* What happens when troubles come your way? How do you respond? Do you tend to let go of God and panic? Or are you learning to hold fast to Him and the promises He has made? What specific "faith builders" do you have in your life to help keep your shield in good repair? Do you read Scripture regularly? Fellowship faithfully at your church? Build strong relationships with fellow believers? How sure is your defense against the fiery arrows of the wicked one?

*The helmet of salvation.* Do you have full assurance of your salvation? Are you convinced that your destiny is an eternity with Christ? Or have the trials, temptations, cares, and concerns of this world drawn your eyes away from your heavenly hope? In what ways can you adjust your daily schedule in order to spend time with the Savior, embrace the promises of His Word, and work at growing in the salvation you have received?

*The sword of the Spirit.* How sharp and polished is your knowledge of Scripture? Of the vital, life-changing doctrines of the Christian faith? Are you able to wield God's Word skillfully when Satan's messengers attempt to confuse you or tempt you? How can you intentionally strengthen yourself in the area of biblical truth?

*The power of prayer.* Finally, how seriously do you take prayer? How often during the day do you commit to persistent, prevailing prayer? Is it something you squeeze into an already packed schedule or tack on at the end of your wearying worldly activities? Or do you focus time, attention, and energy on this singular means of engaging in spiritual warfare?

To close this time of personal reflection, spend some time in prayer right now, asking God to help you put on the armor He has provided. Don't rush through it. It may be one of the most pivotal decisions you make in your Christian life. It will certainly be your defense in the day of evil.

# Wrapping Up Well
## EPHESIANS 6:21-24

NASB

21 But that you also may know about my circumstances, [a]how I am doing, Tychicus, the beloved brother and faithful minister in the Lord, will make everything known to you. 22[a]I have sent him to you for this very purpose, so that you may know [b]about us, and that he may comfort your hearts.

23 Peace be to the brethren, and love with faith, from God the Father and the Lord Jesus Christ. 24 Grace be with all those who love our Lord Jesus Christ [a]with incorruptible *love*.

**6:21** [a]Lit *what*  **6:22** [a]Lit *Whom I have sent to you*
[b]Lit *the things about us*  **6:24** [a]Lit *in incorruption*

NLT

21 To bring you up to date, Tychicus will give you a full report about what I am doing and how I am getting along. He is a beloved brother and faithful helper in the Lord's work. 22 I have sent him to you for this very purpose—to let you know how we are doing and to encourage you. 23 Peace be with you, dear brothers and sisters,* and may God the Father and the Lord Jesus Christ give you love with faithfulness. 24 May God's grace be eternally upon all who love our Lord Jesus Christ.

**6:23** Greek *brothers*.

As in all his letters, Paul wraps up the message to the Ephesians with some personal greetings and an encouraging farewell. Though some would be tempted to rush through the last few verses as a "throwaway" postlude with no doctrinal or practical meat, *don't do it!* Remember that "all Scripture is inspired by God and profitable for teaching, for reproof, for correction, for training in righteousness; so that the man of God may be adequate, equipped for every good work" (2 Tim. 3:16-17).

By the time we're finished with these final four verses of Paul's powerful letter, we'll have seen some principles of Christian life and ministry we can't do without. They center on a somewhat obscure—but by no means irrelevant—ministry companion, the beloved and faithful Tychicus. Let's see how Paul wraps up well, leaving us with a message of grace, truth, and love.

## — 6:21-22 —

Tychicus first appears on the pages of Holy Scripture in Acts 20:4. Immediately after a riot in Ephesus (Acts 19:23-41), Paul departed to Macedonia, continued on to Greece, then returned to Macedonia (Acts 20:1-3). At this point Luke lists the men who were part of Paul's ministry team, some perhaps joining him immediately after the events in Ephesus, some joining the group in the several months that followed. In any case, by the time Paul and his ministry partners arrived in Troas on the northwestern shore of Asia Minor, the following men were among Paul's associates: three from Macedonia—Sopater, Aristarchus, and Secundus; four from Asia Minor—Gaius, Timothy, Tychicus, and Trophimus; and Luke, the physician and author of the Gospel of Luke and the book of Acts.

We can't be sure if Tychicus was present with Paul throughout the remainder of his journey to Rome. But we know from Ephesians 6:21-22 and Colossians 4:7-8 that Tychicus was present with Paul in Rome at the time those letters were written. He served as the courier for both letters, as well as Paul's personal representative to the churches in Ephesus and Colossae. Thus, Paul's mention of Tychicus in Ephesians 6:21-22 is much more than simply a way to wrap up a letter. In fact, it gives us two important insights into a proper approach to ministry.

First, we must never forget that Paul engaged in a *team ministry*. Take the time to read the end of several of his letters to see how many friends he had working with him.[14] In fact, we have no evidence that Paul was truly alone in ministry even during his imprisonments. He had faithful men and women like Tychicus, Timothy, Luke, Mark, Aquila, Priscilla, and Phoebe partnering with him. Sometimes they would stay behind to strengthen the new churches planted by the apostle (Acts 17:14; Titus 1:5). Other times Paul would send them back to churches or send them ahead to a city to prepare for his upcoming visit (Acts 20:5; 1 Cor. 4:17). Many times they served as his messengers, carrying his precious and treasured letters to their destinations (Eph. 6:21-22; Col. 4:7-8).

Second, Paul valued *personal presence* as much as powerful and accurate proclamation. As both "beloved" and "faithful" (Eph. 6:21), Tychicus would add a personal touch to Paul's correspondence with the Ephesians. He would tell them how well Paul was holding up under his arrest and how the saving word of the gospel was spreading even further through Paul's imprisonment. Tychicus would be able to respond to questions, hear and see the genuine concern in the Ephesians' voices and faces, and mediate their thoughts and feelings back to Paul in a tangible way. We shouldn't forget that the apostles preferred personal, physical presence among the people to correspondence. In the conclusion of his third letter, the apostle John wrote, "I had many things to write to you, but I am not willing to write them to you with pen and ink; but I hope to see you shortly, and we will speak face to face" (3 Jn. 1:13-14). And Paul himself wrote in Romans 1:11-13,

> For I long to see you so that I may impart some spiritual gift to you, that you may be established; that is, that I may be encouraged

together with you while among you, each of us by the other's faith, both yours and mine. I do not want you to be unaware, brethren, that often I have planned to come to you (and have been prevented so far) so that I may obtain some fruit among you also, even as among the rest of the Gentiles.

In our techno-crazed world, in which we can carry on virtual "face-to-face" conversations over the Internet, take university courses and earn degrees without setting foot in a real classroom, and get powerful Bible teaching and preaching 24/7 at the touch of a button, we too quickly forget the need for flesh-and-blood presence. Nothing can ever take the place of a real person spending real time and sharing real space with other real people (see 1 Thes. 2:7-9). Paul did not just send Tychicus to Ephesus to share information; that could have been accomplished through a letter. Rather, Tychicus was to share his very self, something that would comfort the hearts of the Ephesian believers (Eph. 6:22).

This ministry of personal presence is exactly how God Himself works in our lives. Think about it: If information were *all* we needed, God could have just left us with the Bible, a book filled with inspired, inerrant information and infallible, reliable answers. Now, don't get me wrong. The Bible is essential for our spiritual growth and health, and we would be lost without it. Yet to leave us with only the written Word of God would have been to leave us as "orphans" (see John 14:18). Without the revelation of Jesus Christ and the presence of the Holy Spirit, we wouldn't be able to make heads or tails of the Bible, nor would we be able to apply it to our lives.

God desires to dwell with us, among us, even *within* us. The Bible is a means to that end: a personal relationship with "God with us." The Son of God—Himself truly God—"became flesh, and dwelt among us" (John 1:14). People heard Him speak, saw Him with their eyes, and touched Him with their hands—the very "Word of Life" (1 Jn. 1:1). Then when Christ ascended to heaven, He deliberately chose not to leave us alone. His personal presence is mediated to us through the Spirit of God—Himself truly God—who has come to indwell believers and the believing community (John 16:7; 1 Cor. 3:16; 6:19).

The practical implications of the principles of team ministry and personal presence are significant. First, those who are tempted to "go it alone" in ministry or the Christian life need to stand against that temptation. God has designed us to live in harmony and to grow in community—to refresh others and to be refreshed, to encourage others and to be encouraged, to care for others and to be cared for, to give empathy and to receive it, to love and to be loved, to be accountable, affectionate, vulnerable, and sociable. Furthermore, there is strength in numbers (see Eccl. 4:9-12). We *need* each other desperately.

Second, those of us addicted to forms of communication that prevent personal presence need to strip away some of these barriers to true incarnational ministry. It might be time to turn off your cell phone, close your laptop, stop staring at your iPad, log off of your social network, and start investing real time with real people. Represent Christ to others. Share the presence of the Holy Spirit as He encourages others through you. Invite others into your private world. Someday, as the shades of your earthly life begin to draw closed, you'll be glad you did.

## — 6:23-24 —

As Paul beautifully began his letter, so he eloquently closes it. He extends a blessing of peace, love, and faith from God the Father and the Lord Jesus (6:23). It's almost as though Paul were summing up the main themes of the entire letter to the Ephesians. Since Christ has established peace with God and between believers (2:14-15), those called by His name are to live out that peace, "being diligent to preserve the unity of the Spirit in the bond of peace" (4:3). This peaceful way of life was first on Paul's mind, and close behind it was love—the basis for achieving peace.

Knowing that all the doctrinal precision in the world meant nothing without love for Christ and for each other (1 Cor. 13:1-3), Paul repeatedly urged his readers to an incorruptible love of Jesus Christ and a faithful love of the brethren (Eph. 6:23-24). How many times had Paul reminded the Ephesians of God's love for them and their love for others? Interestingly, Paul uses the noun for "love" (*agapē* [26]) ten times in Ephesians. In fact, Ephesians averages more references to love per chapter than any of Paul's other writings.

Given this strong emphasis on love, I find it sadly ironic that the church in Ephesus seems to have passed down everything to the next generation but that all-important fruit of the Spirit. About thirty-five years later, Christ Himself, through the apostle John, had this to say to the church at Ephesus: "But I have this against you, that you have left your first love. Therefore remember from where you have fallen, and repent and do the deeds you did at first" (Rev. 2:4-5). What a valuable lesson to learn from the Ephesians! Let's remember to stand firm in doctrinal truth without losing our love for God, our love for fellow believers, and our love for the lost.

Because we have received new life through Jesus Christ by grace through faith alone, let's live out that new life of love by the power of the Holy Spirit. When we yield to His transforming grace, we can be assured that the Spirit will do everything necessary to help us wrap up well. Then we will be able to say the same words Paul said when he wrote his final words to Timothy, by then the pastor of the great church in Ephesus: "I have fought the good fight, I have finished the course, I have kept the faith; in the future there is laid up for me the crown of righteousness, which the Lord, the righteous Judge, will award to me on that day; and not only to me, but also to all who have loved His appearing" (2 Tim. 4:7-8).

# APPLICATION: EPHESIANS 6:21-24
## Positioning Yourself for Practice

Both profoundly theological and practical, Paul's letter to the Ephesians strikes at the heart of the Christian life. The first half (Eph. 1–3) emphasizes our new position in Christ—forgiven and justified by grace through faith. The second half (Eph. 4–6) puts these truths into practice, emphasizing love and good works.

This simple structure clarifies the relationship between faith and practice, between description and prescription, between a firm footing in doctrine and practical steps of faith. If right doctrine and right practice were two guardrails along a straight road, few Christians would stay in the center of their spiritual journeys for very long before they drifted toward one extreme or another, throwing sparks and causing all kinds of damage. As we wrap up our study of this doctrinally rich and practically enriching letter to the Ephesians, ask yourself: *Where do you find yourself on this road?*

There are four basic possibilities:

1. *Puffed up by data* (1 Cor. 8:1). Perhaps you spend your time, energy, and resources acquiring biblical, theological, and historical knowledge. You have a regimented devotional time that looks more like preparing for an exam than spending intimate moments with the personal God you love. At the same time you have few outlets for actually expressing your faith—except, perhaps,

those occasions when you teach, discuss, argue, or debate doctrine. If this describes you, what should you do? Meditate on Ecclesiastes 12:12; 1 Corinthians 8:1-3; and James 1:22-25. How do these passages address the extreme of theological knowledge without practical application?

2. *Zeal without knowledge* (2 Tim. 2:15). Maybe you drift toward the other extreme. You stand against intellectualizing the faith and avoid structured learning in order to "experience" the faith. Perhaps the only kind of theology acceptable to you is "practical theology," and you'd much rather learn from an uneducated pastor with years of *real-life experience* than a seminary professor who has spent most of his life with his nose in a book. Your thirst for practical ministry keeps you engaged in the lives of the needy—but when it comes to responding to deep, profound questions about God, you don't have a clue where to begin. If this describes you, what should you do? Meditate on Ezra 7:10; 1 Timothy 4:13; and 2 Timothy 2:15. How do these passages address the extreme of practical living without doctrinal knowledge?

3. *Broken down or burned out* (Heb. 5:11). Maybe you're pursuing neither knowledge nor practical experience. Perhaps your mental, spiritual, emotional, and physical engines have finally sputtered to a stop, and you're not advancing any longer in the Christian life. Like those who grew "dull" in the letter to the Hebrews, you've stalled out on the road. By this time you should be well advanced in Christian doctrine and practice, but instead you need a fresh dose of baby food. If this condition describes you, what should you do? Meditate on Galatians 6:9-10 and Hebrews 5:11-14. How do these passages exhort you to get up and advance in the Christian life?

4. *Clicking along at a good pace* (2 Pet. 1:8). You may be at a fruitful and productive season in your walk with Christ in which you're maintaining a healthy balance between biblical knowledge and practical application. You're exercising your gifts for the edification of the body of Christ and, in turn, you are being built up in the faith. You seek reconciliation when you sin, and you strive— by the power of the Holy Spirit—to seek the Lord in all you do. If this wholesome condition describes you, what should you do? Meditate on 2 Timothy 3:14-17; 2 Peter 1:5-8; and Revelation 3:10-13. How do these passages encourage you to continue on the straight path?

The book of Ephesians as a whole reminds us that the Christian life is meant to be both *believed* and *lived*. This means we're responsible for both doctrinal truth and practical living—everyday life lived in the light of meaningful theological truth.

# ENDNOTES

# GALATIANS

## INTRODUCTION

[1] Charles C. Ryrie, *Balancing the Christian Life* (Chicago: Moody, 1969), 159.

## CONFIRMING THE TRUTH OF THE GOSPEL (GALATIANS 1:1–2:21)

[1] S. Lewis Johnson, Jr., "The Paralysis of Legalism," *Bibliotheca Sacra* 120 (April–June 1963): 109.

[2] Donald K. Campbell, "Galatians," in *The Bible Knowledge Commentary: New Testament Edition,* ed. John F. Walvoord and Roy B. Zuck (Wheaton, IL: Victor Books, 1983), 589.

[3] John R. W. Stott, *The Message of Galatians,* The Bible Speaks Today (Downers Grove, IL: InterVarsity Press, 1968), 13.

[4] See H. N. Ridderbos, "Galatians, Epistle to the," in *The International Standard Bible Encyclopedia,* ed. Geoffrey W. Bromiley, vol. 2, *E–J* (Grand Rapids: Eerdmans, 1982).

[5] Leon Morris, *Galatians: Paul's Charter of Christian Freedom* (Downers Grove, IL: InterVarsity, 1996), 43.

[6] Campbell, "Galatians," 591.

[7] Josh McDowell and Don Stewart, *Handbook of Today's Religions* (Nashville: Nelson, 1983), 24.

[8] In the Greek text, the subject ("God") is implied.

[9] Stott, *The Message of Galatians,* 34.

[10] This reconstruction is not merely conjecture. Galatians 2:4-5 mentions that these "false brethren" had infiltrated the church in Jerusalem to "spy out" the believers' freedom in Christ.

[11] Campbell, "Galatians," 593.

[12] James Montgomery Boice, "Galatians," in *Expositor's Bible Commentary,* ed. Frank E. Gaebelein (Grand Rapids: Zondervan, 1976), 10:440.

[13] See Eusebius, *Ecclesiastical History* 2.23.

[14] Ibid. 2.23.15.

[15] Walther Günther, "Lie, Hypocrite," in *The New International Dictionary of New Testament Theology* (Grand Rapids: Zondervan, 1976), 2:467–470.

[16] Commentators and Bible translations differ on where Paul's address to Peter

ends. Some end it at the initial rebuke at 2:14 (RSV, ESV, NET). Many, like the NASB, NIV, and NKJV, extend the quotation all the way to the end of the chapter.

17  Stott, *The Message of Galatians,* 64.

18  F. F. Bruce, *The Epistle to the Galatians: A Commentary on the Greek Text,* The New International Greek Testament Commentary Series (Grand Rapids: Eerdmans, 1982), 142.

## DEFENDING THE SUPERIORITY OF THE GOSPEL (GALATIANS 3:1–4:31)

1  Donald Grey Barnhouse, *Romans,* vol. 3, *God's Remedy* (Grand Rapids: Eerdmans, 1954), 208.

2  Thomas Jefferson, Letter to Colonel William S. Smith, November 13, 1787, in William B. Parker and Jonas Viles, eds., *Letters and Addresses of Thomas Jefferson* (Buffalo, NY: National Jefferson Society, 1903), 65.

3  See Boice, "Galatians," 10:465.

4  Stott, *The Message of Galatians,* 93.

5  Morris, *Galatians,* 116.

6  G. Walter Hansen, *Galatians,* The IVP New Testament Commentary Series, ed. Grant R. Osborne (Downers Grove, IL: InterVarsity, 1994), 107–108.

7  Stott, *The Message of Galatians,* 97.

8  Charles C. Ryrie, *Basic Theology* (Chicago: Moody, 1999), 352.

9  Campbell, "Galatians," 600.

10  Stott, *The Message of Galatians,* 100–101.

11  Hansen, *Galatians,* 114.

12  Campbell, "Galatians," 601.

13  See Steve Farrar, *Point Man: How a Man Can Lead His Family* (Sisters, OR: Multnomah, 2003), 29.

14  For a more detailed treatment of these spiritual disciplines, see Charles R. Swindoll, *So, You Want to Be Like Christ? Eight Essentials to Get You There* (Nashville: W Publishing Group, 2005).

15  See Bruce, *The Epistle to the Galatians,* 208–209.

16  Hansen, *Galatians,* 135.

17  John Adair, "What's the Meaning of This? A History of Interpretation," in *Insight's Bible Handbook: Practical Helps for Bible Study* (Plano, TX: IFL Publishing House, 2007), 60.

18  Roy B. Zuck, *Basic Bible Interpretation* (Wheaton, IL: Victor Books, 1991), 29.

19  For Paul's use of allegory, see E. Earle Ellis, *Paul's Use of the Old Testament* (Grand Rapids: Baker, 1981); Colin Brown, "Parable, Allegory, Proverb," in *The New International Dictionary of New Testament Theology* (Grand Rapids: Zondervan, 1976), 2:747–748, 754–756.

20  Joseph C. Aldrich, *Life-Style Evangelism: Crossing Traditional Boundaries to Reach the Unbelieving World* (Portland, OR: Multnomah, 1981), 20.

21  Campbell, "Galatians," 603.

22  C. S. Lewis, *The Great Divorce* (New York: Macmillan, 1946), 72.

## LIVING THE FREEDOM OF THE GOSPEL (GALATIANS 5:1–6:18)

1  The diamond was originally purchased for $312,000.00 (J. Willard Hershey, *The Book of Diamonds: Curious Lore, Properties, Tests, and Synthetic Manufacture* [New York: Hearthside Press, 1940], 101). This equals approximately five million dollars adjusted for inflation (see http://data.bls.gov/cgi-bin/cpicalc.pl).

2  Adapted from Victor Argenzio, *Diamonds Eternal* (New York: David McKay, 1974), 50–52.

3  Stott, *The Message of Galatians*, 135.
4  Eugene H. Peterson, *Traveling Light: Reflections on the Free Life* (Downers Grove, IL: InterVarsity, 1982), 145.
5  Stott, *The Message of Galatians*, 140.
6  Bruce, *The Epistle to the Galatians*, 243.
7  John Calvin, *Commentaries on the Epistles of Paul to the Galatians and Ephesians*, trans. William Pringle (Grand Rapids: Baker, 1996), 162–163.
8  The Greek present active participle always has a continuous aspect, describing an ongoing practice that characterizes a person's life.
9  Boice, "Galatians," 10:498.
10 Bruce, *The Epistle to the Galatians*, 257.
11 Walter Bauer et al., *A Greek-English Lexicon of the New Testament and Other Early Christian Literature* (Chicago: University of Chicago Press, 2000), 871.
12 Hansen, *Galatians*, 185.
13 Bruce, *The Epistle to the Galatians*, 262.
14 Hansen, *Galatians*, 191–192.
15 See ibid., 197.
16 Ibid.
17 Stott, *The Message of Galatians*, 180.
18 Helen H. Lemmel, "Turn Your Eyes upon Jesus," in *The Hymnal for Worship and Celebration* (Waco, TX: Word Music, 1986), no. 335.
19 Campbell, "Galatians," 611.

# EPHESIANS

## INTRODUCTION

1  G. L. Borchert, "Ephesus," in *The International Standard Bible Encyclopedia*, rev. ed., ed. Geoffrey W. Bromiley (Grand Rapids: Eerdmans, 1982), 2:115.
2  Edward M. Blaiklock, "Ephesus," in *The New International Dictionary of Biblical Archaeology*, ed. R. K. Harrison and David R. Douglass (Grand Rapids: Zondervan, 1983), 181.
3  Borchert, "Ephesus," 2:115.
4  E. M. B. Green and C. J. Hemer, "Ephesus," in *New Bible Dictionary*, 2nd ed., ed. J. D. Douglas et al. (Wheaton, IL: Tyndale, 1982), 337.

## SOVEREIGNTY AND GRACE: THE FOUNDATIONS OF OUR FAITH (EPHESIANS 1:1–2:10)

1  Francis Bacon, *The Essays or Counsels Civil and Moral*, 4th ed. (London: Routledge, 1887), 11–12.
2  See John Pollock, *The Apostle: A Life of Paul* (Wheaton, IL: Victor Books, 1985), 14–15.
3  Ibid., 15–16.
4  James Montgomery Boice, *Ephesians: An Expositional Commentary* (Grand Rapids: Baker, 1997), 5.
5  Harold W. Hoehner, *Ephesians: An Exegetical Commentary* (Grand Rapids: Baker, 2002), 173.
6  Boice, *Ephesians*, 6.
7  See Hoehner, *Ephesians*, 144–148.
8  Eph. 6:21-22; cf. Acts 20:4; 2 Tim. 4:12; Titus 3:12.

9  John R. W. Stott, *God's New Society: The Message of Ephesians*, The Bible Speaks Today Series (Downers Grove, IL: InterVarsity, 1979), 22–23.

10  See the very similar greetings in Rom. 1:7; 1 Cor. 1:3; 2 Cor. 1:2; Gal. 1:3; Phil. 1:2; 1 Thes. 1:1; 2 Thes. 1:2; 1 Tim. 1:2; 2 Tim. 1:2; Titus 1:4; and Phlm. 1:3.

11  Walter Bauer et al., *A Greek-English Lexicon of the New Testament and Other Early Christian Literature*, 2nd rev. ed. (Chicago: Chicago University Press, 1979), 322.

12  Thomas Ken, "Doxology," in *The Hymnal for Worship and Celebration* (Waco, TX: Word Music, 1986), no. 625.

13  Warren Wiersbe, *Be Rich: Are You Losing the Things That Money Can't Buy?* (Colorado Springs: Victor Books, 1976), 13–14.

14  Stott, *God's New Society: The Message of Ephesians*, 39.

15  Johannes E. Louw and Eugene A. Nida, eds., *Greek-English Lexicon of the New Testament Based on Semantic Domains*, vol. 1, *Introduction and Domains*, 2nd ed. (New York: United Bible Societies, 1988), § 6.55.

16  Ibid., § 6.54.

17  Hoehner, *Ephesians*, 241.

18  Johnson Oatman Jr., "Count Your Blessings," in *The Hymnal for Worship and Celebration*, no. 562.

19  See Hoehner, *Ephesians*, 247.

20  Ibid., 259.

21  A. Skevington Wood, "Ephesians," in *The Expositor's Bible Commentary, vol. 11, Ephesians—Philemon*, ed. Frank E. Gaebelein (Grand Rapids: Zondervan, 1978), 30.

22  Stott, *God's New Society: The Message of Ephesians*, 56.

23  Because God the Father is a spirit and does not have a literal body (John 4:24; 1 Tim. 1:17), the physical image of Christ sitting at God's "right hand" is probably best understood as a reference to Christ's supreme authority as the appointed heir of all things, as in Psalm 110:1. See Wood, "Ephesians," 30.

24  Charles Haddon Spurgeon, *The Treasury of the Bible* (Grand Rapids: Zondervan, 1968), 7:276–277.

25  R. Kent Hughes, *Ephesians: The Mystery of the Body of Christ*, Preaching the Word Series (Wheaton, IL: Crossway, 1990), 65.

26  Ibid.

27  *Doctrinal Statement of Dallas Theological Seminary*, Article IV.

28  Charles Wesley, "And Can It Be?" in *The Hymnal for Worship and Celebration*, no. 203.

29  See views in Hoehner, *Ephesians*, 342.

30  Ibid., 343.

## RECONCILIATION AND PEACE: THE RESULTS OF GOD'S GRACE (EPHESIANS 2:11–3:21)

1  John Milton, *Paradise Lost* 2.142-143.

2  Josephus, *The Jewish Wars* 5.193-194.

3  Stott, *God's New Society: The Message of Ephesians*, 92.

4  See *1 Clement* 5.3-4; 42.1-3; Ignatius, *Magnesians* 13.1; *Romans* 4.3; Polycarp, *Philippians* 9.1; Tertullian, *Against Marcion* 4.5.

5  "The Muratorian Fragment," in Bruce M. Metzger, *The Canon of the New Testament: Its Origin, Development, and Significance* (Oxford: Clarendon Press, 1987), 307.

6  Stott, *God's New Society: The Message of Ephesians*, 116.

7  Louw and Nida, *Greek-English Lexicon*, § 35.20.

8  Hoehner, *Ephesians*, 449.

9 Max Turner, "Ephesians," in *New Bible Commentary: 21st Century Edition*, 4th ed., ed. Gordon J. Wenham et al. (Downers Grove, IL: InterVarsity, 1994), 1234.
10 See A. Skevington Wood, "Ephesians," 50.
11 Hoehner, *Ephesians*, 489.
12 Samuel Trevor Francis, "O the Deep, Deep Love of Jesus," in *The Hymnal for Worship and Celebration*, no. 211.
13 See Hoehner, *Ephesians*, 489.

## WALKING AND GROWING: THE BELIEVER'S LIFESTYLE (EPHESIANS 4:1–32)

1 Randy White, as quoted in Charean Williams and Tim Price, "Remembering Tom Landry—Reactions from Friends, Players and On-field Foes," *Fort Worth Star-Telegram*, February 14, 2000.
2 Hoehner, *Ephesians*, 504.
3 Louw and Nida, *Greek-English Lexicon*, § 66.6.
4 Stott, *God's New Society: The Message of Ephesians*, 148.
5 Daniel B. Wallace, *Greek Grammar Beyond the Basics: An Exegetical Syntax of the New Testament* (Grand Rapids: Zondervan, 1996), 99–100.
6 See Hoehner, *Ephesians*, 531, 533.
7 W. Hall Harris, "The Ascent and Descent of Christ in Ephesians 4:9–10," *Bibliotheca Sacra* 151 (April–June 1994): 204–214.
8 See J. Armitage Robinson, *St. Paul's Epistle to the Ephesians: A Revised Text and Translation with Exposition and Notes* (London: Macmillan, 1903), 96.
9 See Charles R. Swindoll, *Insights on James, 1 & 2 Peter*, Swindoll's Living Insights New Testament Commentary (Carol Stream, IL: Tyndale, 2014), 220–224.
10 "The Apostles' Creed," in *The Hymnal for Worship and Celebration*, no. 716.
11 On the foundational and temporary nature of the offices of apostle and prophet, see "Are There Apostles and Prophets Today?" on page 207.
12 Ray Stedman with James D. Denney, *Our Riches in Christ: Discovering the Believer's Inheritance in Ephesians* (Grand Rapids: Discovery House, 1998), 188.
13 See Rom. 14:19; 15:2; 1 Cor. 14:3, 5, 12, 26; 2 Cor. 12:19.
14 Stott, *God's New Society: The Message of Ephesians*, 172.
15 Max Turner, "Ephesians," 1239.
16 R. Kent Hughes, *Ephesians*, 141.
17 Boice, *Ephesians*, 161.
18 Stott, *God's New Society: The Message of Ephesians*, 184–185.

## FOLLOWING AND SUBMITTING: THE IMITATOR'S PATH (EPHESIANS 5:1–6:9)

1 Thomas à Kempis, *The Imitation of Christ*, trans. Aloysius Croft and Harold Bolton (Milwaukee: Bruce, 1940), 1.
2 The origins of this humorous story are unknown, but it has been repeated in various forms for decades.
3 Frederick Buechner, *Listening to Your Life: Daily Meditations with Frederick Buechner*, comp. George Connor (San Francisco: HarperSanFrancisco, 1992), 242.
4 Gerhard Kittel and Gerhard Friedrich, eds., *Theological Dictionary of the New Testament: Abridged in One Volume*, trans. and abridged by Geoffrey W. Bromiley (Grand Rapids: Eerdmans, 1992), 865.
5 Wood, "Ephesians," 68.
6 Kittel and Friedrich, *Theological Dictionary of the New Testament*, 30.
7 Ibid., 620.
8 Wood, "Ephesians," 68–69.
9 *Doctrinal Statement of Dallas Theological Seminary*, Article IV.

10  Charles Wesley, "And Can It Be?" in *The Hymnal for Worship and Celebration,* no. 203.
11  Hoehner, *Ephesians,* 687.
12  Charles Hodge, *Commentary on the Epistle to the Ephesians* (Grand Rapids: Eerdmans, 1994), 300.
13  For a full treatment of the biblical doctrine of God's will, see Charles R. Swindoll, *The Mystery of God's Will* (Nashville: Nelson, 1999).
14  Hoehner, *Ephesians,* 705.
15  Stott, *God's New Society: The Message of Ephesians,* 218.
16  Hoehner, *Ephesians,* 786–787.
17  John MacArthur, *Ephesians,* The MacArthur New Testament Commentary Series (Chicago: Moody, 1986), 324.
18  Sam Tsang, *From Slaves to Sons: A New Rhetoric Analysis on Paul's Slave Metaphors in His Letter to the Galatians* (New York: Peter Lang, 2005), 22.
19  Mark Hassall, "Romans and Non-Romans," in John Wacher, ed., *The Roman World* (London: Routledge, 2002), 2:685–700.
20  Tsang, *From Slaves to Sons,* 39.
21  Boice, *Ephesians,* 220.
22  Louw and Nida, *Greek-English Lexicon,* § 35.29.

## CLASHING AND CONQUERING: THE WARRIOR'S STRATEGY (EPHESIANS 6:10-24)

1.  Martin Luther, "A Mighty Fortress Is Our God," in *The Hymnal for Worship and Celebration,* no. 26.
2.  Ibid.
3.  R. Kent Hughes, *Ephesians,* 216.
4.  Christopher Nolan et al., *The Dark Knight* (Warner Bros., 2008).
5.  Stott, *God's New Society: The Message of Ephesians,* 275.
6.  Hoehner, *Ephesians,* 834.
7.  Luther, "A Mighty Fortress Is Our God."
8.  Elisha A. Hoffman, "Leaning on the Everlasting Arms," in *The Hymnal for Worship and Celebration,* no. 354.
9.  Ignatius of Antioch, *Letter to the Ephesians* 13.1., trans. Michael W. Holmes, *The Apostolic Fathers: Greek Texts and English Translations,* updated ed. (Grand Rapids: Baker, 1999).
10.  Hoehner, *Ephesians,* 842.
11.  Stott, *God's New Society: The Message of Ephesians,* 281.
12.  Max Turner, "Ephesians," 1244.
13.  Hoehner, *Ephesians,* 850.
14.  Rom. 16; 1 Cor. 16:19; Col. 4:7-15; 2 Tim. 4:19-21; and Phlm. 1.